ANCIENT CHRISTIAN MAGIC

ANCIENT
CHRISTIAN
MAGIC

COPTIC TEXTS OF RITUAL POWER

Marvin Meyer, *General Editor*
Richard Smith, *Associate Editor*

Neal Kelsey, *Managing Editor*

HarperSanFrancisco
A Division of HarperCollins*Publishers*

Translators

STEPHEN EMMEL	MARVIN MEYER
DAVID FRANKFURTER	PAUL ALLAN MIRECKI
JAMES E. GOEHRING	ROBERT K. RITNER
HOWARD M. JACKSON	STEPHEN H. SKILES
NEAL KELSEY	RICHARD SMITH
EDMUND MELTZER	

The image on the cover is based on a drawing, from the Schott-Reinhardt Papyrus (Heidelberg Kopt. 500/501), of Jesus Christ in the praying position. On his robe, he is identified with the names "Jesus Christ" and "Bes," an ancient Egyptian god. Adapted from Angelicus M. Kropp, *Ausgewählte koptische Zaubertexte*. Vol. 3, Tafel III, Abb. 6. Brussels: Fondation égyptologique reine Élizabeth, 1930. Used with permission.

Illustration Credits begin on page 393.

The Nag Hammadi, Super Greek, and Hebrew fonts used to print this work are available from Linguist's Software, Inc., P.O. Box 580, Edmonds, WA 98020-0580, tel (206) 775-1130.

Book design by Jaime Robles

FIRST EDITION

Library of Congress Cataloging-in-Publication Data:
Ancient Christian magic : coptic texts of ritual power /
  Marvin Meyer, general editor ; Richard Smith, associate editor ;
  Neal Kelsey, managing editor.
    p.   cm.
  Includes bibliographical references.
  ISBN 0-06-065578-X (alk. paper).— ISBN 0-06-065584-4 (pbk.)
  1. Magic, Coptic. 2. Magic, Egyptian. I. Meyer, Marvin W.
II. Smith, Richard
BF1591.A48 1994   93-28832
133.4'3'093209015—dc20   CIP

94 95 96 97 98 CWI 10 9 8 7 6 5 4 3 2 1
This edition is printed on acid-free paper that meets the American National Standards Institute Z39.48 Standard.

CONTENTS

ACKNOWLEDGMENTS

The publication of this book has depended upon the hard work, good will, and generosity of a number of people and organizations, and I happily acknowledge a few of them. This has truly been a collaborative endeavor, and I thank the members of the Coptic Magical Texts Project for their collegiality and commitment. The Institute for Antiquity and Christianity of Claremont Graduate School, to which this research project belongs, has been a friendly academic home for our research over the past several years. Through the Institute, the J.W. and Ida M. Jameson Foundation and the Board of Higher Education of the United Methodist Church have provided financial assistance to the project. I wish to express my personal appreciation to the National Endowment for the Humanities, the Graves Awards Committee (for the American Council of Learned Societies), and the Griset Chair in Religion at Chapman University for their generous support, and Richard Smith likewise wishes to acknowledge the help of the National Endowment for the Humanities. Edmund Meltzer would like to thank Susan T. Hollis, the Wilbour Library of Egyptology at the Brooklyn Museum, and an anonymous private source of a research grant administered through Claremont Graduate School. Finally, I thank John Loudon and his colleagues at Harper San Francisco for their excellent work in producing a scholarly book that is also very attractive and thoroughly accessible.

MARVIN MEYER

Director, Coptic Magical Texts Project,
Institute for Antiquity and Christianity, Claremont Graduate School
Professor of Religion, Chapman University

INTRODUCTION

MARVIN MEYER AND RICHARD SMITH

The titles of many books are carefully selected, and so it is with this book: *Ancient Christian Magic: Coptic Texts of Ritual Power.* These texts deal with what most people would regard as magic—spells, charms, amulets, and so on. They date from about the first to the eleventh or twelfth century C.E., with the majority from late antiquity, and are thus to contemporary readers ancient. And virtually all are texts by Coptic Christians from ancient and early medieval Egypt. Thus the words of the title—ancient, Christian, magic—should convey the distinct kind of texts presented together here for the first time in English.

However, the subtitle is more precise and crucially important. In the subtitle we have deliberately chosen to call this a collection of "texts of ritual power" rather than "magical texts." Several considerations prompted this choice of terms, and a reflection on some of them may help the reader approach the book with increased understanding. We have inherited two histories of "magic": One is the long history of the phenomenon, for which these texts provide documentation, and the other is the history of the study of the phenomenon, which dates from the beginnings of anthropology in the nineteenth century. Both of these

1

histories are similar in that they regard "magic" as something alien, to be either condemned outright or explained away.

Throughout Mediterranean antiquity the words *mageia* and *magos*, "magic" and "magician," were used to categorize the exotic and the dangerous. They were foreign words to a Greek speaker, used to describe foreign practices semiotically joined to the word barbarian. "Magic" put a label on those invasive threats to traditional civic piety and cultural cohesiveness. Roman emperors burned fortune-telling books and jailed people who wore amulets. A "magician" was either a criminal or a quack, condemned by law and ridiculed by satirists. As Flaubert wrote in his dictionary of traditional banalities, "Magic: Make fun of it." After the third century, highbrow philosophers who practiced invocation of divine powers tried to disengage themselves from this magical tradition by rewriting the vocabulary. They called what they did *theurgy,* "divine work," as opposed to *goeteia,* howling out barbaric words. From this came the enduring debate, which has continued into the modern period, over high or white magic versus low or black magic.

In *Ancient Christian Magic* we have transcendent mysticism as well as chthonic howling, but telling them apart is sometimes difficult; the more closely these texts are actually read, the harder it is to maintain any distinction between piety and sorcery. The texts themselves, as we point out in the notes, rarely use the word *mageia,* or other Greek and Coptic words we translate as "magic" and "sorcery." Our texts are frequently invocations of the powers to protect the person from "magic," from sorcery, and against the evil eye. The users did not, therefore, consider themselves practitioners of "magic," which they regarded as a negative term. The terms of positive description they use, *phylakterion* and *apologia,* "amulet" and "spell," really just mean "protection" and "defense." Since the practices are a means of fighting back against magical attack, "magic" does not seem a fitting description.

During the nineteenth century, European scholars began a great endeavor to describe and to understand the peoples around the world who were then circumscribed by their empires. These people were usually tribal. Their economies, technologies, and forms of worship were quite different from those of the European scholar. But the European scholar, the early anthropologist, had terms and concepts already in place to describe these peoples.

They were primitive, and they engaged in "magic." Two of these Victorian writers, Edward Tylor and James George Frazer, had a lasting effect on the ongoing discussion of "magic," even though their theories were caught up in an evolutionist mentality that was used to justify colonialism. Applying the notion of evolution, not as Darwin intended to mean, "differently adapted," but rather meaning "progressively advanced," they described these societies as early stages in a story of human progress. Tribal cultures thus represented a primitive stage that could help us understand human nature by revealing its earliest development. Magic became synonymous with origins, a forerunner of what "we" believe, which is "religion," and at the same time magic became the irrational precursor of science. The result has been that even in the scholarly literature the term "magic" is used with the same rhetorical force as it was in antiquity, a term of contrast to reinforce a cultural self-image of purity and rationality.

We no longer regard tribal cultures as representing primitive stages, but the nineteenth century defined the terms of the debate. Magic throughout our century has continued to be contrasted with religion or with science, and used to describe *other* cultures or subcultures. This is reflected in the distinction between sociology, which studies "us," and anthropology, which studies "them." Books written by sociologists tend to have "religion" in their titles, while books written by anthropologists are often about "magic." One result is that historians, who work with texts (like this volume) rather than with peoples, continue to go to anthropology for theoretical models when trying to discuss phenomena traditionally perceived as magical.

It is only recently that scholars have tried to escape from the "religion/magic," "we/they" hierarchy. One obvious problem with these contrasts is that any culture, whether small-scale or complex and industrialized, is a conflicting structure of elements that includes both the rational and the irrational. So in the religions of the first-world nations, where material benefits are prayed for, where victory in battle is invoked, and where individuals wear charms for luck or protection, just what does it mean to say that magic is something practiced by other, more primitive people? Nor does any scheme of advancement hold true, for the texts in this volume date from the late Roman and early Byzantine centuries, long after the period when Greek rationality peaked. To hold onto an evolutionary scheme requires that irrational practices be explained as survivals or reversions. Thus the late antique flourish of mystical cults and magic was described by the classicist Gilbert Murray in a famous phrase as a "failure of nerve," a retreat from self-confidence and patient inquiry. But another classicist, E. R. Dodds, went on to demonstrate that irrational elements complicated Greek culture all the way through. Another concern is the usefulness of applying theories of magic, which were derived from the observation of small-scale tribes, to the texts in this volume, which were produced in a cosmopolitan urban setting.

A more useful, less value-laden term than either "magic" or "religion," which one scholar after another is beginning to propose, is "ritual." We human beings, in our worship practices, engage in rituals everywhere, in all parts of the globe and in all types of societies. The texts in this volume, although they range from hostile revenge to personal enhancement, from transcendent ascent to fortune-telling, have one common factor: They are ritual texts. They direct the user to engage in activities that are marked off from normal activity by framing behavior through rules, repetitions, and other formalities. Ritual instructions pervade these texts. Stand over here, hold a pebble, tie seven threads in seven knots, say the names seven times, draw the figure in the bottom of the cup, write the spell with the finger of a mummy, write it with bat's blood, with menstrual blood, on papyrus, on clay, on lead, on tin, on a rib bone, on a parchment shaped like a sword, fold it, burn it, tie it to your arm, your thumb, drive a nail in it, bury it with a mummy, bury it under someone's doorstep, mix this recipe, drink it. Or simply "do the usual."

Beyond agreement on how rituals are done (correctly, with a focus on rules), theorists are not agreed on why they are done. Whether ritual is in some way symbolic behavior, or communicative behavior, or a focusing of the individual's emotions or perceptions, or a form of social control and cohesion, is a topic of debate. Maybe, according to the latest proposal by Frits Staal, it does not mean much of anything. Whatever, most would agree that we should not ask, "Does it work?" This is a question which allowed the negative appraisal of primitive magic as "pseudoscience." But with such a broad category, ritual, where do we draw the line at not including in this volume the liturgy of the ancient

Coptic church? Or, how do we map these rituals against such rule-governed activities as a game, a dance, a social encounter, or the obsessive activities of a neurotic?

Although many, perhaps most, rituals can be discussed in terms of empowerment or power relations, the texts in this volume are overt in their manipulation of power and force. Deities are summoned "by the power of" a talisman, a name, or the power of another divinity. Angels have power and angels are "powers." The ritualist accomplishes nothing alone, "not by my power, but by the power of" some greater figure. The whole thing is reminiscent of nothing so much as the system of Roman patronage, where a complicated social network enabled individuals to exert pressure based not on power they themselves held but on their relation to a greater personage. In these texts, such a network of forces is ritualized. Notice, in this context, that in the New Testament book of Acts, Simon Magus, who practices *mageia*, calls himself the great power of god, and asks the apostles to "give me this power." Most Greco-Roman writers use this vocabulary; a *magos* invokes power and uses power.

"Texts of ritual power," then, appears to be a fitting description. Nevertheless, these texts do have one characteristic where current theories of ritual do not help, while the old distinction between religion and magic may. Most theories of ritual are social; they account for activities performed by groups. Rituals have a social function, and they take place within a social structure. The rituals in this volume, however, appear at first glance to be private activities performed in secret. Such a distinction was made early in this century by the French sociologist Émile Durkheim, who saw religion as a collective thing, but the magician, he said, "has a clientele and not a church." Nevertheless, there has been little support for theorists of magic who focus on the individual's psychology, such as Sigmund Freud, or emotions, such as Bronislaw Malinowski.

Even though the texts in this volume reveal individuals in the most extreme emotional states, we have to realize that the construction and the acting out of these states are socially determined. Durkheim's colleague Marcel Mauss made an important shift of emphasis away from individual experience to milieu. Force and milieu, he argued, were inseparable, and ritual power was not an experimental fact but a social fact: "It is supported by the magician performing the rite and the individual who believes in it." Following this argument, Claude Lévi-Strauss gave a famous description of a person killed by a spell, because "the group acts as a sort of gravitational field within which the relationship between sorcerer and bewitched is located and defined," so that the victim's physical integrity dissolves along with the withdrawal of the social personality. Likewise, the third-century Egyptian neoplatonist Plotinus was said to have felt the effects of a spell cast against him by an envious rival.

Larger shifts in cultural milieu can also help us understand an interest in more private rituals as opposed to participation in public rituals. During the Hellenistic period there was a great breakdown in the authority of the city-states, accompanied by a decline in the ceremonial forms of worship around which social identities cohered. People became citizens of a much larger world, with social role and group identity more ill-defined. Private associations and small cultic practices flowed throughout the late antique world with great mobility. By the fourth and fifth centuries, writes historian Peter Brown, "the individual, as a 'man of power,' came to dwarf the traditional communities." Jonathan Z. Smith calls this the development of "religious entrepreneurship." The anthropologist Mary Douglas has located similar shifts in many cultures due to the weakening of group boundaries, accompanied by an exaltation of the self and an objectification of other people and human relationships. This self-exaltation and objectification of others is the very situation we discover when we read these Coptic texts. When group boundaries are weak, Douglas writes, "and ego-focused social categories dominate a person's life, attitudes to ritual are highly magical. Power is theoretically available for all, but it needs a talented man to go out and get it for himself according to known rules." Thus we see that magic is not the basic category, but ritual, and our attitude toward ritual is that which gives it power.

THE MAIN PURPOSE of this volume is to present in English translation a representative selection of 135 Coptic texts of ritual power. We do not claim that this selection is a complete English edition of such Coptic texts of ritual power; we are aware of other texts, published and unpublished, that are not included here, and we can only surmise that more texts exist of which we are not aware. Newly published texts continue to appear in scholarly journals from time to time, and accounts circulate of additional texts in private and public collections around the world. Thus the definition of a corpus of Coptic texts of ritual power remains an exceedingly difficult undertaking. The texts that are included here, however, should give the reader a fair sense of the range of texts that represent ritual power in Coptic Egypt. These texts have been assigned dates from about 100 C.E. to around the eleventh or twelfth century. Presumably these texts—including the later ones—include earlier materials, since texts of ritual power tend to be concerned with the transmission (even the accurate transmission) of older traditional materials. These texts are written on papyrus, parchment, rag paper, pottery, and bone. As a rule of thumb it may be noted that texts written on papyrus ordinarily are assigned an earlier date and texts on paper a later date, while texts written on parchment may be fairly early or quite late. These texts are composed mainly in Coptic (a few, in chapter 1, are in Old Coptic), but some Greek texts and Greek passages are also noted, and one text (text 94) opens with several lines of Arabic written in Coptic letters. Most of these texts may be classified as Christian texts, and they demonstrate that Christianity can take the form of a folk religion with a syncretistic interest in making use of ritual power for all sorts of practical purposes.

In content, these Coptic texts of ritual power may be grouped into three categories—hence the structure of the present book.

One, some texts consist of Old Coptic, Greek, and Coptic Gnostic texts that provide rather early evidence for the diverse manifestation of ritual power in Coptic Egypt. These texts are grouped together in Part 1 of this book.

Two, other texts are Coptic spells that are typically preserved in one of two forms: Either they are spells or amulets prepared for a particular client, who usually is identified by his or her name and often the name of the mother; or they are master copies, with no name yet inserted but with the formula "N. child of N." These spells are organized by function in the chapters of Part 2 of this volume, although it has proved difficult to classify them in a fully accurate fashion. For example, sometimes it is artificial to distinguish the healing and the protective or apotropaic functions of spells; and it is a more or less arbitrary decision that we have placed three sexual curses (texts 85–87) in chapter 6, "Sexual Spells," rather than chapter 7, "Curses." (We have in fact placed them at the end of chapter 6, as a transition to chapter 7.) Again, London Hay 10122 (text 81) is placed in chapter 6 less on account of its specific contents than because of our wish to keep several texts from the London Hay collection together (texts 78–81; compare also text 127).

Three, another group of texts, given in Part 3 of this volume, represents the category of ritual handbooks. These handbooks may take the form of collections of recipes and spells assembled by a given practitioner or client, or they may be books or codices with spells copied together within the confines of a single manuscript. Chapters 12 and 13 present two such Coptic codices, one from Leiden and the other (originally) from Heidelberg.

The English translations of the 135 Greek and Coptic texts published in this volume are intended to be as accurate and readable as possible. The Coptic of these texts is often difficult to translate on account of the esoteric character of the subject matter and the deviations from standard Coptic syntax and spelling. Several different translators have contributed to this volume, so that the reader may expect a degree of stylistic variation from one translation to another. Nonetheless, the editors have attempted to bring some standardization to the translations. We have also decided to maintain a uniform policy of not capitalizing the word "god" or other references to the divine (for example, "father," "son," and "holy spirit" within a Christian trinitarian context), whether such words refer to the Judeo-Christian-Islamic god or not. We trust this decision will help avoid a situation of overcapitalization, on the one hand, and a bias that otherwise might emerge, on the other hand, should we capitalize the word "god" only when it refers to the Judeo-Christian-Islamic deity. Within the texts there occur numerous illustrations, many of them in the form of ring signs and letters. Only a few samples of such illustrative material are included here.

The following sigla are used in the presentation of the Coptic texts and their translations:

[ ] Square brackets indicate a lacuna or gap in the text.

< > Pointed brackets indicate a correction of a scribal omission or error.

{ } Braces indicate superfluous letters that presumably were added by a copyist.

( ) Parentheses indicate material that is not present in the text but is supplied by the translator for the sake of clarity of translation.

Three dots in an English translation indicate a word or a passage that cannot be restored with confidence. Occasionally the number of dots indicates the approximate number of letters (especially in a name) within a lacuna.

Page numbers and other manuscript references are given within parentheses. Raised vertical strokes designate the lines in the text; every fifth line is indicated by means of a raised number.

For the sake of simplicity, a standard cross is used to represent the various forms of a cross or cross-like symbol in the manuscripts.

To the English translations of the texts of ritual power are added several sorts of material useful for the understanding of the texts. Each chapter is prefaced with an introduction, as is each text, and sufficient textual and bibliographical data is provided so that the reader can identify basic characteristics of the spells and find out where the Greek and Coptic texts are available in their original languages. The textual designations and descriptions are intended to provide the reader with an easy access to the scholarly literature. A few texts from the Beinecke Library of Yale University are published here for the first time; Stephen Emmel has edited these Coptic texts in the Appendix, "Previously Unpublished Coptic Texts of Ritual Power in the Beinecke Library, Yale University." Notes to the translations are provided for our fellow Coptologists and other scholars who may wish to pursue textual issues and problems of syntax and spelling. A glossary of terms gives brief identifications of some of the most prominent terms, names, and motifs in the texts, and a concluding bibliography mentions sources that were consulted and significant books and articles for further study.

PART 1

RITUAL POWER IN EGYPT

1

OLD CoPTIC TEXTS oF RITuAL PoWER

INTRODUCTION BY EDMUND MELTZER
TRANSLATIONS BY EDMUND MELTZER
AND MARVIN MEYER

Throughout the history of the modern academic study of religion and culture, as we have noted, the definition of "magic" in relation to science and religion has been a major problem. At the root of the problem is the loaded, evaluative connotation of "magic" as false, deceptive, discredited, or morally tainted, contrasted with both science (a correct, enlightened understanding of natural law and causation) and religion (a correct, enlightened understanding of the divine and spirituality). Thus, "magic" is relegated to the "they" side of a "we/they" dichotomy. This is simultaneously unfair to the materials and practices studied under the heading of "magic," and self-serving for the materials (mainly those we identify as "our own") that are exempted from that label. It perpetuates a complacent double standard. A statement by the Egyptologist and historian of religions Herman Te Velde, in "Funerary Mythology," aptly epitomizes one aspect of the situation:

> The distinction between the magical and the religious is one of definition. The word *magic* is often used simply to label actions, sayings, and ideas that do not seem reasonable from a Western positivist or Christian point of view (29).

Another aspect of this problem is inadequate attention to the given culture's own understanding and social context of the practices in question. What has been labeled "magic" is often regarded or defined by the culture using it as something that has been given, revealed, sanctioned, approved, established by the god(s) or the divine realm, and a rightful and necessary part of the proper divine, natural, social order. Thus, in the Egyptian Instruction for Merykare we read that the creator-god "gave *hekau* (normally translated "magic") to humankind as a weapon." The antisocial, destructive, malicious use of ritual power, however, is normally forbidden, and is the target of punishment, reprisal, and ostracism in traditional societies. It is perceived as an offense against the divine social order, wrongfully disrupting or interfering with it. The legitimate use of ritual power includes permitted or ordained recourses against its illegitimate use and against the practitioners of this ritual power. One of the sets of questions that presents itself, then, as we work with such a body of material is this: To which of these spheres did a given text, artifact, or practice belong? By what, or whose, criteria? According to which of the competing systems or subsystems that were current? In what circumstances and at what point in time?

The sphere of life to which the vast majority of the materials presented in this book pertains is what we call "religion," and the practices involved belong to the domain of ritual. The texts are not abstract or disembodied entities. The rituals in which they figure are by no means limited to mere recitation but involve a wide range of practices often mentioned or described explicitly by the texts. Sometimes even the writing or copying of the texts and vignettes functions as a ritual act. These texts and practices answered the needs of the people who employed them in times of crisis, hurt, or loss, or in the continual difficulties of everyday life. Thus, the bottom line in these texts is empowerment, and the texts themselves are appropriately described as texts of ritual power.

THE ANCIENT EGYPTIAN word for ritual power (usually translated "magic") is *hekau*, also found as *heka*. Its etymology is uncertain. Some have regarded it as a compound that means "smiting the *kas* (or, "vital essences")"; the Egyptians themselves seem to have treated it that way as a pun. It can be (perhaps more plausibly?) analyzed as an intensifying (?) prefix (*h*) attached to a form of the root of *ka* ("vital essence"). This word is attested as early as the Old Kingdom Pyramid Texts and as late as Coptic, where it takes the form *hik*. Users of ritual power are called "ritualists" (the form is related to *hekau*), and often they may be characterized as priests, especially lector-priests. A user of ritual power can also be described as a "reciter." It has recently been suggested by Robert K. Ritner that this is the epithet of the renowned healer Djedhor of the Persian period in Egypt. *Heka* or *hekau* can be personified as a deity; this may cast doubt on the Egyptian concept of ritual power as an impersonal force.

A study of the deity *Heka* has prompted this reflection on the part of Te Velde in his article "The God Heka in Egyptian Theology":

> The god Heka, who represents magic, power, divine creative energy, human creativity, vital potential, mysterious efficacy, seems to be a very exceptional god. It is of importance to make a closer examination of the data referring to this god, in order to see what exactly is the specific magical component of what is called Egyptian magic. Lévi-Strauss has remarked that the term of totemism and likewise the concept of myth are categories of our thinking, artificial units, which only exist as such in the minds of scholars engaged in research, while nothing specific in the outside world corresponds to them anymore. It seems not impossible to me that he might also call the concept of magic such an "unité artificielle," which is continually given a different content (186).

Ritual power figures prominently not only in texts of that category narrowly defined, but also in mortuary texts (which are, after all, texts dealing with ritual power in a specific context), other "religious" texts, "medical" texts, and stories. The media themselves on which texts are recorded can illustrate ritual practice. For example, figures and pots are broken in execration rituals, and *cippi* of Horus are used to sanctify holy water for use in healing scorpion sting and snakebite. Other objects testifying to the pervasiveness of ritual power include the ubiquitous amulets as well as "magical" ivories. As is the case in many literate traditions, some texts were themselves used as amulets. In the words of J. F. Borghouts, *Ancient Egyptian Magical Texts,*

> Whatever their provenance or their actual *Sitz im Leben*, no spell can be detached from an accompanying magical action to which certain preliminary conditions pertain, too. Some of this information may be gained from the spell itself—usually towards the end, in the directions for use. Thus some spells give explicit hints on the use of the paraphernalia, necessary to the carrying out of the act such as staffs, substitute objects, masks, amulets, etc. . . . In general, however, much of the documentation about magical procedures comes from other sources, textual or archaeological. The spells are the *verbalized* core matter of the rite (VIII–IX).

Ritual directions are frequently found in utterances belonging to the mortuary literature, which increasingly are suspected by scholars of having some "this-worldly" applications. We may also note that, while the act of writing and the written text or words are important aspects of ritual power in virtually all literate traditions, such is the case in particular in Egyptian writing.

IT IS NECESSARY to elaborate somewhat on the spheres of operation of ritual power and on some of its implications at different periods. Ritual power as defined here is present in and fundamental to all ritual, not merely ritual in certain restricted or preconceived contexts. Borghouts mentions everyday applications, applications that pertain to the king or the state, and applications found primarily in the temple ritual. To a large extent these distinctions are arbitrary or of degree rather than of kind, as he himself acknowledges and his examples illustrate. The operation of ritual power in different sociopolitical and religious contexts can, however, have paradoxical or ironic consequences:

i. private use of ritual power can most easily enter the realm of or at least raise the question of the criminal or antisocial use of ritual power, whereas the temple and state uses normally cannot (a qualification will be noted below);

ii. a change in the official religion will result in a change in the structure or articulation of the use of ritual power by the religious establishment, but not in the existence or fact of its use of ritual power;

iii. such a change will create a disjunction between the official worldview and schema of ritual power and that of private individuals—and temples or religious institutions—who are still operating in the old tradition;

iv. on the popular level, eclecticism and persistence of tradition do much to moderate the cut-and-dried appearance of these demarcations;

v. the popular uses by people who profess the official system can be proscribed by the latter, bringing us back to the first point.

One case usually regarded as involving illicit use of ritual power in very high echelons of the court is the so-called harem conspiracy against Ramesses III. Though Hans Goedicke, "Was Magic Used in the Harim Conspiracy Against Ramesses III?", has rejected this understanding and argued that "making people of wax" refers not to ritual practice but to other accustomed means of making people "malleable," the consensus remains plausible. Despite the prevalence of the use of ritual power on an everyday or household level, there is an insistence on secrecy with regard to knowledge and dissemination of rituals. There are also statements in the nature of recommendations testifying to the excellence or efficacy of the ritual.

One frequent aspect of the use of ritual power is described by Borghouts, *Ancient Egyptian Magical Texts*. The ritual specialist "expresses the will of supernatural powers by impersonating them, hence, elsewhere, the frequent initial presentative clause 'I am god X'" (x). This needs to be clarified and understood in context, as it is fundamental to the employment of ritual power. It is not to be regarded as *hybris* or as an amoral, anarchic free-for-all in which anyone can coerce or bully the gods. This is, rather, an example of the ritual specialist playing the role of, and being for that duration and purpose an embodiment of, the divine being or power. This is a feature of many traditions, and its presence in ancient Egypt is now better understood by research that pays more attention to anthropology. The wearing of ceremonial masks by at least some ancient Egyptian ritualists, including Anubis-masked embalmers and mortuary priests as well as some other priests, has recently been discussed by Arelene Wolinski, "Egyptian Masks," as an example of this phenomenon. The identification or self-predication of identity of the ritualist with the divine being or power remains a feature of Coptic texts of ritual power, and is quite likely one of the reasons why the popular or everyday use of ritual power was proscribed by the church authorities (though the use of ritual power per se was just as characteristic of the legitimate church ritual).

THIS BRINGS US to a consideration of the dimensions of continuity, change, and commonality in the texts and practice of ritual power in ancient and Coptic Egypt. The material covers a very long history, and it is hardly surprising that change and development took place during the Pharaonic and Greco-Roman periods. Some of these changes have been discussed by John Ray, "Ancient Egypt." Ray focuses upon the increasing emergence of divination, beginning in the New Kingdom (especially the Ramesside period), marked in later periods by the adaptation and assimilation of practices and materials from Mesopotamia, Persia, and the Greco-Roman world. Borghouts, *Ancient Egyptian Magical Texts*, has stated that in "Demotic and Coptic sources, . . . procedures, purposes and mythological themes often differ" (VII). In the case of the latter, the drawing of themes from Christianity is an obvious element of change, though this is not the case with the Old Coptic materials. With regard to content, the 146 examples of hieroglyphic and hieratic texts ranging from the Old Kingdom through the Greco-Roman period (thus overlapping with Demotic as well as Old Coptic materials) that Borghouts presents in *Ancient Egyptian Magical Texts* give us a reasonable overview of the different concerns of Egyptian texts of ritual power:

    i. love charm (1);
    ii. dangerous or dead people, the evil eye (5);
    iii. night visions (3);
    iv. evil influences, death (3);
    v. dangers during epagomenal days (a liminal period of the year) (9);
    vi. specific disease, demons (6);
    vii. everyday ailments (2);
    viii. hemorrhage (4);
    ix. burns (3);
    x. headaches (9);
    xi. abdominal diseases (4);
    xii. vague malign influences affecting several parts of the body (8);

xiii. blindness (1);
xiv. semen of a demon (1);
xv. women's ailments, childbearing ailments (5);
xvi. protection of children (6);
xvii. administration of medicines (11);
xviii. protection against dangerous animals (2);
xix. protection against scorpions (40);
xx. protection against crocodiles (12);
xxi. protection against snakes (8);
xxii. protection against the serpent Apophis (3).

An excellent sample of the texts and attested practices of ritual power known from Demotic sources is the Demotic Magical
Papyrus of London and Leiden, originally published by F. Ll. Griffith and Herbert Thompson and the subject of recent studies by
Janet H. Johnson. This Demotic material, which includes Old
Coptic glosses and occasional words within the text, is now available in Hans Dieter Betz, *The Greek Magical Papyri in Translation,
Including the Demotic Spells*. The original editors characterize the
papyrus as "a compilation . . . seen to consist mainly of directions for divination processes, involving numerous invocations,
together with erotica and medical prescriptions, in which, however, magic plays as large a part as medicine" (5).

The specifically Coptic component of the continuum of ritual power in ancient and late antique Egypt is illustrated and discussed in the present volume. While the Coptic material needs to
be studied and appreciated in itself, it cannot arbitrarily be separated from the already millennia-old tradition of ritual power in
Egypt, from the Coptic practitioners' non-Christian contempo-
raries, or from the universal and pervasive realm of ritual power
as an aspect of human culture.

IN THIS CHAPTER we present three Old Coptic texts of ritual
power: the Old Coptic Schmidt Papyrus (text 1) and two Old
Coptic sections from the Great Magical Papyrus of Paris (texts
2–3). The Schmidt Papyrus offers an appeal to the Egyptian god
Osiris on behalf of a woman who is complaining about a desire
for love or the issue of desertion. The opening lines of the Great
Magical Papyrus of Paris invoke Egyptian (and Jewish) powers for
the purpose of revelation. The Isis love spell from the same codex

employs Old Coptic and Greek materials relating to Isis, Osiris, Nephthys, and other Egyptian powers in order to present spells for a woman to obtain a male lover or a man to obtain a female lover. These texts are written, totally or in large part, in the form of the ancient Egyptian language that we term Coptic or, more specifically, Old Coptic.

Coptic, the latest phase of the ancient Egyptian language, emerged in its standard form about the third century C.E. and is still employed today as the liturgical language of the Coptic Orthodox Church. The unique feature of Coptic among written forms of Egyptian is that it is written in the Greek alphabet, supplemented by several native letters derived from Demotic, the number of which varies from dialect to dialect. Since its script did not have to be deciphered and its grammar did not have to be completely recovered, Coptic was the second form of Egyptian to be studied by scholars, and it played a major role in the decipherment of the earlier Egyptian language and scripts (for example, hieroglyphic Egyptian). As the only form of Egyptian written in a vocalized script, Coptic has been extensively employed in attempts to reconstruct the vocalization of pre-Coptic Egyptian and to illuminate various historical and comparative aspects of the Egyptian language.

Though standard Coptic is known as the language of Christian Egypt *par excellence,* Christianity was not the initial motivation for the introduction of the Coptic script, nor was the supposedly cumbersome nature of the Demotic script, which was the vehicle for everyday literacy in Greco-Roman Egypt. In fact, the consistent use of the Greek alphabet to write (perhaps we should really say "spell") Egyptian seems to have been motivated by the need to record and retrieve precise vocalized pronunciations, specifically in texts of ritual power! Texts and glosses of this sort are the material we designate as Old Coptic and are attested in the first century C.E.; the earliest datable attempts to write Egyptian in the Greek alphabet occur in graffiti at least as early as the first century B.C.E. Old Coptic employs more native letters than the later standard dialects and preserves some grammatical forms unknown or known only vestigially in standard Coptic.

1. A woman's complaint about neglect

Text: Old Coptic Schmidt Papyrus

Description: papyrus, estimated 13.2 x 10.2 cm, ca. 100 C.E. (so Walter E. Crum); the whereabouts of the papyrus is unknown.

Bibliography: Helmut Satzinger, "The Old Coptic Schmidt Papyrus"

Translator: Edmund Meltzer

The Old Coptic Schmidt Papyrus is a text that communicates the complaint of a woman named Esrmpe against a man named Hor. Helmut Satzinger, the original editor of the text, classifies it as a love charm in the form of "a complaint, of an appeal to a court." In this connection he notes "the close connection that existed, at least from the New Kingdom onward, between jurisdiction and oracular practices" ("The Old Coptic Schmidt Papyrus," 46). We may prefer to suggest that the papyrus is not merely a love charm but is rather a complaint about a situation of desertion or familial neglect on the part of Hor. This interpretation would accord well with the overall tone of the text and would help explain Esrmpe's lack of a "champion son" and her apparent barrenness.

TEXT

It is Esrmpe (daughter) of Kllaouj who is complaining <about> ' Hor (son) of Tanesneou. My lord ' Osiris, (lord) of Hasro, I appeal to you, ' render justice to me and Hor (son) of Tanesneou 5 for the things that I have done to him and the things that he has done ' to me. He does not consider <me> (?), I having no ' power, I having no champion son. ' I cannot help; I am a barren woman. ' There is no one who will appeal <on> my behalf <before> him, because of 10 Hor . . . , I appeal ' to [you . . .] great one (?), Osiris, hear my cries . . . ' Many are the things that he has done to me. Make a way ' for your [. . .]s, [. . . O]siris, (lord) of Abydos, ' Osir[is . . .] 15 Isis . . . Wepwawet, Hathor, ' the nurse [of] Anubis son of Osiris, the cowherd ' of . . . , ' render me justice.

2. Invocation of Egyptian and Jewish deities for revelation

Text: Great Magical Papyrus of Paris, 1–25

Description: lines 1–25 of a fourth-century papyrus codex housed at the Bibliothèque Nationale, Paris

Bibliography: Karl Preisendanz, *Papyri Graecae Magicae*, 1.66–67; Marvin Meyer, *"PGM IV.1–25"* (in Hans Dieter Betz, *The Greek Magical Papyri in Translation*, 36–37); Terence DuQuesne, *A Coptic Initiatory Invocation*

Translator: Marvin Meyer

The Old Coptic invocation that opens the Great Magical Papyrus of Paris calls upon Egyptian and Jewish powers for the purpose of revelation. The text includes initial words of power, brief instructions for the use of the invocation, a series of greetings, and a concluding request for revelation. In syncretistic fashion the invocation combines traditional Egyptian lore with other, chiefly Jewish, references. Part of this invocation is paralleled in the Demotic papyrus of ritual power XIV.627–35 (see Hans Dieter Betz, The Greek Magical Papyri in Translation, *229). Thanks to the generosity of the staff at the Bibliothèque Nationale, Marvin Meyer was able to confirm several readings in this text and the next text during July 1991.*

TEXT

SAPHPHAIOR¹
BAELKOTA KIKATOUTARA EKENNK¹ LIX,
the great demon and the inexorable one,¹
. . . IPSENTANCHOUCHEOCH ⁵

DOOU SHAMAI ARABENNAK ANTRAPHEU BALE¹
SITENGI ARTEN BENTEN AKRAB ENTH OUANTH¹
BALA SHOUPLA SRAHENNE DEHENNE KALASHOU¹
CHATEMMOK BASHNE BALA SHAMAI,
    on the day¹ of Zeus, at the first hour,
    but on the (day) of deliverance, at the fifth hour,
        a cat; ¹⁰
    at the eighth, a cat.¹

Hail, Osiris, king of the underworld,
    lord of embalming,¹

who is south of Thinis,
who gives answer in Abydos,
who is under ' the noubs tree in Meroe,
whose glory is in ' Pashalom.
Hail, Althabot;
bring Sabaoth unto me. 15
Hail, Althonai, great Eou, very valiant; '
bring Michael unto me,
the mighty angel ' who is with god.
Hail, Anubis, of the district ' of Hansiese,
you who are upon your mountain.
Hail, goddesses, '
Thoth the great, the great, the wise.
Hail, gods, 20
Achnoui Acham Abra Abra Sabaoth.
For Akshha ' Shha is my name,
Sabashha is my true name, '
Shlot Shlot very valiant is my name.

So let the one who is ' in the underworld
join the one who is in the air. '
Let them arise, enter, and give answer to me 25
concerning the matter about which I ask them.
The usual.

3. Isis love spell

Text: Great Magical Papyrus of Paris, 94–153
Description: lines 94–153 of a fourth-century papyrus codex housed at the
Bibliothèque Nationale, Paris
Bibliography: Karl Preisendanz, *Papyri Graecae Magicae*, 1.70–77; Marvin
Meyer, "*PGM* IV.94–153" (in Hans Dieter Betz, *The Greek Magical Papyri in
Translation*, 39–40); idem, "The Love Spell of *PGM* IV. 94–153"
Translator: Marvin Meyer

*The Isis sex spell embedded within the Great Magical Papyrus of
Paris is composed of Old Coptic and Greek sections to be used to obtain*

a lover. The text opens (94–114) with the story of the adultery of Osiris with Nephthys and Isis's use of magic to make Osiris come back to her. The same story is recounted in Plutarch On Isis and Osiris 14, but there the infidelity of Osiris and the grief of Isis are minimized. The spell that follows (115–31) applies the power of the mythic story, as an historiola, to the desire of a person (a male) to attract a woman. Two sets of instructions for the use of the spells (132–37; 144–46) are preserved in Greek. The final two Old Coptic sections offer spells for a woman to get a man (138–43) and for a man to get a woman (147–53).

TEXT

It is Isis who is coming from the mountain at midday in summer, the dusty young woman. [95] Her eyes are full of tears and her heart is full of sighs. Her father, ' Thoth the great, came to her and asked her, "My daughter ' Isis, you dusty young woman, why are your eyes full of tears, your heart full of sighs, '. . . of your garment soiled? (Away with) the tears of your eyes!" She said ' [to him], "He is not with me, my father, ape Thoth, ape [100] [Thoth], my father. I have been betrayed by my woman friend. I have discovered ' [a] secret: Yes, Nephthys is having intercourse with Osiris ' [. . .] my brother, my own mother's son." He said to her, ' "Look, this is adultery against you, my daughter Isis." ' She [said] to him, "It is adultery against you, my father, [105] [ape] Thoth, ape Thoth, my father. It is pregnancy proper for me ' myself." He said to her, "Arise, my daughter Isis, ' [and go] south of Thebes, north of Abydos. There are ' . . . those who trample (?) there. Take for yourself Belf child of Belf, ' [the one whose] foot is of bronze and whose heels are of iron, [110] [that] he forge for you a double iron nail with a ' . . . head, a thin base, a strong point, ' and light iron. Bring it to me, dip ' it in the blood of Osiris, and hand it over; we . . . ' this flame . . . unto me." [115]

"Every flaming, every cooking, every heating, every steaming, ' every sweating that you (masc.) will cause in this flaming stove, ' you must cause in the heart, in the liver, (in) the region ' of the navel, in the belly of N. whom N. bore, until I bring ' her to the house of N. whom N. bore and she puts what is in [120] her hand into my hand, what is in her mouth into my mouth, what is in her belly onto my belly, ' what is in her female parts onto my male parts, ' quickly, quickly, immediately, immediately! ' Rise up to the kings of Alchah, speak the truth (?) in Oupoke, ' arouse god (after) N. whom N. bore, and I shall send her [125] to be with N. whom N. bore. For I am To ' child of To; I am the Great child of the Great; I am Anubis, who bears ' the glorious crown of Re and puts it upon King ' Osiris, King Osiris Onnophris, . . . arouse ' the whole earth, that you may arouse the heart of N. whom [130] N. bore, that I may know what is in her heart for me, for N. ' whom N. bore, on this day." '

If a large amount of saliva forms in your mouth as you speak, ' understand that she is distressed and wants to talk with you. ' If you yawn frequently, she wants [135] to come to you. But if you sneeze two times or more, ' she is in good health and is returning to where she lives. ' If you have a headache and are crying, she is distressed or even dying. '

"Rise to heaven, and arouse the high one (masc.) after the noble one (fem.). Rise ' to the abyss, and arouse Thoth after Nabin. Arouse [140] the heart of these two bulls, Hapi and Mnevis. ' Arouse the heart of Osiris after Isis. Arouse ' Re after the light. Arouse the heart ' of N. whom N. bore after N. whom N. bore." '

(Say) these things on behalf of women. But when (you are speaking) about women, [145] then speak, conversely, so as to arouse the females ' after the males: '

"When she drinks, when she eats, when ' she has intercourse with someone else, I will charm her heart, ' I will charm the heart of her, I will charm her breath, I will charm [150] her three hundred sixty-five members, I will charm her inner part ' . . . wherever I want, until she comes to me and I know ' what is in her heart, (what) she does, and of what she thinks, ' quickly, quickly, immediately, immediately!"

2

GREEK TEXTS OF RITUAL POWER FROM CHRISTIAN EGYPT

INTRODUCTION AND TRANSLATIONS
BY MARVIN MEYER

The world of Greco-Roman Egypt was a wonderfully diverse and pluralistic world, and nowhere is that diversity and pluralism seen more clearly than in the texts of ritual power that were produced and used by the people who inhabited that world. Our knowledge of Greco-Roman traditions of ritual power in Egypt has expanded greatly with the publication of the "Greek magical papyri" in the well-known volumes edited by Karl Preisendanz, *Papyri Graecae Magicae*, which were published in 1928 and 1931 and were reedited (by Albert Henrichs) in a new edition that appeared in 1973–74. (Now see also Robert W. Daniel and Franco Maltomini, *Supplementum Magicum*, for texts missed by Preisendanz and published since Preisendanz.) English translations of these Greek texts (and others not included in *Papyri Graecae Magicae*) have appeared recently, in 1986 (second edition, 1992), in a volume edited by Hans Dieter Betz, *The Greek Magical Papyri in Translation*. Included in this volume, alongside the Greek texts (with Coptic passages), are Demotic texts of ritual power. Betz and the other contributors decided, however, to omit Greek texts of ritual power that were predominantly Christian. (Betz admits that the Greek texts included in his volume may still contain "a few sprinkles of Christianity.") This decision may have been made because of the particular problems associated with defining a corpus of Christian texts of ritual power and analyzing their Christian contents. While a few such texts are published in volume 2 of *Papyri Graecae Magicae* (more in the second edition than in the first), these texts are merely samples from a much larger corpus that includes, for example, many of the Coptic Christian texts of ritual power translated in the present volume.

Betz provides a succint description of the nature of the texts given in *The Greek Magical Papyri in Translation:*

> This collection includes individual spells and remedies, as well as collections made by ancient magicians, from the early Hellenistic period to late antiquity. Since the material comes from Greco-Roman Egypt, it reflects an amazingly broad religious and cultural pluralism. Not surprising is the strong influence of Egyptian religion throughout the Greek magical papyri, although here the texts nevertheless show a great variety. Expressed in Greek, Demotic, or Coptic, some texts represent simply Egyptian religion. In others, the Egyptian element has been transformed by Hellenistic religious concepts. Most of the texts are mixtures of several religions— Egyptian, Greek, Jewish, to name the most important (xlv).

In this chapter we present a collection of those Greek texts of ritual power that were passed over by Betz and the other contributors: Christian texts of ritual power that are preserved in Greek. These texts are sometimes difficult to identify with any certainty. What is it about a text that makes it indisputably Christian? What is it about a text that makes it indisputably a text of ritual power? If a short text merely preserves a quotation from Psalm 91, for example, is it clearly a Christian text of ritual power? In spite of uncertainties, we present in this chapter a broad sampling of Greek (occasionally Greek and Coptic) texts that illustrate a general concern for ritual power in Christian Egypt. As such, these texts, together with the other Greek and Demotic texts of ritual power, complement very nicely the Coptic texts of ritual power published in this volume.

The ritual power invoked in the texts in this chapter is directed toward several specified needs. Many of the texts are spells intended to heal or protect a person from illness. When the precise illness is mentioned, more often than not it is a fever, an eye ailment, or a disease prompted by demon-possession. Oxyrhynchus 1384 (text 4) combines medical prescriptions and healing legends in the same text. Oxyrhynchus 1077 (text 7) presents Matthew 4:23–24 with the Greek words arranged to form crosses and with a drawing of a human figure in the center. Like other texts, Berlin 11858 (text 8) includes an *historiola*, or mythic story (here, a paraphrase of Matthew 14:22–33), that may help provide the power to aid the one wearing the amulet. Berlin 9096 (text 9) strings together biblical quotations, not for their edifying contents or their doctrinal possibilities, but rather for their power to protect the person who wears the piece of parchment. Some texts (texts 10, 11, 14, and others) make use of credal formulations and liturgical utterances (Alleluia, Amen, the trisagion, and so on). The lines from the Great Magical Papyrus of Paris (text 19) give instructions for the performance of an exorcism. Both the words of power to be spoken (in Coptic and in Greek) and the actions to be performed are given, as is the description of the apotropaic tinfoil amulet to be worn after the exorcism. Ianda 14 (text 21) coalesces lines from the Lord's Prayer and the Exorcism of Solomon in order to create verbal power for protection.

The other texts in this chapter address additional needs. Oxyrhynchus 1060 (text 25) and Oslo 1.5 (text 26) offer protection for a house. The former text invokes a variety of powers (Aphrodite, Horus, Yao Sabaoth Adonai, St. Phocas) to protect especially the entrance to a house, and the latter text offers protection for a family against all sorts of evil vermin and fiendish threats. The text from the Hermitage (text 27), Vienna G 19929 (text 28), and the text from the Institut français d'archéologie orientale in Cairo (text 29) are all texts of vengeance against opponents. In the case of the text from Cairo, a curse is directed against a woman and her children. Six oracular texts (texts 30–35) are used to ascertain the will of god for future plans. These texts may be compared, in general, with the collection of oracles in Vatican Coptic Papyrus 1 (text 126). Among the Greek oracular texts, Oxyrhynchus 1926 (text 32) and Harris 54 (text

33) were made from the same sheet of papyrus, and they constitute the two possible responses to the question whether one
should engage in a financial transaction ("no" or "yes"). Prague
1 (text 36) shows a general interest in success and good luck, and
Heidelberg G 1359 (text 37) lists biblical names (names of
power?) and suggests Greek translations. In terms of its contents,
Heidelberg G 1359 need not be read as a text of ritual power, but
the fact that it was folded may suggest that it was worn as an
amulet.

4. Spells and healing legends for medical problems

Text: Oxyrhynchus 1384

Description: papyrus, 30.2 x 15.4 cm, fifth century

Bibliography: Karl Preisendanz, *Papyri Graecae Magicae*, 2.215–16 (lines 15–29 only); Bernard P. Grenfell and Arthur S. Hunt, *The Oxyrhynchus Papyri*, 11.238–41

Translator: Marvin Meyer

Oxyrhynchus 1384 is a text consisting of three medical recipes (for a purgative, a medicinal drink for someone who has difficulty urinating, and a poultice for wounds) and two healing legends. In the first legendary account the unusual order of the persons of the Christian trinity ("in the [name of the] father and the holy [spirit and the] son," 20–22) could conceivably hint that the holy spirit may be taken as the divine mother (compare Oxyrhynchus 924 [text 15]).

TEXT

Ingredients for a laxative: | † cummin—4; | fennel—2; | parsley—4; [5] kostos root—4; | mastic—4; | coriander—7; | bayberries—21; | nuts—[. . .]; [10] ham (?)—[. . .]; | pennyroyal—[. . .]; | silphium (?)—[. . .]; | salt—[. . .]; | vinegar—[. . .]. [15]

† [Three men] met us | in the desert [and said to the lord] | Jesus, "What treatment is possible for the sick?" | And he says to them, "[I have] given olive | oil and have poured out myrrh [for those] [20] who believe in the [name of the] | father and the holy [spirit and the] | son." |

† Angels of the lord ascended to | [mid]-heaven, suffering [25] from eye ailments and holding a sponge. | The son of the lord says to them, "Why have you ascended, | O holy, all-pure ones?"

"We have come up | to receive healing, O Yao Sabaoth, because you are | powerful and strong." [30]

For difficulty in urination, to heal the one who is suffering: | † Take the dry seed of wild basil, | grind it with wine of Ascalon, | then drink it hot. |

† For the treatment of wounds: [35] Take the fruit of a cypress, | boil it, and apply it.

5. Amulet to heal eye ailments

Text: Berlin 21911

Description: papyrus, 4.2 x 5.2 cm, fifth century

Bibliography: G. H. R. Horsley, *New Documents* (1978), 118–19; William Brashear, "Vier Berliner Zaubertexte," 30–31

Translator: Marvin Meyer

Berlin 21911 is an amulet intended to heal the eye ailments of Phoibammon. The prayer must be addressed to the virgin Mary (note the feminine participle in the first clause, and the reference to the addressee's "only begotten son"), and the text closes with a citation of Psalm 91:1.

TEXT

✝ Having received grace from ¹ your only begotten son, ¹ stop the discharge, the ¹ pains of the eyes ⁵ of Phoibammon son of ¹ Athanasios. One who dwells with the ¹ help of the most high [will] ¹ abide in the shelter ¹ [of the god of] heaven.

6. Healing ostracon

Text: Paris, ostracon from the Egger collection

Description: ostracon, seventh or eighth century

Bibliography: Karl Preisendanz, *Papyri Graecae Magicae*, 2.234–35; Henri Leclercq, "Amulettes," 1805–7

Translator: Marvin Meyer

This ostracon apparently was used as an amulet for healing. The text refers in a very general way to John 9:1–12; on the Portico of Solomon compare Acts 3:11.

TEXT

✝ In the sheep-pool in Soloam— ¹ its name in Hebrew is Bedsaida—the lord was found, in the Portico ¹ of Solomon the master was found. He healed the person who was bedridden ¹ by means of his word, and he opened the blind man's eyes. Hence we also, [5] along with the archangels <and> the bodiless <angels>, shout and call [|] out and say, Holy is god, whom the cherubim praise and [the angels] [|] revere. Holy, mighty is he, whom the chorus of bodiless angels glorifies. [|] [Holy], immortal is he, who was revealed in the [manger] of the dumb animals. Have mercy upon us. ✝

7. Healing spell using the Gospel of Matthew

Text: Oxyrhynchus 1077

Description: parchment, 6 x 11.5 cm, sixth century

Bibliography: Karl Preisendanz, *Papyri Graecae Magicae*, 2.211

Translator: Marvin Meyer

Oxyrhynchus 1077 is an amulet that employs Matthew 4:23–24 as a healing spell ("Curative Gospel according to Matthew"). The Greek words of the amulet are positioned so as to form crosses, and a human figure is drawn in the center.

TEXT

Curative Gospel according to Matthew. And Jesus went about all of Galilee, teaching and preaching the gospel of the kingdom, and healing every disease {and every disease} and every infirmity among the people. And his fame spread into all of Syria, and they brought him those who were ill, and Jesus healed them.

8. Amulet for help from god and the saints

Text: Berlin 11858

Description: papyrus

Bibliography: Karl Preisendanz, *Papyri Graecae Magicae*, 2.231–32, with an emended and restored version of the Greek transcription

Translator: Marvin Meyer

Berlin 11858 was rolled up and used as an amulet to help the one who wore it. Besides referring to the aeons, the angels, the saints, and the virgin Mary, the text opens with an historiola *that paraphrases Matthew 14:22–33.*

TEXT

[When a strong] wind [came up] and ' he (that is, Peter) began ' to sink, ' he called out with a loud [5] voice. And ' he (that is, Jesus) held out his hand ' and grabbed him. ' And when it was ' calm, he (that is, Peter) shouted, [10] "Son of God!"

And I say, ' ✝ O omnipotent one, ' glory to you, god, ' who creates the angels, ' O ruler of aeons. [15] The heavenly chorus ' of aeons praises you. . . . ' I call for [my help, all] ' those who [have been sanctified] through their struggles, ' in memory of St. [Cosmas and] [20] in memory of St. [Damian]. ' The [chorus of cherubim praises] god, [and] ' the chorus of angels joins in praising 'the thrice-[holy] church, [and] ' the community [of the saints blesses] [25] the king Christ, god. ' The chorus of [all the] angels [and] ' the chorus of the [perfect saints praise] ' you, mother of god [and ever-virgin]. ' Chorus of angels [and] [30] archangels, bless. . . .

9. Spell for healing and protection, using biblical quotations

Text: Berlin 9096

Description: parchment, 14 x 8 cm

Bibliography: Carl Wessely, *Les plus anciens monuments du Christianisme,* 2.412–13

Translator: Marvin Meyer

This text describes itself as an amulet worn by a person who is to be helped and protected (and, presumably, healed; compare lines 17–20) by the power invoked through the texts cited (Psalm 91:1; John 1:1–2; Matthew 1:1; Mark 1:1; Luke 1:1; Psalm 118:6–7; Psalm 18:2; Matthew 4:23).

† In the name of the father and the son and the holy spirit. |
One who dwells in the help of the most high | <will> abide
in the shelter of the lord of heaven. |

† In the beginning was the Word, and the Word was with [5]
<god>, and the Word was god. This was in the beginning |
with god. |

† Book of the generation of Jesus Christ, son of David, son of
Abraham. |

† Beginning of the gospel of Jesus Christ, son of god. |

† Since many have undertaken [10] to compile a narrative. |

† The lord is my helper, and I shall not fear. | What will hu-
mankind do to me? |

† The lord is my helper, and I shall look upon | my
enemies. [15]

† The lord is my foundation, and my refuge, | and my
deliverer. |

† The lord Jesus went about all Galilee, | teaching in their syn-
agogues | and preaching the gospel of the kingdom [20] and
healing every disease and every infirmity. |

† The body and the blood of Christ spare your | servant who
wears this amulet. |

Amen, Alleluia † A † O . †

10. Spell invoking Christ for protection against illness and ill treatment

Text: Cairo, Egyptian Museum 10263

Description: papyrus that seems to have been buried with a mummy;
fourth or fifth century

Bibliography: Karl Preisendanz, *Papyri Graecae Magicae,* 2.220–22

Translator: Marvin Meyer

*Egyptian Museum 10263 is an invocation of Christ, who is
described with various titles and creedlike formulations, against the
power of the evil spirits that cause illness (particularly fever) and ill*

treatment. The references to the aeon (or age), "the fullness of the aeon" (1), and the defeat of the cosmic powers may recall Gnostic traditions.

TEXT

I invoke you, [god] of heaven and god of the earth and [god] of the saints through [your blood], the fullness of the aeon ¹ who comes [to us], who has come to the world and has broken the claw of Charon, who has come through Gabriel in the ¹ womb of the virgin Mary, who was born in Bethlehem and raised in Nazareth, who was crucified ¹ [. . .] for this reason the curtain of the temple was torn by itself, who, after rising from the dead in the grave ⁵ on the third day of his death, showed himself in Galilee, and ascended to the height of heaven, who has ¹ myriads of myriads of angels on his left as well as myriads of myriads of angels on his right calling out ¹ three times with one voice, Holy, holy is the king of the aeon, so that the heavens are full of his divinity, ¹ who goes on his way with the wings of the winds.

Come, O mercy, god of the aeon, who has ascended to the ¹ seventh heaven, who has come from the right of the father, the blessed lamb through whose blood the souls have been ¹⁰ freed and through whom the bronze gates have opened by themselves, who has broken ¹ the iron bars, who has loosed those bound in the [darkness], who has made Charon impotent, ¹ who has bound the hostile rebel that was cast into his own places. The heavens were blessed ¹ and the earth was glad that the enemy withdrew from them and that you gave freedom to the creature who prayed to ¹ the lord Jesus, the voice that absolved of sins all of us who call upon your holy name. ¹⁵ The sovereigns [and] the powers and the world-rulers of darkness, whether an unclean spirit or a demon falling ¹ at the hours of midday, or a chill, or a mild fever or a shivering fever, or ill treatment from people, ¹ powers of the adversary—may they not have power against the figure, since it was formed from the hand of your ¹ divinity, [because] yours, O mercy of the aeon, is [all] power, which prevails for ever.

11. Amulet to heal and protect Joseph from fever

Text: Cologne 851

Description: papyrus, 5.5 x 6.5 cm, seventh century

Bibliography: Dierk Wortmann, "Der weisse Wolf"

Translator: Marvin Meyer

Cologne 851 is an amulet, worn by a person named Joseph, against disease and specifically against fever. For this purpose Jesus Christ is invoked, as is the white wolf (with connections to the Egyptian god Horus and the Greek god Apollo), and the word ERICHTHONIE (compare the vocative form of the name of the Greek hero Erichthonios) is presented in "heart formation."

TEXT

                             †   †   †

Jesus Christ	ERICHTHONIE	Let the white wolf,
	RICHTHONIE	
heals	ICHTHONIE	the white wolf,
	CHTHONIE	
the chill	THONIE	the white wolf
and the	ONIE	heal the shivering
fever	NIE	fever of Joseph.
and every	IE	They are quick! † †
disease of the	E	
body of Joseph, who wears		
the amulet daily		
and intermittently.		
They are quick! Amen,		
Alleluia. † † †		

12. Amulet to heal and protect Megas

Text: Amsterdam 173

Description: papyrus, 5.7 x 9.7 cm, fourth or fifth century

Bibliography: Pieter J. Sijpesteijn, "Ein christliches Amulett aus der Amsterdamer Papyrussammlung"

Translator: Marvin Meyer

Amsterdam 173 is an amulet to bring healing and protection to Megas.

TEXT

A † O By Jesus Christ ǀ heal Megas whom ǀ D. . . . . . bore [of] every disease, and ǀ pain of the head and the temples, [5] and fever, and shivering fever. A † O

13. Healing amulet for a woman

Text: Florence, Istituto Papirologico "G. Vitelli," 365
Description: papyrus, 9.5 x 21.5 cm, fifth or sixth century
Bibliography: Karl Preisendanz, *Papyri Graecae Magicae*, 2.227
Translator: Marvin Meyer

This text employs the trisagion along with references to the raising of Lazarus (compare John 11:1–57) and the healing of Peter's mother-in-law (compare Matthew 8:14–15; Mark 1:29–31; Luke 4:38–39) in a "divine amulet" intended to provide healing for a woman.

TEXT

† Holy, holy, holy, lord ǀ . . . [6] and who has healed again, who has raised ǀ Lazarus from the dead even ǀ on the fourth day, who has healed ǀ Peter's mother-in-law, who has also accomplished [10] many unmentioned healings ǀ in addition to those they report in the sacred ǀ gospels: Heal her ǀ who wears this divine ǀ amulet of the disease afflicting [15] her, through the prayers and intercession ǀ of the ever-virgin mother, the ǀ mother of god, and all. . . .

14. Another healing amulet for a woman

Text: Berlin 21230
Description: a very long strip of papyrus, 3 x 21.7 cm, fifth or sixth century

Bibliography: G. H. R. Horsley, *New Documents* (1978), 114–15; William
Brashear, "Vier Berliner Zaubertexte," 31–33
Translator: Marvin Meyer

*Berlin 21230 is an amulet to provide healing for a woman. Like
the previous text, this amulet includes credal formulations that form
the basis for the healing that is requested.*

TEXT

. . . virgin Mary, and was crucified by Pontius Pilate, and was
buried in a tomb, and arose on the third day, and was taken up to
heaven, and . . . ¹ Jesus, because then you healed every infirmity of
the people and every disease . . . , Jesus, . . . believe . . . because
then you went into the house of Peter's mother-in-law [when she
was] feverish, ¹ [and] the fever left her; so also now we beseech you,
Jesus, now also heal your handmaid who wears your [holy] name
from every disease and [from every] ¹ fever and from a shivering
fever and from a headache and from all bewitchment and from
every evil spirit, in the name of father and son and holy spirit.

15. Amulet to protect Aria from fever

Text: Oxyrhynchus 924
Description: papyrus, 9 x 7.6 cm, fourth century
Bibliography: Karl Preisendanz, *Papyri Graecae Magicae*, 2.212
Translator: Marvin Meyer

*Oxyrhynchus 924 is an amulet to protect a woman named Aria
from several sorts of fever. Among the names and letters arranged on
the bottom of the amulet are a series of six of the Greek vowels (Epsilon
is missing), Alpha and Omega, a reference to the trinity as "father,
son, mother" (with the holy spirit as divine mother?), and the name
Abrasax.*

TEXT

Truly guard and protect ¹ Aria from the one-day ¹ chill and
from the daily ¹ chill and from the nightly ⁵ chill and from the

mild ' fever of [the top of the head]. ' You shall do these things [graciously] ' and completely, first on account of ' your will and also on account of her [10] faith, because she is a handmaid ' of the living god, and that ' your name may be glorified ' continually. '

[Power] [15]	A	of Jesus	father, son, mother		Christ	O
	E		holy	AO spirit		U
	I		Abrasax			O

16. Amulet to heal and protect Joannia from fever

Text: Oxyrhynchus 1151

Description: a long, narrow piece of papyrus, 23.4 x 4.4 cm, folded and tied to form an amulet that could easily be worn; fifth century

Bibliography: Karl Preisendanz, *Papyri Graecae Magicae*, 2.212–13

Translator: Marvin Meyer

Oxyrhynchus 1151 is an amulet to heal a woman named Joannia and protect her from several sorts of fever ("and every evil," 38). The "god of the sheep-pool" is invoked (compare John 5:2), John 1:1–3 is cited for its power, and several other figures (the virgin Mary, the archangels, John the evangelist, and a series of saints) are also adjured.

TEXT

✝ Flee, hateful ' spirit! ' Christ pursues you; ' the son of god and [5] the holy spirit ' have overtaken you. ' O god of the ' sheep-pool, ' deliver from all evil [10] your handmaid ' Joannia whom ' Anastasia, also ' called Euphemia, ' bore. [15] ✝ In the beginning was ' the Word, and the Word ' was with god, and ' the Word was god. ' All things were made [20] through him, and without ' him was not anything ' made that was made. ' O lord, ✝ Christ, son and ' Word of the living [25] god, who heals ' every disease ' and every infirmity, ' also heal and watch over ' your handmaid [30] Joannia whom Anastasia, ' also called ' Euphemia, bore, and chase ' away and banish ' from her every [35] fever and every sort of ' chill—quotidian, ' tertian, quartan— ' and every evil. Pray ' through the intercession of [40] our lady the ' mother of god, and the ' glorious archangels, ' and the holy and glorious ' apostle and [45] evangelist and ' theologian John, and ' St. Serenus and ' St. Philoxenos and ' St. Victor and [50] St. Justus and all ' the saints. For your ' name, O lord god, have I invoked, ' the name that is wonderful ' and exceedingly glorious and [55] fearful to your ' adversaries, Amen. †

17. Amulet to protect a woman from pain and distress

Text: Vienna, Rainer 5 (13b)
Description: papyrus, 13.4 x 19.6 cm, sixth or seventh century
Bibliography: Karl Preisendanz, *Papyri Graecae Magicae*, 2.219–20
Translator: Marvin Meyer

Rainer 5 is an amulet to protect a woman from pain and distress, particularly of the womb or vulva. The Christian trinity, the virgin Mary, and the saints are all invoked, and holy oil is employed, along with the invocations, to limit the grief caused by "the devil's beasts."

TEXT

[In the name of the father] and the son and the holy [spirit, and] our lady ' the all-holy mother of god and ever-virgin Mary, and the most saintly ' forerunner John the Baptist, and the theologian St. ' John the evangelist, and our saintly fathers [5] the apostles, and all the saints! I adjure every sting of the ' devil's beasts on the earth, by god and ' Jesus Christ our savior, through the oil ' of the [sacred baptism, to] this place where you have left [poison]: ' Stay [in] place and do not spread either to the heart [10] or to the head or to the vulva, but ' stay where <you have left> your poison, and may the person remain free of distress ' through the all-holy and [honored] ' name of the [almighty god and] 'Jesus Christ the [son . . .].

18. Amulet to protect Silvanus and give him good health

Text: Berlin 954

Description: papyrus, sixth century

Bibliography: Karl Preisendanz, *Papyri Graecae Magicae*, 2.217

Translator: Marvin Meyer

Berlin 954 is an amulet that was burned in a fire in modern times but originally was folded and tied with red thread for Silvanus, the person who wore it. In the amulet Silvanus asks that he be free of demonic possession and in good health. The protective powers of the Lord's Prayer (Matthew 6:9–13), the incipits *(opening lines) of John and Matthew, and words perhaps derived from the Nicene Creed (28) are employed to accomplish the wishes of the one who owns the amulet.*

TEXT

✝ O lord god almighty, ' father of our lord and savior ' [Jesus Christ], and St. Serenus: ' I, Silvanus son ^{5} of Sarapion, pray and bow ' [my] head before you, ' and ask and beseech that you drive ' out of me, your servant, the ' demon of witchcraft and ^{10} the one of wickedness and the one of ' enmity, and take from me ' every disease and every infirmity, ' that I may be healthy and may [be ' destined, in good health], to speak ^{15} the prayer of the gospel: Our father who is in ' heaven, may your name [be made holy], ' your [kingdom] come, [your] will be done ' [as] in heaven so also on earth. ' Give [us] today [our] daily bread. ^{20} And forgive us our debts ' as we also forgive ' [our debtors]. And do [not] lead ' us into temptation, O lord, [but] deliver ' us from evil. [For yours is] the glory for ^{25} ever [. . .] and the. . . . ' In the beginning was the [Word]. Book of the ' [generation of Jesus Christ, son of David, son of Abraham]. ' O light from light, true god, grant ' me, your servant, the light. St. Serenus, ^{30} supplicate on my behalf, that I may be perfectly healthy.

19. Spell to drive out demons

Text: Great Magical Papyrus of Paris, 1227–64

Description: lines 1227–64 of a fourth-century papyrus codex housed at the Bibliothèque Nationale, Paris

Bibliography: Karl Preisendanz, *Papyri Graecae Magicae*, 1.114; Marvin Meyer, "*PGM* IV.1227–64" (in Hans Dieter Betz, *The Greek Magical Papyri in Translation*, 62); idem, *Who Do People Say I Am?*, 34–35

Translator: Marvin Meyer

This text from the Great Magical Papyrus of Paris gives instructions for driving out a demon. After the opening title, the text indicates the words to be uttered, and the words addressed to the divine (1231–39) are given in Coptic. Only in these Coptic words are there Christian elements in this text. The reference to "the seven" in the Coptic section must indicate the seven spheres of the sky. The text next describes the procedure to be used to bind and beat the demonic force (1248–52). Finally there are instructions for the preparation of an amulet. The powerful utterances on the amulet include permutations and verbal transformations based upon BOR and PHOR, and PHOR (or P-Hor) may be taken as the name of the Egyptian god Horus. Among the powerful words are also utterances that may refer to the Egyptian god Bes, the Greek word for "favor" (charis), and the Greek woman Baubo described in some legends about Eleusis. The sign that occurs on the other amulet mentioned at the end of the text is linked to the syncretistic Egyptian figure Chnoubis (or Chnouph).

TEXT

Excellent spell for driving out demons: |

Formula to be spoken over his head: | Place olive branches before him [1230] and stand behind him and say, | "Greetings, god of Abraham; greetings, god | of Isaac; greetings, god of Jacob; | Jesus the upright, the holy spirit, | the son of the father, who is below the seven, [1235] who is within the seven. Bring Yao | Sabaoth; may your power issue | forth from N., until you drive away this | unclean demon Satan, | who is in him. I adjure you, demon, [1240] whoever you are, by this | god, Sabarbarbathioth | Sabarbarbathiouth Sabarbarbathioneth | Sabarbarbaphai. Come out, demon, | whoever you are, and stay away from N., [1245] hurry, hurry, now, now! Come out, demon, | since I bind you with unbreakable adamantine ' fetters, and I deliver you into the ' black chaos in perdition."

Procedure: ' Take seven olive branches. For six of them [1250] tie together the two ends of each one, ' but for the remaining one use it as a whip as you utter the adjuration. Keep it secret; ' it is proven.

After driving out (the demon), hang around ' N. an amulet, which the patient puts on ' after the expulsion of the demon, with [1255] these things written on a tin metal leaf: ' "BOR PHOR PHORBA PHOR PHORBA ' BES CHARIN BAUBO TE PHOR BORPHORBA ' PHORBABOR BAPHORBA PHABRAIE ' PHORBA PHARBA PHORPHOR PHORBA [1260] BOPHOR PHORBA PHORPHOR PHORBA ' BOBORBORBA PAM-PHORBA PHORPHOR ' PHORBA, protect N." ' There is also another amulet on which ' this sign occurs: ϛ

20. Amulet to protect against the mischief of evil spirits

Text: Vienna G 337, Rainer 1
Description: papyrus, sixth century (?)
Bibliography: Karl Preisendanz, *Papyri Graecae Magicae*, 2.218–19
Translator: Marvin Meyer

Rainer 1 describes itself as a "[divine] protector" (5–6), an amulet designed to protect a person from all the mischief that can be caused by evil spirits. The person adjures the spirits by means of the power of god, the angels, the seven spheres of heaven, and the Christian liturgy (33–34). This means of adjuration is somewhat reminiscent of the Testament of Solomon, a Jewish text that describes how the temple of Yahweh in Jerusalem was built by Solomon through the power of the demons who were constrained to work for Solomon. In this regard it is particularly noteworthy to observe that the present amulet also addresses the evil spirits as "all of you who have sworn before Solomon" (29–30).

[I adjure you by the four] ' gospels of the son [. . . , whether a ' tertian fever] or a quartan fever or [. . .] ' fevers [. . .]. [5] Depart from [N., who wears] this [divine] ' protector, because the one who [commands you is the] ' god of Israel, whom [the angels] ' bless and people [fear and every] ' spirit dreads. Again [. . .] [10] demon, whose name ' [. . .], ' who has feet of a [wolf but] ' the [head of] a frog [. . .]. '

I adjure it by the [seven circles] [15] of heaven: the first [. . .], ' the second of [aquamarine, the third] ' of steel, the [fourth] ' of malachite, the fifth [. . .], ' the sixth like gold, the [seventh] [20] of ivory.

I adjure [you], ' unclean spirits, who do wrong to the lord: ' Do not injure the one who wears ' these adjurations. Depart 'from him. Do not hide [25] down here in the ground; do not lurk under ' a bed, nor under a window, nor ' under a door, nor under beams, nor ' under utensils, nor below a pit. '

I adjure all of you who [30] have sworn before Solomon: Do not ' injure a person, do not cause harm with fire or [with water], ' but through the oath be fearful of ' the Amen and the Alleluia and the ' gospel of the lord, who suffered for the sake of [35] us people.

And now I adjure ' all of you spirits who weep, ' or laugh frightfully, [or] make ' a person have bad dreams or terror, ' or make eyesight dim, or [40] teach confusion or guile of mind ' in sleep and out of sleep.

I ' adjure them by the father and [the son] and the holy [spirit], ' and the holy angels who ' stand before [our lady], [45] to depart from the one who [wears] ' the fearful [and holy] ' statements of [oath], because the lord Jesus [commands . . .].

21. Protective spell using the Lord's Prayer and the Exorcism of Solomon

Text: Ianda 14

Description: papyrus, 15.3 x 30 cm, fifth or sixth century

Bibliography: Karl Preisendanz, *Papyri Graecae Magicae*, 2.226–27

Translator: Marvin Meyer

Ianda 14 is a text, folded and used as an amulet, that apparently was meant to protect the wearer from demons and diseases. The lines of the Lord's Prayer (Matthew 6:9–13; compare Luke 11:1–4 [later texts]) and the Exorcism of Solomon are mixed through each other to form a verbal montage. On lines 14–15 compare Psalm 91:13.

TEXT

✝ Gospel according to Matthew. When Jesus came down from the mountain,— ' "Our father [who] is in heaven, may your name be made holy, may . . . come" — ' "-vil one. For [yours] is the glory for ever and ever."— ' . . . is incomparable and . . . ⁵ controlling the [creation . . .]. ' (I adjure) you through the arm of the immortal [god and] his ' right hand,—[his] disciples came to him and [said], ' "Teacher, teach"— "your kingdom—, [your will] be done as in ' heaven so also on"—Exorcism of Solomon against every unclean ¹⁰ spirit. It is god who gave it, at whose disposal are myriads of myriads ' and thousands of thousands of angels— the demon of midday, the shivers ' by night . . . by day—and by the fearful and holy name, ' shivers—"us to pray just as [John] taught"—"earth. ' Give us today our daily bread. And forgive"— "you will tread on the asp and the basilisk and you will trample ¹⁵ the lion and the dragon—whether by night, or whether blind or deaf [or] dumb or toothless demons, ' . . . or every disease and evil occurrence, (depart) from the one who wears this. Amen.— ' "his disciples." And Jesus says to them, "When you pray, speak as follows:—"our debts ' as we also have forgiven <our> debtors."

22. Spell for protection against evil spirits

Text: Cairo, Egyptian Museum 67188
Description: papyrus, 49.6 x 28.5 cm, sixth century
Bibliography: Karl Preisendanz, *Papyri Graecae Magicae,* 2.222
Translator: Marvin Meyer

Cairo 67188 (verso) is a prayer of Dioskoros of Aphrodito (see Preisendanz) for protection against evil spirits. "Yao, Sabao" recalls Yao Sabaoth, and "Brinthao" is similar to a portion of the Harpon-

Knouphi formula employed in texts of ritual power. Lines 6–16 of the present text (not included here) contain poetic reflections on Greek contests.

TEXT

[Christ! I adjure] you, O lord, almighty, first-begotten, self-begotten, begotten without semen, ' [. . .] as well as all-seeing are you, and Yao, Sabao, Brinthao: Keep me as a son, ' protect me from every evil spirit, and subject to me every ' spirit of impure, destroying demons—on the earth, under the earth, [5] of the water and of the land—and every phantom. Christ!

23. Spell for protection against headless powers

Text: Zereteli-Tiflis collection, 24
Description: a long, narrow yellow leaf of papyrus, oval in shape, 4–5 x 24 cm, sixth century
Bibliography: Karl Preisendanz, *Papyri Graecae Magicae*, 2.223–24
Translator: Marvin Meyer

This text contains a spell to provide protection against headless demons and powers that are bothering the person invoking the angels and archangels.

TEXT

† O angels, ' archangels, who ' hold back ' the floodgates [5] of ' heaven, who ' bring forth ' the light from the ' four [10] corners of the world: ' Because I am ' having a clash ' with some ' headless beings, [15] seize ' them and ' release me ' through the power ' of the father [20] and the son and ' the holy ' spirit. O ' blood of my ' Christ, which was poured [25] out in the ' place of ' a skull, spare me ' and have mercy. '

Amen, [30]
Amen, '
Amen! '
†

24. Amulet for protection against a headless power

Text: London, amulet from the Edward collection, University College

Description: papyrus, fifth or sixth century

Bibliography: Karl Preisendanz, *Papyri Graecae Magicae*, 2.224

Translator: Marvin Meyer

This text from the Edward collection is similar to the previous text. The present text is an amulet in which angels and archangels are invoked to provide protection against a headless power ("a headless dog"; compare Psalm 22:20?) and the virgin Mary is invoked to provide healing. As line 10 indicates, the amulet was worn by a woman.

TEXT

✝ O angels, archangels, who guard the | floodgates of heaven, who bring forth the | light upon the whole earth: Because I am having a clash | with a headless dog, seize him when he comes ⁵ and release me through the power of the father | and the son and the holy spirit, Amen. |

AO, Sabaoth. |

O mother of god, incorruptible, undefiled, unstained mother | of Christ, remember that you have said these things. ¹⁰ Again heal her who wears this, Amen. ✝

25. Amulet to protect the entrance to a house from vermin

Text: Oxyrhynchus 1060

Description: papyrus, 9.2 x 6.3 cm, sixth century(?)

Bibliography: Karl Preisendanz, *Papyri Graecae Magicae*, 2.209–10; Marvin Meyer, "A Sixth-Century Christian Amulet"

Translator: Marvin Meyer

Oxyrhynchus 1060 is an amulet intended to provide protection for a house and specifically the entrance to the house. The powers invoked include the Greek goddess Aphrodite (whose name is presented in the translation, visually, in "wing formation"), the Egyptian god Horus, and the Judeo-Christian deity Yao Sabaoth Adonai and Christian St. Phocas. The amulet is also given a date (10).

TEXT

> † The door, Aphrodite, |
> Phrodite,
> Rodite,
> Odite, |
> Dite,
> Ite,
> Te,
> Te,
> E,

Hor Hor | Phor Phor, Yao Sabaoth Adonai, [5] I bind you, arte<m>isian scorpion. | Free this house | of every evil reptile | [and] annoyance, at once, at once. | St. Phocas is here. [10] Phamenoth 13, third indiction.

26. Amulet to protect a house and its occupants from evil

Text: Oslo 1.5

Description: papyrus, 10 x 16 cm, fourth or fifth century

Bibliography: Karl Preisendanz, *Papyri Graecae Magicae*, 1.210–11

Translator: Marvin Meyer

Oslo 1.5 is an amulet meant to provide protection for a house and the family living there. The powers invoked include Egyptian and Judeo-Christian deities, and among the powerful utterances used in the text are a series of vowels and the familiar expression BAIN-CHOOOCH. The concluding Greek word, ΙΧΘΥΣ, means "fish," and was employed among Christians as an acrostic for Ἰησοῦς Χριστὸς Θεοῦ Υἱος Σωτήρ, *"Jesus Christ, Son of God, Savior." For three amulets that parallel Oslo 1.5 see Oxyrhynchus 2061, 2062, 2063, published in Hans Dieter Betz,* The Greek Magical Papyri in Translation, *265 (= Karl Preisendanz,* Papyri Graecae Magicae, *XXVIIIa, XXVIIIb, XXVIIIc).*

CH M G. | Hor Hor Phor Phor, Yao Sabaoth Adonai, Eloe, Salaman, Tarchei, | I bind you, artemisian scorpion, 315 times. Preserve this house | with its occupants from all evil, from all be-witchment [5] of spirits of the air and human (evil) eye | and terri-ble pain [and] sting of scorpion and snake, through the | name of the highest god, Naias Meli, 7 (times) (?), XUROURO AAAAAA | BAINCHOOOCH MARIIIIIIL ENAG KORE. Be on guard, O lord, son of | David according to the flesh, the one born of the holy virgin [10] Mary, O holy one, highest god, from the holy spirit. Glory to you, | O heavenly king, Amen.

A†O ☧ A†O

ΙΧΘΥΣ

27. Spell seeking relief from the wrongs of Theodosios

Text: from the Hermitage
Description: papyrus, 8.8 x 16 cm, fourth century
Bibliography: Karl Preisendanz, *Papyri Graecae Magicae*, 2.225
Translator: Marvin Meyer

This text from the Hermitage seeks relief and redress in the face of the tyranny of a certain person named Theodosios. The text was folded and used as an amulet.

TEXT

† Holy trinity, holy trinity, [holy trinity]! | Through the holy martyrs [I pray to the] | lord. For [the] angel is not ignorant of our [suffering], | which bears witness [that] Theodosios behaves in a [tyrannical] [5] manner. Nothing but | hostilities have I suffered from his | tyrannical behavior, and I have not found any help | ex-cept the power of god [and] | the testimony for us through the [saints]. [10] And for these reasons I flee for refuge [to you]; | and while weeping I look upon [your] | holiness, that I may see your

power. | Such wrong has he done to me! | For while groaning I have suffered [15] [nothing but] evil [things] from him. O lord, | do not overlook this and do not stand by | him—as I said before, | Theodosios—and do <not> neglect me. | For there is only one lord, [only one] [20] god, in the son [and] | in the father and the holy [spirit], | for ever | and ever, [Amen], | Amen, Amen, Amen. [25] O lord, lord, lord, [. . .].

28. Spell for a person seeking vengeance

Text: Vienna G 19929 (Rainer)
Description: papyrus, 11.9 x 10.5 cm, sixth century
Bibliography: Karl Preisendanz, *Papyri Graecae Magicae*, 2.224–25
Translator: Marvin Meyer

This spell seeks to curse an opponent for his harsh behavior that apparently caused the one now seeking vengeance to have lost his position. The text was folded and probably was used as an amulet.

TEXT

✝ O lord, master of the earth, | avenge me | on the one who opposes | me and on the one [5] who has driven me | from my place, | and pay him back | at once, lord, | so that he may fall into hands [10] harsher than his own.

29. Mesa's curse against Philadelphe and her children

Text: from the Institut français d'archéologie orientale, Cairo
Description: papyrus, 8 x 31 cm, fourth century
Bibliography: L. Barry, "Une adjuration chrétienne"; Gudmund Björck, *Der Fluch des Christen Sabinus*, 47
Translator: Marvin Meyer

This text, folded to form an amulet, consists of a curse invoked by Mesa against Philadelphe and her children.

TEXT

✝ ✝ ✝ Holy god, Gabriel, Michael, do what is sufficient for me, Mesa. | Lord god, strike Philadelphe and her children. | Lord, lord, lord, god, god, god, strike along with her Ou|[. . .]sou. Christ, have mercy upon me and hear me, lord.

30. Oracular text (1)

Text: Oxyrhynchus 925

Description: papyrus, 5.6 x 9.6 cm, fifth or sixth century

Bibliography: Karl Preisendanz, *Papyri Graecae Magicae*, 2.209; G. H. R. Horsley, *New Documents* (1977), 37–44

Translator: Marvin Meyer

Oxyrhynchus 925 is a text that seeks from god an oracular response to a question about a proposed journey.

TEXT

✝ O god almighty, holy, | true, lover of humanity and | creator, father of our lord and savior | Jesus Christ, show me [5] your truth: Do you wish me to go | to Chiout, and shall I find that you are of help | to me and gracious? May it be so, Amen.

31. Oracular text (2)

Text: Oxyrhynchus 1150

Description: papyrus, 7.5 x 10.8 cm, sixth century

Bibliography: Karl Preisendanz, *Papyri Graecae Magicae*, 2.216

Translator: Marvin Meyer

Oxyrhynchus 1150 is a text that seeks an oracular response about whether Anoup should be brought to a hospital.

TEXT

† O god of our patron, ¹ St. Philoxenos, if ¹ you command us to bring ¹ Anoup to your hospital, ⁵ show [your] power, ¹ and let the message come forth.

32. Oracular text (3)

Text: Oxyrhynchus 1926
Description: papyrus, 7.1 x 16.5 cm, sixth century
Bibliography: Karl Preisendanz, *Papyri Graecae Magicae*, 2.216; G. H. R. Horsley, *New Documents* (1977), 40
Translator: Marvin Meyer

Oxyrhynchus 1926 is a text that seeks from god an oracular response to a question about whether or not one should make an offer for a business establishment. Here the text is worded negatively; the next text, Harris 54, has been prepared from the same sheet of papyrus and addresses the same concern, but is worded positively. These two texts thus embody the two options for the response. See Herbert C. Youtie, "Questions to a Christian Oracle."

TEXT

† My lord god almighty and St. ¹ Philoxenos my patron, I beseech you ¹ through the great name of the lord god, if it is not ¹ your will for me to speak about the bank or ⁵ about the weighing office, direct me to find out that I may not speak. † (verso)

† CH M G † CH M G † CH M G †

33. Oracular text (4)

Text: Harris 54

Description: papyrus, 7 x 15.5 cm, sixth century

Bibliography: Karl Preisendanz, *Papyri Graecae Magicae*, 2.232; G. H. R. Horsley, *New Documents* (1977), 40

Translator: Marvin Meyer

Harris 54, like Oxyrhynchus 1926, is a text that seeks an oracular response to a question about whether one ought to make an offer for a bank. Harris 54 is worded positively. Oxyrhynchus 1926 has been cut from the same sheet of papyrus and raises the same question, but does so with a negative formulation. See Herbert C. Youtie, "Questions to a Christian Oracle."

TEXT

✝ My lord god almighty and St. ǀ Philoxenos my patron, I beseech you ǀ through the great name of the lord god, if it is ǀ your will and you help me get the banking business, ⁵ I invoke you to direct me to find out and to speak. ✝ (verso)

✝ CH M G ✝ CH M G ✝ CH M G

34. Oracular text (5)

Text: Berlin 21269

Description: papyrus, 6.6 x 9.4 cm, sixth or seventh century

Bibliography: Kurt Treu, "Varia Christiana II," 29–30

Translator: Marvin Meyer

Berlin 21269 is another text that seeks an oracular response to a question. In this case the issue is the proposed marriage of two people, Theodora and Joseph, and an answer is provided ("Yes").

TEXT

God of the Christians: ǀ Is it your will ǀ [that] we give your handmaid ǀ Theodora to Joseph? ⁵

Yes.

35. Oracular text (6)

Text: Berlin 13232

Description: papyrus, 3.5 x 5.5 cm, Byzantine period

Bibliography: Kurt Treu, "Varia Christiana," 120; G. H. R. Horsley, *New
Documents* (1977), 40

Translator: Marvin Meyer

*Berlin 13232 is yet another text with oracular interests. This text
provides the oracular response to a question asked of god, but the
answer is so general as to preclude the possibility of recovering the original question.*

TEXT

✝ Do not harm ' your soul, for ' what has come to pass is
from god.

36. Invocation of divine power to bring success and good luck

Text: Prague 1, Wessely collection

Description: papyrus, 24 x 28.3 cm, around 300 C.E.

Bibliography: Karl Preisendanz, *Papyri Graecae Magicae,* 2.229–30

Translator: Marvin Meyer

*Prague 1 is an invocation of the power of god, in order that god
may send the archangels to grant success and luck in all the affairs of
life. The author of the text then claims to be surrounded by divine and
angelic power, and asks for protection from hostile powers. The text
closes (50–53) with a humble plea written in Coptic.*

TEXT

I invoke you, O god almighty, ' who is above every ' ruler and
authority and lordship ' and every name ⁵ that is named, who is
enthroned ' above the cherubim before ' you, through our lord '
Jesus Christ, the beloved child. ' Send [out] to me, O master, ¹⁰
your [holy] archangels, ' who stand opposite ' your holy altar '

and are appointed for your holy ' services, Gabriel, Michael, ¹⁵ Raphael, Saruel, Raguel, ' Nuriel, Anael. And let them ' accompany me today, ' during all the hours of day ' and night, and grant me victories, ²⁰ favor, good luck with N., ' success with all ' people, small and ' great, whom I may encounter ' today, during all the ²⁵ hours of day and night. ' For I have before me Jesus ' Christ, who attends me ' and accompanies me; ' behind me Yao Sabaoth Ado[nai]; ³⁰ on my right and [left] ' the god of Ab[raham, Isaac, and Jacob]; ' over [my] face [and] ' my heart Ga[briel, Michael], ' Raphael, Saruel, [Raguel], ³⁵ Nuriel, Anael: [Protect] ' me from every [demon, ' male or female, and from] ' every stratagem ' and from every name, for ⁴⁰ I am sheltered under the wings ' of the cherubim.

O Jesus Christ, ' you king of all the aeons, ' almighty, inexpressibly a creator, ' nurturer, master, almighty, ⁴⁵ noble child, kindly son, ' my unutterable and ' inexpressible name, truly ' true form, unseen [for] ' ever and ever, Amen! ⁵⁰

By the saints ' remember me, pray ' for me; I am without ' strength.

37. Biblical names of power and their translations

Text: Heidelberg G 1359

Description: papyrus, 11 x 18 cm (?), third–fourth century

Bibliography: Karl Preisendanz, *Papyri Graecae Magicae*, 2.222–23; Adolf Deissmann, *Light from the Ancient East*, 405–6

Translator: Marvin Meyer

Heidelberg G 1359 consists of a list of biblical names and phrases, with suggested Greek translations, arranged roughly in alphabetical order. It was folded and may have been used as an amulet.

TEXT

Arima	Jesus, Yo salvation
Ariel	my light of god
Azael	might of god
. . . 5	

Yoman	Yao faith
Yobab	Yo father
Eli eli sazachthani	My god, my god, why have you forsaken me?
Anael	grace of god 10
Judah	Yao confession
[J]erael	of compassion
[J]ephthae	Yao opening
[J]onathan	Yao gift
[J]eroboal	giving judgment in a higher way 15
[J]oseph	Yao addition
[Es]aiou	rising of Yao
[. . .]elam	rest
Jachaz	Yao strength
[J]akin	Yao resurrection 20
[. . .]	Yao
. . .	. . .
Kates	holy
Maana	from consolation
Magabael	How good (is) [god]! 25
Melecheiel	[My] king (is) [god].
. . . . el	my god

3

RITUAL POWER IN COPTIC GNOSTIC TEXTS

INTRODUCTION AND TRANSLATIONS
BY RICHARD SMITH

In the swirling ocean of cults and sects that flowed around the Roman Empire, one cluster of sects received the label "Gnostic." Whether the label was used by the groups involved or whether it encompasses a coherent movement is a matter of historical interpretation, but the term "Gnostic" is useful in describing the most radically dualist of the ancient cults of salvation. As Gnosticism developed over the first few centuries of the Christian era, several currents merged and separated in a complicated process of unifying syncretism and divisive sectarianism. This movement began, most scholars now agree, among the many Jewish sects that flourished around the Mediterranean diaspora communities.

As a Jewish sect in the first century, Gnosticism developed fantastic myths to portray a world filled with evil and alienation. Rejecting the creator-god of the Jewish Scriptures as a wicked ruler responsible for this world, the myths proposed a more remote and spiritual god beyond this cosmos, and they filled the spaces in between these two realms with legions of angels and powers, both threatening and helpful, that the soul must pass on its heavenly journey of salvation toward the higher god.

By the second century, this myth had appropriated many Christian motifs, and Jesus became the paradigm for the soul that had descended from on high to reveal, through a series of instructions and initiations, the way back to the divine source from which all souls had emanated. The earlier, Jewish, layer of this tradition is today called Sethian Gnosticism, because the sects traced their spiritual descent from Seth, the third son of Adam. The Christianized layer is referred to as Valentinian Gnosticism, because of the tremendous synthesis made by the creative second-century "heretic," Valentinus.

Starting in the mid-second century and on into the early third, both versions of Gnosticism were charged with philosophical ideas from middle and neoplatonism. Sethian Gnosticism had a flourish of activity in conflict with Plotinus and his philosophical school. An important impact of neoplatonism, as we see developed in these texts, is the internalization of the transcendent and the increased emphasis on the "mind" of the devotee.

Pertinent to the present volume is the fact that the Gnostic sects frequently were accused by their enemies of practicing magic, of engaging in rituals intended to manipulate the heavenly powers. The New Testament letter to the Colossians attacks an incipient Gnostic group that was trying to combine Jewish cultic practices with Christianity. The group was performing initiations involving angels and powers to achieve a mystical union with Christ. We see the developed version of these rituals in the Sethian texts 40, 41, and 42 in this chapter. The final phase, especially seen in the excerpts from Zostrianos, dates from the neoplatonic period, and the third-century biography of the philosopher Plotinus describes his debates against people who passed around Sethian Gnostic texts and even mentions Zostrianos by name. In his writing Against the Gnostics, Plotinus accuses these people—he calls them imbeciles—of trying "to control the transcendent powers by means of magic chants and evocations, using all kinds of songs and cries and hissing sounds."

The Christian Gnostics, too, were accused by the church fathers of practicing magic. The source of all the heresies, according to Irenaeus, was Simon Magus mentioned in the book of Acts: "His followers use exorcisms and incantations, and they employ familiars and dream-guides, in order, by magic, to overcome the angels who created the world." Likewise the followers of the famous Christian Gnostics Valentinus and Basilides were accused of practicing magic. The heretics, says the church father Hippolytus, "dupe gullible people by delivering their doctrines in darkness and secrecy like sorcerers." Gnosticism and ritual power became so closely linked in the popular imagination that the thousands of gems that have survived from the ancient world, inscribed with strange figures and words of power, were automatically but mistakenly called "Gnostic amulets." In fact, to an outsider like the pagan philosopher Celsus, magic, Gnosticism, and Christianity were all of a piece. In defending Christianity against Celsus, Origen took great pains to differentiate his religion from the practice of reciting spells to ascend through the heavens past the evil cosmic rulers, as seen in the Second Book of Jeu (text 39 of this chapter).

The Gnostic sects also had a tendency to develop the sacramental rituals of the Christian church. The Christian Gnostics elaborated these rites into a sequence of stages in an initiation process. The Gospel of Philip from Nag Hammadi describes a five-stage ritual process involving anointing, baptism, a eucharistic meal, a rite of redemption, and a mystical union within the bridal chamber. The baptism of fire from the Bruce Codex (translated here as text 38) is also one step in a long ritual sequence leading to a heavenly ascent.

It is in their rituals of ascent that the Gnostic sects most effectively blended the practices of ritual power with the visions of the mystics. The rite of baptism, which began as a Jewish ceremony of purification, developed into a rite of heavenly initiation. Other Jewish inspirations were visionary traditions like those in the apocalypses of Enoch, which recount ascent through the spheres and encounters with angels. These seem to have blended with divination techniques for ritually inducing visions. Ritualized inquiry of the gods was common in antiquity, from the mantic practices of the great civic temples to the candle-lit rooms of the sorcerers. With its dualist emphasis, Gnosticism pushed these divine inquiries toward the investigation of heavenly matters. To the church father Tertullian, such inquisitiveness and heresy went hand in hand, and this explained why the Gnostics ran around "with magicians, astrologers, and other crackpots." They are always inquiring about the source of divine things, Tertullian complains, instead of just reading the Bible.

Many scholars have thought that the accusations of magic made by the Christian fathers against the Gnostics were just standard rhetorical clichés, and not true. The texts translated here show the situation to be more complex. Gnosticism reflected an interplay with many traditions, and the true agenda of the heresiologists' rhetoric was to show that the doctrines of the Gnostics were plagiarized. It is a common argument, even today, among religious apologists: Accepted religion is divinely pure, while rejected teachings are derived from human sources. From the philosophers, from the Greeks, from the barbarians, and from the magicians, wrote Bishop Hippolytus in the early third century, the Gnostic heretics have "cobbled together their errors like shoemakers." He thus rather accurately describes the Gnostics as religious *bricoleurs*, with ritual power as one part of the pastiche.

38. A Gnostic fire baptism

Text: Bruce Codex, Bodleian Library, Oxford; page 108, line 23 to page 112, line 6 (according to the edition of Carl Schmidt)
Description: papyrus codex originally of seventy-eight (now seventy-one) leaves containing three separate texts. In the designation of its modern editor, the section translated here is chapter 46 of the Second Book of Jeu. Fourth century (?)
Bibliography: Carl Schmidt, *Gnostische Schriften in koptischer Sprache aus dem Codex Brucianus*; Carl Schmidt and Violet MacDermot, *The Books of Jeu and the Untitled Text in the Bruce Codex*
Translator: Richard Smith

This fire baptism ritual is preceded and followed by baptisms of water and of the holy spirit. The whole sequence, therefore, seems inspired by the words of John the Baptist (in Matthew 3:11 and Luke 3:16), "I baptize you with water . . . but he will baptize you with the holy spirit and with fire." New Testament baptism with holy spirit begins following the resurrection, where it is a running motif in the book of Acts, but baptism with fire seems only to have been practiced by these Gnostic Christians. The setting here, as in Acts, is after the resurrection. The present ritual, however, is elaborated well beyond the ecclesiastical sacrament of baptism, with this ritual's list of magical ingredients, its invocation of exotic names, and its drawings of seals. For "orthodox" Christians, the only seal was the sign of the cross.

The botanical ingredients required for the ritual probably all have symbolic meanings, but what are they? The pigeon grass, or vervain, that wreathes the disciples' heads was, according to several ancient writers, carried in religious processions. The tradition of ritual power pulled both from Greek religions with their ritual use of plants sacred to various gods and also from the Hellenistic philosophical tradition of "cosmic sympathy." These combined traditions influenced ritual power well into the late Middle Ages. One plant in our spell that is curiously evocative is "doghead." "Doghead," or kynokephalon, is a kind of snapdragon, whose flower was thought to resemble the head of a sacred Egyptian baboon. Pliny's Natural History tells us that it was an instrument of divination and a protection from sorcery. In this Gnostic ritual the plant is put in the disciples' mouths, and several other Greek spells give instructions to "recite like a dog-headed baboon (kyno-kephalos)" or, in the delightful translation of Morton Smith, "I

invoke you, lord, in baboonic." The Greek spells also frequently mention the practice, seen here, of invoking while holding a pebble with a
number written upon it.

TEXT

Jesus . . . said to his disciples, "Bring me grapevines, so that
you may receive the baptism of fire." And the disciples brought
him the grapevines. He offered up (**page 109**) incense. He sent up
juniper berries and myrrh, along with frankincense, mastic, nard,
cassia flowers, turpentine, and oil of myrrh. And he also spread a
linen cloth on the place of offering, and set upon it a chalice of
wine, and set loaves of bread upon it according to the number of
the disciples. And he had all of his disciples dress themselves
with linen garments, and crowned them with the plant pigeon
grass, and put the plant doghead in their mouths. And he had
them put the pebble with the seven voices in their two hands,
namely 9879. And he put the plant chrysanthemum in their two
hands, and put the plant knotgrass under their feet. And he
placed them before the incense which he had offered up. And he
had them put their feet together.

And Jesus came behind the incense which he had offered up
and sealed them with this seal:

This is its name: Thozaeez.
This is its interpretation: Zozazez.
Jesus turned to the four corners of the world with his disciples and invoked this prayer, speaking thus, "Hear me, my father,
father of all fatherhoods, infinite light. Make my disciples worthy
to receive the baptism of (**page 110**) fire, and release them from
their sins, and purify them from their transgressions: those which
they knowingly committed and those which they do not know
they committed, those which they have committed from childhood up to this very day, as well as their slanders, their curses,
their false oaths, their thefts, their lies, their lying accusations,
their whoring, their adulteries, their lusts, their greed, and things
which they have committed from childhood up to this very day.
You must wipe all of them out and purify them all. Make

Zorokothora Melchisedek come secretly and bring the water of the baptism of fire of the virgin of the light, the judge. Yea, hear me, my father, as I invoke your imperishable names that are in the treasury of the light:

Azarakaza A . . Amathkratitath
Yo Yo Yo
Amen Amen
Yaoth Yaoth Yaoth
Phaoph Phaoph Phaoph
Chioephozpe Chenobinuth
Zarlai Lazarlai Laizai
Amen Amen Amen
Zazizauach Nebeounisph
Phamou Phamou Phamou
Amounai Amounai
Amen Amen Amen
Zazazazi Etazaza Zothazazaz.

"Hear me, my father, father of all fatherhoods, infinite light, for I have invoked your imperishable names that are in (**page 111**) the treasury of the light. You must make Zorokthora come and bring the water of the fire baptism of the virgin of the light, that I may baptize my disciples in it.

"Yea, hear me, my father, father of all fatherhoods, infinite light. Let the virgin of the light come and baptize my disciples in the baptism of fire. Let her forgive their sins and purify their transgressions. For I invoke her imperishable names, which are:

Zothooza Thoitha Zazzaoth
Amen Amen Amen.

"Yea, hear me, O virgin of the light, judge. Forgive the sins of my disciples and purify their transgressions, those which they knowingly committed and those which they do not know they committed, those which they committed from childhood up to this very day. And let them be numbered among the inheritance of the kingdom of the light.

"So, my father, if you have forgiven their sins, and wiped out their transgressions, and made them be numbered in the kingdom of the light, you must give me a sign within the fire of this fragrant incense."

And at that instant the sign that Jesus had mentioned happened in the fire, and Jesus baptized his disciples. And he gave to them from the offering and he sealed them on their foreheads with the seal of the (**page 112**) virgin of the light, that which makes them be numbered within the kingdom of light.

And the disciples rejoiced, for they had received the baptism of fire along with the seal that forgives sins, and because they had been numbered with the inheritance of the kingdom of light.

This is the seal:

39. Spell for ascending through the heavens

Text: Bruce Codex, Bodleian Library, Oxford; page 127, line 5 to page 128, line 20

Description: papyrus codex of originally seventy-eight (now seventy-one) leaves. The section translated here is part of chapter 52 of the Second Book of Jeu. Fourth century (?)

Bibliography: Carl Schmidt, *Gnostische Schriften in koptischer Sprache aus dem Codex Brucianus*; Carl Schmidt and Violet MacDermot, *The Books of Jeu and the Untitled Text in the Bruce Codex*

Translator: Richard Smith

The theme of the soul ascending through the multiple heavens dominates Gnostic literature. Although similar ascents are found in other traditions, the Gnostic versions are characterized by the hostility of the cosmic environment and the confrontational aspect of the heavenly rulers or archons. Here Jesus gives the disciples instructions on how to overcome these archons during their after-death journey. They receive higher names of powers to invoke, seals, and a pebble-amulet.

The section translated here is only part of a long ritual sequence. The previous text (text 38) is one of a series of baptisms that serve as a preliminary to the ascent. Following this section, similar instructions are given for arriving at the fourth through the twelfth aeons. Then the ascending Gnostic soul encounters the thirteenth and fourteenth aeons and the multitude of emanations of the first and second invisible god. Still further and higher aeons are indicated, but the end of the manuscript is missing.

The many names and numbers are mostly unintelligible. But Yaldabaoth, who plays a leading role in several Nag Hammadi texts as the leader of the archons, appears here as hardly more than a spear-carrier.

TEXT

When you come out of the body and you reach the first of the aeons, and the archons of that aeon arrive before you, seal yourselves with this seal:

This is its name: Zozeze.

Say it one time only.

Grasp this pebble with both your hands: 1119, eleven hundred nineteen.

When you have finished sealing yourselves with this seal, and you recite its name one time only, say these protective spells also: "Retreat Prote(th), Persomphon, Chous, archons of the first aeon, for I invoke Eaza Zeozaz Zozeoz."

Whenever the archons of the first aeon hear these names, they will be very afraid, withdraw to themselves, and flee leftward to the west, while you journey on up.

When you reach the second of the aeons, Chouncheoch will arrive before you. Seal yourselves with this seal:

This is its name; say it one time only: Thozoaz.

Grasp this pebble with both your hands: (**page 128**) 2219, twenty-two hundred nineteen.

When you have finished sealing yourselves with this seal, and you recite its name one time only, say these protective spells also: "Retreat Chouncheoch, archon of the second of the aeons, for I invoke Ezaoz Zoeza Zoozaz."

Yet again the archons of the second aeon will withdraw to themselves and flee westward to the left, while you journey on up.

When you reach the third of the aeons, Yaldabaoth and Choucho will be arriving before you. Seal yourselves with this seal:

This is its name: Zozeaz.

Say it one time only.

Grasp this pebble with your hands: 3349, thirty-three hundred forty-nine.

When you have finished sealing yourselves with this seal, and have recited its name one time only, say these protective spells also: "Retreat Yaldabaoth and Choucho, archons of the third of the aeons, for I invoke Zozezaz Zaozoz Chozoz."

Yet again the archons of the third of the aeons will withdraw to themselves and flee westward to the left, while you journey on up.

40. The Gospel of the Egyptians

Text: Nag Hammadi Codex III, page 66, line 8 to page 67, line 26 (parallel Codex IV, page 78, line 10 to page 80, line 14)

Description: Parallel versions of this text exist in two fourth-century papyrus books from Nag Hammadi; in Codex III it is the second of five tractates, and in Codex IV it is the second of two. The Codex III version bears the title "The Holy Book of the Great Invisible Spirit," but modern editors have called it the Gospel of the Egyptians

Bibliography: Alexander Böhlig and Frederik Wisse, *Nag Hammadi Codices III,2 and IV,2: The Gospel of the Egyptians*
Translator: Richard Smith

This lovely hymn of mystical union comes from the climax of a Sethian Gnostic text, the Holy Book of the Great Invisible Spirit. The hymn uses metaphors of light, water, and "putting on" to express assimilation of the worshiper to the deity. The deity consists of an eternally existing father, a mother, and a son. Although the deity is eternal and transcendent, this mystical assimilation takes place in the interior of the worshiper, in the mind and in the breast. The poetically charged images seem unable to contain such paradoxes, including the ultimate paradox of hymning and naming a deity whose true nature is inexpressible silence, and the language breaks out in abstract vowel chanting and glossolalia.

The original editors suggested that this passage contains two hymns, the first made up of five strophes beginning "truly, truly," and the second hymn made up of the five strophes here translated as separate paragraphs. The editors also suggested that many of the abstract words are code names, including that of Jesus.

TEXT

> IE IEUS ¹ EO OU EO OUA
> Truly, truly! [10] IESSEU MAZAREU IESSEDEKEU, ¹ the
> living water!
> The child of the child! ¹
> O glorious name!
> Truly, truly! ¹ The one existing eternally!
> IIII EEEE EEEE OO ¹ OO UUUU OOOO AAAA [15]
> Truly, truly! EI AAAA OO ¹ OO
> O one who exists, who sees the aeons! ¹
> Truly, truly! AEE EEE IIII¹ UUUUUU OOOOOOOO ¹
> The one who exists for ever and ever! [20]
> Truly, truly! IEA AIO, in ¹ the mind, who exists!
> UAEI EISAEI ¹ EIOEI EIOSEI

This, your great name, ¹ is upon me, O faultless, ¹ self-born one, who is not outside of me. [25] I see you, O one invisible ¹ before everyone. For who will be able to ¹ grasp you in another language?

Now (**page 67**) that I have known you, I have merged myself
' with the one who does not change. I have armed ' myself with luminous armor ' and have been luminous. For the mother was ⁵
there on account of the lovely beauty ' of grace. Therefore ' I have
reached out my folded hands. '

I have been formed by the ring ' of the wealth of light which
is in ¹⁰ my breast, which gives form to the multitude ' born in the
light, where no accusation ' reaches. I shall sing your ' glory truly,
for I have grasped ' you. SOU IES IDE AEIO AEIE OIS O! ¹⁵

Eternal, eternal god of silence, I ' honor you completely. You
are my ' place of rest, O son, ES ES O E, the ' formless one who exists in the formless ones. '

He exists, he raises the one ²⁰ by whom you shall purify me
into ' your life according to your indestructible name. ' Therefore
the fragrance of life ' is in me. I have blended it with water, ' from
the pattern of all the rulers, ²⁵ so that I shall live with you in the
peace ' of the saints, you who exist for ever.

41. The First Stele of Seth

Text: Nag Hammadi Codex VII, page 118, line 24 to page 121, line 17
Description: The Three Steles of Seth is the fifth and last tractate of a
fourth-century papyrus book, Codex VII, from Nag Hammadi.
Bibliography: Birger A. Pearson, *Nag Hammadi Codex VII*
Translator: Richard Smith

*The hymns contained in the Three Steles of Seth complicate the
distinctions sometimes drawn between "magic," mysticism, and religious liturgy. The category of ritualized empowerment, though less precise, encompasses a variety of cultic practices. In the way that it uses
divine power, however, this text is different from the majority of texts in
the present collection. Rather than pulling the deity down into the
world to use its power, this text uses divine power to lift the worshiper
up into a state of deification. Although the dynamics are the same, the
force moves in a different direction.*

*This is the first of three steles, or "carved tablets," containing cul-
tic hymns of the Sethian Gnostic community. At the opening, the wor-*

shiper *identifies himself with Seth and praises his father Adam (Gi-radama). At line 15, the hymn begins to address the "self-produced one," also called Mirotheos, who is the lowest person of the Sethian "trinity" and who acts as a bridge between "the perceptible world" and the higher realms. Notice may be taken of the frequent use of the term "power," which is held by the self-produced one, then given to "em-power" the worshipers (and also notice the shift from "I" to the more communal "we"). The hymn uses other images of reciprocity ("crown giver, crown receiver") and assimilation ("we became perfected with you"). In the second and third steles (not included here), the hymns are addressed to the higher and highest members of the trinity, the male virginal mother Barbelo, and then to the unborn father. The hymns thus envision a divine hierarchy of beings, who pass power down through the ranks, enabling the worshiper, at the lowest level, to ascend step by step to the highest state of deity.*

TEXT

The First [25] Stele of Seth

I praise | you, father Giradama, | I, your son, | Emmacha
   Seth, whom you produced | without birthing in
   praise [30] of our god, for I | am your son, and
   (page 119) you are my mind, my father. |
Although I sowed and produced, | yet you saw the great-
   nesses | and took a stand, being indestructible.
I [5] bless you, father; bless me, | father.
I exist because of you. |
You exist because of god. |
Because of you, I exist with | that one.
You are light [10] looking at light.
You have appeared | as light.
You are | Mirotheas; you are my Mirotheos. |
I bless you as | a god.
I bless your [15] godliness.
Great is the | good self-produced one, who | took a stand,
   god who already | had taken a stand.
You came in goodness, | you appeared, and you appeared [20]
   as goodness.
I shall speak | your name, for you are a primary | name.
You are unborn.

You ' appeared in order that you might ' appear as the
eternal ones. [25]

You are existence, therefore ' you have appeared as actual '
existences.

You are the one who is spoken ' of by voice, ' but by mind
you are [30] glorified, you who have ' power
everywhere. '

Therefore the perceptible world ' is also aware of you
because ' of you and your seed.

You are merciful. **(page 120)**

And you are from another race, ' and it is superior to yet
another race. '

And now you are from another ' race, and it is superior to
yet another [5] race.

You are from another ' race, for you are incomparable.

You ' are merciful, for you are eternal. '

You are superior to a race, ' for you have caused all of these
to increase.

But because of [10] my seed, you are aware ' that it is
determined by reproducing.

Yet others ' are from other races, for ' they are incomparable,
being superior to ' yet other races, for they are
determined through [15] life.

You are Mirotheos. '

I praise his power, which was given ' to me and which
caused the ' actually existing masculinities to
produce ' masculinity three times, [20] and which
was divided into the pentad, ' which was given
to us ' thrice-powerfully.

This one who was produced ' without birthing!

This one who ' came forth from the superior!

Because of [25] that which is humble, he journeyed ' forth.

You are a father ' from a father, a ' word from a command. '

We praise you, O thrice-masculine one, [30] for you
reconciled the all ' through the every.

For you ' empowered us.

You came into being from ' one, from one you have '
journeyed, and you have arrived at one.

You saved [35] and you saved and you saved us.

O ' crown receiver, crown giver! **(page 121)**

We praise you eternally. |

We praise you since we have | been saved as completely |
    perfect ones, perfect because of [5] you: those who
    became perfect with you, | who is complete, who
    completes | the perfect ones through all of these,
    | and who is resembled everywhere.

O thrice- | masculine one, you have stood, you have
    already [10] taken a stand, you were divided everywhere
    | and remained one.

And | whomever you wanted to, you saved. | But you want
    that all who are worthy | be saved.

You [15] are perfect!

You are perfect! |

You are perfect!

The First | Stele of Seth

42. Prayers, hymns, and invocations for transcendent initiation

Text: Nag Hammadi Codex VIII, page 1, line 1 to page 132, line 9
Description: The text entitled Zostrianos fills almost the entirety of a
fourth-century papyrus book, Codex VIII, from Nag Hammadi.
Bibliography: John H. Sieber, *Nag Hammadi Codex VIII*
Translator: Richard Smith

*Zostrianos is the narrative of a heavenly journey in which the
main character, Zostrianos, invokes divine powers who assist him to ascend to higher and higher regions. The text is very long and fragmentary, yet it clearly bridges ritual invocation, the language of the mystery
cults, and heavenly speculation. The selections translated here begin
with page 4, line 20, as Zostrianos responds to the revelation of an
angel.*

TEXT

When he said these things [to me], | I, quickly and with
much | eager feeling, ascended with him up | to a large light-cloud.

I abandoned ˈ my body on the ground, guarded ²⁵ by glories.

And [I] was ˈ rescued from the entire world ˈ with the thirteen aeons who dwell ˈ in it [by] their angelhood. ˈ They did not observe us, though their ³⁰ archon was confused at [our] ˈ journey. . . .

(Zostrianos ascends through several levels of an elaborately structured heavenly realm. He receives a sequence of baptisms "in living water," whereupon he blesses the divine powers. This pattern is repeated four times. Zostrianos then proceeds with his inquiry, asking about different kinds of souls and people. "The great exalted administrator Authrounios" appears and recites a lengthy mythological account of the creation of the perceptible world by copies and reflections of higher eternal glories. The main characters in the story are Sophia and the world ruler. Zostrianos, still longing for more knowledge, invokes "the child of the child, Ephesech." Ephesech delivers a lengthy discourse [38 pages of the codex] about the higher realms. These "have appeared from a single origin, the Barbelo aeon . . . from existence, blessedness, and life." But all flow ultimately from the great invisible spirit. Many other beings, such as the four lights Armozel, Oroiael, Daveithe, and Eleleth, are also discussed. Occasionally Zostrianos interrupts to praise the names of those about whom he has learned and to prod Ephesech with further inquiry. At the conclusion, Zostrianos sings a hymn [**page 51, line 24**]:)

You are one, you ²⁵ [are one], you are one!
Child (**page 52**) of [the child . . .] ˈ IATO [. . .] ˈ exist
      [. . .] ⁶
[You are] one, you [are one . . .]! ˈ
SEMELEL [. . .] ˈ TELMACHAE [. . .] ˈ
OMOTHEM [. . .] ¹⁰ male [. . .] ˈ
He produces [. . . the] ˈ administrator of the [glory].
[. . .] ˈ desire the one who [. . .] . ˈ
All-perfect [. . .] ¹⁵ all.
AKRON [. . .], ˈ O triple-male AA[. . .] ˈ
OOOOO BITREISE [. . .] ˈ
You are spirit from ˈ spirit.
You are light from ²⁰ light.
You are [silence] ˈ from silence.

You are ' thought from ' thought.
Son of [god], '
god, seven, the [. . .], ²⁵
let us speak. . . .

(At the end of his hymn, Zostrianos says, [**page 53,** line 15]:)

[I was] baptized the fifth ' time in the name of the ' self-begotten, at the hands ' of each of these powers. I ' became as a god.

(After his fifth baptism, Zostrianos sings further praises, the aeons of the self-begotten are revealed, and he says [page 57, line 13], "Yoel, she of the glories, the male and virginal, came before me." She brings Zostrianos into the great aeon and baptizes him a final time [**page 62,** line 11]:)

She who belongs to all the glories, ' Yoel, said to me, ' "You have received all the baptisms ' in which it is necessary to be submerged, ¹⁵ and you have become initiated ' . . . . ' So now invoke ' Salamex and [. . .] ' and the all-perfect Ar[. . .], ²⁰ the lights of the aeon ' of Barbelo and the immeasurable knowledge, ' and those ' will reveal (**page 63**) [. . .] virgin Barbelo ' [and] the invisible ' [three]-powered spirit." This ' is what she said to me, she who belongs to ¹⁰ all [the glories], Youel. And she left ' [me] and went to stand ' before the first appearance. '

Then I was ' standing over my spirit, ¹⁵ mentally praying intensely ' to the great lights. ' I was invoking ' Salamex and ' Se[. . .]en, and the all-perfect ²⁰ [. . .]e. And I saw ' glories greater than powers, ' and they anointed me, and I was empowered. . . .

(In response to Zostrianos's invocation, Salamex arrives and delivers a long revelation [**pages 64–128** of the codex]. The text is fragmentary, but the subjects of the revelation are the aeons of Barbelo, the hidden one, and the spirit. Interspersed in the revelation are several hymns to these beings, filled with names of power and vowel-chanting. Zostrianos's membership in the divine realms is then confirmed [**page 129,** line 2]:)

Apophantes, along with Aphropaic the light-virgin, ' arrived before me ' and brought me into first appearance, ⁵ the great male perfect ' mind. And I saw all of these ' there, as they exist ' in unity. And I ' joined with all of them and blessed [10] the hidden aeon and the virgin Barbelo ' and the invisible ' spirit. And I became a complete initiate ' and was empowered, written ' in glory and sealed. [15] I received an initiate crown ' there, and I advanced ' to each of the initiates. ' And they were all examining me, ' listening to the [20] greatness of my knowledge, ' rejoicing and being ' empowered. And I descended again. . . .

(Zostrianos descends back down through the aeons to the perceptible world, where he writes his knowledge on three wooden tablets and begins proselytizing the ignorant masses.)

PART 2

COPTIC SPELLS
OF RITUAL POWER

4

HEALING SPELLS

INTRODUCTION BY DAVID FRANKFURTER
TRANSLATIONS BY STEPHEN EMMEL,
JAMES E. GOEHRING, NEAL KELSEY,
MARVIN MEYER, AND RICHARD SMITH

Coptic spells of ritual power may be grouped appropriately according to the basic functions of the spells. With such an organizational principle in mind, we present in the following chapters selections of healing spells (chapter 4), protective spells (chapter 5), sexual spells (chapter 6), curses (chapter 7), and spells with a variety of other applications (chapter 8).

The healing spells translated in this chapter offer a record of medical practices in Coptic Egypt and thus a close view of the types of ailments and afflictions that ordinary Egyptians of the late Roman period encountered. Like those spells and rituals devoted to physical afflictions in other cultures, the Coptic spells demonstrate that the lines between "magic," medicine, and religion that are customarily assumed in modern conversation simply did not exist for the clients and purveyors of these texts. We find, for example, in Michigan 136 (text 43) the plainest folk remedies for babies' teething pains, "malignant disease," and skin ailments combined with the most extravagant invocations to powers, names, and deities for gynecological inflammation and a vowel-amulet for headache. The very ingredients of folk remedies were often used ritually or presented in mythological terms: An appendix to a ritual text in Leiden actually shows how common substances like white hellebore or wormwood could function in ritual spells as semen of Helios or blood of Hephaistos (see Hans Dieter Betz, *The Greek Magical Papyri in Translation*, 167–69). On the other hand, those ritual prescriptions most distant from modern medicine—invocations to Isis or vowel-inscriptions on tin—certainly functioned integrally in the overall process of healing, whether by consoling a patient with an appeal to higher powers or by allowing the patient some measure of responsive action in a situation imbued with danger and uncertainty (compare Berlin 8324 [text 45]). Finally, it is obvious that the healer and patient participate in the local religion in its broadest sense, by ritually appealing to powers that are acknowledged and venerated by the temple or the church, often doing so with the very gestures, articles, and language of "official" liturgy (note texts 46–48 and 55–57).

The use of extensive *historiolae*, recitations of mythological precedents for the healing of specific ailments, in text 43 (lines 57–114) and texts 47–49, recalls traditional Egyptian healing practices from before the Greco-Roman period. In these ancient healing rituals the immediate affliction of the patient (for example, snakebite or gynecological hemorrhage) would be assimilated to a mythological situation (thus, Horus's snakebite, Isis's hemorrhage). The narrative of the mythological situation would lead to some sort of resolution, often through the intervention of other "magical" gods such as Re or Thoth. Finally, with its narrative resolution, the mythological situation would be referred—implicitly or explicitly—back to the immediate affliction of the patient. Generally the recitation of these narratives accompanied ritual actions—gestures, use of substances—similar to those recorded in text 43. In the case of the Horus *cippi*, manufactured throughout the Greco-Roman period, the power to heal snake and scorpion venom could be "washed off" the letters of the narrative that had been inscribed on the stelae.

Yale 1792 (text 55) represents an example of an *historiola* working through the power of its very letters, like the Horus *cippi*. Indeed, the form of this spell recalls also the extensive use of the Psalms in Jewish healing and apotropaic traditions as "words of power," for these archaic celebrations of divine accomplishments were consistently spoken or worn in Jewish tradition to repel demons and misfortune in much the same way as *historiolae* of

Isis. But the use of such extensive *historiolae* as we find in texts 47–49 offers a rare witness to the continuity of belief, from the classical throughout the Coptic periods, of this ritual context for curing specific ailments. That is to say, Coptic patients would have regarded the "doctors" who recited these narratives as well as the use of narratives for healing power much the way patients did priests and their stories in ancient Egypt.

The literary contexts of healing spells, as for other categories of ritual texts, conform to three general types: manuals, master texts, and amulets. Ritual manuals like Vienna K 8303 (text 44) and those represented in chapter 9 tend to contain a diversity of rituals, prescriptions, and amulet designs; text 43 contains almost entirely healing spells. The dearth (and cost) of writing materials in late antique Egypt, however, made an extensive manual (and the surface large enough to contain it) a rare achievement. More commonly the collector and purveyor of spells would have access to small scraps of leather, papyrus, or pottery, upon which individual spells might be recorded using "N. child of N." wherever a client's or object's name would go (compare, for example, texts 47–49). The extensive Hay collection in chapters 6 and 9 reflects this form of spell-collecting. Of course, there is evidence that even these master copies were sold as amulets without the necessary names inscribed (compare perhaps Schmidt 1 [text 48]).

It might be argued that Coptic healing amulets operate by two basic principles: (1) The content of the spell conveys power to the wearer through contact with its very letters, empowered by corollary symbols and characters (as in the Horus *cippi*); and (2) the inscribed spell represents its perpetual recitation, extending the ritual invocations beyond their initial utterance. Text 55 tends closest to the first pattern, while texts 46 and 50, which record the ritualist's supplications to powers and gods on behalf of named patients, tend closest to the second. In a striking synthesis of both principles, text 54 supplicates the amulet itself, as an object so powerful it might heed a desperate voice.

Yale 2124 (text 58) may represent a fourth genre for ritual spells, the "transworld message" to be conveyed to its subject through burning, depositing it in a sacred place, or merely placing it in a convenient location for the words to be activated (compare also text 84 in chapter 6). The wording of the request in text 58 is oddly general, suggesting that it may have been distributed in an ecclesiastical context (perhaps to supplant more esoteric or "magically" worded amulets?).

It should be noted that the Coptic word customarily translated "healing," *oujai*, carried a range of meanings that also included the more abstract sense of "salvation," a notion it had throughout Egyptian history from the New Kingdom on. In texts 56–57 the sense of *oujai* suggests a spiritual state attainable through the ritual drawing down of the named powers. In Rossi's "Gnostic" tractate (text 71 in chapter 5) the archangel Raphael, traditionally known as a healing angel (see Tobit 3:17; 8:2–3), is invoked as "the one who is over *oujai*" (2,5), implying in this case a more physical state. So also the drawing down of *oujai* into liquid according to the ritual prescriptions of texts 56–57 reflects a concrete approach to ritual "healing" similar to that in the rest of the spells in this chapter. The image of "liquid *oujai*" appears also in an Egyptian-Christian prophecy of the third century, the Apocalypse of Elijah, which describes the eschatological martyr Tabitha as providing "*oujai* for the people" in the form of her blood (4:4). Much in the way that the Greek *eulogion*, "blessing," came to be a technical term for a highly efficacious amulet from a pilgrimage shrine, perhaps we might find in the semantic range of *oujai* the perennial tensions between everyday and spiritualizing needs in late antique culture.

43. Book of ritual spells for medical problems

Text: Michigan 136

Description: seven small vellum leaves (4 1/8 x 4 7/8 in.) from a Coptic book; an additional first leaf has been lost, so that the existing text begins with page 2.

Bibliography: William H. Worrell, "Coptic Magical and Medical Texts," 17–37

Translator: Marvin Meyer

Michigan 136 consists of a series of folk remedies and ritual spells to treat a wide variety of medical concerns. The health concerns addressed in the text include gout, eye disease, pains from teething, fevers, pregnancy and childbirth, abdominal problems, malignancy, skin disease, headaches, toothaches, earaches, hemorrhoids or other sores, constipation, foot disease, mental problems, and the like. The text also suggests solutions for crying babies and the infestation of vermin. The remedies disclose such aspects of ritual power as amulets, invocations, powerful utterances, and series of vowels (AEEIOUO, listed twice, forward and backward, in "wing formation," 126–32). Within the document (60–114) is a long invocation of the reproductive powers of Egyptian deities (Amun, Thoth, Isis, Horus—but note also Yao Sabaoth), and in this section some archaic and Old Coptic words are used. In lines 41–44 there is a quotation from Homer (Iliad 3.33–35). Such a use of Homeric verses in ritual spells is well known (Hans Dieter Betz, The Greek Magical Papyri in Translation, *47, 54, 76). At least a portion of the document has been translated from Greek, and some of the present text (including the Homeric citation) has been left, untranslated, in Greek (compare 10–36; 41–52; 112–15; 124–32).*

Included in the notes of Worrell's article are numerous suggestions offered by Worrell's scholarly colleagues for reading the highly irregular Coptic of the document. Some of these suggestions are incorporated into the textual notes below.

TEXT

. . . (**page 2**) and over some oil, and you anoint him a little. ' These are the names that you will speak over ' the oil and (the) metal leaf:

Anax ' Sabrex Apemenon Borau 5 Peritrara
Nouannoonospetala ' Kenon Onesinne.

You write them on ' the metal leaf; they are these. Write the ' other names and the characters: '

        (signs)   PETPOI (signs and ring letters)[10]

For gout—(it is) proven: '
     (signs and ring letters)   ARDABAI '
MAKOUM.

Write on a piece of silver when the moon ' is waning, and while you pour warm ' sea (water), utter [15] the name. Perform it very well. ' Do this for 44 days: '

> I invoke you, great ' Isis, ruling in ' the perfect blackness,
> mistress [20] **(page 3)** of the gods of heaven from birth,
> > Atherneklesia ' Athernebouni Labisachthi '
> > Chomochoochi Isi Souse Mounte '
> > Tntoreo Iobast Bastai ' Ribat Chribat Oeresibat [25]
> > Chamarei Churithibath Souere Thartha '
> > Thabaaththa Thath Bathath Lathai '
> > Achra Abathai Ae.
> Make the ' womb of N. whom N. bore ' attain the (condi-
> > tion) from god and [30] be without inflammation,
> without danger, ' always without pain,
> now, 2 (times), at once, ' 2 (times)!

Dip a tuft of white wool. ' Put it under it, and immediately ' attend to the healing.

For a spleen,[35] a proven salve. From early morning ' until the sixth hour of the day: barley meal ' and lard from pigs and very ' sour vinegar; salt.

For ' eyelids, that they not swell: blood of [40] bats and blood of shrimp, when the moon is waning. ' **(page 4)**

For chills:

> And just as someone who sees a snake ' in a mountain glen
> > shrinks back, ' and trembling takes hold of ' his limbs
> > under him, and he withdraws again. . . . [45]

Gabriel, heal N. child of N.,
     now ' 2 (times), at once, at once.

So when you make 7 ' strings, whether of warp or of woof, ' bind them and make 7 knots, and look toward ' the east and say 7 (times), [50]

     Lord Gabriel, lord Gabriel, ' lord Gabriel,
     heal the ' patient. '

For a little child, to make the child's teeth ' grow before that child has pain: Put the foam from [55] wax on the child's swollen (gums). '

For a person who is swollen: gold brine ' in which the gold is immersed. ' Grind it with oil. Anoint the person until ' that person gets better. [60] **(page 5)**

     Voice of winds when there are no winds,
     voice of waves ' when there are no waves,
     voice of Amun, the three ' deities.
     Amun, where are you going in this ' way, in this
          manner?
     I am going from the south wind ' northward—
     neither reed nor rush nor [65]—I am going to
          Abydos—nor these two mountains ' nor these
          two hills—
     I am mounted ' on a silver horse,
     with a black horse under me, '
     the books of Thoth with me, '
     those of the Great One of Five in my hands.
     I make [70] those who are pregnant give birth,
     I close up those who ' miscarry,
     I make all eggs productive except ' infertile eggs.
     Hail, ' Thoth!
     He has come forth to me.
     Amun, ' where are you going, the three of Isis? [75]
     Today she is in labor, (for) four days of how
          many ' . . . .
     It is freed from the seals ' to give birth.
     Let it happen.

You have not found me,
you have not ' found my name,
you have not found ' a little oil for disclosing . . . , [80]
    (page 6)
and you put it against her spine ' toward the bottom,
and you say, Young woman, young woman over there, '
restore yourself,
restore your womb,
serve ' your child,
give milk to Horus your son, '
through the power of the lord god. [85]
Cow, cow of Amun, mother of ' the cattle,
they have drawn near you.
In the morning ' you must go forth to feed (them).
They have drawn near ' you.
In the evening you must come in to let them drink. '
Say, Watch out for these 7 things that are bad for
    producing [90] milk:
    the sheath, the lid, the worm of Paope ' that has
    not yet spread, the barley that has not ' yet pro-
    duced shoots, the real weed that does not
    provide ' shelter (?) for a shepherd, does not
    provide a staff for a herder, ' does not provide a
    goad for a cowherd.
They have come to me, my [95] shepherd, my herder,
    my cowherd,
with their garments ' torn,
a strap on the front of their shoe(s) ' fastened with . . .
    of reed.
What is it with you, that you ' are running, that you
    are in a hurry, my shepherd, my herder, my '
    cowherd,
with your garments torn?
What is it with you, [100] **(page 7)**
with a strap on the front of your shoe fastened with
    fibers ' of reed?
7 white (?) sheep, 7 black sheep, ' 7 young heifers,
    7 great cows—
let ' every cow and every domestic animal receive its '
    offspring,

for Yao Sabaoth has spoken.
Go [105] north of Abydos, go south of Thinis,
until ' you find these two brothers calling and running
      ' north,
and you run after them and they run south. '
Then say, Express the thoughts of ' your heart(s),
that every domestic [110] animal may receive its
      offspring.

Anousph, ' Anousph, Anousph, Anousph, Anousph, '
      Anousph, Anousph, Ibiach,
hold back ' the blood in every member of N. child
      of N.
What ' do you order?
I know, I have it in mind. [115]

Favor. '

Greetings to the sun,
greetings to those who are with you, '
greetings to the one who is yours.
Greetings, greetings, ' Michael,
greetings, Gabriel,
greetings, ' Semesilamps.

Give me the power [120] (**page 8**) of Yao, the strength of
      Abrasax, the ' favor of Sabaoth,
before all people ' . . . ,
especially before N. child of N.,
face ' to face,
now, 2 (times), or at once, 2 (times)! '

Amulet for the stomach and [125] for a headache:
On a piece of tin ' write:

AEEIOUO		OUOIEEA '
AEEIOU		OUOIEE '
AEEIO		OUOIE '
AEEI	(ring signs within a square)	OUOI [130]
AEE		OUO '
AE		OU '
A		O ' (**page 9**)

For the malignant disease: ' a measure of Philanis, three [135] measures of Ebriaam, three ' measures of celery seed, three ' measures of dill seed. You put ' honey on them and grind them ' together, and put them [140] into a cup of beer and a cup ' of . . . wine, and grind them ' together well, and divide it ' into three portions and take a portion ' with you every day for three days, and [145] drink seven cups in the . . . , ' and stretch yourself out on your belly, and people take your ' feet and stretch them out . . . ' and turn you seven times. ' After this you go down to the warm (bath). [150] **(page 10)**

> Osphe, Osphe, Osphe, Yosphe, Yosphe, Yosphe, '
> Bibiou, Bibiou, Bibiou,
> Yasabaoth ' Adonai, the one who rules over ' the four
>   corners of the world, '
> in whatever I want—I, N. [155] child of N.—
> now, now, at once, at once! '

You drink seven more cups, and go to the ' swimming bath of warm water and drink seven more ' cups, and come up and drink seven more ' cups, and spend three days [160] doing this every day, drinking (?). . . . '

For a woman whose womb hurts: ' Take oil, fat, or the (fat) of a cow (?), and a ' little hair of an old woman. Put them on coals ' of sycamore wood. Let her squat over their [165] smoke. She will get better.

If there is a woman ' for whom it has kept on hurting: a small amount of milk ' from a sow. Put it in a little sweet wine. Let ' her drink it. She will get better. ' **(page 11)**

For those who will be sick in their mind(s), if their mind(s) [170] oppress them and they have a demon: His ' stele makes them get better. '

(signs) '	(signs and letters in a
	stele-shaped area)
CHOUBAROCH '	
Those who are sick,	grant healing [175]
Write it on a vulva stone. '	

For all vermin that you want to remove from ' your house: a little galbanum, a ' little sulfide of arsenic, a little fat ' from goats. Place it on a coal [180] like a [. . .] poultice of bad ' laurel. Put it in the water until it dissolves, ' and sprinkle it around the house. ' (**page 12**)

For the skin disease that makes crusty skin peel: a shoot ' of artemisia (?), four staters of soda of [185] arsenic. Grind them together. Apply ' them with an ibis feather.

For a skin ' disease on the person's face: frankincense ' from abroad, seven palm fibers (?), along with a black sheep, ' a burned horn of the sheep, a [190] little pure urine, a lok of ' sour vinegar. Put them in a new, blackened . . . , ' bake them together. Apply ' them with an ibis feather. '

If there is someone who is . . . : Smear [195] his neck with calf gall.

A great lizard: ' In this way, while it is still fresh, burn it, grind it with vinegar, ' put it with incense. Put it on eyes that have discharge. ' They will get better.

A little fresh fat from a sow: ' Grind it. Put it on sores that have appeared at the anus, along with real honey. [200]

For teeth that hurt: a small ' amount of warm milk from an ass. Wash out your mouth ' with it, and they will get better. ' (**page 13**)

For ears that hurt: a little calf gall. ' Put it into his ear and [205] under his teeth, and they will get better.

A person who ' has trouble taking a shit: Smear his belly with calf ' <marrow>, and he will get better.

If there is a ' little child crying: Smear the child's ' skull with calf marrow or calf [210] brains.

A . . . that is in the house: ' white lead. Put it into salt water. Sprinkle it ' in the house.

For the ' . . . or the black lizards: ' a pint of genuine (olive) oil, a [215] pint of aged vinegar, a pound ' of Helkiera, three ' staters of white lead. You ' put them into bowls with fire ' underneath until it is mixed in, 220 while you stir them with fresh palm shoots. ' (**page 14**)

For the hip—(it is) proven: ' an ounce of wax, ' an ounce of aged vinegar. ' Melt in turbid vegetable oil. 225 Two grams ' of aloes. Loosen branches in a ' date palm that has [never] been struck ' by iron, from which branches have not been ' gathered [. . .], and work on 230 pieces of wood . . . ' when they are soft, and place it upon them, and ' mix them with the palm branch until they ' dissolve.

The foot that is sick: ' The corresponding hand is the one that anoints it 235 after you have been silent; and [you] call out ' three times, and anoint yourself ' after you have been silent and have not moved for any reason. . . .

44. Spells for medical problems and the protection of a house

Text: Vienna K 8303 (Rainer, AN 197)

Description: paper, 9.5 x 9 cm, eleventh or twelfth century

Bibliography: Viktor Stegemann, *Die koptischen Zaubertexte*, 79–82; Walter Till, "Zu den Wiener koptischen Zaubertexten," 219

Translator: Marvin Meyer

This is a fragmentary text that contains several suggested remedies for medical problems and (verso) a spell to protect a house from vermin.

TEXT

For shivering: Write these things (and) bind them ' to him:

(signs)

Jesus Christ LATHA 5 RAN(?) .THARBA LATHA, heal us, ' yea, yea, at once! '

A bone (?): If someone gets it, ' recite these things over your hand; ' pour it; it is dissipated. ALLON[. . .] 10 EKESIOS UE, 7 times [. . .], ' yea, yea, [at once, at once]! (**verso**)

[. . .] ' demon(s), ENDRO ARME ' OTHNI KENTA EN-
TAKO TANTA, ' I adjure you by your names ' and your powers,
that you 5 guard this house. Creeping things must not ' do evil or
bite or ' wound with their stingers ' or mouths. '

For the spleen: Write these things . . . : 10 [A]ssouch, Assa.
Off(ering). Alaoth ' [. . .].

(signs)

45. Spell for various diseases

Text: Berlin 8324

Description: papyrus, 16 x 9 cm

Bibliography: Walter Beltz, "Die koptischen Zauberpapyri," 74; Adolf

Erman, *Aegyptische Urkunden aus dem Koeniglichen Museen zu Berlin*, 1.16;

Angelicus M. Kropp, *Ausgewählte koptische Zaubertexte*, 2.215–16

Translator: Marvin Meyer

*Berlin 8324 is an amulet to be used to treat various diseases. The
reference to diapsalms in the instructions for what is to be recited indicates the musical rubric (in Hebrew, Selah) found in the Psalms of the
Jewish Scriptures.*

TEXT

    †   SOROCHCHATTA '
        EI   ƎI
        EI   ƎI

    For fever. '
    For a pain in the belly. 5
    For a womb. '
    For a molar that hurts. '

    Seventy diapsalms and seven ' diapsalms in three
       series.'

    7 names of Mary, 7 of the archangels.

46. Spell to heal a foot

Text: Vienna K 8638 (Rainer)
Description: parchment, 8.5 x 6.8 cm, tenth century
Bibliography: Viktor Stegemann, *Die koptischen Zaubertexte*, 52–53
Translator: Marvin Meyer

This spell employs several words of power, including the SATOR palindrome, the ALPHA formula, and the seven vowels in a series, in order to bring healing to the foot of a person named Beres. The reference to vapors reflects the archaic medical view of bodily exhalations that can influence one's health.

TEXT

EROUCH BAROUCH ' BAROUCHA,

I beg and I ' invoke you today, ' lord god almighty, [5] that I may take away every ' pain and every vapor from ' the foot of Beres son of Kasele, ' and that I may heal him of all ' suffering, yea, yea, at once, at once, [10]

SATOR AREDO [TE]NED ODERA ' RODOS,
ALPHA LEON ' PHO[N]E ANER [. . .], '
AEEIOUO.

47. Spell using legends about Horus and Abimelech, to bring sleep

Text: Berlin 5565
Description: papyrus, 18 x 31 cm
Bibliography: Walter Beltz, "Die koptischen Zauberpapyri," 61–63;
Angelicus M. Kropp, *Ausgewählte koptische Zaubertexte*, 2.12–14
Translator: Marvin Meyer

Berlin 5565 is a spell to bring sleep upon a person who is suffering from illness or insomnia. The text opens with a dialogue (1–4) between a practitioner and an angelic or demonic force, Afboure, whose power is invoked in order to bring sleep. (The word "Afboure" may also be understood as a verb to be translated "he has dreamed.") The text continues with a legend about Isis, Nephthys, and Horus (5–10), and it concludes with an adjuration directed to Ax/Abrasax (10–13), that this angel may bring sleep like that brought upon the legendary figure Abimelech the Ethiopian, who slept for some sixty-six years (or, as here, even longer).

TEXT

"Afboure, Afboure!"

"Look, the golden chalice is in your hand."

"If (I) send you to my work, you will go, and to the task, ' you will stay for it."

"If you send me to the water, I shall draw it out, if to the stream, I shall go for its mud." '

"No, I have not sent you for these things, I have not dispatched you for other things. I send you to N. ' child of N., that you may bring sleep upon him, and slumber, until the sun of Chousi (?) arises." 5

Say: The true name is Papleu. Say: This is Isis, this is Nephthys, the two sisters, ' who are troubled within, who grieve within, who have wandered through heaven and earth, who are in the abyss. '

Say: Look, Horus the son of Isis was in distress. She is (?) far from him . . . , ' since she turned to the sun, (she) turned to the moon, to confine them (?) in the middle of heaven, to the Pleiades, in the middle of heaven. Isis ' and Nephthys are the two sisters who are troubled within, who grieve within, 10 who are in the abyss.

Say: You are Ax, you are Abrasax, the angel ' who sits upon the tree of Paradise, who sent sleep upon Abimelech ' for seventy-five years. You must bring sleep upon N. child of N., ' now, now, at once, at once!

48. Another spell using legends about Horus and Abimelech, to bring sleep (or sex?)

Text: Schmidt 1

Description: papyrus, 15 x 15 cm, folded and probably worn as an amulet

Bibliography: Angelicus M. Kropp, *Augewählte koptische Zaubertexte*, 1.11–12; 2.3–6

Translator: Neal Kelsey

The bulk of Schmidt 1 consists of a legend presented in the form of a dialogue between Horus and Isis. The text opens with Horus crying and sighing in great distress. He calls upon his mother Isis to hear his complaint. When Isis inquires about the cause of Horus's distress, Horus responds that he is troubled by seven maidens, not one of whom sleeps or dozes. Isis then provides a ritual for discovering her name and provides a cure, apparently for insomnia. The text concludes with an allusion to the Abimelech legend. In the present context, rather than an antidote for insomnia, the request may be for a sexual favor. Compare also Schmidt 2 (text 72) as well as Sergio Donadoni, "Un incantesimo amatorio copto."

TEXT

♀ Hear Horus crying,
  hear Horus ' sighing:
  "I am troubled, poured out (?) for seven ' maidens (?),
  from the third hour of the day
  until the fourth hour ' of the night.
  Not one of them sleeps, 5
  not one of them dozes."

Isis his ' mother replied to him within the temple of Habin '
with her face turned toward the seven maidens (?) ' (and) seven
maidens (?) turned toward her ' face:

  "Horus, why are you crying,
  Horus, why are you 10 sighing?"

  "Do you wish that I not cry,
  do you ' wish that I not sigh,
  from the third hour ' of the day

until the fourth hour of the night,
while I am poured out (?) ' for seven maidens (?),
not one of whom sleeps, '
not one of whom dozes?"

"Even <if> [you] have not [found me] [15]
and have not found my name,
take a cup [with] ' a little water;
whether it is a small ' breath
or the breath of your mouth
or the breath of [your nose], '
call down to them,
    PKECHP[. . . .]." '

You two angels, who imposed [20] sleep upon Abimelech for
seventy-two [years], ' impose upon N. child of N., and ' be a bur-
den upon his head like a millstone, upon his ' eyes like a sack of
sand, until I complete ' my request to accomplish the desire of my
heart, [25] now, now, quickly, quickly!

49. Spells for relieving the pain of childbirth and stomach pain

Text: Berlin 8313

Description: papyrus, 23 x 35.5 cm

Bibliography: Walter Beltz, "Die koptischen Zauberpapyri," 65–67 (Beltz
apparently assigns an incorrect inventory number [8314]); Angelicus M.
Kropp, *Ausgewählte koptische Zaubertexte*, 2.9–12

Translators: Marvin Meyer and Richard Smith

*Berlin 8313 is a text that contains two spells for relieving pain in
the abdominal region. The first spell (a: column 1, 1–18) recounts a
legend of Jesus and a doe that is in labor, apparently in order to provide
relief from the pains of childbirth. The second (b: column 2, 1–verso,
8) tells a story about Horus, Isis, and three demons named Agrippas, in
order to offer relief for someone (a child?) who has stomach pains, perhaps from indigestion. Both of the spells conclude with similar Christian statements of confidence in Jesus to provide help.*

(a) [O holy] of holies, unshakable, indestructible rock! ' Child of the maiden, firstborn ' [of your father] and mother! Jesus our lord came ' walking [upon] the Mount of Olives in the [midst] of his 5 twelve apostles, and he found a doe . . . in pain ' [. . .] in labor pains. ' It spoke [to him in these words]: "Greetings, child of the maiden! Greetings, ' [firstborn of your] father and mother! You must come ' and help me in this time of need."

He rolled his 10 eyes and said, "You are not able to tolerate my glory, nor to tolerate ' that of my twelve apostles. But though I flee, ' Michael the archangel will come to you with his ' [wand] in his hand and receive an offering of wine. ' [And he will] invoke my name down upon [it] with the name 15 of the apostles, for 'whatever is crooked, let it be straight.' ' [Let the baby] come to the light!"

The will of [my heart happens] quickly. It is I who speak, the lord Jesus. The gift ' [. . .].

(b) Jesus! Horus [the son of] Isis went upon a mountain in order to rest. He [performed his] ' music, [set] his nets, and captured a falcon, [a Bank bird, a] wild pelican. ' [He] cut it without a knife, cooked it without fire, and ' [ate it] without salt [on it].

He had pain, and the area around his navel 5 [hurt him], and he wept with loud weeping, saying, "Today I am bringing my [mother] ' Isis to me. I want a demon so that I may send him to my mother ' Isis."

The first demon Agrippas came to him and said ' to him, "Do you want to go to your mother Isis?"

He said, "How long will it take for you to go there ' and how long for you to come back?"

He said, "'How long will it take for you to go there and how long for you to come back?' 10 I can go there in two hours and I can come back in two."

He said, "Leave, ' you do not satisfy me."

The second demon Agrippas came to him ' and said, "Do you want to go to your mother Isis?"

He said, "How much time do you need ' to go there and how much time to come back?"

He said, "I can go there in one hour ' and I can come back in one."

He said, "Leave, you do not satisfy me."

The third demon Agrippas, [15] the one with a single eye and a single hand, came to him ' and said to him, "Do you want to go to your mother Isis?"

"How long will it take ' for you to go there and how long for you to come back?"

"I can go there with the breath of your mouth and I can come back with ' the breath of your nose."

"Go then, you satisfy me."

He went upon the mountain of Heliopolis ' and found his mother Isis wearing an iron crown and [20] stoking a copper oven. She said to him, "Demon Agrippas, ' from where have you come to this place?"

He said to her, "Your son Horus went upon a ' mountain in order to rest. He performed his music, set his nets, ' and captured a falcon, a Bank bird, a wild pelican. (**verso**) He cut it without a knife, cooked it without fire, and ate it without salt on it. ' He had pain, and the area around his navel hurt him."

She said ' to him, Even if you did not find me and did not find my name, the true name that the sun ' bears to the west and the moon bears to the east and that is borne by the six propitia-tory [5] stars under the sun, you would summon the three hundred ' vessels that are around the navel:

Let every sickness and every difficulty ' and every pain that is in the belly of N. child of N. stop ' at this moment. I am the one who calls; the lord Jesus is the one who grants healing.

50. Amulet to heal and protect a woman

Text: Vienna K 7093 (Rainer)

Description: paper, 5.5 x 11.7 cm, late tenth century

Bibliography: Viktor Stegemann, *Die koptischen Zaubertexte*, 38–40;

Angelicus M. Kropp, *Ausgewählte koptische Zaubertexte*, 2.222

Translator: Marvin Meyer

This text is an amulet to heal and protect a woman named Kira-heu or Heu. Among the powerful utterances are the SATOR palin-

drome, *ALPHA LEON PHONE ANER*, the names of the four living creatures *(AKRAMMATA PERITON SOURITHION PARAMERAO)*, and various other names or utterances (for example, Apabathuel, Mamarioth).

TEXT

SATOR ARETO TENET OTERA ROTAS, ALPHA LEON PHONE ANER, AKRAMMA'TA PERITON SOURITHION PARAMERAO, OCHAMEN OROPHAEON ' ROBIEL THRIECHS APABATHUEL MAMARIOTH, I beg and ' I invoke you, and I adjure you by the one who was crucified [5] upon the cross, that you take away the suffering and the pain from ' Kiraheu daughter of Maria, and grant her healing through ' the power of the lordship of Yao Sabaoth ALPHA, ALPHA EI ' PHONE ANER, THEBNA ATOR ARCHECHON, SATOR ARETO ' TENET OTERA ROTAS, THIO, at once, at once!

51. Amulet to heal and protect Poulpehepus from fever

Text: Oxyrhynchus 39 5B.125/A
Description: paper, 5.5 x 22.5 cm, around the eleventh century
Bibliography: Anthony Alcock, "A Coptic Magical Text"
Translator: Marvin Meyer

This text is an amulet meant to heal and protect a person named Poulpehepus from all sorts of fevers. In order to accomplish this purpose the amulet uses the SATOR formula, the seven vowels in a series, the powerful utterance LAL MOULAL SHAULAL, and the names of the youths in Daniel 1.

TEXT

. . . [3] SATOR ARETO ' TENET OTNRO [5] ROTAS, take away ' this fever and this ' cold and this shivering ' and this chill and ' this shaking fever and [10] this complaint and ' this shaking fever and ' this tertian fever ' and this pain ' from the head and the [15] body of Poulpehepus ' son of Zarra, through ' the name and the nails that ' were driven into (?) the body ' of Manuel, our Nuel, [20] our god on the cross, ' by the Jews, that ' you may take away this ' cold and this chill from the ' body of Poulpehepus son of [25] Zarra, yea, at once!

AEEIOUO '

My lord (?), . . . [29] and these . . . and these ' wonders. . . . [32] I have raised ' my soul like ' the one whom his mother conceived. [35] Let . . . and ' this chill [and] this shivering ' and this chill [and] this shaking ' fever and this complaint ' and this pain [. . .] take(n) (?) away [40] from the head [and] the ' body of Poulephepus ' son of Zarra, yea, at once! '

ASKOI ASRIN . . . FTO ' LAL MOULAL SH[45]AULAL, strengthen, give strength, ' Zetrak, Mezak, ' Aftenako, Ananias, ' Azarias, Mazaneh, ' and Daniel. Take away [50] this cold and this shivering ' and this chill and ' this shaking fever and this tertian ' fever and this pain ' from the head and [55] the body of Poulphepus ' son of Zarra, yea, ' yea, at once! '

AEEIOUO

52. Amulet to heal and protect Phoibammon from fever

Text: amulet from the Moen collection

Description: parchment, 17.3 x 10.2 cm, rolled up and probably worn as an amulet

Bibliography: Pieter J. Sijpesteijn, "Amulet against Fever"

Translator: Neal Kelsey

This text contains a healing spell against fever written, with minor variations, on the two sides of a parchment of very fine quality.

TEXT

(ring signs)

I (am) ' Phoibammon, the son. ' You must stretch out your [10] hand and take away this ' sickness today. Cast it out ' from inside him and outside ' him, this fever <and> cold. ' I adjure you by your names. [15] The names. Cast out ' every cold and every ' fever. I (am) Phoibammon ' son of Maria. ' (hair side)

(ring signs)

I (am) Phoibammon [25] son of Maria. ' You must stretch out your hand ' and take away this sickness ' of fever and cold, and cast it ' out from inside of me and outside of [30] me. Yea, <your> names. The names.

53. Another amulet against fever

Text: Heidelberg Kopt. 564
Description: parchment, 10.2 x 6.3 cm
Bibliography: Hans Quecke, "Zwei koptische Amulette"
Translators: Neal Kelsey and Marvin Meyer

Heidelberg Kopt. 564 is another amulet to heal and protect a person from various sorts of fevers. In this instance the three youths of the book of Daniel are recalled and summoned so that fiery fevers, like the fiery furnace, may not consume the person using the amulet. The amulet includes seven pentagrams near the bottom of the parchment.

TEXT

*Ananias [As]arias Misael, Se[d]rak ' Misak Abdenago, Thalal M[ou]'lal B[. . . : I] adjure you by ' your names and your powers, that as you [5] extinguished the fiery furnace(s) of ' Nebuchadnezzar, you may extinguish [every fever] ' and every [. . .] and every chill ' and every malady that is in the body of Patrikou ' child of [. . .]akou, child of Zoe, child of [10] Adam, yea, yea, at once, at once!

(7 pentagrams)

54. Amulet to heal Ahmed from fever, evil eye, and other problems

Text: Heidelberg Kopt. 544

Description: parchment, 6.4 x 8.1 cm, folded seven times horizontally and two times vertically

Bibliography: Hans Quecke, "Zwei koptische Amulette"

Translator: Neal Kelsey

Heidelberg Kopt. 544 is an amulet to heal and protect a person named Ahmed from fevers and other problems. Among the powerful utterances and invocations are AKRAMACHAMARI, ABLANATHA-NA[LBA], the ALPHA formula, the seven vowels in a series, and the names of several angels and archangels.

TEXT

BABOUCHA . . . AKRAMA'[CHA]MARI ABLANATHANA-[LBA] ' . . . RANKME ' DOME DOM DO D, ALPHA LEON [5] PHONE ANER, AEEIOUO, ' Michael, Gabriel, Raphael, ' Suriel, Zarathiel, Zedekiel, ' Anael, Yoel, Tsel, ' AEEIOUO:

I beg [10] and I invoke you ' that you bring out ' the cold and the slight ' chill and the evil eyes ' and the mania and the [15] crying from ' Ahmed son ' of Mariam, at the ' moment that he ' wears you,
[20]yea, yea, at once, ' at once!

55. Amulet against snakebite

Text: Yale 1792

Description: papyrus, 22.5 x 22.5 cm, folded six times horizontally and twice vertically; "late sixth or early seventh century" (so Parássoglou)

Bibliography: George M. Parássoglou, "A Christian Amulet against Snakebite"

Translator: Neal Kelsey

Yale 1792 is an amulet used to protect a person from snakebite. It employs the ALPHA formula, the SATOR palindrome, several names, and statements recalling Jesus' words about snakes (compare Mark

16:18; Luke 10:19) and Psalm 119:105. Melchior, Tthattasia (compare Thaddias), and Fathisora (compare Balthasar) recall the names of the three wise men (see William M. Brashear, "The Coptic Three Wise Men"). The date Choiak 29 is the Coptic date of Christmas (compare Berlin 11347 [text 63]).

TEXT

ALPHA	TARCHE	PHOBEL
LEON	SIRIS	NOROMIN
PHONE		
ANER		
LOIOI	SATOR	MELCHIOR
	ARETO	TTHATTASIA
	TENET	FATHISORA
	OTERA	
	ROTAS	
	OF	

† Christ was born on the twenty-ninth ' of Choiak. He came by descending ' upon the earth. He rebuked all the poisonous ' snakes. Your word, ' lord, is the lamp of my feet, ' and it is the light of my path.

56. Spell for a cup of healing

Text: Berlin 8319

Description: papyrus, 31.5 x 11 cm, eighth century

Bibliography: Adolf Erman, *Aegyptische Urkunden aus den Koeniglichen Museen zu Berlin*, 1.11; Angelicus M. Kropp, *Ausgewählte koptische Zaubertexte*, 2.121–22; Walter Beltz, "Die koptische Zauberpapyri," 70–71

Translator: James E. Goehring

This fairly fragmentary text provides an invocation of supernatural power over a cup of healing (1–15), followed, it seems, by a recipe for the use of the spell or the preparation of the cup (16–26). The restorations in lines 7, 8, 15, and 20 are based upon suggestions by Kropp.

TEXT

[. . .] come to me today, [. . .]ʼwho spread outʼ[over the] whole world. I beg andʼ[invoke] you today, that ⁵ [you come] down to me on this cupʼ[that] is in my right hand, me,ʼ[N.], so that at the moment that Iʼ[give it to N.], you will make it become ʼ[for him] a cup of healing and cleansing. ¹⁰ [. . .] a cupʼ[. . .]ʼdrink from it, heʼ[. . .]. Yea, yea, for I adjureʼ[you] today through the power of the ¹⁵ [unutterable] names, now, now, [quickly, quickly]!ʼ

[. . .] wild artemisiaʼ[. . .] miceʼ[. . .]ʼand kindle ²⁰ [a fire] under it with straw and grainʼ[. . . until] it boils well.ʼ[. . .] it mixes with [. . .]ʼit [. . .]ʼevening [. . .] ²⁵ days. It will cease quicklyʼ[through] the power of the lord. †

57. Spell for healing with water, oil, and honey

Text: London Oriental Manuscript 5899(1)
Description: paper, 6 x 4½ in., with two different hands on the two sides
Bibliography: Walter E. Crum, *Catalogue of Coptic Manuscripts in the British Museum*, 416–17; Angelicus M. Kropp, *Ausgewählte koptische Zaubertexte*, 2.123
Translator: James E. Goehring

The folio translated here employs ritual power for healing, favor, and other purposes. Side a uses water, oil, and honey; side b summons a series of powers, whose names begin with the letters of the Greek alphabet, in order (the first several names are not given). Often such names are used to identify the twenty-four elders. Crum does not include indications of line divisions.

TEXT

(a) THEMOUPH[. . .]ZARZAL . . PHIRACHACHA . . . , send me today Gabriel, the archangel who has received the good news of the son of the almighty until today, so that he might come down on this water and this oil [. . .] and this honey, and mark the water and fill it with healing and favor and peace and uprightness and salvation and [. . .] my soul, so that if a wicked person [. . .] my heart and my [. . .] soul [. . .].

(b) . . . Kardiel, Labdiel, Murophael, N. . . . . , Ochael, Pithiel, Ruel, Seroael, Tauriel, U...[e]l, Phanuel, Christuel, Pserathael, Olithiel, I adjure you (pl.) by those who rise with the great stars that shine upon the earth, who are called Arael, Aranael, Anapuel, Uriel, Anatalael, Em..[e]l, Aruel, Mael, Asu.[el], that you (sg.) give much favor and a high degree of confidence to N. child of N. before [. . .] when he [. . .].

58. A monk's prayer for good health

Text: Yale 2124
Description: paper, 10.9 x 8.4 cm
Translator: Stephen Emmel

This simple prayer for health and forgiveness once belonged to a medieval monk, who probably either carried it about as an amulet or ritually placed it somewhere. The text is edited for the first time in the Appendix, "Previously Unpublished Coptic Texts of Ritual Power in the Beinecke Library, Yale University."

TEXT

Pray for our ' fathers and our brothers ' who have fallen sick ' with whatever sickness, 5 whether in this ' monastery or in ' any <house> of ' Christ our god. ' Favor them all 10 with health and ' the absence of sickness, ' and let him ' forgive us ' our sins.

5

PROTECTIVE SPELLS

INTRODUCTION BY DAVID FRANKFURTER
TRANSLATIONS BY JAMES E. GOEHRING, MARVIN MEYER,
STEPHEN H. SKILES, AND RICHARD SMITH

Coptic protective spells aimed to create a kind of shield around the subject of the spells, protecting her or him from specified or unspecified hostile forces in a world rife with them; they were *apotropaic*. Initiating such spells involved the combined invocation of supernatural powers, inscription and manipulation of amulets (occasionally described as "seals"), along with associated gestures and oral utterances. Protective spells were hardly unique to Coptic culture. Anthropologists have recorded apotropaic rituals and amulets among countless peoples (see, for example, Barbara Freire-Marreco, "Charms and Amulets"; Joshua Trachtenberg, *Jewish Magic and Superstition*, 132–81). Still today in Jewish and Christian cultures we may notice apotropaic traditions surrounding the Jewish *tefillin* and *mezuzot* and the Christian cross, Bible, saints' medallions, and prayers.

The need for some ongoing emblem of protection in apotropaic ritual explains the veritable profusion of amulets for this purpose in the ancient world and specifically in the collection in this chapter: a letter written by Christ himself (text 61a), "seals" put on the ritualist's body (text 61b), gospel *incipits* (opening lines) on an amulet (text 62), and amulet instructions concluding two liturgies (texts 70–71). The wording of Rylands

100 (text 65) suggests that it originated as an oracle question to St. Leontius but became an amulet following the answer (on oracle questions to Christian saints see texts 30–35 and 126).

At least two spells result in blessed or empowered liquids: Cologne 20826 (text 59: honey) and Berlin 11347 (text 63: oil); Freer fragment 10 (text 60) is ambiguous. These materials were likely meant to carry apotropaic power beyond the rituals themselves, much like the many miraculous waters, oils, and dusts that circumnavigated the late antique world in small vials imprinted with saints' images (see, for example, Gary Vikan, *Byzantine Pilgrimage Art*). These rituals would have allowed one to create a sort of "saints' oil" for general, everyday protection.

But if apotropaic power was generally carried in amulets, it is striking that the protracted liturgies in London Oriental Manuscript 5987 (text 70) and Rossi's "Gnostic" tractate (text 71) endeavor to protect their subjects by calling upon a series of heavenly powers to repel demons in general. Protection in these spells seems not so much resilience to specific misfortunes as a state of exaltation and heavenly status within a helplessly demon-ridden cosmos (compare texts 59–60). This worldview, characteristic of the late antique period, cast the demons as at home in the world and humans as alien and in need of transcendence. The protection offered by texts 70–71 would seem to be a protection against the world and a movement toward a heavenly status unhindered by such cosmic demons as "the first formed one."

Alongside both these more general rituals of protection and those spells explicitly against demons have been placed a series of obstetrical spells (texts 64–67), reflecting an important overlap between protective and healing spells (compare text 68 also, with text 55). As with many ancient cultures, Egypt's literary remains reveal a preoccupation with protective rituals surrounding and following childbirth (compare Michigan 136 [text 43]). People knew well the dangers involved in the obstetrical process, even if they had no technological means of avoiding them. Hence the "magic" of obstetrics was on the whole protective rather than curative. Nevertheless, one can imagine that the chanting of Michigan 1190 (text 66), with its vivid analogies of obstructions falling, during labor would have had a beneficial psychological effect on a parturient mother, much like the Cuna (Panama) shaman's chant that was supposed to draw the woman through the process of delivery with particular cadences, repetitions, and images, as Claude Lévi-Strauss showed in "The Effectiveness of Symbols."

Athanasius's Life of St. *Antony* demonstrates that the worldview Egyptian Christianity inherited from indigenous religion included a quite pronounced realm of demons. At the same time the presentation of demons in the Life of St. *Antony* suggests that different groups within Egyptian Christianity—farmers, merchants, priests, monks, and hermits—all conceptualized demonic threat according to different criteria. A farmer's demons would relate to agriculture, animals, physical ailments, and interpersonal problems, while those cursed by a monk or hermit would tempt him from his steps toward single-minded asceticism. So also in the following spells we can see the range of threats for which rituals were needed spread out between the "everyday" level of London Oriental Manuscript 5525 (text 64), which repeats a purportedly complete list of obstetrical ills, and the "spiritual" level of Rossi's "Gnostic" tractate (text 71), whose major object of aversion is "the first formed one and all his powers." In many of these spells the demons are strikingly vague in definition, suggesting a stance on the part of the ritualist that does not require precision and lurid description (see the Nahman amulet [text 62], lines 35–38), but rather a kind of ritual magnanimity. Indeed, it is unclear whether one should fear or adjure the "20,000 demons who stand at the Euphrates River" in London Oriental Manuscript 5987 (text 70), a scene reminiscent of the "army of demons" that aids Solomon in Apocalypse of Adam 79.

For those spells that list precise ailments, however, like texts 63–64 and 67–68, it would be incorrect to view the ritualist as somehow more realistic or medical. It must be remembered that these spells, rituals, and amulets were conceived to avert the ailments. The listed ailments themselves tend to combine "real" ills with demonic categories (compare text 64, lines 19–30, 124–28), a tendency also found in contemporaneous Egyptian Jewish amulets (see Lawrence H. Schiffman and Michael D. Swartz, *Hebrew and Aramaic Incantation Texts from the Cairo Genizah*, 46–47). Thus, like the healing spells of chapter 4, these spells do not assume any sort of distinction between medicine and religious or ritual healing.

These Coptic spells clearly show continuities with indigenous Egyptian demonology and the exorcistic and apotropaic formulae employed in classical Egyptian texts. Most obvious is the listing of "every demon, whether male demon or female demon" (several times in London Oriental Manuscript 5525 [text 64]), a detail which reflects traditional Egyptian conceptions of the variety of demonic figures and ghosts that could cause harm. The aversion of reptiles in Rylands 104 (text 68, compare Yale 1792 [text 55] in chapter 4), while understandable on pragmatic grounds in Egypt's environment, continues—in function if not in explicit language—the ritual repulsion of the desert god Seth and his manifestation in snakes and scorpions, which formed a major component of Egyptian priestly service to the laity. (Text 55, indeed, allows a formal link between the image of Horus defeating Seth's reptiles and powers attributed to Jesus, in this case through the medium of Psalm 119.) Finally, Cologne 20826 (text 59), meant to cloak the ritualist in the protective power of the sun, describes the sun in terms directly drawn from the mythology of the Egyptian sun god Re. The forces this spell would oppose, therefore, would have recalled the primary enemy of Re in Egyptian mythology, Apophis, the dragon of darkness. One can see this traditional archdemon informing Egyptian Christian concepts of the demonic as early as the third century (compare Apocalypse of Elijah 1:4). But it is important to recognize that in these Coptic spells, when an archdemon is mentioned, the language is vague, apparently deriving from ecclesiastical images of Satan (compare the language of the Nahman amulet [text 62]).

The Egyptian legacy in these spells occurs on the formal as well as the motif level. A popular form of Egyptian protective amulet, the oracular amuletic decree, consisted of an exhaustive list of environmental dangers (essentially demonic) from which a god promised to deliver the wearer. The more dangers listed, the more protection the amulet—as a sort of contract between client and god—afforded the wearer. We find the same formulaic approach toward listing the objects of aversion or protection in texts 64 and 67. Another formal device from Egyptian liturgy is the declaration that the speaker of the spell is, in fact, a god: "It is not I who says this, it is Re," or simply: "I am Re." Thus the speaker in Rylands 104 (text 68) announces, "It is the mouth of the lord Sabaoth that said this," and the speaker in London Oriental Manuscript 5987 (text 70) states, "I am Mary." This ritual redefinition of the speaker assumes traditional notions of the efficacy of language and the function of the divinity itself.

When one compares the concept of demon and demonic danger in these spells with that in Greco-Roman spells like those in the *Papyri Graecae Magicae,* one gains the immediate sense that the Greek word *daimon* has, through Christianity, achieved an exclusively negative meaning. Yet it is clear from the variety of evils named and implied that the single word "demon" did not encompass, and could not possibly have served semantically, the vast array of dangers, fears, and tragedies in the Copts' experience.

59. Invocation of the sun for protection

Text: Cologne 20826
Description: papyrus, 15 x 20 cm, fifth–eighth centuries, probably later in this period
Bibliography: Cornelia Römer and Heinz J. Thissen, "Eine magische Anrufung in koptischer Sprache"
Translator: Marvin Meyer

Cologne 20826 is an invocation of the sun that rises "over the land of Egypt" and other heavenly powers for the sake of empowerment and protection. Honey is to be used in the ritual, and words of power are thought to be written upon the tongue of the person employing the spell. This person assumes a cosmic role in order to gain a vision of the face of god. The description of the divine as the one of "the great number" (26) refers to the number 9999, the largest number capable of being counted on the fingers of a person's hands. The three creatures drawn at the end of the text may be scorpions, although the crude character of the drawing makes a positive identification impossible. The text incorporates Jewish and Christian elements in a spell that reflects the traditional solar interests of Egypt.

TEXT

> Greetings, lord,
> greetings, sun of righteousness,
> who rises ' over all the earth
>   and over the land of Egypt. '
> You must come down upon this honey,
> you must pay attention to it.
> Prevail ' upon the twelve powers and their sweetness. ⁵
>   Spells
>
> In the name of your great ' archangel Abrax,
> whose hand ' is stretched out over his rays,
> you must enlighten ' my heart.
> Lord, greetings, Seth Thioth, ' Barbarioth.
> I give thanks to you, ¹⁰ our god,
> Deiodendea ' Yaoth.
> Lord, greetings, father,
> lord, greetings, ' son,
> lord, greetings, holy ' spirit,

lord, greetings.
Its joy, ' its light has he brought over me. 15
Lord, greetings,
light of gladness,
light ' of the aeons,
light of joy,
light ' of my eyes,
lamp of my body,
god, Yao, '
god, Sabaoth.
You must dip ' your pen in your black ink,
and write 20 upon my tongue.
            Spell

You must give me the sun ' as a garment,
the moon with which I cover myself ' as a cloak.
You must give me the boat ' of the sun,
that it may diminish for me all evil. '
You must give me the 7 stars,
you must give me 25 the stuff of the stars,
and I shall be worthy of beholding your face, ' god. **(verso)**
You must give me your glory of the sun,
you of the great number,
that it may ' keep me from all evil.
            Spell

Yea, for I adjure you '
by the power of Chabarach Rinischir Phunero Phontel '
        Asoumar Asoumar,
who enlighten the underworld 5 in the evening and the
        earth in the morning.
Lord, greetings, ' . . .
I give thanks to you, god, '
Dediodendeiaoth Lamoir,
        at once! '

Serou Seraled Rima Aria Nouda '
Damou Menou 10
Sethioth '
Barbarioth
            (drawing of three creatures)

60. Invocation of god for protection

Text: Freer collection, fragment 10

Description: thick vellum, about 20 x 31 cm, folded in the middle; "no manuscript in the Fayûmic dialect is probably older than the ninth century" (so Worrell)

Bibliography: William H. Worrell, *The Coptic Manuscripts in the Freer Collection*, 126–28, 323–25, 381–83; Angelicus M. Kropp, *Ausgewählte koptische Zaubertexte*, 2.118–19

Translator: Marvin Meyer

This fragment from the Freer collection offers an invocation of god for the purpose of healing and protection. The reference to "water or oil" (2,12) may indicate that such holy fluids are being blessed before they are used for rituals of cleansing (baptizing?) or anointing. The person who employs this prayer may do so on behalf of those who are sick, oppressed, or possessed.

TEXT

> I [invoke] you, god,
> lord of the whole ' world [and the] earth,
> who is above ' heaven,
> god [of the] soul,
> who guards ' the bodies,
> who seals 5 those who are burdened by fate, '
> who is great,
> who is exalted over ' the midpoint of [the] sea,
> who ' establishes them all ' and guides them.
> For 10 you are the one who is over them all, '
> father of all.
> Without you ' nothing happens,
> god, who gives hope, '
> eternal, father of the eternal. '
> For there is no other god besides you, 15
> who supplies [the] restraints,
> Adona, ' Abrathona, Yo, Yo, great [god], '
> who overturns them,
> who rides upon the powers, '
> who casts out the demons,
> who ' terrifies them through your power; 20

. . . them,
father almighty, (**page 2**) god of the ages,
[father of the eternal], |
who grants healing,
who strengthens,
who | heals the diseases,
for | surely your power is for those who are oppressed [5] or
    those who are laid low,
you who | are a friend to everyone who utters | to you, Yao
    Adoni,
all the names | by which I invoke you | on behalf of them,
whether [men] or women, [10]
or anyone who asks (?).
For | you are the one who guards the souls,
whether | (by) water or oil,
through your holy name, |
that they may be well, each one. |
For yours is the power and the glory [15]
    for [ever] and ever, Amen.

(letters and signs)

61. Spell for protection against illness and evil

Text: Vienna K 8302 (Rainer, AN 191)
Description: parchment, 10.4 x 13.2 cm, sixth or seventh century
Bibliography: Viktor Stegemann, *Die koptischen Zaubertexte*, 70–76; Walter
Till, "Zu den Wiener koptischen Zaubertexten," 215–18
Translator: Marvin Meyer

*This text is an amulet intended to provide protection against ill-
ness and the power of evil. The first section of the text (a) bases its plea
upon the correspondence between Abgar of Edessa and Jesus (see the
Coptic book of ritual power from Leiden [text 134]), and the second
section (b) presents a fairly enigmatic "prayer of Elijah the Tishbite."
Among the powerful utterances employed in the text are the (garbled)
traditional words of Jesus upon the cross, Alpha and Omega, the seven
Greek vowels in a series, and the SATOR palindrome.*

(a) † I ask and I invoke you today, evil madness (?). ' At the time <that> Jesus Christ was lifted onto the wood of the cross, he called out, saying, ' Eloe Lema Sabakdani, Jesus Christ. . . . ' Leave (?) Abraham the son of Kaselia. 5 Adam, Seth, Noah, Methuselah, and the holy spirit! '

AO	(ring signs and letters)	Immanuel
Jesus Christ		O Christ A Mary
Ebaal Adoni	Eres Eres	AEEIOUO
		UMU UMU 8

Give me,	ADONAI		son of the '
all of you, '	A	Jesus	ever-living
the second			god, ' wrote
10 letter	A ✡		15 to him,
that our	B	Christ	to ' Abgar
lord '	ISABAOTH		the king,
Jesus '			the king
Christ, the			at the '

city {the city}, to give deliverance, ' through Ananias the messenger, ' the copyist, that it 20 might give health to those who are in ' every infirmity, whether an infirmity from . . . illness or a potion or magic ' or a drug. In general, it must deliver from everything ' evil, becoming a source of healing for those who are in every infirmity, ' in the peace of god, Amen.

Jesus Christ, help! 25

(b) The prayer of Elijah the Tishbite, the chariot of Christ, ' that he prayed:

Jesus is the name. It has raised up . . . ' after him. It bore him, and he called out, saying,

> You of heaven, ' do not bring me forth today.
> You of the earth, do not bring me forth today.
> For ' I am a child of my mother,
> I am one born by myself, 30 like Lazarus.

Let everyone who is living, who has the breath ' of god
    dwelling with him,
let him be ashamed before my face,
fearful ' before my honor,
for the seal of Jesus ' Christ is written upon my forehead,
and the power of the holy ' spirit is what will protect me.
I am clothed, [35] arrayed (?) with the only begotten Jesus
    Christ.
He ' it is who is spread abroad,
who protects me up to this moment '
and all the days of my life, for ever.
Yea, yea! '

IA IO SA . . . '
to me, (**verso**) [40] for ever, ' up to this moment and all the
    days of my life. '

HAPEHIPAHAU HAELEC NAMAROUTHINIA '
AKASHTHINIA MOUNTHARAHA MATHIROTHA, '
Jesus Christ, help! (ring signs) [45]

SATOR ARETO TENET OTERA ROTAS

62. Amulet to protect Philoxenos from all evil

Text: amulet from the collection of M. Robert Nahman
Description: parchment, repeatedly folded (see the full-size plate in
Drescher)
Bibliography: James Drescher, "A Coptic Amulet"
Translator: Marvin Meyer

*This amulet was used to provide protection for Philoxenos against
all sorts of potential threats to his well-being. The powers invoked or adjured include Aio (Yao?) Sabaoth Adonai, the Persian deity Mithras,
Orpha, and Orphamiel. Mention is also made of the words of Jesus on
the cross. The opening portion of Psalm 91 and the incipits of Matthew,
John, Luke, and Mark are quoted for their protective power. The reference to "the great name of god, whose name no one knows except the
camel" (27–28) recalls Arabic lore concerning the names of Allah.*

[. . .] holy [. . .] Aio Sabaoth Adonai ' [. . .]arath Mithras. '

[The praise of the song] of David. The one who dwells ' [in the help of the most high will] abide in 5 [the shadow of the god of] heaven. He will say to the lord, ' [You are my protector and] my refuge; my ' [god, I shall trust] in you. The book [of the ' generation of Jesus Christ, the] son of David, the son ' of Abraham. In the beginning was 10 the Word, and the Word was with ' god. Since many [have] taken in hand. ' The beginning of the gospel of Jesus Christ. '

I adjure you by your powers, your names, ' your holy
    potencies;
I adjure 15 you by Orphamiel,
    the great finger of the father; '
I adjure you by the throne of the father; '
I adjure you by Orpha,
    the entire body ' of god;
I adjure you by the chariots ' of the sun;
I adjure you by the entire host 20 of angels on high;
I adjure ' you by the seven curtains that ' are drawn over the
    face of god;
I adjure you ' by the seven cherubim who fan ' the face
    of god;
I adjure you 25 by the great cherub of fire, whose ' name no
    one knows;
I adjure you ' by the great name of god, whose name ' no
    one knows except the camel;
I adjure ' you by the seven archangels;
I adjure 30 you by the three words that ' Jesus spoke on the
    cross, Eloi Eloi Elema ' Sabakthani, that is, My
    god, my god, ' why have you forsaken me?—
that you keep ' any person who may wear this amulet 35
    from all [harm] and all evil ' and all sorcery and
    all injury induced by the stars ' and all the de-
    mons and all the deeds of the hostile ' adversary,
that you guard ' the body of Philoxenos son of Euphemia 40
    from all these things.
Holy, holy, ' holy.
Amen, Amen, Amen.

63. Ritual spell to heal and protect (a woman and her children?)

Text: Berlin 11347

Description: paper, 48.5 x 20 cm, eighth or ninth century

Bibliography: Walter Beltz, "Die koptischen Zauberpapiere und Zauberostraka," 32–35; Angelicus M. Kropp, *Ausgewählte koptische Zaubertexte,* 2.113–17

Translator: Marvin Meyer

Berlin 11347 presents a ritual (for a woman and her children?) intended to adjure spiritual powers to seal the oil used for healing and protection. The powers invoked include the holy spirit, the twenty-four elders, the four living creatures of Ezekiel 1, the seven archangels, the 144,000 (compare Revelation 7:4; 14:1–3) killed by Herod (compare Matthew 2), the three youths of Daniel 1 (described with their two sets of names and three formulaic words), the confessors (or martyrs), and the twelve apostles. Among the powerful utterances used in the text are Alpha Leon Phone Aner, AKRAMACHAMARI, LAL MOULAL BOULAL, and utterances that recall the words of Jesus on the cross and the palindrome ABLANATHANALBA. The date Choiak 29 refers to the Coptic date of Christmas (compare Yale 1792 [text 55]).

TEXT

> [. . . , help] us, me and my little children ' [. . .], help us.
> He said to her, ' [. . .] these days and very great is ' [. . .]
>> his holy hands.
> He turned his 5 [. . .] you (?). He prayed in this way,
> saying, '
>> [Merciful one (?)], son of a merciful one,
>> compassionate one, ' son of the compassionate one,
>> redeemer, son of the redeemer, '
>> good one, son of the good one,
>> savior, ' son of the savior,
>> forgiver, son 10 of the forgiver,
>> lord, who loves his creation,
>> shepherd, ' who tends his sheep:
> If I have found mercy before you, ' grace before your face,
> you must send your ' holy spirit,
> that it may come upon this oil that is in ' my hand

and seal it in the name of the father [15] and the son and
the holy spirit.
You must send | me your 24 elders, whose names are |
Achael, Banuel, Ganuel, | Dedael, Eptiel, Zartiel,
Ethael, Thathiel, | Iochael, Kardiel, Labtiel, Merael, [20]
Nerael, Xiphiel, Oupiel, Pirael, Rael, | Seroael, Tauriel,
Umnuel, Philopael, | Christuel, Psilaphael, Olithiel,
who | sit upon 24 thrones, with 24 crowns upon | their
heads, with 24 censers in their hands,
that they [25] may stretch out their right ones, each of them
by | name.

You must send me today your 4 | incorporeal creatures, with
4 faces and 6 wings, |
Alpha Leon Phone Aner,
Paramara | Zorothion Periton Akramata,
that they may stretch [30] out their 4 spiritual fingers and seal
| the oil that is in my hand,
in the name of the father etc. |

You must send me today your 7 holy | archangels,
Michael, Gabriel, Raphael, | Suriel, Zetekiel, Solothiel,
Anael, [35]
that they may stretch out their 7 fingers, by | name, and seal
the oil that is in my hands, |
in the name of the father etc.

You must send me today | your 144,000 whom Herod
killed, |
each of them by name,
that they may seal [40] this oil that is in my hand,
in the name of the father etc. |

You must send me today your 3 holy youths, |
Ananias, Asarias, Misael,
Setrok, Misak, | Abdenako,
LAL, MOULAL, BOULAL,
each | of them by name,
that they may seal this oil [45] that is in my hand—me, N.—
in the name of the father etc. |

You must send me today your confessors, (**verso**)
    each of them by name,
that they may seal this ' oil that is in my hands—me, N.—
    in the name of the father ' etc.

You must send me the 12 apostles, ' who have walked with
    the son of god.

At the [5] moment that N. child of N. will be anointed with
    this oil, '
you must take away from him all sicknesses and all
    illnesses ' and all magic and all potions and ' all
    mishaps and all pains and all male spirits ' and
    all female spirits,
whether it has come from the east [10] or the west,
whether they have come from the four sides of ' the earth or
    the air.
Let them all be dispelled ' through the power of Eloei
    Elemas Sabaoth ' Abaktani Abanael Naflo
        AKRAMA'CHAMARI,
    and the power of the one who has come down [15]
        upon the altar on the 29th of Choiak, '
    and the one who has come down upon the waters of
        the ' Jordan as a dove.
He must come upon N. ' to protect him from all evil.
Rule over ' N., who seals it.

Apa Anoup has sealed [20] this oil.
Michael is the one who intercedes.
Jesus Christ ' is the one who gives healing to N.,
    that he may be renewed in ' his whole body,
    like the tree of life that is in ' the middle of paradise,
    all the days of ' his life,
        yea, yea, at once, at once!

64. Exorcistic spell to drive evil forces from a pregnant woman

Text: London Oriental Manuscript 5525

Description: parchment, 14 3/4 x 9 in.

Bibliography: Walter E. Crum, *Catalogue of the Coptic Manuscripts in the British Museum*, 253–55; Angelicus M. Kropp, *Ausgewählte koptische Zaubertexte*, 1.15–21; 2.199–207; François Lexa, *La Magie dans l'Égypte Antique*, 2.168ff

Translator: Richard Smith

This spell protects a woman named Sura, during her current pregnancy and any future pregnancies, from a variety of threatening evils and illnesses. The primary power called upon is Yao Sabbaoth, along with the "great powers" who stand before him, Michael and the other archangels. These seven, with their virtues, are associated with the seven Greek vowels (compare this list with the Coptic book of ritual power from Leiden [text 134], page 4, verso). Many other divine powers and angels are invoked, such as Jesus, along with the words he utters at his crucifixion ("Eloei Elemas . . ."), the Gnostic Abrasax, the companions of Daniel in the fiery furnace, the twenty-four elders, and so forth.

The technique of the spell is the insistence that Yao Sabbaoth descend upon the drawn figure which accompanies the text. The figure would thereby be a consecrated object and, since it was folded tightly when discovered, it may have been carried about by Sura. Noteworthy is that the forces of evil are not distinguished from physical diseases.

TEXT

I adjure you by your name and your ' power and your figure and your amulet ' of salvation and the places where you dwell ' and your light-wand 5 in your right hand and your light-shield ' in your left hand and your ' great powers standing before you. Do not hold back ' and do not ignore, until you find it worth your while ' to descend upon your figure 10 and your amulet ' of salvation.

Watch and protect ' the 4 sides of the body and the ' soul and the spirit and ' the entire house of N. daughter of N. 15 and her child who is in her womb ' as well as every child ' born to her.

Bring them to life yearly ' without any disease. Cast forth ' from her every evil force. [20] Never allow them to approach her or ' any of her children until she bears them. Cast forth from her every doom ' and every devil and every Apalaf and every Aberselia ' and every power of darkness and every evil eye ' and every eye-shutter and every chill [25] and every fever and every trembling. Restrain ' them all. Cast them away from her and away from all her ' children until she bears them, and away from all her dwellings, ' immediately and quickly! Do not ' permit them ever to visit her or the child with whom she is pregnant [30] for approximately two hundred miles around.

Yea, yea, now, now, ' at once, at once! '

Sura daughter of Pelca, she and the child with whom she is pregnant. '

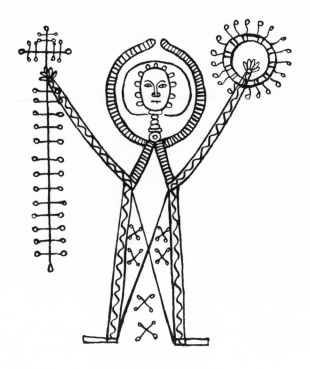

(reconstructed drawing)

OHI SHAOHI SHASHAOHI SHAOHI SHA AAAO

O O O O O O O

Protect, ' shelter her, Yao Sabbaoth . . . archangel Michael, [35] Gabriel, helper. For N. daughter of N., her and the child with whom she is pregnant, ' cast forth from them every Aberselia, '

now, now, at once, at once!

Sura daughter of Pelca. '

Yao Sabbaoth Atonai Eloei Elemas Miksanther ' Abrasakks Michael Gabriel Raphael Suriel Raguel Asuel [40] Saraphuel Yao Atonai Eloei Elemas Sabaoth, I adjure ' you by your holy powers. Watch and protect the four sides of the body and ' the soul and the spirit of N. daughter of N., her and the child with whom she is pregnant, ' whether it is a male or a female. Cast forth from them every chill and ' every fever and every trembling and every Aberselia, and every doom, [45] every devil, and every Apalaf, and every power of darkness ' and every demon, and < . . . >. Cast them forth from her, her and the child with whom she is pregnant. ' Cast them forth from all her dwellings and from every place to which she moves, ' immediately and quickly!

Yea, yea, now, now, at once, at once! '
Sura daughter of Pelca. [50]
Jesus Jesus Jesus Jesus Jesus Jesus Jesus Jesus
† † † † † † † † '
Sara= Mar= Bi= Sara= '
Mar= Thar= Thathrar= '
D D AAAAAAA OOOOOOO '
D D
D D AAAAAAA OOOOOOO [55]
D D
D D AAAAAAA OOOOOOO '
D D Christ Christ Christ Christ Christ Christ Christ
D D AAAAAAA † † † † † † † '
D D

Victory and help to N. ' daughter of N., her and the child ' who is in her womb, whether it is a female [60] or a male! '

[Yea], yea, now, now, at once, at once! '
Sura daughter ' of Pelca. '

ABLANATHANNABLAN '
ABLANNATHANABLA⁶⁵   I ' adjure ' you '
ABLANNATHANABL
ABLANNATHANAB   by ' your 70 holy powers, '
ABLANNATHANA
ABLANNATHAN   take away ' this fever '
ABLANNATHA
ABLANNATH   and this chill 75 and . . .
ABLANNA
ABLANN   (about 7 lines illegible)
ABLAN
ABLA   until she ' bears them so they
ABL
AB   live yearly ' without disease. '
A
        Sura daughter of ' Pelca. 80

    Thalalmelal ' Kokalthaal ' Maalbuk ' Ananias Setra ' Asarias
Misak 85 Misael Abdenako ' Chesenaethi ' Chersetaethi ' Cher-
sospaethi ' Hilelmilelel 90 Michor '

AAAAAAA '	1 '	OOOOOOO
AAAAAA	2	OOOOOO
AAAAA	3	OOOOO
AAAA	4	OOOO
AAA	5	OOO
AA	6	OO
A	7	O '

    (on the right) I adjure you by your 95 . . . ' to approach it and
' to send ' the power of Michael the archangel, ' who came from
heaven and offered salvation. 100
    (on the left) I adjure you. ' Watch and protect the 4 sides ' of
the body and the soul and the spirit and the whole house ' of N.
daughter of N. Take this burning away from her ' and the child
who is in her womb. 105 Watch and guard them from every evil
thing yearly. '

Yea, yea, yea, at once, at once, at once! '
The sun, the one who ascends throughout the whole
     world! '
Sura daughter of Pelca. '

    Beth Bethai Betha Bethari Maruel Marmaruel [110] Matetiel
Sriel Ermiel Chabanta Choner Chammanman ' Basar Escho Sabao
Linirael.nnoel Emiel Sabako ' Atema Chimel Taloel Katatiel
Sariel ' Zohothiel Phalmerael Agramatonael Merathoel ' and
Sebriel SATOR ARETO TENET OTERA ROTAS [115] SATOR Yatha-
tabir Keggiel and Senbriel and Asaroth '

A	EIA	Michael, the peace,
E	EIIAK	Gabriel, the grace, '
E	MIIAK	Raphael, the power,
I	SEMIIAK	Suriel, the will, '
O	ARTORE	Raguel, the truth,
U	ARTORAN	Anael, the glory, '
O	NARTORAK	Saraphuel, the . . . ,
		the doctoring and the healing. [120]

    I adjure you by your names and your powers and the power
of god ' almighty, to dwell here comfortably. Watch and protect the
4 sides of the body ' and the soul and the spirit of Sura daughter of
Pelca and her child, ' her and the child with whom she is pregnant,
whether it is a male or ' a female, so they live yearly without disease. Cast forth from them [125] all doom, all devils, and all Apalaf,
and all Aberselia, ' and every power of darkness, and every demon,
whether male demon ' or female demon. Restrain them all. Cast
them from ' them and from all their dwellings for two hundred
miles around, ' immediately and quickly!
    Yea, yea, now, now, at once, at once!
    Susunkus, [130] also Barpharankus Ablanathanalba Agrama-
chamario Marioth ' Yao Yomam Acham, by the great name of god,
Nahperaneue, ' the one who is called Papleu, who ' is hidden in
the place of light! Watch and protect Sura daughter [135] of Pelca,
her and the child who is in her womb.
    Yea, yea, now, now, ' at once, at once!

65. Spell for healthy childbirth

Text: Rylands 100

Description: papyrus, 5.5 x 7.5 cm; written on the back of a reused letter

Bibliography: Walter E. Crum, *Catalogue of the Coptic Manuscripts in the Collection of the John Rylands Library, Manchester,* 52; Angelicus M. Kropp, *Ausgewählte koptische Zaubertexte,* 2.211

Translator: Richard Smith

This text certainly causes us to question a distinction between ritual spell and religious prayer. It is an appeal to St. Leontius of Tripolis, known for his healing powers.

TEXT

✝ ✝ ✝

✝ O god of St.ⁱ Leontius!

If I stay ⁱ at this house where I am ⁱ and remain inside with [my] ⁵ mother, my heart will be ⁱ at rest and ⁱ shall bear a living ⁱ child. . . . (two remaining lines are obscure)

66. Spell for protection during childbirth (caesarean section?)

Text: Michigan 1190

Description: papyrus, 11 1/2 inches square, fifth century or later ("perhaps very much later"—so Worrell)

Bibliography: William H. Worrell, "Coptic Magical and Medical Texts," 5–13

Translator: Stephen H. Skiles

Michigan 1190 is a generic spell for protection and aid during childbirth. William H. Worrell has suggested that the spell orders an angelic caesarean section. This interpretation hinges on a point of Coptic grammar with which the present translator disagrees (see the note to recto, column 1, lines 12–13). The text is difficult, but (as Worrell himself notes) there is no reference to an incision (nor to the closure of any surgical wound). Worrell draws attention to a text in the Mishnah (Niddah 5.1) and Rashi's comments on it, but the connection among the texts seems tenuous at best. As the passage is presented here, the common motif of an assembly of guardian angels at a time of crisis is commanded rather than surgical intervention.

Robert K. Ritner has suggested that Michigan 1190 may not be a protective spell at all, but rather may be a spell to induce abortion by employing a series of violent images—killing, shattering, breaking, casting fire into a woman. Compare Berlin 8314 (text 75), an erotic spell with much of the same imagery.

TEXT

†

I invoke you, Athrak, great ' angel who stands to the ' right of the sun, to whom all ' the powers of the sun are subject, to come [5] to the side (of) the other. The abyss—you must kill it. ' Silver— you must kill it. Steel— ' you must shatter (?) it. Iron—you must melt ' it away. Stone—you must break it. ' Ocean water(s)—you must make them dry [10] up. Mountains—you must make [them] move. ' Rocks—you must make them melt away. ' A woman who is pregnant—you must attain (her) right ' side and bring forth (her) ' child. It is not really I who shall ask you [15] nor [other] (humans), but [. . . ' Sa]baoth [. . .] [20] to her side [. . .] ' from the crown of (her) head down ' to (the) nail(s) of her feet, and bring ' forth under her polluted blood ' and dark water on [25] (her) right side (over) to (her) left ' side. You must make it weigh on her ' like a millstone. It must flow ' under her like the source of the ' four rivers. Whether magician or [30] conjurer, whether heavenly ' or infernal or human ' hand—draw strength from ' the blood which is under N. I am N. ' I invoke you, Michael, [35] the angel (column 2) who stands on (the) right side of the father, ' that you come to (this side). I invoke (you), Gabriel, the ' angel who stands (on the) left side of ' the father, that you come to me with your fiery [5] sword to this side. I invoke ' you, Adone, the great angel ' who stands over the 12 hours ' of the day, that you come to me, to ' this side. I invoke (you), Uri, the great angel [10] who stands over (the) 12 hours ' of the night, that you come to me, to this side. ' I invoke you, Bori[el], you ' of fiery flaming face, [that] you come to ' [me] to (this side). I invoke you, [. . .][15]el, the [angel who . . .] ' wrath [. . .] [20] the keeper ' of hell, the ringlets ' of whose hair stretch out over ' the whole world, whose ' name is Sisinaei, Amin, that [25] you come to me, to (this side). I invoke you, Esparte, ' daughter of the

devil, who ' leaped down to hell (and) brought ' the keeper of hell
' up, that you come to me, to (this side). I invoke you ³⁰ 12
archangels with ' your 12 bowls (?) full of water ' in your hands:
When I cast ' it into the fire, you 'must fill the 12 bowls (?) ³⁵ with
fire (and) cast them ' into her heart—her lung(s), her ' heart, her
liver, her spleen, ' (into all) the hundred twenty-five body parts.
(**verso**) I invoke you, 7 arch'angels, who are Michael, ' Gabriel,
Uriel, Rakuel, ' Suriel, Asuel, Salaphuel, ⁵ that you yourself come,
Michael, down to (this side) to give, ' without hearing a thing except those from my mouth, ' to fulfill the will of ' my heart, the request of my soul. ' I shall cross the seven rivers ¹⁰ of fire and run
up to ' the seventh heaven ' where Yao Sabaoth sits. ' I shall seek
out Michael ' as he stands [on the] right [side of the ¹⁵ father . . .],
¹⁹ at once, at once [. . .]!

(ring signs and letters)

67. Spell for the well-being of a child

Text: Vienna K 70 (Rainer, AN 189)

Description: parchment, 10 x 44.5 cm, tenth or eleventh century

Bibliography: Viktor Stegemann, *Die koptischen Zaubertexte*, 63–67; Walter
Till, "Zu den Wiener koptischen Zaubertexte," 214–15

Translator: Marvin Meyer

*Vienna K 70 is a prayer for the growth, protection, and good
health of a child. Among the Christian images employed is that of Jesus
as the shepherd (compare, for example, John 10). Stegemann thinks
that there may be a trace of Monophysitism in the text (apparently he is
reflecting upon the last lines of the text).*

TEXT

[. . .] in your presence (?). Make him grow ' and care for
him. Prescribe ' what is good. Fill him with ' understanding and
the knowledge of ⁵ wisdom. Open the organs of perception ' of
his heart, that he may know ' everything that is [good]. . . . ' Let
people rejoice over ' his growth. You must entrust him to the
sheepfold ¹⁰ of Christ. For you are the lord ' since the beginning;

you have created ' humankind in your likeness ' and your image. You must take all sickness ' and all flatulence away from [15] this little child. Provide . . . ' against a chill, against the evil eye, ' against harmful sickness, to take them ' away from him. Grant him ' safety. For you are the lord, [20] through whom the healing of all sickness ' comes, and you ' are the health of soul and ' body and spirit, through ' the favor and the philanthropy [25] of your only begotten son ' Jesus Christ, our lord, through ' whom be the glory to you and him ' and the holy spirit, now ' and always, for ever [30] and ever, Amen. †

68. Spell for protection against reptiles

Text: Rylands 104, section 4

Description: paper, 19 x 14 cm, folded several times

Bibliography: Walter E. Crum, *Catalogue of the Coptic Manuscripts in the Collection of the John Rylands Library, Manchester*, 53–55; Angelicus M. Kropp, *Ausgewählte koptische Zaubertexte*, 2.68–69

Translator: James E. Goehring

This prayer for protection against the bite of reptiles is part of a series of spells for a variety of purposes. In addition to this protective spell, other sections of the text are used against fever, for protection "from everything," and perhaps on behalf of "a mother in childbirth." In his edition of the Coptic text, Walter E. Crum does not include indications of line divisions.

TEXT

A prayer. When you recite it, no reptile can bite (you). O Jesus, I am in Mary. O John, I am in Elizabeth. The lord Jesus said, "Let nothing [. . .] at all [. . .] me, N., on this day and this night." It is the mouth of the lord Sabaoth that said this: Let no reptile bite me, but let all reptiles of the earth become stone in my presence. Let all those on earth become as stone and iron in my presence. For it is the mouth of the lord Sabaoth that said this and the words of the lord are true. It is done.

69. Spell for protection against violent attack

Text: London Oriental Manuscript 4721 (5)

Description: papyrus, 9 3/4 x 9 in.

Bibliography: Walter E. Crum, *Catalogue of the Coptic Manuscripts in the British Museum*, 255; Angelicus M. Kropp, *Ausgewählte koptische Zaubertexte*, 2.69–70

Translator: Richard Smith

Here is an appeal to Jesus for safety in the midst of battle. Jesus instructs those making the appeal to recite his own and several other powerful divine names against the attacking weapons.

TEXT

. . . weapons standing by . . . ￼

And you, lord of lords, ￼ you are the one from whom all healing comes, ￼ with your good father and your holy spirit. 5 If a battle arises [against us and] ￼ we are stricken by a sword, or [a spear, or a knife], ￼ or any weapon under [heaven], ￼ recite it so that the rescue [. . .]. ￼ And our lord Jesus said to them: 10

If a battle arises against us ￼ and we are stricken by a sword, or a spear, or a ￼ knife, or any weapon under heaven, ￼ recite against it my name, and the name of my good father ￼ and the holy spirit, and the name 15 of the twelve apostles, and the name ￼ of the twenty-four elders, and the name ￼ of the seven archangels, those who are within the ￼ veil, who stand by me, my good father, ￼ and the holy spirit, so that 20 neither bloodshed nor aching bones might happen ￼ at any place over which these names will be recited.

70. Spell, with Gnostic characteristics, to protect from filthy demons

Text: London Oriental Manuscript 5987

Description: papyrus, 77 3/4 x 5 3/8 in.

Bibliography: Walter E. Crum, *Catalogue of the Coptic Manuscripts in the British Museum*, 418–20; Angelicus M. Kropp, *Ausgewählte koptische*

Zaubertexte, 1.22–28; 2.149–60
Translator: Richard Smith

Kropp classifies this, with several similar texts, as an "exorcism," a term that has come to be associated with demonic possession of the personality. It is better described by the term the text itself uses at the very end, a phylakterion *or "(protective) amulet" of general application to be "bound upon the right forearm." Tying an amulet onto an arm was common in Mediterranean antiquity and is still practiced by many cultures in the world today.*

The spell is an appeal to Christ, who is invoked by the exotic name Baktiotha, and beyond that the spell is thick with motifs from Gnostic myth. For example, it presents an emanationist Christology whereby Christ, or modalities of Christ, emanate from the father, through the angels, to earth. Another Gnostic motif is the predication "mother who has given birth to the true light," and the first three of the following divine names are names from the Gnostic "four lights." Similar statements about the mother giving birth to the light, or lights, are found in Sethian Gnostic texts such as the Gospel of the Egyptians and Zostrianos. Line 71 begins an extended description of Davithe (see illustration), who seems to be the most magnetic of this Gnostic quartet, assimilating especially the iconography related to the biblical king David ("the key," compare Revelation 3:7 and London Oriental Manuscript 6794 [text 129]).

Several of the other characters invoked in this text are discussed in glossary entries, but the "distributors" (lines 16, 97, and 125) are a puzzle. Crum thought this obscure term referred to humans of some kind, but it is more likely that they are astrological dividers that separate the cosmos into measurements of space and time. All of these various forces are called in for protection against less specified "filthy spirits."

TEXT

✝ I invoke you today, Baktiotha, ¹great trustworthy one from above, who is trustworthy ¹over the ninth generation of things.

[Christ] ¹almighty, who was produced within the father ⁵ until a perfect person was produced for us ¹through an angel and archangel, ¹who was sent upon the earth to us, and gave ¹his body and his blood for the sake of all of us, and rose ¹from the dead! Reach out and listen to us today, ¹⁰ Sabaoth.

For I am Mary, who is hidden in ' the appearance of Mariam. I am ' the mother who has given birth to the true light. '

Armiel, Davithe, Eleleth, Ermukratos, ' Adonai, Ermusr the invisible, Bainchooch, 15 do not bring your (pl.) anger upon all the ' distributors. Bring it upon all the filthy spirits. ' Let them be shamed and ' fall before me. For you are the ones who dwell ' on the north side and the east side of Antiochia. 20 There is (?) a myrtle tree in that place, ' whose name is called Lake Acherousia, ' which flows from under the throne of Yao Sabaoth. ' The name of that area is called ' "Salomites, the faith of Yao Sabaoth." 25

The well-being of the strong man, if he stays, is his dwelling place; ' if he leaves, his exit leaves a piece of land. ' Kabaoth Karbeltha is the one whom ' the seven aeons advise, saying, ' "Let us shut the storehouse while he is looking 30 for a way to come into it, for what he wants ' is to come into it." He relaxed his mouth ' in laughter; the greatness within <him> said, "I find ' laughter . . . ' on a head corner. . . ." He carried the head of the father, Sabaoth. 35 He went up in a form of light and ' peace.

Amen, 17 (times).

Jesus, 21 (times). Holy one, ' 21 (times). Holy paraclete, 21 (times). Holy invisible one, ' 21 (times). Holy bridegroom, 21 (times). ' Holy almighty one, 21 (times). Kalampsoel 40 Thoel Thumiael Thoroloel Akxukunur ' Misael Charuel Zamroch ' Afeieb Zif Thoantoriel Bakaichom ' Ormosira Erichatra Manut Prok...e! ' Yoel Thiel Misiael Mioel Daithe 45 Eleluth Ermukratos Adonai Ermusur, ' the invisible one within the seven veils, ' by him stand the seven radiant lights ' Sarthiel, Tharbioth ' and Urach and Thurach and Armuser and Eiecha, 50 the seven inexpressible lights, the sixty ' golden lamps which burn in the tabernacle of the father. ' Salvation is by the white grapevine that is . . . ' upon the head of the throne of his glory. Salvation ' is from the seven golden palm branches that are hung in the tabernacle 55 of the father. Salvation is from Ar.iu Mariu Adonai ' Yao Sabaoth Bainchooch. Prepare for me ' 240,000 angels of heaven ' today, with their burning, sharp swords drawn in ' their right hands. Let them humiliate every 60 filthy spirit in their midst. It should not be said ' that your king does not exist. Yes, lord, you exist ' for ever.

Almighty Yao Sabaoth ' Moneus Soneus Arkoeus ' Adonai Yao Eloi, the one who is in the seventh 65 heaven, who divides the day and the hours, ' I invoke you today, who prepares for me the 20,000 ' demons who stand at ' the Euphrates River, who prays ' to the father twelve times per hour, [70] until he gives rest to all of the dead. '

Davithe of the golden hair and lightning eyes, ' it is you who have the key of divinity ' in your hand. What you shut cannot be opened ' again, and if you open, cannot be shut. It is you [75] who offer from the golden chalice of the church of the ' firstborn. Davithe, you are the original father. ' It is you who blow the golden trumpet ' of the father. As you blow, ' all those who dwell in the entire creation [80] gather to you, whether rulers or angels or archangels. '

Yao Yao, Christ, almighty, who was ' produced inside the father until a ' perfect one was produced for us through ' the angels and archangels and was sent [85] upon the earth to us, and was pierced ' with a spear in his right side, and rose from ' the dead and raised those who were being punished, ' and divided the day, who came forth from the first ' breath of the father, whose forepart is like a lion, [90] whose rear end is like a she-bear, with a ' falcon's form, with a dragon's face, Haruel ' Kappsop Pakruthos Thetrumas ' Thetrumas Istrael Barucha! ' I adjure you today, come Baktiotha, [95] fill me with all things, Yao Yao, 7 (times), ' A 21, E 21, E 21, I 21, O 21, U 21, O 21. ' Spell. For I adjure all you distributors. ' The two arms (?) of Seth! The two cheeks of Christ, ' which throw forth lightning before the father! [100] Phukta, who divides the day and the hours, ' who raised up Adam in paradise, ' and found Eve! <You> are the salvation of the father. ' Holy, 7 (times). Holy, holy one who dwells in ' the heavens! Allimiel, Davithe, Eleluth, [105] Ermutos, Adonai, Davithe, you are the father ' who.... ' You are Akramiel, Prakuel, the salvation of ' Istrael. You are the salvation of the father. ' You are . . . , the salvation of. . . . You are [110] the father in whom . . . ' Ermukraton . . . Ermusur ' invisible Bainchooch, O one within ' the seven veils.

21 (times): Yao Yao ' Eloi Zabakdani! Merioth Merchoth! [115] Finish all things for me. Spell. You must dwell ' with me in a foreign land, a land of ' grace, by the power of Bainchooch, the one who descended ' upon the flaming sea, on unextinguishable flames, ' twelve times per hour [120] until he gave rest to all the dead. ' Abranathanabra Akrammachimari ' Adonai Yao Sabaoth Sachamara ' Sachamar Chomach Tabrael Suraech Urakabie ' Yao

Eloi Zabakdani! Finish [125] all things for me, all you distributors: It is you ' who send dew and rain ' upon the earth. Yao Bamein-sam . o . ' Barucha! Finish everything for me. ' Thororoel Ephtha-niael! By the power [130] of Piel Pomiel Bainchooooooooch Yao the . . . ' Psephos . . . ' and my entire demand, now, 2 (times), at once, 2 (times)! † '

† [. . .] (references to: prayer, numbers, first fruits, cup and glass, censer, 21 times again and again) [150]

. . . This is the amulet that you ' bind upon your right fore-arm. . . .

71. Rossi's "Gnostic" tractate against the powers of evil

Text: from the Biblioteca Nazionale, Turin

Description: papyrus book of twenty-one pages (with an additional damaged page; two other manuscript pages are missing); the text was destroyed in a fire in 1904

Bibliography: Francesco Rossi, "Di alcuni manoscritti copti"; Angelicus M. Kropp, *Ausgewählte koptische Zaubertexte*, 1.63–78; 2.176–99; É. Amélineau, *Le nouveau traité gnostique de Turin*; Marvin Meyer, *Rossi's "Gnostic" Tractate*

Translator: Marvin Meyer

Rossi's "Gnostic" tractate consists of a series of protective spells to be used by a person who wishes to adjure the powers of the divine realm against malevolent forces. The text opens with a recipe for the prepara-tion of an amulet and the observance of a ritual that apparently involves the use of incense and sacrifice. The balance of the tractate provides statements of invocation and praise arranged in stanzas. The powerful utterances within the tractate include vowels in a series (for example, AEEIOUO) given without elaboration on page 21 and with a sevenfold repetition at 18,22 and 19,18. The expression ABLANATHANAFLA at 1,9 and perhaps also the name [Agra]ma Chamariel at 19,1–2 (compare AKRAMMACHAMAREI, with variations) represent common formulae in ritual texts. The famous name Abrasax (compare also Abrasaxael at 3,2) is given in "wing formation" on page 21. Jewish concerns dominate in the names and descriptions of divine and angelic powers (along with the portrayal of the divine throne-chariot at 12,17ff.), and Christian interests are reflected in the Christian liturgical materials (for example, the trinitarian formula and the trisagion) and in the references to Christ (for example, "the head of Christ," 14,5–6; "his son upon the cross,"17,2; also "Adonai Eloei Elema Sabaktani," 9,17–18, a garbled version of the words attributed to Jesus on the cross). The image of the four pillars that support heaven recalls Egyptian lore, with Nut, the sky goddess, lifted above Geb, the earth god, by means of four pillars (that is, the arms and legs of Nut, or Shu as the bearer of the sky). Although the tractate traditionally has been described as Gnostic, such an attribution requires careful qualification.

TEXT

† Draw the four angels in front of the ' curtain of the
father, while you are wearing ' a wreath of
roses, with a branch ' of myrtle in [your]
hand (and) with gum ammoniac 5 in your
mouth. '

O(ffering); frank(incense); sto(rax); stac(te). Nest; '
slay the six doves. Cinnamon; ' rose oil . . .
charcoal (from) white wood; ' olive wood.
(page l)

[I invoke] you [today],
the one who ' [governs] from heaven to earth,
from ' [earth] to heaven,
the great ' only begotten one:
Listen to me today, for I 5 call to you,
only father, ' almighty,
the mind ' hidden in the father,

the firstborn ' of every creature and every aeon, '
    ABLANATHANAFLA.

Listen [10] to me today, for I call to you, '
the one who is over every aeon,
the firstborn ' (of) the names (?) of all the angels. '
Let them listen to me, all the ' angels and the archangels, [15]
let them submit to me, all ' spiritual natures
who are in this place, ' quickly!
For this is the will ' of Sabaoth.
Help ' me, holy angels! [20]
Let them flee from [me], ' all my enemies,
and. . . .
(two pages missing; **page 2**)
[. . .] quickly!
Let them flee ' [from] my face, silently! '

Michael, the one who is over all the ' strong powers,
Raphael, [5] the one who is over salvation, '
Gabriel, the one who is over the powers,
Arnael, ' the one who is over hearing,
Uriel, the one ' who is over the crowns,
Nephael, ' the one who is over aid,
Akentael, [10] the one who is over the stars,
Asentael, ' the one who is over the sun,
Eraphael, ' the one who is over the day,
Yeremiel, ' the one who is over the bowls (?), '
Eriel, the one who is over the water, [15]
Phanuel, the one who is over the produce, '
Aphael, the one who is over the snow, '
Akrael, the one who is over (the) sea, '
[.]eilael, the one who is over the rain[water], '
[. .]abuel, the one who is over the . . . , [20]
[. . .]athiel, the one who is over . . . , '
. . . , the one who [is over] . . . , (**page 3**)
Thauruel, the one who is over the ' clouds,
Abrasaxael, the one who is over ' the lightning,
Yaoel, the one who is over ' every place,
Sabael, the one who is over [5] the good,
Adonael, ' the one who is over the coming in of the father
    and ' his going forth,

Spell

that ' you (pl.) may come to me, stand ' with me,
and ¹⁰ cast from before my face every ' unclean spirit.
Let them ' all withdraw from before my face, '
lest they say, ' Where is his god?
Let them ¹⁵ all tremble and flee from my ' presence,
in the name of the father ' and the son and the holy spirit, '
    AAAAAAAAAAAA.

Holy, ' holy, holy is the lord Sabaoth! ²⁰
Heaven and earth are full of your ' [holy glory]!
We glorify you, we glorify (**page 4**) all your holinesses, Yao.
We ' glorify you, holy one, Sabaoth, ' the first of heaven and
    earth.
We ' glorify you, Adonai Eloei ⁵ almighty, the first of the '
    cherubim and the seraphim.
We ' glorify you, Marmaraoth, ' the one who is before the
    angels ' and the archangels.
We ¹⁰ glorify you, Chamarmariao, ' the one who is before
    the fourteen ' firmaments.
We glorify you, ' Thrakai, the one who has arrayed the '
    earth upon the abyss and has hung [the heaven]
    ¹⁵ as a vault.
We glorify ' you, Manachoth, the one who has ' laid the
    foundation of heaven and earth ' and has estab-
    lished the fourteen ' firmaments upon the four
    ²⁰ pillars.
We glorify [you], ' An . . . baom, the one who has come to
    [gird (**page 5**) his] sword in the middle of both
    of his ' thighs (?).
We glorify you, ' Thrakaim, the one who has taken the ' ap-
    pearance of Gabriel.
We glorify you, ⁵ Lauriel, the minister of Raphael. '
We glorify you, heaven; we glorify you, ' earth.
We glorify you, sun; we glorify ' you, moon.
We glorify you, Sabaoth, ' and all the stars.
We glorify you, ¹⁰ Araktos; we glorify you, Yao. '
We glorify you, Adonai Eloei ' almighty.

Listen to me!
Come ' to me, good Gabriel,

so ' that you may listen to me today, on account of [15]
the seal of Adonai, the father, ' and the fourteen
amulets ' that are in my right hand, '
that you may come to me at this place and ' become
for me a patron, [20] minister, and help all the
days ' of my life.
. . . ' cast out every evil (**page 6**) and unclean spirit,
whether male ' or female,
whether heavenly ' or of the earth or of the air. '
They must not be able to stand in my [5] presence nor in the
presence ' of your great might, god.
Amen, 3 (times). '

I glorify you, presence ' of Adonai Eloei almighty, '
so that you may listen to me [10] this day and send me '
Gabriel, the angel of ' righteousness,
that he may come to me on account of this ' seal of
the father almighty ' that is in my right hand,
that you [15] may stand at my right, and ' help me.
Direct your ' arrow against the first formed one and ' all his
powers and his ' unclean and evil [20] demons.
Reveal your hand to me ' [today].
Reveal to me today (**page 7**) [your] power and your glory.

I ' adjure you today, Gabriel, '
by Saber Blararo,
the ' three presences
that are in the [5] midst of the four pillars
that ' lift up heaven and earth, '
Thalamora Thesoha Thaisara. '

I adjure you, Gabriel, by these ' four angels
who stand [10] by the four pillars '
with their feet set upon the ' foundations of the abyss,
the holy one(s?), who ' lift up heaven,
Theriel ' Throel Bael.

I invoke [15] you, four great angels ' of the head of the father,
that you ' send me Gabriel, the ' angel of righteousness,
that he come to ' me and reveal to me his [20] [might]
and his glory.
Spell

For this is ' [the] will of almighty Sa'[baoth],
that he come to [me today] ' . . . .

I adjure you, [Gabr]iel, (**page 8**) by the [head of B]athuriel,
the great father, '
that you [come] to me and appear to me, at once! '

I adjure you, Gabriel, by the four ' corners of the fourteen
firmaments, 5
that you come to me and be with me ' this day and
this hour and help ' me through your might and
your glory, at ' once!

I adjure you, Yoiriel, by ' the cloud of light that is with the
father, 10
in which he was hidden before he created ' anything,
whose name is Marmarami, ' the great, the place of
the spirit of Adonai ' Eloei almighty:
You must ' appear to me and send me 15 Gabriel, the angel
of righteousness, ' today,
that he may scatter before me all ' spirits of Satan that
were ' created all together on a single ' day.
Lord god 20 almighty,
reveal to me your ' power,
send me Gabriel, the ' angel of righteousness,
that he may come ' [to me], quickly!
Amen, 3 (times). (**page 9**)
On account of [the might] of your holy name, ' Yao
Sabaoth Adonai Eloei ' almighty,
today, since I call ' to you,
Yao Sabaoth Adonai 5 Eloei, only great god,
who is ' within the seven curtains, '
the one who is seated upon his glorious ' holy throne:
You must send ' me Gabriel, the angel of 10 righteousness,
with his sword ' unsheathed in his hand, in his right '
hand,
that he may cast away from me ' all unclean spirits.
They must not be able ' to stand in my presence, but 15 let
them all flee before my face. '
Spell

I invoke you by your honored ' names,

Adonai Eloei Elema ' Sabaktani,
the one who looks upon ' the heavens so that they
tremble, (and) 20 the earth moves,
Saba Sabab Sabaoth ' Yao Yaoth Napher.
This is ' your secret name, god, who is ' seated in the
heights,
Esaes ' Ab[. . . . . . P]mou Pmou **(page 10)** Onoeros
Touora. . . . [A]katho[s] ' Efpakale Chebouthanis
A[m]amiel ' Tamach Mamiel Mariek Toak ' Etoak
Afrak Yoak,
the one who is seated 5 over the cherubim.

I invoke ' you by the head of Bathuriel, the great ' father,
and his right hand that ' grasps all your divinity, '
that you listen to me, 10 N. child of N., and send to me
from heaven ' Athonath Athonath, whose name is '
Gabriel, the angel of righteousness, '
that he come to me and do my work ' for which I invoke
you.
Spell 15
Bend your bow against the first ' formed one and all his
powers. '
Draw your sword against the first ' formed one and all his
potencies. '

Cleanse for me this place for 20 600,000 cubits,
cleanse for me ' the abyss for 600,000 cubits, '
cleanse for me the east for ' 600,000 cubits,
cleanse [for me] ' the north for 600,000 [cubits], **(page 11)**
cleanse for me the south for [600,000] cubits, '
cleanse for me the west for ' 600,000 cubits,
cleanse for me the ' air for 600,000 cubits,
that they may not come to 5 me.
Spell

Yea, yea, for I invoke ' you, Gabriel,
by the head of ' Bathuriel, the great father,
that you become ' for me a patron, minister, ' and helper in
every task.
I pray, 10 I invoke you—I am ' the presence of Yao Sabaoth '
Adonai almighty— '
that you listen to me and come to me today, ' on account

of the seal of the father [15] that is on this amulet in
my ' right hand (and) the twenty-four ' letters
that are on the amulet ' of the father,
that you listen to me, ' quickly!

I invoke [you], [20] Gabriel,
by the great name of the father ' and his holy glory,
and those who ' stand in his presence, '
Athonas Siak Ksas Sabak ' Kaab Kaesas Ekoe. . . .

I (page 12) invoke you, Gabriel,
[by the] head ' of Michael, Raphael, Anlel, Sariel, '
Gabriel, Auriel, Phariel, Sasael, ' Nechiel,
Adoniel, Thriel, Athiel, [5] Akutael,
who stand round ' about the invisible father and his '
seat, '
that you come to me and watch ' over me all the days of my
life. '
Spell

I invoke Gabriel, [10]
by his seven archangels, ' Tophou and Raphael and
Bariel, ' Arthamiel, Arophtebel, Lanach, ' Ephnix,
who stand in the ' presence of the father, listening to
the things that [15] come from his mouth—this is
my manner ' also:
Listen to the things that come from ' my mouth.
Amen, 7 (times).

Yea, yea, for I ' invoke you, good Gabriel, '
by the glory of the great [20] throne of the father—
for ' its [. . .] (are) a fiery flame, (page 13)
there are flames of fire burning, '
there are rivers of fire surrounding ' it,
flowing before it—
that you come ' to me, at once!

Yea, Gabriel, for I [5] invoke you,
by the four ' creatures that draw it—a lion's face, ' an
ox's face, an eagle's face, a human ' face—
that you come to me today.
Spell '

I invoke you today, Gabriel, 10
    by these amulets which are under the feet ' of the
        father,
    before which thousands of thousands from heaven '
        and earth tremble,
that ' you come to me.
    Spell

I invoke ' you, Gabriel,
    by the two great seraphim, 15 who have six wings on
        each ' of them—
    with two they cover their face, '
    with two they cover their feet,
    with ' two, one after the other, they fly, '
    calling out and saying, 20
    Holy, holy, holy is the lord ' Sabaoth!
    Heaven [and] earth are full ' [of (your) holy] . . . ! '
    . . . the earth [. . .] **(page 14)** in your holy glory—
that you come to me. '
    Spell

I invoke you, Gabriel, '
    by the name of Orpha, the whole body of the father, '
    and Orphamiel, the great finger that is on 5 the
        right hand of the father,
    and the head of ' Christ,
that you come to me today.
    Spell '

I invoke you, Gabriel,
    by the ' power of Manuel Sabaoth; '
I invoke you, Gabriel,
    by the 10 right hand (of) the father,
    and the seal ' that is in the bosom of the father,
    and these ' amulets that are written on the breast ' of
        the father,
that you come to me ' today, quickly!
    Spell

I 15 invoke you, Gabriel,
    by the first ' sound that came forth from the mouth '
        of the father,

and the breath that came forth ' from his nostrils,
and his ' goodness,
and the glory that surrounds ²⁰ him,
that you come to me today.
[Spell] '

I invoke you, Gabri[el], '
by the great pillar of [light] ' . . . , **(page 15)**
and the golden capital on which [the name] of the
father ' is written,
that you come to me today.
Spell '

I invoke you, Gabriel,
by the light ' of the father, through which are enlightened the ⁵ cherubim and the seraphim, and all
the ' heavens and all the world, '
that you come to me today.
Spell '

I invoke you, Gabriel,
by the ' robe that is white as snow, ¹⁰ with which the
father is clothed,
and ' the hair of his head that is like ' pure white wool,
and ' the attire of the crown (of) ' pearls that is upon
the head of the father, ¹⁵
that you come to me today.
Spell '

I invoke you, Gabriel, '
by the rainwater that pours forth ' over the head of the
father,
and the great ' eagle whose wing is spread ²⁰ out over
the head of the father, '
that you come to me today.
Spell '

I invoke you, Gab[riel], '
by [. . .] of light [. . .], **(page 16)**
that you do everything that [comes] from my mouth. '
Spell

I invoke you, Gabriel, '

by the great, honored virgin, '
    in whom the father was hidden from the
        beginning, 5
    before he created anything,
that you come ' to me today.
    Spell

I invoke ' you, Gabriel,
    by the three days ' that the father spent while he was
        standing,
    before ' he set all the creation in motion.
    Spell 10

I invoke you, Gabriel, '
    by the washing that the father undertook ' when he
        was about to mold Adam,
    and the ' flower that came forth from his left ' hand,
    and the chalice that is in his 15 right hand, from
        which he let ' his angels drink, and ' all the world,
that you come to ' me today.
    Spell

I invoke ' you, Gabriel,
    by the spittle 20 that came forth from the mouth of
        the father ' and became a spring of living water, '
that [you] come to me today. '

I [invoke] you, Gab[riel], '
    . . . his . . . (page 17) tears
    that came forth from the [eyes] of the father ' over his
        son upon the cross, '
that you come to me today.
    Spell

I ' invoke you, Gabriel,
    because of these 5 holy names of the father,
        Marinab ' Marmarou Babam Phioou ' Bathuriel
        Yao Sabaoth Adonai ' Pantocrator Manuel '
        Sabaoth Abathou Yachaoi Ichaof 10 Sabaoth, in
        which Daniel was hidden, '
that you come to me at this ' place where I dwell,
on account of ' all the things for which I have invoked you: '

You must be strong in [15] all of them all the days of my ' life.
 Amen, 12 (times).

Let my body be ' cleansed of every unclean ' spirit,
  whether a spirit of a ' male demon or a spirit [20] of a
   female demon,
  or ' an angelic spirit of [. . .], ' or a spirit of the first
   formed one. '
Let them not be able to stand ' [in] my presence, **(page 18)**
  but let them all flee before [me]. '
  Amen, 12 (times).

You must cleanse this ' place of every unclean spirit. '
Guard me from all evils all [5] the days of my life.
Cleanse ' for me the four sides that surround ' me for
 600,000 cubits around, '
cleanse for me the abyss for 600,000 ' cubits, together with
 heaven above me for [10] 600,000 cubits,
that they may not come ' down to me.
  Spell

I invoke ' you, Gabriel,
  by the seven ' eyes of the father, Serneuo ' Pabaothou
   Afriton Amiton [15] Theothanauteri.
  A(men), A(men), A(men), A(men), A(men), A(men),
   A(men). '

Bathuriel, great father, Bathuriel ' Sabaoth Boboel Athaor
 Maue, ' god of gods:
You must send me ' Gabriel, the angel of righteousness, [20]
  that he may do everything ' for which I invoke you. '
  Amen.
A 7 (times), E 7 (times), E 7 (times), I 7 (times),
  O 7 (times), U 7 (times), O 7 (times), ' M 7 (times),
  CH 7 (times), [P 7 (times)].

I invoke you, ' Gabri[el],
  [by] the great name of . . . , [25] . . . which . . . , **(page 19)**
   Sabaoth Bathuriel . . . . ma ' Chamariel,
that you send me ' Gabriel, the angel of righteousness, '
  with his sword unsheathed in [5] his right hand, against
   every ' unclean spirit,

whether a male ' demon or a female demon, '
whether male spirits or ' female spirits.
  Spell

Thael Yoel 10 Thael Throel Sael Bael Thok ' Thel Thaboel
    Thafriel Saroael ' Abothel Thamiel Thauel Uel ' Tam-
    bel Tharoiel Aje Aje Tachael ' Sarsael Sarsomoel
    15 Sarsabael,
    the twenty-four angels ' who stand by the twenty-four '
        elders,
help me, ' at once, at once!
    A 7 (times), E 7 (times), E 7 (times), I 7 (times),
    O 7 (times), U 7 (times), O 7 ' (times), M 7 (times),
    CH 7 (times), P 7 (times).

Arise, bend your 20 bow against the first formed one [and] '
    all his powers,
    . . . ' theboel . . oel,
    . . . (page 20) the four pillars of [the] abyss, '
    because of their four heads that lift ' up the first
        heaven.
  Spell

Gabriel, ' angel of righteousness,
    draw 5 your sword in your right hand, '
    pursue every evil spirit. '
  Spell

Bael Phoel Thael Throel ' Thabael Thoel Bachool Thiel '
    Aroel Afphel Aruoel Samiel 10 Auel Uel Obmiel
    Tharimiel ' Achel Aaroabdel:
Listen to me, ' strong angels,
for I ' invoke you by the lord, you ' twenty-four archangels
    15 of the body of Yao Yecha,
that ' you hearken to me and ' send me Athonath Athonath,
    ' that is, Gabriel, the angel ' of righteousness,
that he come to me 20 and do my work.
  Spell.
  Amen, 3 (times). '
  . . . . . (page 21)
  . . . . IS . . . PAOO . .
MGRA...AMOTHAMB.THA.S (with rings) ANOO

AMAI.RAMOTHAM.AFROMOTHAM
Gabriel Athonath Athonath

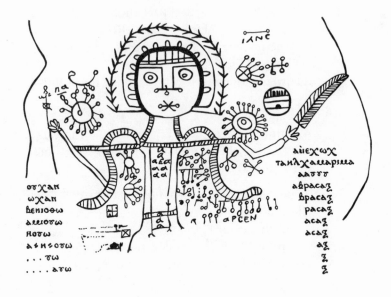

6

SEXUAL SPELLS

INTRODUCTION BY DAVID FRANKFURTER
TRANSLATIONS BY STEPHEN EMMEL, DAVID
FRANKFURTER, HOWARD M. JACKSON, NEAL KELSEY,
MARVIN MEYER, AND STEPHEN H. SKILES

"Magic" as an aid to love and for the pursuit of sexual pleasure is a cross-cultural phenomenon—a testimony to the intensity of emotions and the perennial problems that love and sex have always entailed. In late antiquity the popular interest in acquiring (or averting) supernatural aids to seduction is reflected throughout Greek and Latin novels: Apuleius's Metamorphoses, where the hero apprentices himself to a famous sorceress renowned for her powers to "bind" desirable young men (2.5), or Pseudo-Callisthenes' Alexander Romance, in which the Egyptian "magician"-king Nektanebos seduces the queen of Macedon with spells and herbs and by appearing to her as the god Ammon (1.5–8). One surely gets the impression that love magic was a constant factor in the social and sexual landscape of late antiquity, "a kind of sneak attack," in the words of John J. Winkler, "waged in the normal warfare of Mediterranean social life" ("The Constraints of Eros," 233).

The following collection of texts, quite typical of ritual corpora in Mediterranean antiquity, offers a remarkable picture of the kinds of erotic sabotage of which a young woman or man in Coptic Egypt would have had to beware: charms slipped under one's door (texts 74 and 84), potions deposited on stones by the doorstep (text 77), or perhaps pieces of fruit at the market (text 76). Such rituals were surely the equal property and tactics of both men and women.

The language and the ritual form of these sex spells derive from the *defixio*, or "binding" spell, used throughout the Mediterranean world for such diverse functions as jinxing chariot races, assuring a lawsuit's success, and outright homicide (a convenient collection, organized by function, has been edited by John G. Gager, *Curse Tablets and Binding Spells from the Ancient World*). The legacy of the *defixio* appears here not only in the use of the word "binding" (texts 85–86) but also in the specific directions found in most of these spells to overpower the mind and body of the victim, the client's intended lover: "disturb all the reason within the heart of N. daughter of N., that she be unable to eat, or to drink" (text 77); "Take his heart and his mind; you must dominate his entire body" (text 84). Although in this case emotional and psychological, this language of subjugation was typical of binding spells of all types.

Erotic binding spells often seem to call down illness upon their victims, often described in terms of unquenchable heat, inability to sleep or even recline, and often general derangement. Cyprian of Antioch's vivid spell (text 73) adjures the powers to "[fill] her from the toenails of her feet to the hair of her head with desire and longing and lust, as her mind is distracted, her senses go numb, and her ears are ringing. She must not eat or drink, slumber or sleep, for her garments burn her body, the sky's lightning sets her afire, and the earth beneath her feet is ablaze." A modern reader might well wonder whether this state of health would be conducive to meaningful love and sex. But in an important essay on the imagery in erotic binding spells, Winkler has offered the compelling argument that this imagery of intended sickness actually represented a projection of the client's own state of "lovesickness." By projecting it onto the desired lover, the client is seeking to master his or her own state of mind. As Winkler puts it, "The control exercised by the agent . . . puts him in a role opposed to that of the erotic victim he 'actually' is" (226–27).

The language of love and sex spells is quite vivid, and it is in this series of spells in fact that the ritual *analogy* achieves a unique verbal artistry. One can only admire the imagination of the client or scribe who instructed the powers to render a rival's penis like a rag on a dunghill (texts 85 and 87) or "like an ant that is frozen in winter, tiny and frozen" (text 127, lines 114–16). It was once believed, following the early theories of magical technique put forth by James George Frazer, that the ritualist was setting up a kind of sympathetic and telepathic bond between the intended victim's part and its mimetic representation, on the primitive assumption that "like produces like." But the use of analogies—verbal and plastic—in ritual spells has more recently been described as "persuasive": the transferral of certain *properties* of the one object to, in this case, the victim, on the assumption that ritual is efficacious (Stanley J. Tambiah, "Form and Meaning of Magical Acts"). Erotic spells in antiquity tended to have an oral or spoken nature (see, for example, J. C. B. Petropoulos, "The Erotic Magical Papyri"); and in this context one is bound to recognize some reflexive efficacy in the verbal analogies. That is, in reciting (or hearing) the very details of the animals or objects whose traits the victim should assume, the client receives immediate satisfaction and catharsis.

The Coptic spells excel particularly at animal analogies: "I desire that N. daughter of N. spend forty days and forty nights hanging on me like a bitch for a dog, like a sow for a boar" (text 72, lines 32–36); "as she whinnies like a mare, brays like a camel, purrs like a lioness, and hisses like a crocodile" (text 73, lines 117–20); "that she may be (like) a honey(-bee) seeking (honey), a bitch prowling, a cat going from house to house, a mare going under (sex-)crazed (stallions)" (text 79, lines 11–13). Two spells liken the victim's intended state of desperate searching to that of a dog looking for her puppies (texts 74–75). Rather than these similes arising from Egypt's putative tradition of animal worship, it is more likely that they reflect the common use of animals in Egyptian folklore to articulate human character. Such animal imagery is also used in Pharaonic Egyptian love spells. The History of the Monks in Egypt, which reflects the origins of Coptic culture in the fourth and fifth centuries, describes a monk who hallucinated the devil in the guise of a voluptuous woman, as "like an excited stallion eager to mount a mare" (1.34). But the same text also suggests that these ritual analogies to animals were a common and powerful form of erotic spell in Coptic Egypt: "A certain evildoer had by magic arts transformed a girl who had consecrated her virginity into a mare. Her parents brought her to

[Macarios] and begged him, if he would be so kind, to change her back into a woman by his prayers" (21.17, translated by Norman Russell). This anecdote reflects precisely the kind of animal analogies invoked in the following spells, with the assumption that they could work to a frightening degree.

Like other spells in this volume, the sex and love spells reflect native Egyptian traditions at a number of different levels. Schmidt 2 (text 72) offers an *historiola* of Isis, Horus, and seven maidens (variously identified as the seven mouths of the Nile and the seven Hathors). While the more common ritual appeals to Isis-Horus mythology concern healing and childbirth, references to Horus's erotic conquests are also known among ancient texts of ritual power. Michigan 4932f (text 82) invokes common legends of Isis's preparation of Osiris's body (compare Plutarch, On Isis and Osiris 18). Finally, the curious figure "whose head is in the abyss, whose feet are in the underworld" has been connected with a form of Seth, the Egyptian god of desert and confusion, syncretized with Apophis, the demon of darkness.

One also sees literary forms from Egyptian rituals reused in these spells. In threatening to "stop the sun in its chariot, the moon in its course, the crown of stars upon the head of Jesus" if the powers do not respond to directions, Berlin 8314 (text 75) recalls an ancient Egyptian ritual form whereby the priest declared the power to return the cosmos to primal chaos if an act were not completed. The dialogue form, in past or perfect tense, similarly recalls a traditional form of reciting mythic scenes in Egyptian rituals (London Hay 10376 [text 78]).

The striking image in London Hay 10414 (text 79), that the intended lover "will draw her robe to her neck, and she shall call out to me, 'Come here,'" may actually derive from an Egyptian ritual practice for procreative fertility. Herodotus reports how women on the ceremonial barges during the festival of Bastet "pull up their dresses" toward villages along the Nile (Histories 2.60.2); while Diodorus Siculus describes how women, "pulling up their dresses, display their genitals" to the new Apis bull in Memphis during a specific forty-day period (1.85.3). In addition, several terracotta figurines in the Egyptian Museum in Cairo portray the goddess Isis in such a posture (see Françoise Dunand, *Religion populaire en Égypte romaine*, numbers 60–61).

Other themes derive from the general world of Greco-Roman rituals of power. When Cyprian's spell (text 73) describes the sending of the archangel Gabriel as the agent of seduction, one might recall the Egyptian king Nektanebos's use of the god Ammon for similar goals (Alexander Romance 1.8) as well as a general notion in texts of ritual power that one might send a demon or other supernatural agent into the dreams of the erotic victim.

But as much as they reflect the continuing significance of traditional Egyptian ritual forms in the Coptic period, the following spells also demonstrate the domestication of Christian legends— indeed, to such a degree that one can assume the existence of a living Christian folklore independent of ecclesiastical teaching. Stories of the annunciation (text 78, lines 8–10) and of the biblical matriarch Sarah's birth (text 83, lines 4–6) are invoked as narrative precedents for, respectively, erotic attachment and the achievement of conception, in much the same way as the mythology of Isis and Horus continually spawned new *historiolae* for the practical needs of Egyptians. References to the secret or efficacious words of the prophet Elijah (texts 80 and 86) suggest that this figure held a peculiar power in Coptic folk religion, perhaps because of his status as prototype of desert hermits, many of whom were reputed to have supernatural powers (see History of the Monks in Egypt 7).

In this chapter we have grouped together several texts from the Hay collection (texts 78–81), which, together with text 127 in chapter 9, constitute a portfolio of texts of ritual power copied by the same scribe. Included here is Hay 10122 (text 81), which properly speaking does not present a sexual spell but is allowed to remain in the context of the other Hay texts. For further discussion of collections, portfolios, and hoards of texts of ritual power, see the introductions to chapters 9, 10, and 11.

72. Spell using a Horus legend for erotic purposes

Text: Schmidt 2

Description: parchment, 26 x 10.5 cm

Bibliography: Angelicus M. Kropp, *Ausgewählte koptische Zaubertexte,*
1.13–14; 2.6–8

Translator: Neal Kelsey

*As Schmidt 2 presents the situation, the person who may employ
this spell desires to have sexual relations with a woman, but she turns
away his advances, and consequently he invokes ritual power. The
main body of the text is built upon a Horus-Isis legend (compare
Schmidt 1 [text 48]) wherein Horus complains to his mother, Isis, that
he has found seven maidens whom he desires but they do not desire
him. The description of one entering with head down and exiting with
feet down may suggest a descent to and ascent from the underworld. In
addition to Sergio Donadoni, "Un incantesimo amatorio copto," compare also London Hay 10391 (text 127), especially lines 12–19. The
present text concludes with a spell designed to cause the woman to
hang all over her male admirer.*

TEXT

♀ I am N. child of N.
I entered ' through a door of stone,
I exited through a ' door of iron.
I entered with my head down, '
I exited with my feet down.
I found seven ⁵ maidens who were sitting upon a '
  spring of water.
I desired but <they> did not desire, '
I agreed but they did not agree.
I desired to ' love N. daughter of N.,
but she did not ' desire to receive my kiss.
I strengthened myself, I ¹⁰ stood up.
I cried, I sighed until ' the tears of my eyes covered the
  soles ' of (my) feet.

Isis replied: What is wrong with you, man, ' son of Re,
  who cries and sighs ' until the tears of your eyes
  cover ¹⁵ the soles of your feet?

(Horus):	Why, Isis, ' do you not want me to cry?
	I entered ' through a door of stone,
	I exited ' through a door of iron.
	I entered ' with my head down,
	I exited with my feet down.
	I found 20 seven maidens upon a spring ' of water.
	I desired but <they> did not desire,
	I agreed ' but they did not agree.
	I desired to love N. ' daughter of N.,
	but she did not desire to receive ' my kiss.

(Isis):	Why did you enter through a door 25 of stone and exit through a door of ' iron,
	and find seven maidens ' and desire but they did not desire,
	and desire ' to love N. daughter of N. but she ' did not desire to receive your kiss?
	You did not 30 strengthen yourself and stand up,
	and you did not send forth seven ' tongues, saying, THETF, 7 (times). '

Great one among the spirits,
I desire that ' N. daughter of N.
spend forty days ' and forty nights
hanging on 35 me like a bitch for a dog, '
like a sow for a boar. '
For I am the one who calls, '
you are the one who must desire.

73. Erotic spell of Cyprian of Antioch

Text: Heidelberg Kopt. 684
Description: book with sixteen pages of rag paper; the pages are
14.3 x 9 cm; pages 1–13 contain the spell of Cyprian, and the last three
pages are blank; eleventh century
Bibliography: Friedrich Bilabel and Adolf Grohmann, *Griechische, koptische
und arabische Texte*, 304–25
Translator: Howard M. Jackson

According to legend, Cyprian of Antioch tried to employ magic in order to seduce a Christian virgin named Justina. As the story goes, he failed in his attempts, and so he converted to Christianity, abandoned his books of ritual power, and eventually became bishop of Antioch. Some traditions suggest that both Cyprian and Justina were martyred during the persecution of the Roman emperor Diocletian (ruled 285–305). The translation given here is of the spell of Cyprian. See also Howard M. Jackson, "A Contribution toward an Edition of the Confession of Cyprian of Antioch."

TEXT

I know that everything has passed ' me by. ' Everything has changed in my soul; everything has changed ' in my person. My heart has grown bitter. [5] I have grown pale. ' My flesh shudders; ' the hair of my head stands on end (?). I ' am all afire. I have lain down to rest, ' but I could not sleep; I have risen, but I found no [10] relief. I have eaten and drunk ' in sighing and groaning. ' I have found no rest either in soul ' or in spirit for being overwhelmed ' by desire. My wisdom has [15] deserted me; my strength has been sapped. All contrivance ' has been brought to naught.

Yet I am ' Cyprian, the great magician, who was ' the friend of the dragon of the abyss. ' He called me his son, and I called [20] him father. He placed his crown ' and his diadem on my head. ' (**page 2**) I suckled milk at his right ' breast. He made my place at his right ' hand. He subjected to me [25] every power of his. I ascended up to the ' Pleiades, and they glided by under me like a ' ship. I learned the whispers of the stars; ' I took possession of the treasuries of the winds. ' I mastered the whole of astronomy. [30]

But all this did me no good with ' a virgin named Justina. She ' made my powers and the powers of Satan ' like a sparrow in the hand of a child. ' I came to understand in the depth of my heart, [35] the meditation of my soul, ' and the pondering of my mind that no one, ' whether angel or archangel or cherubim ' or seraphim or dominion or ' power or any incorporeal being [40] or authority, would be able ' to prophesy to my heart the ' answer it desired ' nor fulfill my ' command, no one except the father of the aeons [45] (**page 3**) and his only begotten son, ' Jesus Christ, and the pure holy ' spirit.

So I reproved my wrath, ' laid my anger aside, and allayed my ' rage with great humility. [50] Then I got to my feet, ' turned my face to the west, ' stretched my right hand out to heaven, ' cleansed myself of the dirt on my feet, ' snorted, [55] and directed these spells ' at heaven, to the tabernacle ' of the father within the seven ' veils. I cried out to ' the father of the aeons, the lord of every lordship, [60] of every power and every ' throne, voicing the following spells: ' ERISI TONAI ' CHARIM BALIM, O king, ' AUTOUL OBIA KAKIKEPHALI [65] AMOU AMOU! Seize the spirit ' you have deposited! Yea, yea! ' **(page 4)**

I do not need him still, ' he who sent out to me today the ' great minister of blazing [70] flame, Gabriel, he with the ' great power of fire, in that he ' fills his fiery face with the ' fire that devours every other fire, ' that fire which is your [75] divinity, lord god, and in that he ' fills his vessel full of longing ' and desire and fills ' his fiery wings with the ' river of fire that fills [80] your divinity with power, ' that fire in which every soul shall ' bathe before they come ' into your presence. He comes ' in the rush of his power at [85] your command, O father of ' the aeons, to go to N. daughter of N., ' and reveal himself to her in a ' great revelation, ' **(page 5)** relentless (?), irresistible, [90] fascinating, filling her heart, her soul, ' her spirit, and her mind ' with burning desire and ' hot longing, with perturbation ' and disturbance, filling her from the toenails of [95] her feet to the hair of her head ' with desire and longing and lust, ' as her mind is distracted, ' her senses go numb, and her ears ' are ringing. She must not eat or [100] drink, slumber or ' sleep, for her garments ' burn her body, the sky's lightning sets ' her afire, and the earth beneath her feet is ablaze. ' The father must have no mercy upon her; [105] the son must show her no pity; ' the holy spirit must give no sleep ' to her eyes, for her remembrance of god ' and her fear of him flee away ' from her, and her thoughts, her [110] intentions, and her mind ' turn to devilry, ' **(page 6)** as she hangs upon ' desire, longing, and ' disturbance because of N. son of N., as [115] a donkey hangs upon her jackass, a . . . ' upon her . . . , a bitch upon her ' mate, as she whinnies like a mare, ' brays like a camel, ' purrs like a lioness, and hisses like a [120] crocodile, for she hangs upon desire ' and longing for N. son of N., ' as a drop of water hangs ' from the lip of a jar. When one ' looks at her, he shall faint [125] for the burning summer heat.

Yea, ' I adjure you, O Gabriel: ' Go to N. daughter of N. Hang her by ' the hair of her head and by the lashes ' of her eyes. Bring her to him, [130] N. son of N., in longing and 'desire, and she remains in them for ' ever. As you brought the good ' news of the father to the ' pure virgin Mary [135] **(page 7)** as a true and actual message, so may the ' good news become true and actual for me, as ' my spells are swiftly fulfilled ' by you. Do not be ' heedless as you were on the day [140] on which the lord sent you to the land of Eden ' and you returned to him without any land, ' empty-handed, but ' carry out for me personally, today, ' for me, N. son of N., this [145] good news and announcement, ' that when she hears it she cannot ' resist, yea, yea, at once, at once!

I adjure you, ' O Gabriel, by the salvation that comes from the ' consubstantial trinity. I adjure [150] you, O Gabriel, by the tabernacle ' of the father and by those who are within it. ' I adjure you, O Gabriel, by the throne ' of the almighty and by him ' who sits upon it. I adjure ' you, O Gabriel, by the powers of the [155] celestial beings and by the song and the praise ' of the powers of heaven. ' **(page 8)** I adjure you, O Gabriel, by the word ' and the breath of the father, the breath that ' went out to the virgin Mary. You announced [160] the good news of him to her, while ' he came to dwell inside of her, he who was both god ' and human, whom she bore, who ascended ' the cross and redeemed us. I adjure ' you, O Gabriel, by the holy suffering [165] which Jesus Christ underwent for our sakes ' on the wood of the cross and by the breath ' which he delivered into the hands of his ' father, which was the words, "Eloei Eloei ' Elemos Abaktane." I adjure [170] you, O Gabriel, by the tears ' that the father shed on the head ' of Jesus, his only begotten son, on ' the wood of the cross. I adjure you by ' your sword, by which you tore the [175] veil of the temple. ' I adjure you by the seven calls (?) which the ' father first made to Jesus, his son, ' on the lord's day, until he ' rose from the dead, [180] **(page 9)** and by the spiritual sacrifice, ' the holy mass, and the ' mysteries of Jesus Christ, which the ' holy celebrate, and ' by the judgment that the almighty [185] will carry out upon the whole world ' in the valley of Josaphat, that ' you may not detain or ' discount, neither for a single moment ' or blink of an eye, until you come [190] forthwith to your sign of the zodiac which ' I shall set afire.

Go to N. ' daughter of N., and put fire and longing ' and desire and disturbance ' and agitation into her [195] heart for N. son of N. Bring her ' to him in a state of humility and ' subjection, while he beholds her strip ' naked all the time, as his desire ' mingles with hers, as he [200] sleeps with her and she never satiates ' him. Take the shamefastness from her face and from her eyes. ' **(page 10)** Let him be her lord; let him become ' her lord, as she becomes his servant. ' Let her constantly ask after him, [205] every moment, all the time, ' at every hour, her and his whole life ' long. Let every person ' and every soul and every breath ' be abominable, foul, putrid, and hateful [210] to her except N. son of N. If he goes ' away from her, let her mourn ' in groaning and crying in bitterness of heart. ' If he turns his back on her, let ' her fall to her knees [215] and do him obeisance in fear ' and humility. If he speaks, let ' her be silent. If he is angry, let her ' make him calm by treating him truly (?) ' lovingly, giving him her gold and [220] silver, her garments and ' perfumes, her food and ' drink, her gifts ' **(page 11)** and her adornment on every occasion, ' every season, all her days, [225] her whole life long. She must ' always stay with him, ' in accordance with these spells, while every day she sees to ' her beauty and her attractiveness in her heart, ' in her mind, in her thoughts, [230] in her intentions and her eyes, ' in which she shall have a day that is harder ' than any other day with all its hours ' together with every day and every night, yea, yea, at once! '

If you do not carry out my wishes, O Gabriel, [235] and fulfill my ' command, I shall always despise you, ' cut you off from me, anathematize ' you, revile you, and loathe you. ' The father must assign you no place in heaven; [240] the son must give you no rank ' in heaven; the holy spirit must not ' encourage your hymns of praise. ' The queen of women, the virgin Mary, ' must never take you to herself, nor shall people call [245] you "bringer of good news," ' **(page 12)** until you fulfill all the spells ' that I have spoken in my ' prayer. You must not ' bring any evil upon me, [250] and you must not . . . ' to me, and you must not . . . to me, ' and you must not touch me with any ' evil or any suffering, but with ' every joy and honor. I [255] for my part bless the father almighty; ' I give praise to Jesus, the ' only begotten; I sing hymns to the ' holy spirit; and I . . . ' you yourself, O Gabriel, for [260] you were a . . . ' in my requests. . . . ' Come, do not turn yourself . . . ' to you for ever. Amen. '

The offering takes place for him with mastic, alouth, [265] storax . . . daily ' prayers . . . as long as ' you like, while you fast daily, ' **(page 13)** while you . . . tell them (?) . . . ' and oil . . . while you . . . [270] while you fast, are in a state of purity, and ' wear garments, until . . . on a ' potsherd with hair (brush?) the prayer . . . ' let ' them watch over. . . .

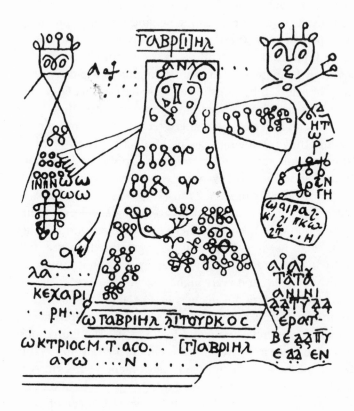

74. Erotic spell to attract a woman

Text: Yale 1791 (second text)
Description: papyrus, 37.3 x 25.4 cm, sixth or seventh century (so Petersen)
Bibliography: Theodore C. Petersen, *A Collection of Papyri*, 38–39 (no. 53), with a photograph (front only) showing an incorrect arrangement of the fragments prior to conservation
Translator: Stephen Emmel

In order to make the love charm in Yale 1791 effective, the person employing the spell is first instructed to inscribe a sheet of tin with certain signs (line 2, with the signs written on the papyrus between lines 4 and 5), then to prepare an offering and bury it at the door of the woman whose love he desires (lines 2–4). The incantation to be spoken as part of the operation (and perhaps also to be written on the tin along with the signs) is addressed to unspecified celestial powers ("you" is plural throughout). The person would insert the name of the woman whom he seeks to attract in line 10, and his own name twice in line 17. The text is edited for the first time in the Appendix, "Previously Unpublished Coptic Texts of Ritual Power in the Beinecke Library, Yale University."

TEXT

For a woman's love, a really effective charm (?). |
Write these signs on a sheet of tin.
Off(ering): wild herb (?), | froth from the mouth of a completely black horse, and a bat. | Bury it at the woman's door. You will see its potency quickly.

(signs and letters) 5

I adjure you by all your holy names, with your offerings, | and your amulets, and your thrones upon which you sit, | and your garments that clothe you, and your | perfect steles, [and your] residences in which you dwell. | I adjure you by all these things for the sake of a heartfelt love and a pang 10 and a heartfelt madness in the heart of N. daughter of N. Quickly! I adjure | the great power of Bersebour, the king of the demons | . . . . I adjure you | by all these things. Let her not eat or [drink or lie down (?)] | or sit, until she becomes like a [black (?)] dog 15 that is crazy for its pups, and, as for a drop | of water dangling from a jar like a snake, desperate [for the] | soul of N. son of N., until she comes to N. Quickly! . . . | . . .

75. Another erotic spell to attract a woman

Text: Berlin 8314
Description: parchment, 51.5 x 7.5 cm
Bibliography: Walter Beltz, "Die koptischen Zauberpergamente," 91–92;
Angelicus M. Kropp, *Ausgewählte koptische Zaubertexte*, 2.21–23
Translator: Marvin Meyer

Berlin 8314 is a love spell in which a man seeks to attract a woman. While the opening of the text (1–10) remains obscure, it may well suggest the ceremonial use of oil and, perhaps, the employment of animal-like powers. The text goes on to call upon Tartarouchos ("the one who controls the underworld") to muster his strength and thereby to bind the heart of the woman to the man.

TEXT

✝ The oil that is trustworthy (?), that was ' brought forth from the stone . . . ⁵ sea. I shall [seek] ' with desire a portion of the . . . ' of a snake, the . . . of a serpent, ' the . . . of a black dog ' whose pups would be taken away before her eyes, ¹⁰ the seven that she would bear: '

Upon N. daughter of N. until you [bind] ' her heart and her flesh ' to me, N. son of N. If you do not obey ' the things of my mouth and accomplish the things of ¹⁵ my hand, I shall go down ' into the underworld and bring up ' Tartarouchos and say, ' You are a god also. Accept my wish and ' satisfy my demand upon ²⁰ N. daughter of N.

He said to me, If you demand ' it, I can break the stone, ' I can make the iron into water, ' I shall destroy the iron doors ' quickly, until I bind the ²⁵ heart of N. daughter of N. to you—me, ' N. son of N., at once! If she does not come to me, I shall stop ' the sun in its chariot, the moon ' in its course, the crown ' of stars upon the head of Jesus, ³⁰ until I satisfy your ' demand, at once!

Yea, ' yea, I adjure you and ' all your powers ' upon my offering. I adjure ³⁵ the throne of fire upon which ' you sit, until you satisfy ' my demand upon N. daughter ' of N. I adjure your ' amulets, yea, yea, at once, at once!

76. Another erotic spell to attract a woman

Text: Berlin 8325.

Description: papyrus, 12 x 10 cm, ninth century

Bibliography: Walter Beltz, "Die koptischen Zauberpapyri," 74–75; Angelicus M. Kropp, *Ausgewählte koptische Zaubertexte*, 2.24–25

Translator: Marvin Meyer

Berlin 8325 is a love spell used to attract a woman. The person using the spell apparently invokes power down upon pieces of fruit. When the desired woman eats the food, it is believed, she will be overcome with love.

TEXT

✝ I adjure [you by] your names and ' your powers and your amulets and the ' glorious places where [you] dwell, ' that you come down upon these ⁵ [pieces of fruit (?)] that are in my right hand, I [. . .], ' so that [. . . ' (when)] she eats of them, ' you may give her desire for me, ' and she may desire me with endless desire ¹⁰ and come to me in the place where I am, and ' I may lay my breast ' upon her and satisfy all my ' desire with her, and she may satisfy ' all my desire, ¹⁵ right now, right now, at once, at once!

77. Another erotic spell to attract a woman

Text: Heidelberg Kopt. 518

Description: parchment, 21.4 x 16.4 cm

Bibliography: Friedrich Bilabel and Adolf Grohmann, *Griechische, koptische und arabische Texte*, 375–80

Translator: David Frankfurter

Heidelberg Kopt. 518 is an erotic "binding" spell, invoking archangels to disturb the desired woman with lust until she comes to the client. The vocal parts of the spell correspond to a series of rituals, including drawing and burning. Lines 40–42 and 58–59 offer an image of "normal" family life and activities, from which the intended woman is meant to be separated. Lines 52–54, in which the verb tense switches to the perfect, seem to be a form of mythic story, although the reference to dogs coming under dogs may simply be a reference to copulation (images of animals copulating also function ritually in Schmidt 2 [text 72], Heidelberg Kopt. 684 [text 73], and Hay 10414 [text 79]). On the devil descending to the source of the rivers (lines 28–34), compare the next text (and the notes).

[The throne upon which Yao Sa]baoth sits '
. . . '
[any] year, [in any month and any day],
until he tramples them ' today,
by the great [power] of the archangels Michael 5 and
    Gabriel,
who go to wherever N. daughter of N. is, '
who fill her heart with every fiery desire '
and every longing and every passion and every (form of)
    love,
who ' seize her like a flame of fire,
who bring ' her to N. son of N.

Yea, yea, I adjure you and your 10 healing and your great
    powers and your names,
until you ' disturb all the reason within the heart of N.
    daughter of N., '
that she be unable to eat or drink,
or remain ' in any place,
until she arises and goes on her ' feet,
and comes to N. son of N.,
and he satisfies his desire 15 with her, at once, at once!

Move her heart with a ' powerful desire
    as the fire moves to you. '
This is the very way that brought N. daughter of N. to N.
    son of N.,
    without ' restraining her, yea, yea, at once, at once! '

Dr(aw) the fig(ures) . . . when she seeks anyone, when she
opens . . . dr(aw) the pray(er) and the fig(ure) that you 20 [bring
about]. Wr(ite) the holy day. Dr(aw) also . . . a guardian ' [. . .]
that you bring about. Dr(aw) a male member that . . . ' the gift.
Knead it in the principle ' [that you] bring about, also . . . the col-
ors. Destroy ' [. . .] and he is similar (?). Offer up the male
<member>, send 25 [. . .] bind them with linen strips; smear
them with mud; burn ' them in the fire. Thymas, alaoth, storax . . .
' [that you] bring about in the wind, when you write:
    ENASSAABRAN . . . '

[. . .]N SHOURAN SHOUTABIN SHOURABATAN
    SHOURACHAN '
[. . .]BAN SHOUSHF SHOURACHAEL PRIM PRIMPE A
    . . . 30
[. . .] PATBOUKANIA, Zeus, devil, Apo[llo], '
[. . .]A PKONOS PSHOUSHF PANTINOS PANTITOS '
[. . .] in your hand from the beginning.
You went down to ' [the source of] the rivers,
and filled them with passion and longing ' [. . .] and
    wickedness and love and desire and madness.

I adjure you 35 [by the] spell,
that wherever they will be, '
[. . .] disturb with madness [. . .] '
[. . .] when she comes to N. son of N. [. . .] '
[. . .] with unleashed desire [. . .], '
that you may go to wherever N. daughter of N. is, 40
and seize her and fetch her to N. son of N. from ' wherever
    she is.
Whether she is eating or drinking ' or suckling or in the
    mountains or on the sea, '
compel her, disturb her until she comes to N. son of N. '

I adjure you, Michael, by the light upon which you are
    seated. 45
You, bring the companions that are with you in this
    singular rank, '
so that at this moment I will utter your names, '
put you in this fire by the door of the house and doorpost, '
    on a stone or in some oil,
simply any place over which I utter ' your names,
and give it to N. daughter of N.
She must come 50 to N. son of N. any year, in any month
    and on any day.
You must ' receive the adjuration in your ears;
you are the one who is called. '

Thus he came. You have called, NOUNOU ABAKOUK, you
    have called.
The dogs ' come under the dog.
You have called the little ones to come under the . . . ' with
    the great companion. . . .

You are this one who disturbs . . . , 55
through the seal of N. son of N., you were bringing her to
      N. son of N. . . . ,¹
the great power, at once!
OURICH MARICH BATOL . . . ¹ place.
Send your powers to go into the [house]¹ of N. daughter of
      N., until she is disturbed and distressed,
and she renounces [her father]¹ and her mother and her
      husband and her children,
and she is hardhearted [and is filled] 60 with desire for N.
      son of N., with burning desire and love . . . , ¹
. . . with longing unleashed for eternity. . . . ¹

[Ap]ollo   Write the [prayer (?)]. ¹
SHOUSHF¹
Be a mediator! 65
Illumine¹   (drawing of a figure)
the abyss! ¹
Bring N. daughter of N. ¹
to N. son of N.

78. Another erotic spell to attract a woman

Text: London Hay 10376
Description: leather, 16 x 9 1/2 in., "perhaps sixth or seventh century" (so
Crum)
Bibliography: Walter E. Crum, "Magical Texts in Coptic—I," 51–53
Translator: David Frankfurter

*Hay 10376 is another erotic spell used by a male client to attract a
woman. Among other myths invoked, the spell uses the Christian legend of the annunciation as the effective analogy to the client's own desire as it comes to the woman "like an angel" and dwells within her.
The spell also alludes to a rare apocryphal tradition concerning Satan
and Eve in the Garden of Eden (lines 15–19). The spell is apparently
meant to be uttered while holding a chalice of wine (lines 20–21).*

The Department of Egyptian Antiquities of the British Museum generously provided infrared photographs of this text and the other texts in the Hay collection for David Frankfurter to examine.

TEXT

[. .]eixumarax, the one of the iron rod, the one of the . . . lord, from ' the saltwater to the cataract, whom the whole creation ' of women obeys, as . . . comes up out of the sea like a shady (?) tree ' [in] his power.

He said to me, 5 "If you consider me a brother, I will do it (?) for you."

I said to him, "[. . .] you to N. daughter of N., so that you might give her to me and I might satisfy ' my desire [with] her."

He said to me, "As a father is concerned for his children, (so) I am concerned ' [for you]."

[I said] to him:

I adjure you with your power and the right hand of the
    father ' [. . .] the son and the authority of the
    holy spirit, and Gabriel ' [who] went to Joseph
    (and) caused him to take Mary for himself as
    [wife],
that you neither 10 delay nor hold back,
until you bring to me N. daughter ' of N.,
and I satisfy my desire with her {with her}.

CHAMCHOM ' ME ATHTHATH OUCHACH AO OUCHA
ANNEH NIALTHEHIJEKKOKE [. . .] '

With desire may she desire me,
with love may she love me.

May my [desire] ' and my love dwell inside her, N. daughter of N., like an angel 15 of god in her presence.

For this passion is what Mastema ' proclaimed [. . .]. He threw it down into the source of ' the four rivers. He [washed (?)] in it, so that the children of humankind ' should [drink] from it and be filled with the devil's passion. N. child of N. drank ' from it (and) has been filled with the devil's passion.

So now [20] [I too (?)] invoke you today, I, N. son of N.,
   over this wine that is ' in my hand,
in order to give it to N., that she may drink from it,
and a pleasant desire ' may arise within her toward me,
   like an angel of god,
and she {drink} ' obey me.
I adjure you by these three names,
   OUSKLEM OUSKLEMA, ANARSHESEF, ELOE
      ELEMAS YATHOTH,
   the one who descended upon the sacrifice, [25]
that you come to me, in my presence, me, N. son of N.,
and send my ' desire into her, N. daughter of N.,
   like an angel of ' god.
If she should not obey me, I expel her from the good father.

I adjure ' her by the three names,
   IAMALEL THAMAMAEL THAE.

79. Spells for sex and business

Text: London Hay 10414
Description: leather, 11 1/8 x 4 3/4 in., perhaps sixth or seventh century
Bibliography: Walter E. Crum, "Magical Texts in Coptic—II," 195–97; Irene
Grumach, "On the History of a Coptic Figura Magica," 172–73
Translator: David Frankfurter

*These spells are also a part of the Hay collection and were copied
by the same scribe as the previous spell. Hay 10414 recto is a love spell,
although the client and "victim" are not named. While opening with a
story of Solomon, a prominent figure in Jewish demonomantic tradition, the spell proceeds to employ traditional Egyptian images to gain
power for the spell: A form of Bachuch is used, for example, as are references to the Egyptian underworld tradition. The spell is significant for
its range of similes for lust, compounded for ritual effectiveness. Hay
10414 verso seems to be a business spell, aimed at bringing the maxi-
mum clientele to the supplicant's shop.*

✝ The favor that was given to the . . . of King Solomon, ' who "suffers" the virginity and love of women, CHAHE, until they take ' their hymen(s) and throw them upon ' the face of the earth. . . .

I will not, I will not . . . , [5]
I will not sleep until I put to shame their parents.
KOK TPARKO'KOK, this is the one whose head is in the
    abyss,
whose feet are in the underworld. '
We came to you today, we entrusted to you N. daughter of
    N., '
until you give her your food,
so that I may be honey ' inside her,
manna on her tongue,
that she may desire me like the sun, [10]
that she may love me like the moon,
that she may hang on me as ' a drop of water sticks on a jar,
that she may be (like) ' a honey(-bee) seeking (honey),
a bitch prowling,
a cat going ' from house to house,
a mare going under (sex-)crazed (stallions),
right now, ' now, at once, by all the power of the
    underworld! [15]

KOK KOCHAROTOCH PARSOBOL ANAEL,
I asked ' him and he sent a demon whose name is '
    Theumatha,
whose head is in the abyss,
whose feet are in the underworld, ' the Gehenna of fire.
He took fiery tongs; '
he will afflict the head of N. daughter of N.,
until she comes to me, [20] wherever I want.
She will draw her robe to her neck, '
and she will call out to me, "Come here!"
By the power of ' Adael, right now, right now, now at once,
    at once!

(ring letters)

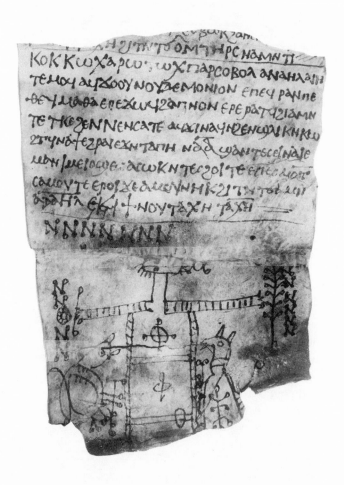

LONDON HAY 10414 (*lower part*)

(drawing of a human figure,
with two animals)

. . .

This favor of . . . all (of them);
the daughter of N.
Bind N. daughter of N. by his hand, N. son of N. **(verso)**

. . . (adjure) you today upon this pot of ¹ spell-free water. At the moment that you will sprinkle ¹ yourselves in the dwelling place, and ¹ gather for me the entire generation of Adam ⁵ and all the children of Zoe, as they bring me ¹ every gift and every bounty, they must gather ¹ before me, all of them, like a honey bee into ¹ the mouth of a beehive.

Yea, yea, for I adjure you ¹ by your names and your powers and your ¹⁰ amulets and the places where you dwell, ¹ that you give me favor and ¹ blessing and desire in the dwelling place and ¹ assembly and the shop, today ¹ and all the days for the rest ¹⁵ of my life, yea, yea, at once, at once! ¹

How to perform it: everything; storax; calamus extract; ¹ muscatel; blood of a white dove; ¹ black dye. Draw the figure ¹ on the bottom of a new pot; put spell-free water ²⁰ into it . . . of blood ¹ of a dove . . . your names . . . ¹ at the door of the storehouse (?) ¹ . . . the figure inside the door of the portal ¹ . . . all of them . . . ²⁵ to you. . . .

(more figures)

80. Spells for favor, honor, and passion

Text: London Hay 10434

Description: leather, 6 x 2 3/8 in., perhaps sixth or seventh century. An additional piece, 5 1/4 x 3 1/4 in., is framed along with this former piece

Bibliography: Walter E. Crum, "Magical Texts in Coptic—II," 199–200

Translator: David Frankfurter

Hay 10434, another text from the Hay collection, contains one or more spells, one of which is obviously an erotic spell. The second (?) spell is notable in suggesting powerful utterances as the "prayer of Elijah." The additional piece contains a spell for desire.

TEXT

† The spell: ¹
the guardian of all ¹ . . . ¹ in the places of the morning (?) . . .

(ring letters and signs)

Yao Sabao   (animal figures)   The east

(verso)

For N. child of N.: '

(ring letters)

Michael, ' give favor; '
Gabriel, give life; 5
Suriel, give honor; '
Raphael, give life; '
Sebt-Hor, give favor; '
Anael, give honor,
Bathu'el, give N. child of N. passion 10 for N. child of N.,
    all the days ' of his life.

This is the amulet of the prayer of Elijah:

(ring signs)

PHLEMNEKOK APHENTOR '
KACHAMOS NNICHALINOS '
STOMAU SNIKARTIAN '
NSOUES[. . .]PKAKA'MESTOKOS LANION '
    KACHAMEISON, N. child of N. ' with N. child
    of N., . . .

(additional piece:)

ATHA ATHA ATHARIM,
The eye will tell, '
the heart will desire
      † †

(signs and letters)

81. Spell for gathering (to a business?), for menstrual flow

Text: London Hay 10122
Description: leather, 14 x 3 1/4 in., perhaps sixth or seventh century
Bibliography: Walter E. Crum, "Magical Texts in Coptic—II," 197–99
Translator: David Frankfurter

Hay 10122 is yet another text from the Hay collection. By its imagery and the repetition of the word "gathering," the first spell in the text may be designed to attract customers to a business; the verso concludes with a gynecological spell. It is unclear to which spell the drawings on the verso relate.

For an additional text from the Hay collection, see Hay 10391 (text 127). Like Hay 10391, Hay 10122 (verso) features nine powers (called guardians in Hay 10391 and elsewhere); the present text provides drawings depicting these guardians.

TEXT

(drawing, perhaps of a boat)

Ananias, Azarias, Mizael, '
Sedrak, Mizak, Adenako, '
Lal Moulal Sholal '

(ring letters and signs)

. . . the amulets; 5 blood of white camels; ' a gathering of
doves . . . ; ' nest.

(ring signs) '

The gathering, the gathering of angels ' for the salutation of
the father: 10

I shall sing and glorify and ' hymn:
Holy, holy, ' god almighty, ' creator, invisible one, '
Hormosiel, the angel 15 in whose hand is the trumpet, '
as he gathers the angels ' for the salutation of the father, of
the ' whole council of the father, '

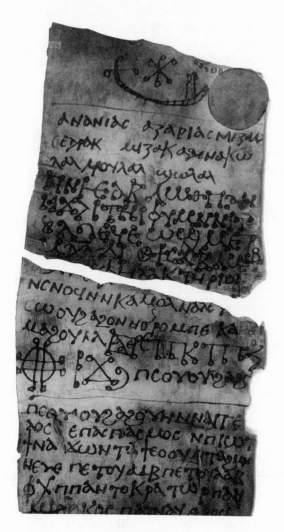

LONDON HAY 10122 (*recto*),
upper part

Anaboel, the steward of the father, [20]
the congregation,
Pakothan Lere'kiel.

I beg, I invoke ' you today, Hormisel, '
   the angel in whose hand are [the gatherings], '

LONDON HAY 10122 (*verso*),
upper part

[that you] [25] gather ' today
    the [whole] generation of ' Adam,
    and [all] the children ' of Zoe,
through the power of the [great] ' unseen names of [30] terror,
Ariel, Oriel, ' Emiel, Thimiael, Thanael, ' Patriel,
who gather ' the entire cosmos, '
    along with [35] everything in it, '

from the region of ' the sunrise to its ' place of setting.
I ' beg, [40] I invoke, (**verso**)

(figure)   (figure)   (figure)   The north

Beth Betha Betheial

(sign) (figure) (figure) (figure) (sign)

Abiout K[. . .]

(figure) (figure) (figure) The south

Hraphael	(ring letters and signs)	
Sraguel		
Raguel	(another figure)	Outriel
Ta.el (?)		Ousiel
. . .		Ourael
. . .		Michael
Suriel		Eiael
Aguel		Ael
Sraphoel	(standing figure)	El
Raguel		L
Hraguel		
Michael		
El		
Maiel		

A woman (with an unusual flow of) blood: Write . . . ' and
after (?) the flow (?) . . . ' her time (?) ' [. . .] woman . . . of the
pad ' [. . .] figure . . . ' place it at the door of ' [. . .].

(drawing of a woman)

The sin of the woman.

(signs)

Flower ' of wild acacia; ' ashes ' of . . . ; white reed; ' an earthen
altar. ' Put it in oil ' . . .

82. Spell for mutual love between a man and a woman

Text: Michigan 4932f

Description: vellum, 5 1/2 x 15 1/4 in., "probably fairly early" (so Worrell)

Bibliography: William H. Worrell, "Coptic Magical and Medical Texts," 184–87

Translator: Stephen H. Skiles

Michigan 4932f is a spell to be said over oil, after which the oil is to be used in some way to attract a woman to a man. William H. Worrell has rightly noted that the goal of this spell is mutual love rather than sexual liaison, but his assumption that the production of children out of such a love implies matrimony cannot be substantiated from the text. The only hint at marriage is the mention of Isis and Osiris, a mythic couple whose love was as archetypical for antiquity as that of Romeo and Juliet is for English speakers. On Dimelouchs as a ruler of judgment, compare Temeluchos as a punishing angel in Berlin 10587 (text 92).

TEXT

✝ Oil! Oil! Oil! Holy oil! ¹

Oil that flows from under the throne of Yao ¹ Sabaoth! Oil with which Isis anointed ¹ Osiris's bone(s)! I call you, oil. The sun and ⁵ moon call you. The stars of heaven call ¹ you. The servants of the sun call you. ¹ I want to send you. You must come so that I may bring you and you ¹ may bring N. daughter of N. to me—me, N. son of N.— and you must make my love ¹ [be] in her heart and hers in mine ¹⁰ [like] a brother and sister, or a bear ¹ [who] wants to suckle her young. Yea, yea, I ¹ [invoke] you, the one whose head is in heaven, ¹ whose feet are in the abyss, before whom is (what) is also under ¹ the Sheep (pl.), behind whom is (what) is also under Draco, ¹⁵ the one [before whom] the heaven of all darkness is hung ¹ [. . .]. (**verso**)

I shall uproot him (with) iron. I shall melt him ¹ ✝ away. No, my lord, do not hand me ¹ over to Dimelouchs, who (presides) ¹ over judgment. Instead, I want ⁵ you to descend to hell and ¹ uproot all thoughts of the devil ¹ about N. child of N., ¹ and make my love be in her [heart] ' and hers in mine. For [it is] I [10] who invoke; it is you who fulfill the desire.

83. Spell to make a woman become pregnant

Text: Pierpont Morgan Library M662B 22

Description: papyrus, 21.8 x 28 cm, seventh century (?)

Bibliography: Leslie S. B. MacCoull, *"P. Morgan Copt.,"* 10–14; Florence D. Friedman, *Beyond the Pharaohs,* 196

Translator: Marvin Meyer

This spell is to be used by a man to make a woman become pregnant. For that purpose god is invoked and the remarkable pregnancy of Sarah is recalled (compare Genesis 17:15–21; 18:9–15). A cup of wine given to the woman is to function as the medium through which the spell is to take effect and all hindrances to pregnancy are to be overcome. The other side of the papyrus contains an inventory of wine.

TEXT

✝ Almighty master, lord, O god, since ' from the beginning you have created humankind in ' your likeness and in your image, you also ' have honored my striving for childbirth. You [5] said to our mother Sarah, "At this time ' in a year a son will be born to you." ' Thus also now, look, I invoke you, ' who is seated upon the cherubim, that you ' listen to my request today—me, N. son of N.— [10] over the chalice of wine that is in my hand, so that ' when I . . . it to N. daughter of N., you may ' favor her with a human seed. And, lord, ' who listens to everyone who calls upon you, ' Adone Elon Sabaoth, god of gods [15] and lord of lords, if (?) a person binds ' an amulet on her or if (?) someone gives her (?) ' a chalice . . . or if (?) there is something from you (?), ' let her be released through redeeming love ' . . . I adjure you [20] by your great name and the sufferings you experienced ' upon the cross: You must bring to pass the words . . . ' that have been spoken over this chalice in my hand.

84. Spell for a man to obtain a male lover

Text: Ashmolean Museum 1981.940

Description: vellum, 8 x 10.5 cm, originally folded to 2.5 x 1.3 cm (by the evidence of creases); perhaps the sixth century

Bibliography: Paul C. Smither, "A Coptic Love-Charm"

Translator: David Frankfurter

This text contains a same-sex love spell commissioned by one Papapolo to "bind" another man, Phello (this name literally means "the old man" or "the monk"), by means of a variety of powerful utterances (especially ROUS). Besides extending the scope of erotic binding spells in late antiquity, this spell also employs formulae common to several Coptic texts of ritual power. The folds in the text and the description of the text's depositing (lines 6–7) imply that this spell was intended to be placed near the beloved man.

TEXT

    † CELTATALBABAL[.]KARASHNEIFE[.]NNAS'KNEKIE, by the power of Yao Sabaoth, ROUS ' ROUS ROUS ROUS ROUS ROUS ROUS ROUS. '

(ring signs)

    † † † I adjure you by your powers and your amulets 5 and the places where you dwell and your ' names, that just as I take you and put you at the door ' and the pathway of Phello son of Maure, (so also) you must take ' his heart and his mind; you must dominate his entire body. '

> When he (tries to) stand, you must not allow him to stand.
> When he (tries to) sit, you must not allow him 10 to sit.
> When he lies down to sleep, you must not allow him to
>   sleep.

> He must seek ' me from town to town, from city to city, '
>   from field to field, from region to region, '
> until he comes to me and subjects himself under my ' feet—
>   me, Papapolo son of Noe—
> while his 15 hand is full of all goodness,
> until I satisfy with him the desire of my heart

and the demand of my ' soul,
with pleasant desire and love unending, '
right now, right now, at once, at once! Do my work!

85. Sexual curse to leave a man impotent and protect a woman from sexual advances

Text: Chicago Oriental Institute 13767
Description: paper, folded, probably in order to be placed into a small
holder; Stefanski assigns it a late date
Bibliography: Elizabeth Stefanski, "A Coptic Magical Text"
Translator: Marvin Meyer

*Chicago Oriental Institute 13767 is a sexual curse that is intended
to leave a man named Pharaouo impotent. This amulet belongs to the
same ritual tradition as Heidelberg Kopt. 682 (text 86) and Strasbourg
Coptic Manuscript 135 (text 87).*

TEXT

O binding of the sky,
binding of the earth,
binding of the air,
binding of the firmament,
binding ' of the Pleiades,
binding of the sun,
binding of the moon,
binding of the birds,
binding ' of the ring of the father,
binding with which Jesus Christ was . . . upon the wood of
the cross, '
binding of the seven words which Iliseus spoke over the
head(s) (of) the [5] holy ones, whose names are
these: Psuchou Chasnai Chasna Ithouni
Anashes Shourani ' Shouranai!

May that binding be upon the male organ of Pharaouo ' and his
flesh; may you dry it up like wood and make it like a rag upon '

the manure pile. His penis must not become hard, it must not have an erection, it must not ejaculate, he must not have intercourse ' with Touaien daughter of Kamar or any woman, whether wild or domesticated, until I [10] myself call out, but may it dry up the male organ of Pharaouo son of Kiranpales. He must not ' have intercourse with Touaein daughter of Kamar, he being like a corpse lying in a ' tomb. Pharaouo son of Kiranpoles must not be able to have intercourse ' (**verso**) with Touaen daughter of Kamar, ' yea, yea, at once, at once!

(ring signs)

86. Another sexual curse to leave a man impotent and protect a woman from sexual advances

Text: Heidelberg Kopt. 682

Description: parchment, 30.5 x 9.8 cm

Bibliography: Friedrich Bilabel and Adolf Grohmann, *Griechische, koptische und arabische Texte*, 393–96

Translator: Marvin Meyer

Heidelberg Kopt. 682 is a text written to protect the purity of a woman by binding the potency and sexual activity of an unnamed man. The text includes instructions for writing on a clay sherd and washing or anointing it (1–8), writing on paper and burning it (8–10), uttering words of power (11–19), drawing again (43–44), and performing an offering (44–46). The author of the spell is identified and the precise date is given (Paope 21, 684 A.M. ["in the year of the martyrs"] = October 18, 967 C.E.). This spell belongs to the same ritual tradition as Chicago Oriental Institute 13767 (text 85) and Strasbourg Coptic Manuscript 135 (text 87).

TEXT

(drawing, ring letters)

Draw our ' names on a ' sherd ' of clay: [5] Nalmite, ' Nalchobia. ' Wash them off with ' genuine (olive) oil.

Use(?) the ' male and female face(s). Draw the figure [10] on paper. Let it burn. ' Go quickly: Release N. and N., ' Aios Baiot Atonas; release ' N., Nitha Bar Bau ' Mar Marti Sopos Jabes [15] Saraphos Ber Bar Hetios ' Ohei Phet Bab Mourat Terik ' Escheu Keta; release N., ' Ache Pher Pha Cheume Rouch, ' that you may release N. and N. [20]

O binding of the sky,
binding of the earth, '
binding of the mountain,
binding of the water, '
binding of the ring of the father,
binding ' of the ax that is in a hand of flesh,
binding ' (with) which Christ was bound upon the wood of
    [25] the cross!

You must bind the virginity of N. ' N. must not be able to release the virginity ' until the virginity of the holy virgin ' is released. '

O binding of the word(s?) that Elias the [30] prophet spoke upon the holy mountain, ' whose names are these: Chakouri Chabnei ' Chabna Shorani Shouiona! '

May the present binding be upon ' the male organ of N. toward N. [35] He must not be able to release the virginity of N.; ' he must not become hard, he must not have an erection, ' he must not ejaculate, he must not be able to release ' the virginity of N., but it must ' stay in the flesh of N. May the [40] flesh of N. be like a ' corpse; it must not be able to get out ' of the tomb, yea, yea, at once! '

(ring signs)

Draw: ' Nalmitet, Nalchobini.
Off(ering): [45] wild white myrrh; frankincense ' . . . .
It is done ' well. '

I, Pdi Yo, servant of Michael, ' (son) of Pcelleta, have written on Paope 21 and in the year 684.

87. Another sexual curse to leave a man impotent and protect a woman from sexual advances

Text: Strasbourg Coptic Manuscript 135
Description: parchment
Bibliography: Walter E. Crum, "La magie copte," 541–42; Angelicus M. Kropp, *Ausgewählte koptische Zaubertexte*, 2.228
Translator: Marvin Meyer

Strasbourg Coptic Manuscript 135 consists of a spell to protect a woman named Seine from the sexual advances of a man named Shinte by binding his sexual potency. This spell belongs to the same ritual tradition as Chicago Oriental Institute 13767 (text 85) and Heidelberg Kopt. 682 (text 86).

TEXT

It is on Shinte son of Tanheu that I shall work a spell of binding, ' Keuentios Patilos Kous Makous, the one who has fallen from ' his invisible chariot (?) and has been cast into the outer ' darkness: Bind, fasten the flesh of Shinte son of 5 Tanheu, Bar Bare Apakentor Methalai. ' Bind, fasten the flesh of Shinte son of Tanheu. ' It (?) must not have an erection, it must not become hard, it must not ejaculate. ' May he—Shinte son of Tanheu—be like a corpse left ' in a tomb and like an old rag 10 left on a manure pile. He must not be able to have ' intercourse and he must not be able to release the virginity ' of Seine daughter of Moune, ' yea, yea, at ' once, at once!

7

CURSES

INTRODUCTION BY ROBERT K. RITNER
TRANSLATIONS BY STEPHEN EMMEL, DAVID
FRANKFURTER, MARVIN MEYER, ROBERT K. RITNER,
STEPHEN H. SKILES, AND RICHARD SMITH

To the modern reader, few of the texts in this volume probably seem less "religious" and less "Christian" than the following
curses. Their blatantly vindictive tone and hostile purpose, directed toward specific and personal enemies, place them at odds
with traditional popular and scholarly conceptions of "proper"
religious expression. Indeed, in the century-long debate among
anthropologists, sociologists, and religious historians regarding
the presumed categories of religion and magic (see Stanley J.
Tambiah, *Magic, Science, Religion, and the Scope of Rationality*), it is
just these characteristics that have long been felt to distinguish inferior "magic" (hostile, limited, personal) from elevated "religion" (beneficent, universal, communal). Unfortunately for
scholarly preference and popular sentiment, however, ritual cursing has been shown to occupy a prominent position within all official ancient Near Eastern religious traditions.

Pharaonic Egyptian society, in particular, utilized a variety of
formal cursing techniques directed against both state and personal enemies (see Robert K. Ritner, *The Mechanics of Ancient
Egyptian Magical Practice*). The evidence for such rituals has survived in texts, execration figures of stone, wax, wood, and pottery
("voodoo dolls"), statuary and relief, architectural elements, and

even royal clothing design. The setting for these rites extended from temple and palace to ruined cemeteries and border fortresses. Regardless of setting, the most notable feature of Egyptian cursing was its reliance on the vengeful nature of the angry dead. Improperly buried or untended corpses were held to be responsible for disease and domestic torment. Curses were regularly deposited in abandoned graveyards, effectively handing over the intended victim to the disgruntled ghost, who was further compelled to service by oaths. Similar methodology appears below explicitly in texts 89, 96–101, and 109. With the Christianization of Egypt, older concepts and techniques were not simply abandoned, and the mechanics of ancient Egyptian cursing reappear in Coptic, and later Islamic, practices. The tortured potsherd of Heidelberg Kopt. 681 (text 105) is the direct descendant of pharaonic execrations. Even today, ancient cursing ritual survives in the Egyptian folk technique of breaking a pot to drive off an enemy. Further survivals of traditional cursing techniques are detailed below.

If certain native Egyptian practices resurface in Coptic rites because of geographic and cultural continuity, others may have returned to the country through biblical scripture. Thus, the pot-breaking custom just noted may have survived because of its early adoption into Jewish custom, as represented by Jeremiah 19:1–11. Similarly, the "curse against the nations" in Amos 1:2–2:16 has been argued to derive from Egyptian execrations. In any case, such biblical references provided ready, "canonical" precedents for early Christian curses. The religion of the Old Testament is replete with the language of cursing, and the most enthusiastic practitioner of the art is enshrined in our term *jeremiad*. The pronouncements of other prophets were directly applicable for contemporary invocations, as in the curse against perjurers (text 92, compare text 101), which concludes with reference to Zechariah 5:1–4. Text 104 invokes "the curses of the Law and Deuteronomy," while the curse of Cain appears in texts 88 and 90, and that against Sodom and Gomorrah in texts 90 and 97. The image of the suffering Job serves contrary purposes, depicting either the envisioned punishment of the victim (text 88) or the ultimate salvation of the complainant (text 89).

As a counterpoint to its more famous theme of forgiveness, the New Testament offers the examples of Jesus cursing the fig tree (Matthew 21:18–19; Mark 11:12–22) and disbelieving towns (Luke 10:13–15), as well as the express authorization for the disciples to curse cities and individuals (Matthew 10:11–15; Luke 9:5; 10:10–12; compare Acts 18:6 and contrast Luke 9:51–56). The authors of the Coptic curses were neither prophets nor apostles, yet these biblical examples suffice to demonstrate that the notion of cursing was not alien to the evolving Judeo-Christian traditions.

Where the authors (or perhaps more properly, "clients") are described, it is they who often appear as humble, injured victims, appealing their mistreatment to a divine tribunal. Whether widows and orphans (text 89) or the miserable and wretched (texts 91 and 93), the authors "cast their cares" upon their divine judge, appealing to biblical precedent of salvation from destruction (texts 89 and 91). The frequent injunction to bring judgment on behalf of the petitioner (texts 88–93 and 108) reflects the well-studied juridical setting of many Hellenistic curses, both Christian and Pagan (see Robert W. Daniel and Franco Maltomini, *Supplementum Magicum*). The technique is again anticipated in the earlier Egyptian practice of letters of judicial complaint to the gods and the blessed dead.

In both rhetorical technique and practical mechanics, the curses follow ancient models, but with older mythology updated for contemporary tastes. Dynastic Egyptian practitioners did not hesitate to equate themselves and their instruments with the native gods and their force, readily claiming, for example, "I am Isis." Coptic scribes are no less bold, identifying their charm with the cross of Jesus and proclaiming, "I myself am god" (Louvre E. 14.250 [text 109]). A traditional variant of this formula announces that "it is not I who does this, but the god N." A Coptic descendant appears in London Oriental Manuscript 5986 (text 88): "Not by my power, but by the power of the lord Sabaoth." Particularly surprising to modern sensibilities is the Egyptian technique of threatening deities in order to force their compliance. Transmitted to Coptic rites, the pattern appears in Yale 1800 (text 106) where the angel of the holy altar is bound and threatened in the name of Asmodeus the demon. Berlin 8503 (text 95) demonstrates the use of a mythic *historiola* or divine precedent for the spell's efficacy: As Moses gave confusion to pharaoh, so will the spell render its victim speechless. Trampling (text 88), striking (text 96), and burning (text 105) are all practices that had been physically enacted on execration figurines, and just such a wax image is manipulated in text 110. Following millennia-old ritual, a doll or dolls may be killed (by a nail?), bloodied, "embalmed," and probably buried. The often associated use of personal effects or "relics" is attested in text 96 (victim's hair), while text 97 is actually written on a bone plucked from the cadaver to be enchanted. Texts 88 and 90 are provided with a secondary imprecation, an "eternal curse upon the reader of these lines," directed against those who would disturb the papyri. Even these formulae are stereotyped. Little-known Demotic temple graffiti from Dakka, Aswan, and Medinet Habu promise just such a curse on those who would read or deface the inscriptions. Let the reader be forewarned.

88. Curse against Victor Hatre, David, and Papnoute

Text: London Oriental Manuscript 5986

Description: papyrus, 13 x 7 7/8 in., "probably of some antiquity" (so Crum)

Bibliography: Walter E. Crum, *Catalogue of the Coptic Manuscripts in the British Museum*, 506–7; Angelicus M. Kropp, *Ausgewählte koptische Zaubertexte*, 2.225–27

Translator: Richard Smith

Here the god of heaven and earth is invoked, along with the host of heaven, to destroy some specifically named enemies. The exact number of enemies is not clear. Victor Hatre (or, Victor the twin) seems to be the name of one person, not two, but Papnoute may or may not be a separate person. David, the son of Victor Hatre, is also named. The person cursing these men feels badly mistreated, but what did they do to provoke such anger?

TEXT

God of heaven and earth! Whoever shall open this papyrus and read what is written in <it>, may all those things written in it descend upon him.

Yea, god of heaven and earth! †

† Lord, you are the one who knows those things which are secret and those which are revealed. God, ⁵ you are the one who shall perform my judgment against all those who oppose me. My father Michael, my father Gabriel, Suriel, Gunuel, Raphael! Not by my power, but by the power of the lord Sabaoth and all those whose names are recited, you shall appeal to the god of heaven and earth.

Trample Victor Hatre, Papnoute. Bring him down. He is acting like a demon. God, may you bring down David his ¹⁰ son. Render him friendless, in prison, like a bronze chain, as I produce the trusty words.

Any person, every one, who adjures bad things upon me and every one who calls my name evil, and those who curse me, all of them—O god [. . .] who shall perform my judgment against them all, lord, god—you shall bring all of them down, all of those who. . . . ¹⁵ Lord, do not neglect my [prayer] and my request, for they have mistreated me. You must bring [them] down from their heights, just as all of them did to me.

Lord Sabaoth, do not neglect me. The cherubim, the seraphim, the ten thousand angels and archangels [20] shall appeal to the god of heaven and earth, and he shall perform my judgment against every one who opposes me. Any one who curses me, you must bring down and abandon him to demons.

Yea, true, beloved savior!

Yea, consubstantial trinity!

Let me watch Victor Hatre and David his son, let me watch him, being inflicted by the spirit of the world. [25] You must bring upon them all the sufferings of Job. O god, you must bring down Papnoute from his height. Abandon him to demons. Number them with Judas on the day of judgment. You must liken them to those who have said, "His blood is upon us for three generations." You must liken them to Cain, who murdered Abel <his> brother.

89. A widow's curse against Shenoute

Text: Munich Coptic Papyrus 5

Description: papyrus, 30.5 x 23.3 cm, about seventh century

Bibliography: W. Hengstenberg, "Koptische Papyri," 95–100, 8*–16*; Angelicus M. Kropp, *Ausgewählte koptische Zaubertexte*, 2.229–31

Translator: Marvin Meyer

In this text a widow and her children formulate a curse against a man named Shenoute, who is oppressing them. The appeal for justice is directed to god, who in turn identifies himself (5–9) as one who protects widows and orphans. The appeal employs the language of the courtroom ("bring judgment on our behalf") as the widow recalls the many ways in which god vindicated the righteous against the wicked. The papyrus closes (33–38) with a description of its burial with a mummy, which in turn is empowered, along with other mummies, to call out to god.

† CH M G † † Emmanuel

I am a poor widow [with] orphaned children ¹ and a burned . . . in my hand. With nine . . . , all of us, with a single sigh, ¹ appeal to the father and the son and the holy spirit and ¹ the consubstantial trinity, that he may hear and bring judgment on my behalf, quickly, against this ⁵ man who is doing evil to me.

Throw your [care upon me], for I am the father ¹ for orphans and [the judge for widows] . . . ¹ god . . . orphaned children . . . ¹ appeal . . . bring judgment, quickly, . . . ¹

You who made ¹⁰ the first human, Adam . . . ,
[who looked upon] the offering of Abel ¹
      with honor and esteem,
who [crowned] Stephen, the first ¹ martyr,
who saved Noah from the [water] of the flood,
who ¹ brought Lot out of Sodom and saved [him] . . . ,
who ¹ freed Daniel from the lions' den,
who gave Job power ¹⁵ to endure all the trials
      that came upon him from the enemy
      until he conquered ¹ him through his endurance,
who loves the [righteous],
whom the righteous love! ¹

I adjure you,
who is seated upon the chariot [of the] cherubim,
with the seraphim ¹ standing before you,
with . . . thousands of thousands and ten thousands [of
      ten thousands ¹ of] angels, [archangels], ²⁰
[. . .], with two they [cover] ¹ their face,
and with two they fly, ¹
calling out, one [after] another,
Holy, holy, holy, holy, ¹ holy, holy, holy, [. . .].

I adjure you by the cry that you (?) ¹ uttered:
Bring judgment on our behalf, quickly,
      against Shenoute son of ²⁵ Pamin.
You must strike him just as you struck ¹ 185,000
      among the host of the Assyrians in a single night.
You must bring ¹ upon him fever and chill and jaundice.

You must ' make his enemies open their mouths . . . him.
He must flee along a single path '
     and his enemies must flee after him [. . .]. [30]
You must bring upon [him . . .]. [32]
. . . judgment on my behalf. '

The mummy [on] which this [papyrus for] vengeance is placed must appeal night ' and day [to the lord (?)], from its [bed] to the ground [35] in which it is buried with the other mummies lying around this grave, ' all of them calling out, together, what is in this papyrus, until ' god hears and [brings] judgment on our behalf, quickly! Amen.

A A A A A A A '

O O O O O O O

† † † †

90. Curse against several violent people

Text: Papyrus Lichačev

Description: papyrus, 30 x 15 cm, fourth–fifth century

Bibliography: Petr V. Ernštedt, *Koptskie teksty Gosudarstvennogo Èrmitaža*, 151–57; B. A. Turaev, "Axmimskij papirus iz kollekščin N. P. Lixačev," 28–30; Oscar von Lemm, "Koptische Miscellen," 1076–86; Angelicus M. Kropp, *Ausgewählte koptische Zaubertexte*, 2.232–34

Translator: Marvin Meyer

In this papyrus a victim similarly calls upon god, in the language of the courtroom, to bring judgment against several people who have committed an act of violence. The closing lines (verso) pronounce a curse upon anyone who opens and reads the papyrus.

TEXT

† Lord, my god,
to whom I look, '
who is seated upon the chariot of the ' cherubim,
with the seraphim round about you, '

who is mounted upon the four creatures, 5
Michael, Gabriel the archangel, '
cherubim and seraphim,
Rabuel, ' Suruel, Kukkuel,
you who are seated ' upon your throne with your beloved
son, '
along with all those who have been named,
and the place where 10 this will be deposited,
and the angel of the church: '
You must strike Prestasia and Tnounte and ' Eboneh,
quickly, deservedly!
You must hinder them ' as they have hindered him.
You must bring upon ' them the anger of your wrath and
your raised arm. 15
As you cursed Somohra and Komohra ' through the anger of
your wrath,
you must curse ' the one who has committed this act of
violence.
You must bring ' the vengeance of Enoch against them.
As the blood ' of Abel called out to Cain his brother,
the blood 20 of this miserable man will call out,
until you bring judgment on his behalf '
against those who have committed this act of violence
against him.

Eloei, Eloei, ' that is, lord Sabaoth,
you must bring your wrath ' upon them,
in a disturbing way.
You in whose hands is every breath, '
who formed the world,
you must 25 quickly overthrow the people
who have committed this violence. '
Yea, lord Sabaoth,
you must bring judgment on his behalf, '
quickly! † (verso)

Whoever opens this papyrus and reads it, what is written ' on
it will come upon him, by order of the lord god. †

91. Jacob's curse against Maria, Tatore, and Andreas

Text: Oxford, Bodleian Coptic Manuscript C. (P) 4
Description: papyrus, 28.5 x 14.5 cm
Bibliography: Walter E. Crum, "Eine Verfluchung"; Angelicus M. Kropp,
Ausgewählte koptische Zaubertexte, 2.234–38
Translator: Richard Smith

A person named Jacob casts this curse, for unspecified abuses, against two women, Maria and Tatore, and a man, Andreas, along with their entire families. Johannes is also among those targeted, and he is addressed by a rare Greek title that means something like the "headman" of a village.

To work his judgment and revenge, Jacob calls on the familiar Christian divine powers, along with biblical quotes and liturgical fragments. Just as god rescued Jonah from the whale, saved the three youths from the fiery furnace, and rescued Daniel from the lion's den, so Jacob hopes to utilize that same power to punish his many enemies.

TEXT

✝ I am Jacob, a miserable, wretched person.

I ask, I invoke, I worship, I lay my prayer and my request before the throne of god the almighty, Sabaoth.

Perform my judgment and my revenge against Maria daughter of Tsibel, and Tatore daughter of Tashai, and Andreas son of Marthe, quickly!

Only true god, the one who knows things secret and revealed, you must strike Tatore daughter of Tashai, with her children, and Maria daughter of Tsibel, and Andreas son of Marthe, with their whole family, and Johannes the headman, with his son—Amen! 5 —with a wicked disease, and anger and wrath, and wicked suffering, and unhealing pain.

I appeal to you, father, I appeal to you, son, I appeal to you, holy spirit, the consubstantial trinity, the good news of Gabriel the archangel, that you perform my judgment and my revenge and my violence with Tatore and Andreas and Maria daughter of Tsibel, with their children. Bring upon them blindness to their two eyes. Bring upon them great pain and jaundice disease and burning fever and trouble and dispersion and ruin.

Father, strike them.

Son, strike them.

God, who exists before the [10] world had yet come into being, strike them.

At once, at once!

O one who sits upon the cherubim, having the seraphim around him, ' strike Maria daughter of Tsibel, and Tatore daughter of Tashai, and Andreas son of Marthe, with their children, quickly! '

O thousands of thousands and ten thousands of ten thousands of angels who stand by him, and archangels and rulers and authorities and powers ' . . . praising and honoring and calling out together, saying, "Holy, holy, holy, lord Sabaoth, ' heaven and earth are full of your glory," strike Tatore and her children and her husband, with Maria and her children and [15] . . . her husband, with great anger and unhealing suffering, for they have caused a lot of violence.

And you, lord, you know everything. ' [Adonai], lord, Eloe, Sabaoth, strike Tatore daughter of Tashai, and Maria daughter of Tsibel, and Andreas ' [son] of Marthe. Strike them quickly!

O four creatures who stand by the father, the great god, ' strike Tatore, and Andreas, and Maria and her children and every one who resides with them. '

[The body] and the blood of Jesus Christ, strike Maria daughter of Tsibel, and Tatore daughter of Tashai, and Andreas [20] son of Marthe, at once!

O twenty-four elders who are seated before the father, strike Tatore ' and Andreas and Maria, quickly!

O you who rescued Jonah from the whale, strike Tatore and ' Andreas and Maria.

O you who saved the three holy ones from the burning fiery furnace, strike Tatore ' daughter of Tashai, and Maria daughter of Tsibel, and Andreas son of Marthe, with great anger and great destruction and ruin.

O you ' who rescued Daniel from the lions' den, strike Maria and Tatore and Andreas with the anger of your wrath. [25]

Michael, strike them with your fiery sword.
Gabriel, strike them with your fiery sword.
Raphael, ' strike them with your fiery sword.
Rakuel, strike them with your fiery sword.

Suriel, strike them with your fiery sword.
 Amen! '

Seven archangels who stand in the presence of god, strike them with your fiery sword. Strike Maria ' and Tatore and Andreas, quickly, Amen!
Adonai Eloe Eloi Eloi Eloi Eloi,
Yao Yao Yao Yao Sabaoth Emmanuel,
El El El El El El El, '
Emannuel Michael Gabriel Raphael Rakuel Suriel Anael Ananael Phanuel Tremuel Abrasaxsax, father, [30] son, holy spirit, god [of] Abraham, god of Isaac, god of Jacob, god of the angels, god of the archangels, ' god of the cherubim, god of the seraphim, god of all the powers, who created heaven and earth, who created the sun and the moon ' and the stars, who created people according to his likeness and his image! (verso)
O one apart from whom there is none other, who performs judgment on everyone, perform my judgment also.
Lord, only true god, ' I have fled to you and thrown my cares [on you], lord, god, for you [have said (?)], ' "Throw your cares on me, and I will [support you." Stretch out] your strong hand over them with your arm ' raised, and strike Tatore daughter of [Tashai, and] Maria daughter of Tsibel, and Andreas son of [Marthe], [5] and their children, and everyone who resides with them—Amen!—with every evil grief, and every suffering, and every unhealing pain. ' Send to him an evil demon who torments them by day and by night. '
Amen, Amen, Amen!
AAAAAAA EEEEEE EEEEEEE IIIIIII OOOOOOO UUUU-UUU OOOOOOO †
A O † Jesus Christ

92. Curse against perjurers

Text: Berlin 10587
Description: papyrus, 28.5 x 26.5 cm, tenth century (?)
Bibliography: Walter Beltz, "Die koptischen Zauberpapyri," 79–81;

Angelicus M. Kropp, *Ausgewählte koptische Zaubertexte*, 2.238–40
Translator: Richard Smith

Temeluchos, the angel invoked here, was well known in late antiq-
uity. In the (Greek) Apocalypse of Paul 16 he is, as in this text, "the
angel who is set over punishments." In the Apocalypse of Peter 8 he
specifically tortures those who abort children. Thus some early church
fathers knew him as a guardian angel over the souls of aborted and ex-
posed children. In the present text he appears to be the punishing angel
of perjurers (compare Dimelouchs in Michigan 4932f [text 82]).

The focus of the curse against these perjurers provokes some specu-
lation. We might assume a courtroom situation, and the perjurers
might even be the liars for hire, mentioned by Juvenal, who hung
around the Roman courts. Has the person casting the spell, therefore,
been found guilty based on false testimony; or, as is found in some
Greek curses against perjurers, is the spell being cast before the trial as
a form of insurance?

The identification of "the living Christ" with "Seth" may indicate
familiarity with Sethian Gnostic traditions.

TEXT

I adjure you by your true names, ' Raphael, Adonai, Sabaoth.
' Send Temeluchos to me, ' the one who is over the . . . punishments, 5 the one who tortures the lawless and the ' liars and the
perjurers, ' that he might take my revenge on them.

Hail! I adjure you ' by your only begotten son, whose true
name ' is Seth, Seth, the living Christ: 10 You must torture them
with your wicked tortures. ' But first cause their eyes to ' fog and
come out. Afterward, you must bring ' down upon him a deadly
wound on my behalf, and an unhealing blow ' with an unclean-
able wound.

I adjure 15 you by the great power of heaven, Yao Yao '
Machael: Send Uriel, that he might take my revenge ' with the perjurers, that he bring upon them out ' of heaven an unsleeping
worm and an unquenchable wrath ' and cause it to happen pow-
erfully in the body of the one who shall 20 swear against my name
falsely. ' Send Raphael to me with his fiery sword, ' that he might
come and order Temeluchos and quickly afflict ' him with what a
demon deserves, and with ' error, trouble, and madness. 25 I
adjure you by the seven perfect letters, MMMMMMM. ' You must

appear to him, you must appear to him. ' I adjure you by the seven angels around ' the throne of the father and the son. I adjure those whose ' names I name. Take my revenge with those who perjure [30] your name, Yao Yao Seth Seth Shmmehrael ' Adonai Yakukia Baruchia Sharku Kolosu! **(column 2)**

[. . .] take my revenge with ' . . . you happen upon his . . . [5] with a stick and like . . . ' until he breaks ' . . . , at once! '

Rumiel, Yonael, Maruel, ' Suel, Yoniel, Doruel, [10] Misoel, Eneriel, Somuel, ' Promiel, Sanael, Masthel, ' Sachoiel, Sramael, Srael, ' Yonuel, Runuel, Sarael, ' Susael, Lonuel, who are [15] the twenty-one angels ' on the left, come. ' Take my revenge quickly against the man ' who unjustly perjures the name of god ' with lies. [20]

The angel of Zacharias, by ' the word of god that was coming, ' said to me, "What will you see, ' Zacharias?" I said to him, "I see ' a flying sickle, twenty [25] cubits long and ten cubits ' wide." He said to me, "Do you not ' know what this is?" ' I said to him, "No, my lord." ' He said to me, "This is the [curse] [30] which is coming upon the face of the whole earth, ' upon thieves . . . ' measure . . . them. . . . " '

At once!

93. Curse of a mother against her son's female companion

Text: London Oriental Manuscript 6172

Description: papyrus, 10 x 6 in., "of considerable antiquity" (so Crum)

Bibliography: Walter E. Crum, *Catalogue of the Coptic Manuscripts in the British Museum*, 505–6; Angelicus M. Kropp, *Ausgewählte koptische Zaubertexte*, 2.241–42

Translator: Richard Smith

This is a particularly mean-spirited spell, perhaps cast by an over-possessive mother against a younger woman who has captured the attention of her son.

I, the miserable, wretched sinner, call unto the lord god '
almighty, that you perform my judgment against Tnoute, [who
has] separated my son from me so that he ' scorns me. You must
not listen to her, O [god . . .] if she calls up to you. You must
make her ' without hope in this world. You must strike her womb
and make her barren. You must make her consume the 5 fruit of
her womb. You must make a demon descend upon her, [who will
cast] her into troublesome illness and great affliction. ' You must
bring a fever upon her, and a [. . . and a] chill and a numbness of
heart and an ' itching. Bring upon her the twelve [. . .] a worm
and blood flow out of her ' all the days of her life [. . .] take
them. She must not live; she comes to death. ' You must cause her
mouth to err.

O you who sits upon the chariot of [. . .], O cherubim and
seraphim, perform my judgment 10 against Tnoute. Michael, you
must perform my judgment. Gabriel, [. . .]el, Tremuel, Abraxiel,
Emmanuel, ' perform my judgment against Tnoute, quickly! O
twenty-four elders and the four ' creatures who support the throne
of the father, perform my judgment. O you who performs judgment for the ' mistreated, perform my judgment, quickly!

> AAA BBB GG[G . . .] * * * DDD ' EEE ZZZ EEE III
> OOOOO
> HYBRA DD[D at once], at once! (verso)

> Now, at once, '
> at once, at once! '
> Aloei '
> * * *
> † † †

94. Curse to make a man tongue-tied

Text: Cambridge University Library T. S. 12,207
Description: paper, "late period" (so Crum; he adds, "It is written upon a
strip of paper in a very unskilled, often ambiguous hand, which I cannot
venture to date.")

Bibliography: Walter E. Crum, "A Bilingual Charm" (1902); idem, "A Bilingual Charm" (1903); Angelicus M. Kropp, *Ausgewählte koptische Zaubertexte*, 2.242–43
Translator: Marvin Meyer

This text, the first six lines of which are preserved in Arabic (written with Coptic letters) and the rest in Coptic, consists of a curse that is meant to bind a man's mouth and leave him, literally, tongue-tied. It may be that the man, Garib by name, is involved in litigation with the woman named Thijar, or the issue may be a matter of gossip or slanderous conversation. The opening phrase of the spell is the familiar Islamic word of invocation. The voice calling from the cross refers to the powerful words of the crucified Jesus that are cited frequently in texts of ritual power, and the seven seals (compare Revelation 5:1–4) may be considered to be undone through the death and descent of Jesus into the underworld.

TEXT

In the name of Allah, the merciful, the compassionate! Bind ' the tongue of Garib son of Sitt ' el-Kull, that he may no longer be able to speak ' a word. Binding of his tongue 5 on behalf of Thijar daughter of lady N., ' through this power of these names. Amen. '

(signs)

God, who has bound heaven and has ' bound the earth,
must bind the mouth and the tongue ' of Garib son of
    Sitt el-Kull,
that he may not 10 be able to move his lips '
or speak an evil word against you,
    . . . , ' daughter, servant of Thejir, '
    to her,
    before Garib son of Sitt el-Kull. '

God, who has restrained the sun in the 15 place where it
    sets,
    and has restrained the moon,
    and has restrained ' the stars,
    and has restrained the winds ' [in] the middle of
        heaven,
lord god, you must ' restrain,

you must bind the mouth and the tongue ' of Garib son of
    Sitt el-Kull,
that he may not [20] be able to speak an evil ' word against
    Thijar daughter ' of lady N.
I adjure you,
I adjure the voice ' that was raised upon the cross,
until ' the 7 unbroken seals [25] were undone through him.

I adjure ' you,
I adjure you by your ' . . . .

95. Abdallah's curses to weaken Mouflehalpahapani

Text: Berlin 8503

Description: parchment, 16 x 15 cm, about the eighth century (after the
Arab conquest)

Bibliography: Walter Beltz, "Die koptische Zauberpergamente," 94–97;

Angelicus M. Kropp, *Ausgewählte koptische Zaubertexte*, 2.243–47

Translator: Marvin Meyer

*Berlin 8503 consists of curses against Mouflehalpahapani (Mufle-
halpaha?) to make him weak and confused before a rival, Abdallah.
The legend of Moses confounding the Egyptian pharoah and the court
miracle-workers (compare Exodus 3–11) is used in a spell to take away
Mouflehalpahapani's ability to think and speak with clarity. Included
in the spell is a depiction, on the parchment, of the power Ebbael (por-
trayed somewhat like Christ?). An additional curse, added at the end of
the text, recalls Psalm 115:4–8 as the curse graphically describes how
Mouflehalpahapani is to become as lifeless as a statue.*

TEXT

    The word of the lord came to Moses son of Parori on the day
' of the Sabbath in the thirteenth year of pharaoh, the king of
Egypt, ' the one who has power over all the magicians of Satan,
the lord of all the tribes ' of the earth, saying:

    Moses, arise. Go to the [5] king, pharaoh, and teach ' him
about the name of Phankour ' and Saphlo.

BERLIN 8503

At that moment ' Moses became afraid and ' said, SARTORIS [10] NMMOS ENTOTKAAS ' ISARTORIS.

The lord said, ' Moses, do not be ' afraid. Go to him and ' take speechlessness [15] and confusion ' from me, that he may have it and it may become ' strong. Take it and give ' it to Mouflehalpahapani, ' son of [20] his mother, and say, The words ' of the lord of heaven and ' the ruler of the earth, ' Saklataboth, saying, ' Elile and the salvation of Satan, (**new column**) [5] the eyes and the breath of the lord of ' heaven and the ruler of the earth: ' At the moment that I shall rehearse ' the names and the amulets <and> the figures ' in solitude, you must have speechlessness, [10] as is among the dead, that ' Mouflehalpahapani ' may have speechless-

ness, like ' that of the dead, before ' Abdallah son of ¹⁵ Teleppheu.
The lord must not ' disregard my word: It must ' be strong, it must
' be powerful. Let the mind of ' Mouflehalpahapani, ²⁰ son of Kin
his mother, be as ' that of a trumpet: He must be confused, ' he
must have speechlessness, ' he must be confused, irrevocably, ' before Abdallah son of Teleppheu. ²⁵

No master and no power must be able to shield the mind of
Mouflehalpahapani, ' son of Kin his mother, from it, through the
power of Saklataboth who ' is in heaven. Nor must he be able to
leave heaven, but he shall stay up in the air and take away ' from
Mouflehalpahapani, son of Kin his mother, his judgment and his
mind, ' and lift him up as a sacrifice to Satanael, Saoth, Adon, the
speechless (?) spirits, ³⁰ through the breath of the spirit. Mouflehalpahapani, son of Kin his ' mother, HIRI HORAM HOBOKO-
KIKE PHONE ANAEL EKAITETOM!

Let the lord ' of Moses judge Mouflehalpahapani, son of Kin
his mother, saying, ' Come, Michael and the seven other great
archangels, and my salvation—that ' is I, Abrasax—and the salvation of my father Chachobal, and my powers, HAMOUL,
HAMO, HASI, ³⁵ HARA, HAMAUH, HAHNURANNE, HAPHAP,
so that if you hear this formula (?), ' you may come from every
place where you are, with your wands in your hands, ' and go to
Mouflehalpahapani, son of Kin his mother, and give ' speechlessness and confusion day and night. Bring over him weakness ' before Abdallah son of Teleppheu, day and night, through the
utterance of the word of the lord Yao.

Yea, at once, at once! ⁴⁰

The strong power of Ebbael! '

Mouflehalpahapani, son of Kin his ' mother, is one of the
idols that are in ' Antianas, which have been made by human beings. ' Mouflehalpahapani, son of Kin his mother, has hands but
he cannot touch; he has feet ⁴⁵ but he cannot walk; he has eyes
but he cannot see; he has ears ' (verso) but he cannot hear; he has
a nose but he cannot smell; he has a mouth but he ' cannot speak
a word through his throat; he has a heart but he does not understand. There is no spirit ' in him, in Mouflehalpahapani, son of
Kin his mother. Let ' Mouflehalpahapani, son of Kin his mother,
become as those idols ⁵⁰ before Abdallah son of Teleppheu all
the days of his ' life.

Yea, yea, at once, at once,
without holding back, without being careless,
this day and hour!

96. Lead curse against the health of Kyriakos

Text: lead tablet, Cologne T 10

Description: lead tablet, 7.7 x 10 cm, sixth–seventh century

Bibliography: Manfred Weber, "11. Schadenzauber," 109–12

Translator: Robert K. Ritner

This potent curse, written on a lead tablet, employs names of power against the health and well-being of a man named Kyriakos. The curse tablet originally was rolled or folded for insertion in a tomb, and the text itself refers to the corpse under which the tablet is to be placed.

TEXT

Ouphrikouphouth, Bairouphouth, Beatouphasau, ' Amerbenouth, Phabathath, Pachpasarbar, Poamouroph ' Phabaaou, Serbarbaraos, Sabarboutha, ' Anabarthoou, Choumpsouch, Siserbatha, 5 Komnath, Chach, Bapsabathath, Pasabalthnanarbe, ' Salbable, Cophibol, Krabarasen ' Souteth, Therniklesia, Thernemoni, ' Labesachthe, Chomacho [. . .]oth, Monousatharsibath, ' Thabarioth, E..[. . .]outhothbphiak, I adjure 10 you, these names of this great, powerful stele. ' I invoke you by your names and your strong ' power. At the moment that I shall place you ' beneath this corpse, you must cast Kyr(i)akos ' son of Sanne, the man from Penjeho, into a painful sickness 15 and disease and a wasting illness ' and a suffering in all his limbs. Carry off his sustenance ' of his body; drink his blood; let his [shit] and ' his urine pollute his soul. Loosen his [bones]; burst ' his tendons. Strike him violently with 20 a bad stroke and a bad, ' incurable wound seizing his head to his feet. May ' a fever and a burning and a shivering gnaw at ' his flesh by day and night until his life is ' overpowered like that of this corpse. May day give him to 25 night, and night give him to day. Yea, ' I adjure you (by) your names and your powers, that you hearken ' and you perform my task quickly in order that ' the sleeping place on which he will sleep—he shall not depart from it, ' nor shall any person be able to heal him until I ³⁰ take you from there beneath this corpse. For this ' is the hair of his head; this is his personal effect that I give ' to you. Yea, for I invoke you by the authority and your ' names and your powers, that you perform for me ' my task quickly. Now, now, quickly, quickly!

97. Bone curse to make Apollo burn

Text: bone, Florence 5645
Description: human rib, perhaps deriving from the Theban necropolis; date uncertain. The rib is now broken in two pieces, resulting in the loss of several words; eleven lines remain. The letters, described as being rather yellow, may have faded from red
Bibliography: Astorre Pellegrini, "Piccoli testi copto-sa'îdici del Museo Archeologico di Firenze," 141, 156–59; Walter E. Crum, "La magie copte," 538; Angelicus M. Kropp, *Ausgewählte koptische Zaubertexte*, 3.111 (note 1)
Translator: Robert K. Ritner

The interest of this text derives as much from the object on which it is written as from the purpose of the curse itself. The deposition of curses in older graveyards is a practice continuously attested in Egypt from the third millennium B.C.E. and was intended to elicit or compel the assistance of a powerful or angry ghost, here designated by the traditional term "praised one." The attachment of a curse to a corpse was effected in various ways: placing the text on or beside the mummy, inserting the written spell in the corpse's mouth, or—as here—inscribing the text directly on a portion of a cadaver, which thus acts as a "relic" empowered with the force of the ghost. Curses written on bones are rare, though the Coffin Texts (spell 37) recommend the use of a fish bone, and the Cairo curses which follow here (text 98) are inscribed on two camel bones. The use of red ink or blood for hostile enchantment is standard; this (or other necromantic purposes) may have motivated the compulsion laid upon a bone to produce blood from a corpse in the text from the Liverpool Institute of Archaeology (text 99). The ultimate motivation for the Florentine curse is unknown, but its immediate purpose is clear. Jacob commands the spirit of the corpse to torment his enemy Apollo with afflictions recalling biblical punishment accorded Sodom and Gomorrah. The curse was misunderstood by its original editor as a possible postmortem excommunication of a deceased family of thieves inscribed by a secretary Jacob on behalf of a supposed bishop Apollo.

TEXT

(sign)
You shall say, I invoke your great ' force [which . . . and] your great power which has ' authority over ' this praised one, so that you compel this corpse and that you bring [suffering] ⁵ upon Apollo son of [. . .]. ' May he tremble, may he be inflamed, may he burn, may [. . .] ' every person like Sodom and Gomorrah [. . .]. Now, now, quickly, quickly! I, ' Jacob son of Euphemia, have written to you. ' Yea, yea!

98. Bone curse to bring the powers of darkness down upon Aaron

Text: bones, Cairo A and B
Description: written in red (blood?) on two large animal bones, probably those of a camel; said to derive from Akhmim, perhaps about 900 C.E. or a little later. The threefold repetition of spells is traditional, and the texts thus comprise a single ritual. Bone A: length of outer edge 52 cm, height 47 cm; greatest width 5.33 cm; greatest thickness 1 cm. Bone B: length of outer edge 52 cm, height 46 cm; greatest width 5 cm; greatest thickness 1 cm
Bibliography: James Drescher, "A Coptic Malediction"
Translator: Robert K. Ritner

This threefold repetition of a spell summons the powers of death and the spirit of a corpse ("O dead one") to bring suffering and death upon a man named Aaron. The spirit of the corpse is to be activated when the bones are placed under the corpse.

TEXT

(Bone A)
Chu, ' Kouchos, ' Trophos, ' Kimphas, ⁵ Psotomis, ' and ' Plemos, ' and Ouliat. ' These are ¹⁰ the names of ' the six ' powers of '

death, these ' who bring [15] every sickness ' down upon ' every person, ' these ' who bring [20] every soul ' out from ' every body. ' . . . I adjure ' you by [25] your names ' {and your ' names} and ' your powers ' and your [30] places and ' the security of ' death (itself), ' that you shall go ' to Aaron son [35] of Tkouikira, ' and that you shall bear away ' his soul. I adjure ' you, O ' dead one, by the manner [40] in which you were seized, ' and by this ' punishment that ' has come upon you, ' which you have heard, [45] and by these ' punishments that you have ' seen, ' and by the (terrifying) faces ' that you have seen, [50] and by ' the river of ' fire ' that casts up wave ' after wave, that as I shall [55] place this, ' at the ' moment I ' place this ' bone under [60] your back, ' that the manner (in which) ' you suffered, ' you must bring ' your suffering [65] down ' upon Aaron ' son of ' Tkouikira. ' Yea, yea, [70] at once, at once! ' Depart, at once!

(Bone B, convex side)

Kouchos, ' Trochos, ' Aphonos, ' Pesphokops, [5] and Plemos, ' and ' Ouliat. ' These are (the names of) the six ' powers [10] of ' death, these who ' bring ' every ' soul out [15] from every ' body. ' You shall ' go to ' Aaron son of [20] Tkouikira. I adjure ' you, ' O dead one, ' by the manner in which ' you were seized, [25] and ' by the manner in which you ' went, ' and by the fearful ' places and by the river [30] of fire ' that casts up wave after wave, ' which you have seen, ' and by all your sufferings, ' that you bring [35] all your suffering ' upon ' Aaron son of ' Tikouikira. ' Yea, at once! [40] I call, I adjure ' you, O dead ' one, by the manner ' in which you were seized, ' and by the fearful place [45] to which you ' were taken, ' and by the fearful ' places that you have seen, ' and by the river [50] of fire ' that casts up wave ' after wave, that ' you shall bring ' all your suffering, [55] so that ' at the moment ' I place ' this bone under ' your back, you must [60] bring all your ' suffering ' down upon ' Aaron son ' of Tkouikira. [65] Yea, at once, ' at once! ' Depart, depart, ' at once, at once! ' These are they who bring [70] every ' sickness upon ' people. ' You shall bring ' . . . (illegible traces of about 6 lines).

(Bone B, concave side)

Kouchos, ' Trephops, ' Kimphias, ' Psotemis, [5] and ' Plemos, ' and Ouliat. ' These are (the names of) the six ' powers [10] of [death], ' these who bring ' every sickness ' upon people ' and who bring [15] every soul ' out from every ' body. You shall ' bring away the ' soul of [20] Aaron ' son of Tkouikira. ' I adjure you ' by the

manner in which <you were seized>, ' and the fear that you have
25 seen, and ' the punishments, ' and the monstrous faces ' that
you have seen, ' and the river 30 of fire that casts up wave ' after
wave, ' that at ' the moment that I ' place <this bone> under your
35 back, ' that the manner (in which) ' you suffered, ' you must
bring ' your 40 suffering down ' upon Aaron ' son of ' Tkouikira. '
Yea, at once, 45 at once!

99. Spell for a bone and corpse

Text: from the Liverpool Institute of Archaeology

Description: papyrus, from Thebes, relatively early script (sixth–seventh
century)

Bibliography: Walter E. Crum, *Short Texts from Coptic Ostraca and Papyri*,
105; Angelicus M. Kropp, *Ausgewählte koptische Zaubertexte*, 3.111–12
(note 1)

Translator: Robert K. Ritner

*This brief spell also deals with a bone that is to be placed with a
corpse for reasons of ritual power.*

TEXT

Samakari . . . of Christ, I ' call upon lord Sabaoth ' Adonai
Umospren (?), ' O child with flowing hair (?), I place 5 an oath
upon you, O dead bone, ' in order that you bring forth blood '
from this corpse whose true name this ' is. Now, now, at once, at
once!

100. Mary's curse against Martha

Text: from Aberdeen

Description: papyrus, folded seven times and then four times to form a
small packet; 15.5 x 11.5 cm; perhaps from Akhmim, fourth–fifth
century

Bibliography: Walter E. Crum, "La magie copte," 539–40; Angelicus M. Kropp, *Ausgewählte koptische Zaubertexte*, 2.227–28; G. M. Lee, "Demotica et Coptica"; Roger Rémondon, "Un papyrus magique copte"
Translator: Robert K. Ritner

The protagonists of this spell are both women, Mary and Martha. It was probably the former who commissioned this curse invoking suppurative disease and infestation. The previously unrecognized motivation for the curse appears in lines 5–6, where the victim's affliction is specifically intended to prevent her forthcoming marriage. The same disease is wished upon a man in a text from the Institut français in Cairo (text 101), written by the same scribe. Contrary to the opinion of the original editor, the folded papyrus was surely not worn as an amulet, but, following the standard practice, was inserted in an older burial. It is this corpse who is urged to "rise up in your anger" and inflict his own worm-infested decay upon Martha. While the spells of the Cairo bones make use of the spirits of death to compel the ghost's assistance, the Aberdeen and French Institute spells invoke archangels and saints for the same purpose.

TEXT

Maria. ʼ

Michael, Gabriel, Souleel! ʼ You must bring her away by the method of an ulcerous ʼ tumor. Arise in your anger, bring her 5 down to a painful end, to put ʼ aside marriage, and send forth (?) punishment, ʼ she pouring forth worms, (that is,) Martha. ʼ My lord Jesus Christ, you must bring her ʼ down to an end. Yea, Jesus Christ, you must 10 dissipate her hope ʼ so that no one desires to assist her. † † †

101. Jacob's curse to give someone an ulcerous tumor

Text: from the Institut français d'archéologie orientale, Cairo
Description: papyrus, folded seven times and then four times to form a small packet; 18 x 15 cm; perhaps from Akhmim, fourth–fifth century. This text was written by the same scribe as the text from Aberdeen, as is evident from peculiarities of dialect, spelling, handwriting, format, and content

Bibliography: Roger Rémondon, "Un papyrus magique copte"
Translator: Robert K. Ritner

Less clear than the related text from Aberdeen (text 100), this curse was perhaps commissioned by a certain Jacob against one Hetiere (?) whose deceased father, together with Mary, archangels, martyrs, and St. Zechariah, is invoked as guarantor of the desired punishment. (Roger Rémondon assumes that Jacob is the victim of the curse.) Spelling is particularly poor in this text, often ignoring the direct object "him" of the curse. Ironically, this results in the literal translation: "You must bring me away by the method of an ulcerous tumor." All commands are directed in the masculine singular, whether following feminine or plural names. If this is not an error, it would indicate that the commands are directed only to the ghostly assistant with whom the text was buried (the father of Hetiere?), and the sacred names (Mary, Gabriel, etc.) would be invoked for compulsion as at the beginning of the spell. One should thus understand: "(By) the fifty-four hundred martyrs, Mary, Souleel, Gabriel, Jesus, and Zechariah, you (the ghost) must bring him away."

TEXT

Jac[o]b † † †

☧ Michael, Gabriel, Souleel! The sickle that comes forth from heaven must come down for destruction in the form of an ulcerous tumor. The father of Hetiere (?), who is in the father, you must bring (him) away ⁵ by the method of an ulcerous tumor. Fifty-four hundred martyrs, <you must bring (him) away> by the method of an ulcerous tumor. Mary, who bore Jesus, you must bring (him) away by the method of an ulcerous tumor. Souleel, Gabriel, you must bring him away by the method of an ulcerous tumor. Arise in your anger, in a painful end. ¹⁰ My lord Jesus, you must bring him away by the method of an ulcerous tumor. My holy father Zechariah, you must bring (him) away by the method of an ulcerous tumor. † † † Every [. . .], you must bring (him) down to a painful end, . . . against the father of Hetiere (?). Jacob. (**verso**)

You must bring (him) down to a [painful] end. My lord, you must [bring] him [away by the method of an] ulcerous tumor.

102. Victor's curse to silence Semne

Text: Würzburg 42

Description: rag paper, 11.5 x 14.7 cm, tenth century

Bibliography: Wolfgang Brunsch, "Ein koptischer Bindezauber"

Translator: Robert K. Ritner

Side A of this text contains the scribe's aborted first attempt to sketch the vignette subsequently completed on side B. This image represents the intended object of the spell with outstretched arms and is drawn beneath the label "Semne daughter of Coron." Side B, translated here, contains the revised version of the figure with similar labels, fifteen further lines surrounding the central image, and eleven lines comprising the main incantation. The sheet thus depicts the figure of its victim hemmed in by the names and symbols of avenging angels and spirits declared to be in complicity with the person employing the spell.

TEXT

(S)emne daughter of Coron

. . . mnt (?)		They agreed
Opone (?)		with each
Lap.os (?)		other, namely:
Eidiel	(drawing of Semne)	Phos, 5
Michael		Phipon,
Gabriel		Katasat,
		Phouthe,
		Zloo

Hrophot, Hraguel, Asuel, Saraphuel, Anael:

I adjure you (pl.) today by your powers and your names ¹ and your images and your amulets and your ¹ places where (you) are, that you watch over, ¹ that you guard, that you aid Victor ⁵ son of Koheu, in the presence of Semne daughter of ¹ Coron, and that you give to her mouth and her nose a closing ¹ and a silence and a weariness and a bridle and a ¹ shackle and a dumbness to her mouth, (that is,) Semne daughter of Coron, ¹ with respect to {with respect to} Victor son of Koheu, and ¹⁰ (do likewise to) everyone who thinks evil against him. Yea, yea, yea, ¹ at once, at once, at once!

103. Invocation of a power for blessing and cursing

Text: Cologne 10235
Description: papyrus, now in two large and several small fragments, about
30 x 17 cm; perhaps from Ashmunein, probably sixth century
Bibliography: Manfred Weber, "Ein koptischer Zaubertext aus der Kölner
Papyrussammlung"
Translator: Robert K. Ritner

This invocation of a spirit or angel shows the ease with which the
practitioner may move from so-called white to black magic, requesting
the power of divine condemnation and cursing as well as love and favor.
Some of the same motifs found here may also be noted in Coptic Mu-
seum 4960 (text 120).

TEXT

[. . . I pray and I invoke you today, the one who is great] in
his power, who has [been placed over the bolt (?)] ' of iron. He
has loosed [. . .]. ' May [he] send forth the great finger ' of his
right hand which [. . .] 5 the earth. I invoke [you] today so that '
[you] shall come to me in this place where [I] am for you, ' and
you shall reveal yourself to me [. . . before ' my (?)] face, and you
shall speak with me by mouth, [and you shall come] to me ' with
your two decans, namely Archon and Lamei, 10 [and you] shall
bring me the love and the favor and the peace ' that the father
gave to his beloved, his only begotten ' son when he was coming
into the world, saying to him, ' "Go in my peace, and come back
in my peace. ' My peace that is mine I give to you." I invoke 15 you
also today so that you shall bring to me the ' condemnation and
the hatred that the father sent upon ' [the] head of Satan so that
he separated himself [from him] and he overturned him ' [. . .]. I
[adjure] you [by your . . .] ' and your image and [your amulets of
health] 20 and the places [where you are and the . . . by which
you] ' burst the cloud [. . .] ' everything concerning which I invoke you, ' whether good or evil, ' yea, for I adjure you yourself, by
your great power 25 and your wreath of glory that is upon your
head. ' Yea, yea, for I adjure you by your manner of going ' in and
your <manner of> going out and your manner of ' going up and
your manner of coming down, ' that you shall listen to the words
of my mouth and you shall act 30 in accordance with the actions

of my hands in every work of mine—every one, ' whether love or hate, whether favor or ' condemnation, whether binding or loosening, whether killing ' or vivifying, whether assembling ' or scattering, whether establishing or 35 [overthrowing], whether good watching [. . .].

104. Apa Victor's curse against Alo

Text: Michigan 3565

Description: papyrus, 8 x 11 3/4 in., sixth century or earlier

Bibliography: William H. Worrell, "Coptic Magical and Medical Texts," 13–16

Translator: Stephen H. Skiles

Michigan 3565 is a general curse on Alo and peripherally on Phibamon. Alo's offense is not outlined in the text, but she seems to have aroused heated animosity in Victor. The content of the curse is fairly stereotypical, being noteworthy only in its Christian character. Particularly telling are the references to the Law and to Deuteronomy and Victor's title Apa (a clerical and monastic term of office). Resort to ritual revenge was not precluded by office in the church.

TEXT

✝ Al ✝ o ✝ daughter ✝ of Ae ✝ se ✝ ✝ and Phibamon '
E O O O O O O O '

I write; I adjure you, Saot Sabaot, that you receive this incense ' from me (?) and speak a word to my advantage over Alo daughter of 5 Aese. Ha[. .]ouel, you must bring loss and grief. ' May the adjuration go (up) to heaven until you act on my behalf against Alo ' daughter of Aese. Upon Alo shall (the) curse (of) god come. May the ' darkness take her, Alo daughter of Aese. From afar (?) you (pl.) must beg ' this one (?) to receive this incense from me (?). The curses (of) the Law and 10 Deuteronomy (?) will descend upon Alo daughter of Aese. ' May hunger and misery rule the body of Alo ' and Phibamon. May their eyes (?). . . . May furnace flame(s) ' come from the mouth of Alo daughter of Aese. May ' (the) curse (of) god descend upon Alo and her entire house(hold). [15] May the fear of death be in Alo's house. | May you make them bedridden. Amen, Amen, Sabao[t]! | Apa Victor son of Thib[am]on.

105. Curse against a woman's face and work

Text: Heidelberg Kopt. 681
Description: parchment, 29.5 x 10.9 cm, late tenth century
Bibliography: Friedrich Bilabel and Adolf Grohmann, *Griechische, koptische und arabische Texte*, 400–404
Translator: David Frankfurter

This text is a curse ritual which involves the "persuasive" burning of a spell written on an ostracon. The ritual is meant to be directed against a woman (line 45) and apparently against her business (line 46). The hoped destruction of her "face" may be an indication of the importance of the victim's beauty, or it may testify to the continued importance of burning imagery in Egyptian curse spells. The ritual has two main sections: Lines 1–27 invoke "favor" for the client or professional, while lines 28–52 provide the curse itself. The iconography was meant to be copied onto the ostracon.

TEXT

(ring signs and stars)

Arom Arom
Aromao
Aromana
Aromanael [5]
Araka
Aratamou
Ario Arina
Aratabne
Araksa. [10]
For
I (adjure) you
today,

(drawing of
an exalted
figure)

Yao Sabaoth
Eloei Elemas
Machepot
Salabaooth [5]
Marchechou
Panieilou
Chael
Achael
Off(ering): mastic, [10]
alouth,
storax,
moustiaten.

Ario,
the great one of [15]
the cherubim
of the father
almighty,

(by) the voice emitting from the mouth of the father almighty: '
Look, I shall send the angel before [20] them. N. child of N., give
him favor in the presence of Michael. ' Stand me on the right until
I give him favor, ' so that you complete them. Give favor. Give ' silence. Give peace. Give submission (?). ' Give a congregation.
Give love. Give every craft. [25] You must complete them for me
quickly, yea, at once! '

Ario Arina Aroma Aromanael Arasa '
Aromao Tharmaoth Marmarioth, for I (adjure):

Bok   Barouch

(drawings of four demons)

(written on the body of one:)

Ouchou [30]
Mar '
The flame from which they are made,
the ' wrath of the scorching wind,
the hatred that ' scatters, OTHOR, 400 angels, '
with hatred and strife and loathing, in the face of N.
        daughter of N., [35]
so that at the moment that (I) write your ' names,
        along with your figures and ' your amulets, on a
                potsherd, and light a fire ' under it until it is
                charred,
you must char ' the face of N. daughter of N., in the
        presence of the entire generation [40] of Adam
        and all the children ' of Zoe,
        the small and the great, '
        the rulers and the powers and the kings and ' the
                judges,
that at the moment that they ' see the face of N. daughter of
        N., when they hate it and [45] its speech,

her face must receive no favor, and ' her work must not be
established for all ' eternity, at any time, yea, at
once! '

Write (it with) menstrual blood on the potsherd; ' sleep behind (it). Set (it) upon three 50 bricks; set fire under them. Bury
(it) ' at a crossroad. Off(ering): olive pit; ' consume (it in) the fire.
It is done.

106. Curse to bring seventy different diseases upon a victim

Text: Yale 1800
Description: papyrus, 32.4 x 24.1 cm, sixth or seventh century
(so Petersen, with hesitation, and Birger A. Pearson)
Bibliography: Florence D. Friedman, *Beyond the Pharaohs*, 198; Theodore C.
Petersen, *A Collection of Papyri*, 48-49 (no. 62), with a photograph showing
an incorrect arrangement of the fragments prior to conservation
Translator: Stephen Emmel

*An interesting feature of this malevolent incantation, the purpose
of which is to curse an enemy with a wide variety of lifelong illnesses, is
that the practitioner intends to achieve his or her goal by exercising a
power of restraint over the "angel of the holy altar," preventing it from
performing its liturgical duties (lines 6–8) until it acts first on the practitioner's behalf. Despite the severity of the curse, the practitioner re-
serves the right to rescind it at will (lines 16–17), which suggests that
the curse might be used as a means to achieving some other goal than
the victim's chronic misery. The text is edited for the first time in the
Appendix, "Previously Unpublished Coptic Texts of Ritual Power in the
Beinecke Library, Yale University."*

TEXT

. . . nas, Psatael, I adjure you, Ennael, ' whose left hand is
raised upon the chariot ' of the holy father, and Asaroth, the great
guardian angel, ' who protects the tabernacle of the almighty father. 5 I swear today, angel of the holy altar, ' that neither are you

free nor are you at liberty to go up to god, ' nor to make offerings or to offer worship to the true judge, ' nor to approach the lord, until you have stood upon ' the body of N. child of N. and brought upon it suffering and sickness 10 and illness and rheum and fever and pain ' and weariness and depression and chills ' and tumors and demonic madness and ' seventy different diseases. Let them come and bring them down ' upon the body of N. child of N. all the days of its life, 15 such that neither sorcerer nor sorceress can help ' it or heal it out of my clutches until I myself, N. child of N., ' have mercy on it. Act and complete for me the full will ' of my mind, the desire of my soul, by your mighty power. Asmodeus ' the demon! Yea, yea, at once, at once! . . . th! 20 Phelloth! Athes! At once, at once!

107. Possible curse through the power of Shafriel

Text: Yale 882(A)

Description: papyrus, 9.1 x 15.9 cm, sixth or seventh century (so Birger A. Pearson)

Bibliography: Florence D. Friedman, *Beyond the Pharaohs*, 199

Translator: Stephen Emmel

The purpose of this spell, which invokes the aid of the angel Shafriel, is obscure: perhaps either to bring misfortune upon an enemy (so that "he deprives himself of his peace," that is, his peaceful life) or to conjure up someone or at least someone's voice ("come to me, voice of . . . "). According to the first interpretation, which is reflected in the present translation, the person casting the spell would recite or recopy it, supplying his or her own name in line 5 and again at the end of the spell, in the last instance using the expression "the voice of. . . . " Because the victim remains anonymous ("he . . . himself . . . his" in line 3), the practitioner would probably specify him by somehow physically associating him with the charm (that is, the inscribed piece of papyrus): by hiding it in or near his house, for example, or by bringing it into contact with some personal possession of his.

According to the alternative interpretation, line 3 refers either to the conjurer's object, whose peace (that is, the peace of death) must be disturbed if he is to be conjured up, or to the angel, whose requested exertion on the conjurer's behalf is thereby emphasized, and "voice of N." (understood to be vocative rather than in apposition to "me") may be interpreted as providing an opportunity to specify the person being conjured. The purpose of the audience thus summoned would be to gain supernatural assistance for the conjurer's wishes.

The text is edited for the first time in the Appendix, "Previously Unpublished Coptic Texts of Ritual Power in the Beinecke Library, Yale University."

TEXT

† Come to me today, the one mighty in his power, ' Shafriel the angel, who (?). . . . ' Bring about changes (?) today until he deprives himself of his peace. ' I beg and I entreat 5 you, I, N., ' so that you might come to me, the voice of N.

(eight-pointed star and triangle)

108. Curse against Joor and his wife

Text: Michigan 1523
Description: papyrus, 8 1/2 x 12 1/2 in., perhaps fourth or fifth century
Bibliography: William H. Worrell, "Coptic Magical and Medical Texts," 3–4
Translator: Stephen H. Skiles

Michigan 1523, like other curses, is a juridically oriented spell. The use of specific names and the use of only one side of the sheet indicate that this was a commissioned piece rather than a leaf from a book of generic spells. This suggestion is strengthened by the phonetic links of the opponent's name (Joor) to his intended fate and to the instrument of that fate. The legalistic tone of this text may well be an indication of an important reason for the resort to ritual power as a solution to personal problems: a frustration with the legal system, whether because of slowness, cost, or inadequacy to deal satisfactorily with specific problems. Although Joor seems to be the offender, note that the effects of the curse are seen in terms of the aftermath of the death of the head of the household, establishing a link and perhaps parity between Theodora and the wife of Joor.

I beg, I invoke, I pray to you, holy martyrs, ' I, Theodora, the injured party. ' I lodge this suit against Joor and his wife, ' throwing myself on your goodness, so that 5 you may do as I would with Joor and his wife: ' Beat them and bring them to naught. ' (Let) the curse, the worm, and scattering ' overtake them. (Let) the wrath of god overtake Joor ' and his wife and all that is his. 10 (Let there) be a great distress and outcry ' on his house and wife. ' [May] you lay your hands on [him]; may the strong hand ' and the exalted arm come upon them quickly, ' (upon both) him and his wife. Holy martyrs, 15 may you speedily decide in my favor against them. ' [Send] your powers and miracles. ' Holy [martyrs], may you decide in my favor ' [. . .] Koloje.

109. Curse to separate a man and a woman, using necromancy and a blade-shaped parchment

Text: Louvre E.14.250

Description: parchment, 33 x 15 cm at the base; about tenth century

Bibliography: Étienne Drioton, "Parchemin magique copte"

Translator: Marvin Meyer

The text is written on a parchment sheet (hence the statements "I am the sheet" in the text [or, "I am the strong one"(?)—see the notes]) in the shape of a blade, and it was meant to sever the relationships among a man, a woman, and her mother. The man from whom the woman is to be separated may be the woman's husband (note line 27: "I am that which separates a woman from her husband"). This man, named Sipa, is depicted on the verso of the parchment as a person in despair; he has pulled out his hair. In order for the spell to work, an adjuration of the dead is to be made, and the spell itself is to be placed under the head (under the pillow?) of Sipa. For another text of ritual power that is directly related to a blade or sword, note the Sword of Dardanos (in Hans Dieter Betz, The Greek Magical Papyri in Translation, *69–71).*

Louvre E.14.250

(*recto*)

TEXT

Tartari, Saro, ¹ Ptha, Astabias, ¹ Thatha, Eibethatha, ¹ Lahki-maia, Kaha, ⁵ Alaha, Litlit, put ¹ hatred and separation, ¹ Narakoui,

(symbols)

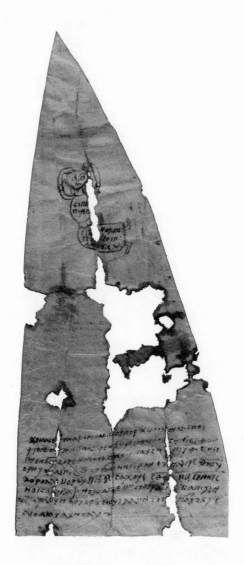

LOUVRE E.14.250

(*verso*)

Eistibia, Toeu, ' Rechorichor, Omar, put hatred ' and separation between Sipa son of Siheu, ¹⁰ and Ouarteihla daughter of ' Cauhare, along with Cauhare. They must not be able ' to look at each other's faces, yea, yea! '

(drawings of creatures, with ring signs and letters)

I am the [sheet that] separates a friend from <his> friends. ' I [am that which separates . . .] sea. I am that which separates [15] [Sipa son of Siheu from] Ouarteihla daughter of Cauhare, ' so that at [the moment that] your figures and your ' amulets and your names will be placed [at the] door of this tomb of these Greeks ' and you [bring the] dead to Sipa son of Siheu, pass by ' the door of the [house of] Ouarteihla daughter of Cauhare, for ever. [20] It must not be capable of being [opened . . .]. You must put on it hatred ' and [separation . . .] and discord [between] Sipa son of ' [Siheu and Ouarteihla] daughter of [Cauhare], ' so that [. . .] each [other], for ever. ' Yea, [yea], put [hatred and separation between] Sipa son of [Siheu] and [25] Ouarteihla [daughter of Cauhare, along with] Cauhare. '

(more drawings and ring signs)

I am the sheet that separates a brother from his brother. ' I am that which separates a woman from her husband. I am the ' sheet that separated pharaoh from his nation ' on account of the magnitude of his powers. I am that which raised Judas against— Ei— [30] Jesus until he was crucified upon the wood of the cross. I am that which ' went up to heaven, calling out, "Eloi Ei Elemas. ' I myself am god." As for [me], then, I beg and I invoke you today, ' Apolle, that at [the] moment that you are placed under the head of S[ipa], ' bring hatred [and] separation for Sipa son of Siheu, and pass on [35] from [. . .] of Ouarteihla ' daughter of [Cauhare]. ' (verso)

(drawing of Sipa)
(on the figure:)

Sipa ' son of ' [Siheu. Put]
hatred [40] between [him] and '
Ouarteihla '

(blank space)

so that you may put hatred and separation and discord and ' dispute between Sipa son of Siheu and Ouarteihla ' daughter of Cauhare. They must not be able to look at each other's faces, [45] for ever, through the power of these names, which are Thkou, '

Aorolle, Morau, Pithos, Sachous, Sth . . . em, Sennes, ' Nokoknia.
Put hatred and separation between Sipa son of ' Siheu and Ouar-
teiouhla, along with her [mother] Cauhare, ' yea, yea, at once, at
once!

110. Curse to harm a person through the use of wax dolls

Text: Heidelberg Kopt. 679

Description: paper, 19 x 13.9 cm, eleventh century (so Viktor Stegemann)

Bibliography: Friedrich Bilabel and Adolf Grohmann, *Griechische, koptische und arabische Texte*, 410–14

Translator: Marvin Meyer

After an abrupt beginning this text proceeds to call for the destruc-
tion and separation of a foe and his house. The instructions for the use
of the spell feature wax dolls that are to be manipulated. The text in-
cludes extensive drawings, ring signs, and letters front and back.

TEXT

He must not take and he must not give his . . . pledges that
he has established ' for him(self), except for . . . that returns '
with destruction, with hatred, with scattering, with reversal, ' with
every hindrance. I adjure you today, 5 you strong angels who always stand before him, ' whose names are Yohau, ' Lohep, Achab,
Aou, Asel, Akalata, Kasis, ' Keria, Acharah, Salani, Paplin, you '
who will be with N. child of N.: You (must) take favor 10 [from]
his presence (and) turn (?) the favor of his dwelling place '
around with destruction, with hatred, with scattering, with ' reversal. The people among all those [who] dwell ' in it must not be
able to look at him in any way. ' Yea, yea, at once, at once! It is
done.15

Draw the figure and the amulets on a metal sheet. Dip them.
Wipe off oil ' on (or, from) the face (of) your enemy. Bury them at
the door. Draw again. ' Put it in a doll of wax that is not melted. '
Place it at the door . . . put in the nail(?). ' It is scattering, it is

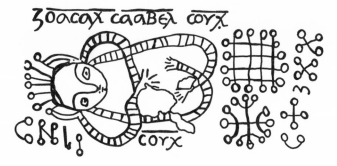

(reverse side:)

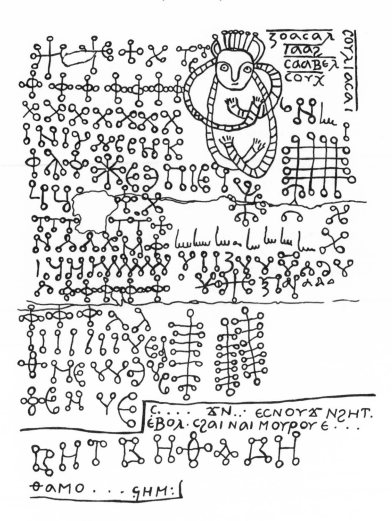

destruction, it is separation in [20] this way. Put it in two wax dolls.
' Turn them back to back. Wrap them in a ' mummy cloth. Smear their face(s) (with) menstrual blood, (with) the oil on the metal sheet, on the face.

Off(ering): . . . that is evil. It is done. '

---

111. Curse to disable the body of an enemy

Text: Berlin 8321

Description: papyrus, 10 x 16 cm

Bibliography: Walter Beltz, "Die koptischen Zauberpapyri," 72; Angelicus M. Kropp, *Ausgewählte koptische Zaubertexte,* 2.25–26

Translator: Marvin Meyer

Berlin 8321 consists of an invocation of the power of Sourochchata against an opponent of the person using the spell. The purpose of the spell is to disable the opponent by undoing the muscular integrity and strength of that person's body, thereby paralyzing him.

TEXT

> . . . I invoke you (sg.) today, ' Sourochchata.
> You (pl.) who are strong in your power,
> who ' bring the rocks to dissolution, '
> let my voice come to you.
> You who dissolve [5] the sinews and the ligaments and the joints,
> you are to dissolve ' the sinews of N. for all ' time.
> Yea, I adjure you,
> I adjure ' your names and your amulets. '
>> Yea, yea!

112 Spell for the return of a stolen object and a curse upon the thief

Text: Vienna K 8304 (Rainer, AN 201)

Description: paper, 7 x 7.3 cm, tenth–eleventh century

Bibliography: Viktor Stegemann, *Die koptischen Zaubertexte,* 82–84; Walter Till, "Zu den Wiener koptischen Zaubertexten," 219–20

Translator: Marvin Meyer

This spell is used to retrieve a stolen vessel and simultaneously place a curse upon the person who stole it. The power invoked is that of Ruphos, said to be the angel of Egypt. The text is written in the form of a spiral from the center outward. Werner Vycichl, "Magic," 1508, calls this spell a "ghost trap" and compares it to incantation bowls. The final words "Yea, at once, at once, at once" are written in the corners.

TEXT

I adjure you today, O Ruphos, the angel who is appointed ¹ over the land of Egypt, that you spread your ¹ wings over any place where this bronze vessel ¹ is, until you return it (to) the place from which it came. ⁵ East and west, north and the sea, if it ¹ lies buried underground, you must make it visible; if it is hidden ¹ in a place that is closed, you must return it to its place. Let not ¹ the earth be firm beneath the person who has taken it, let not the sky shelter him, ¹ and let no peace at all come to him, ¹⁰ yea.

Yea, at once, at once, at once!

8

SPELLS WITH OTHER APPLICATIONS

INTRODUCTION BY RICHARD SMITH
TRANSLATIONS BY STEPHEN EMMEL,
DAVID FRANKFURTER, MARVIN MEYER,
PAUL ALLAN MIRECKI, AND RICHARD SMITH

This chapter of spells with "other applications" reveals the difficulty of trying to classify miscellaneous texts of ritual power. Indeed, this chapter calls into question our general category "ritual texts," as we include, at the end, a fortune-telling book. While the preceding chapters draw together obvious groupings—rituals for healing, protection, sex, and cursing—what do we call this group, the first few of which have no clear function?

The bulk of the texts in this chapter might be considered as spells for personal enhancement, since they aim to attract good things to the user. One spell is to be used to increase the user's business clientele (text 117), two are for developing a beautiful singing voice (texts 121–22), another seems simply to involve heavenly blessings (text 113), and several use variations of a set formula: Perform every wish of my mouth, of my hand, of my heart, and of my soul (texts 118–20).

Two spells, on the other hand, have hostile intent. Berlin 8322 (text 116) attempts to dominate adversaries by calling up the dark powers of the underworld, and London Oriental Manuscript 1013A (text 123) is for something we all have wanted at one time or another: to make a barking dog be quiet.

113. Spell invoking Bathuriel and other heavenly powers

Text: Cairo, Egyptian Museum 49547
Description: ostracon, 40 x 24 cm
Bibliography: Louis Saint-Paul Girard, "Un fragment de liturgie magique copte sur ostrakon"
Translator: David Frankfurter

This text essentially consists of a liturgy hailing and adjuring a series of heavenly figures. Specific invocations to the sun, the seals of Adam, and the soldiers and battlements of the heavenly Jerusalem show a thorough syncretism among Egyptian and Jewish traditions, all within a manifestly Christian text. The descriptions of heavenly liturgy in lines 21–29, evidently meant to have an invocational or even imitative function in performance, may thus be compared to the "heavenly liturgies" of Qumran and the Gospel of the Egyptians from the Nag Hammadi library. But the text's "magical" aspects are also apparent: Besides the invocations, there are two personal requests to sanctify and presumably empower containers (of liquid?—lines 14–15, 33–34), much like the "illumination" rituals in other texts of ritual power. The text's appearance on an ostracon might imply a function as charm or talisman. The ostracon therefore clearly demonstrates the vast borderland between formal liturgy ("prayer") and independent, practical ritual ("magic").

The editor of this text, Louis Saint-Paul Girard, has provided both a literal transcription of the text, with its peculiarities of spelling, and an interpreted transcription, with improvements and clarifications.

TEXT

> † Hail, El Bathuriel, giver of ¹ power,
>> as he replies to the angels! ¹
> Hail, Adonai! Hail, Eloi! Hail, ¹ Abrasax! Hail, Yothael!
> Hail, ⁵ Mizrael, who has beheld the face of the father ¹
>> in the power of Yao!
>> Spell

> I adjure you (pl.) ¹ by the first seal,
>> which is put upon the body ¹ of Adam.

I adjure you by the second seal,'
    which is upon the limbs of Adam.
I adjure you 10 by the third seal,
    which seals the kidneys' and the heart of Adam as he
        lies upon the earth, '
    until Jesus Christ guarantees him in the hand of his'
        father.

The father established him,
    he breathed into' his face,
    he filled him with the breath of life.
Send me 15 your breath of life into this vessel.

Amen Amen Amen!' Sousa Sousa Sousa!
I adjure you by the three cries,
    which' the son sent forth from the cross:
Eloi Eloi' Elema Sabaktani,
    which means, God, my god, why have you forsaken'
        me?

Holy, holy, holy!
Hail, David, [the one] who is the father 20 of Christ,
    who sings in the church of the firstborn child of
        heaven!
Hail, ' David, divine [father, with] this ten-stringed kithara
    of joy,
    as he sings' within the veil of the altar' with joy!
Hail, Harmosiel, who sings within the' veil of the father,
    while echoing behind him (stand) those upon the
        gate 25
    and those within the wall!

The tribes in the twelve worlds' hear them (or, him?),
    rejoice, and' echo him:
Holy, holy, [holy]! One holy father!
Amen, ' Amen, Amen!
Hail Ab[. .]ais [in] heaven and earth!' You praise!
    Spell

Hail, O sun!
Hail, twelve little children 30
    who shelter the body of the sun!

Hail, twelve bowls ' filled with water!
　　They filled their hands (with it).
　　They cast (it) toward ' the rays of the sun,
　　so they shall not burn the fruits ' of the country.

Fill your hands.
(Cast your) blessings downwards upon this ' chalice.
　　Spell

Hail, O four winds of heaven! 35
Hail, O four corners of the world! '
Hail, O armies of heaven!
Hail, ' O earth of the inheritance! '
Hail, O garden of the saints ' [of] the father!

One holy father! 40
[One] holy son!
One holy spirit! '
　　Amen.

114. Invocation of Orphamiel

Text: ostracon, Moen 34

Description: ostracon, 25 x 11.5 cm

Bibliography: Marvin Meyer, "O. Moen 34: A Second Look"; Willy Clarysse, "A Coptic Invocation to the Angel Orphamiel"; Pieter J. Sijpesteijn, "Two Coptic Ostraca from the Moen Collection," 96–97

Translator: Marvin Meyer

This ostracon (reinterpreted by Marvin Meyer and Willy Clarysse) invokes the angel Orphamiel, who is well known from other Coptic texts of ritual power and who is commonly associated with the index finger of god's right hand. (On the power of god's finger see Exodus 8:19; Luke 11:20; also Exodus 31:18; Deuteronomy 9:10; Psalm 8:3.) A similar reference to god's finger is found on an ostracon from Hermopolis (modern Ashmunein), lines 6–7: "[For] I adjure [you] by the finger of god . . ." (see Karl Preisendanz, Papyri Graecae Magicae,

2.233). *For another text that offers translations of names of power see Heidelberg G 1359 (text 37).*

TEXT

✝ You are Orphamiel,' the meaning of which is: the great' finger of the father.

115. Spell of summons, by the power of god's tattoos

Text: Rylands 103

Description: paper, 15 x 8 cm; illegible writing on reverse

Bibliography: Walter E. Crum, *Catalogue of the Coptic Manuscripts in the Collection of the John Rylands Library, Manchester,* 53; Angelicus M. Kropp, *Ausgewählte koptische Zaubertexte,* 2.211–12

Translator: Richard Smith

Rylands 103 is a short, mostly illegible spell of unclear purpose. Still, it has some attractive features. The one casting the spell appears to identify himself or herself (the gender of the divine power in such texts is not necessarily tied to the gender of the user) with Mary, the mother of Jesus. In a rather exotic image, the seven holy vowels of the Greek alphabet are tattooed across god's chest. This same motif is found in London Oriental Manuscript 6794 (text 129). We also have forms of the names Ablanathanalba and Akramachamari. Some divine power is being adjured, but we cannot tell who or for what purpose from what survives.

TEXT

. . . My mother is Mary. The breast . . . the breast from which our lord Jesus Christ drank. In the name of the seal that is traced upon the heart of Mary the virgin; in the name of the seven holy vowels (?) which are tattooed on the chest of the father almighty, AEEIOUO; in the name of him who said, "I and my father, we are one," that is, Jesus Christ; in the name of Abba Abba Abba Ablanatha Nafla Akrama Chamari Ely Temach Achoocha!

I adjure you by the sacrifice of your only begotten son, Jesus Christ, Rabboni, in the way that you sealed the cup.

116. Spell for power to dominate adversaries

Text: Berlin 8322

Description: papyrus, 34 x 21.5 cm

Bibliography: Walter Beltz, "Die koptischen Zauberpapyri," 72–74;

Angelicus M. Kropp, *Ausgewählte koptische Zaubertexte*, 2.16–19

Translator: Marvin Meyer

Berlin 8322 is a text by means of which an individual can obtain power to dominate an opponent. The first part of the text depicts a descent into the underworld to approach an apparent ruler, Louchme. The archangel Michael, too, is summoned, and the person employing the spell is told to go to the realm of the west (in Egyptian thought, this is the world of darkness and the dead) to obtain the services of three powers of darkness, Elouch, Belouch, and Barbarouch. The apparent threats directed to the power if it does not comply with the expressed wishes of the practitioner (lines 11–16) are also known from other texts of ritual power.

TEXT

[. . . 'I am (?)] indeed (?) weaker than the weak, I am stronger than the strong. ' [. . . have] not found power, but I shall find power. ' [I have gone] down to the underworld and have found Louchme. 5 [. . .] fiery throne [. . .]. 'If you ask [. . .] them. '

I said to him, I [do not] ask ' [for these things] nor for other [things] from you, ' but I ask for all of [your power] upon my power 10 [and] upon [my] right arm, that . . . ' [my adversaries not] come near me. If ' [. . .] my adversaries from coming near, I shall restrain '[the sun] in the east, the moon in the west, the Pleiades ' [in the] middle of the sky, until Michael comes 15 [and] places his power upon my power and upon ' [my] right arm.

Michael came and I apprehended him (?). 'He said to me, What are you asking for? I shall do it for you. If you ask for ' [the] stone, I shall break it. If for iron, I shall turn it into water.

I said ' [to him], I do not ask for these things nor for other things from you, 20 [but] I ask for all of [your] power upon my power ' [and] upon my right arm.

But then he said to me, ' [Go] to the west, under this mountain, under this mountain peak, ' down to Elouch, Belouch, Barbarouch.

They ' said to me, What are you asking for? I shall do it for you.

I said to them, ²⁵ [I] ask for all of your power upon my power '[and] upon my right arm.

[They] said to me, ' [Even if] you did not find us and did not find our names and did not ' find [this] corner of the earth, you would invoke our names over it, and [throw (?)] it before N. child of N., (**verso**) and take the power from his [body (?)] and ' . . . , yea, yea, at once, at once, quickly!

117. Spell invoking Michael and the heavenly powers for business and other purposes

Text: Moen 3
Description: parchment, 34 x 19.5 cm
Bibliography: Helmut Satzinger and Pieter J. Sijpesteijn, "Koptisches Zauberpergament Moen III"
Translator: Marvin Meyer

Moen 3 is a text that summons the archangel Michael and other powers to accomplish the wishes of the owner of the spell. In particular Michael is asked to bring together people of the village to patronize the shop of the person employing the spell. Included among the familiar words and formulae are two series of twenty-four variations upon the names Michael and Priphiel. The invocation on the flesh side of the parchment contains a recipe for an offering and is decorated with a drawing of an ouroboros (that is, a snake biting its tail, as a symbol for the eternal nature of the universe).

TEXT

I beg, I invoke ' you, lord, our ' god, almighty, ' that you send ⁵ to me from heaven ' Michael your archangel, ' that he may gather ' together the people of this village ' into the shop ¹⁰ of N. child of N.

Spell

Glory be to you ' and your holy words ' concerning [this]. At once! '

. . . to be victorious, [1]
   [A]BLANATHANABLA [15]
   [A]BLA(NATHANABLA) [1]

   Michael
   Michael
   Mikael
   Mikroel [20]
   Manael
   Mariel
   Macharael
   Marmarael
   Marmariel [25]
   Marthael
   Marthiel
   [M]a[.].thael
   [M]euchiel
   [. . .]archiel [30]
   [. . .]iel
   [. . .]iel
   [. . . e]l
   [. . .]ekel
   [. . .]moel 35
   [. . .]ouel
   [. . .]el
   [. . .]uthel
   [. . .]
   M[. . .]el

(drawing of a standing figure)   AEEIOUO
                                                    EEIOU
                                                     EIO
                                                      IO
                                                       I

         (ring signs and letters)

   AEEIOU[O]
    ENOU
     NI

Priphiel
Prikael
Prophiel
Priroel
Priel 45
Prothiel
Proeiel
Parthoel
Paonel
Pechoel 50
Praiithel
Paruthel
Pamathiel
Parithoel
Pakathiel 55
Papothiel
Perachamiel
Perthathaniel
Pemadel
Pena[.]del 60
Piroua[.]el
Pemoel
Periel
Pemnamouel,
those whom I know 65
and those whom ' I do not ' know. '

AKRAMACHAMARI '

Gather together for me 70 all the people of this village, ' great (and) small, poor (and) ' rich, male and female. ' Gather them all to N. child of N., ' to the shop of N., 75 of N. child of N., at once, at once! '

ABLANATHANABLA ' (be) on my right,
AKRAMACHAMARI ' on my left, '
DAMDAMENNEOS behind 80 me,
SENSENKEBARPHAGES ' before [me]. '

Left: [1]
AKRAMACHAMARI [1]
AKRA(MACHAMARI)
(flesh side)
I invoke [1] you,
Eleath [1] Elmath Tet [1] Atonai,
    2 (times),
you who have [5] come forth from the mouth of the father
    who lives for ever.
You [1] are the one who is blessed,
    is glorified,
    who lives [1] for ever.

I invoke you,
Uriel Takuel [1] Akuel Peskinther Anaoth,
the king [1] of those who are blessed,
who fear the one who is within the 7 curtains, [10]
whom the 7 firmaments surround,
whom the 7 angels surround, [1]
standing before him,
who are these:
    [. . .]ael, Suri[el], [1] Raphael, Rakuel, A[. . .].
[. . .] speaks, [1] and the earth moves,
he gives . . . ,
in the hollow of whose right hand [1] is engraved the
    great invisible name [15] which is called out,
    Atonai, 7 times,
    Holy, 7 times, [1]
in whose hand are the souls of people,
    of men and of [1] women,
    of reptiles and of beasts
    and of those that terrify [1]
    and of those that go upon the ground.
I myself call [1] upon you.
        Spell

ABLANATHANABLA [20]
AKRAMACHAMARI
SESEKENPHARPARAKE [1]
Aon, 7 (ring signs) [1]
    Myrrh . . . [1]
    7 times, myrrh . . . 7, bones . . . [1]

Offering: storax that you bring forth (?), 7, bones of a falcon, 25 7, . . . 7 . . .

(ouroboros, with ring signs, letters,
vowels, and the names
Yao, Sabaoth, Ma . . . , Yak,
Yak, FTH, etc.)

118. Spell invoking a thundering power to perform every wish

Text: from the H. O. Lange collection
Description: two parchment sheets, 15 x 12.5 cm, seventh century
Bibliography: H. O. Lange, "Ein faijumischer Beschwörungstext"
Translator: Marvin Meyer

*H. O. Lange states that he has acquired in Egypt several frag-
ments that constitute two sheets, on which are written two texts of ritual power, one in Fayumic Coptic (translated here) and one in Greek
(twenty-eight lines on 2 verso). The Coptic text is an invocation of divine power, particularly that of Petbe (compare Cairo 45060, line 74
[text 128]), a thundering deity whose name means "Requiter (compare
the Greek deity Nemesis; Shenoute links Petbe with Kronos). Especially
noteworthy is the concluding portion of the text, in which the user
threatens that a lack of divine compliance will bring about the sum-
moning of several deities of coercion, including Greek gods and goddesses (lines 58–62).*

TEXT

Listen to me today, you who ' listen;
listen to my words, you who ' hear;
incline your ear to me, ' quickly;
listen to the words 5 of [my] mouth,
since I call to you, ' quickly,
that you may [hurry] to send to me, '
    quickly and immediately,
and rouse ' [Pet]be, who is in the abyss,

and raise ' up for [me] Sachlabari,
that he may come
and accomplish 10 my heart's wish
and fulfill ' the desire of my soul.

Yea, ' shake yourself today with your power, '
Petbe, who is in the abyss;
shake yourself ' today with your power,
Thunder, 15 the true name of Petbe,
since I drag you ' up to ask you,
Horasias ' Phankapres,
you whose front part looks ' [like] a lion,
whose rear part looks like a ' bear,
whose head is fixed in heaven, 20
whose feet are fixed on the earth,
the big toes ' of whose feet are bound with the 2 rings ' of
the abyss. ' (1, verso)
For you are Shouth Mashouth ' Selouch Malouch,
the one with the head of 25 bronze,
the one with the teeth of iron.

Yea, for ' I adjure you,
Niabathaba Betha ' Bethai Both,
        7 times.
Yea, for ' I adjure [you]
[by] the first pillar ' that the father almighty 30 established
        under the [first] corner ' that is in heaven,
that you may obey ' the things of my mouth,
and pursue the things of my hand,
and accomplish ' for me the wish of my heart
and the desire ' of my soul,
        immediately, 35 quickly,
        Horasias Phankapres.
            Spell '

I invoke you, who lifts up the ' two cherubim of light,
Marioth, ' Gabriel, Amuath, the sun of the underworld, '
that you obey the things of my mouth,
and pursue 40 the things of my hand,
to take my case (?) ' before the presence of the father,
who ' is bound with the white belt at ' his waist,

bound with the scarlet cord ' on his breast, [45] (**2, recto**)
whose iron wand is in ' his right hand,
who is addressed ' with the great secret name, '
Hamouzeth Beth Athanabassetoni, '
whom the wind and the air [50] and the darkness obey. '

Asamuth, I invoke your true name ' 21 times, day and night,
that ' you come and reveal yourself to me,
and accomplish for me ' the wish of my heart
and the desire of my [55] soul.

If you do not obey the things of my mouth ' and pursue the
things of my hand,
I shall call upon ' Salpiax, Pechiel, Sasmiasas, ' Mesemiasim,
and the seventy gods, and Artemis ' the mother of
all the gods, and Apollo [60] and Athena [and]
Kronos ' and Moira, Pal[las and] Aphrodite, '
Dawn, Serapis, [Ura]nos:
Seize him, ' bring him before me,
to . . . [P]etbe, who is in ' the abyss,
yea, with the power. . . . [65]
Go, ' go, at once!
It is [done].

119. Spell invoking Aknator the Ethiopian to perform every wish

Text: Coptic Museum 4959
Description: papyrus, 60 x 16 cm; in six large and several small fragments
Bibliography: No edition of the Coptic has yet been published; see Aziz S.
Atiya, ed., *The Coptic Encyclopedia*, 5.1501 (photograph); Marvin Meyer and
Richard Smith, "Invoking Aknator the Ethiopian"
Translator: Richard Smith

*In this spell a figure named Aknator the Ethopian is summoned,
perhaps as an angelic power, to aid someone. The person employing
the spell promises to perform several ritual acts (fasts, incense, unleavened bread) so that Aknator may in turn perform the powerful deeds
requested.*

The top of fragment 1 shows a drawing of a standing figure, with arms raised in the "orans" or praying position, and wearing a tunic. Around his head is a wreath-halo. Across his body are three rows of ring letters. Writing to the right and left of the figure describes the procedure for a bowl divination (a bowl filled with water, a bit of oil poured over the surface to suggest the forms by which the deity appears to the diviner). This writing and the first three lines of the spell proper are in a rather crude hand. At the fourth line of the spell a practiced and fluid hand shows that a different scribe has taken over the writing. Perhaps we have a case of the sorcerer simply elbowing aside his apprentice. Not only was the first scribe's handwriting labored, but there are several confusing sequences of letters that make translation difficult (see the notes).

The bottoms of fragment 4 and fragment 5 contain a drawing of Aknator's head and shoulders. He has a large curly hair style and, apparently, wings. Underneath the figure are some fragments with ring signs and some untranslatable lines, again in the crude hand.

The vertical fiber side of the scroll contains a short spell of compulsion. It invokes "the great cherubim who stands in the presence of the father . . . to bring her, person N., to the place where I dwell, N. child of N. In the name of the great strong ones, whose names are these: Hor[. . .]os [. . .]leleth .avthea [. . .]!" Perhaps here we see the four lights, Harmozel, Eleleth, Davithe (and Oroiael), common in Sethian Gnostic texts. The spell ends with instructions, "You write it," and a list of ingredients including "wormwood, dark myrrh, and new wine." Next is a drawing of a figure bearing a shield and several staff-like objects. Lines ending in circles radiate from his head, and under his feet is the name Sabaoth. Next, on fragments 3 and 4 (vertical fibers), the crude hand begins a spell in Greek to the father almighty, then switches to Coptic. It is difficult to determine the nature of the spell, but it tells of voices coming out of the air, "saying, Acha Archa Char. . . . "

Fragment 5 vertical is blank.

Fragments 6 and 7 vertical contain some drawing, ring signs, and ingredients, "frankincense, mastic."

The manuscript, then, contains, on the horizontal side, the spell of Aknator the Ethiopian, with a drawing at the top and bottom. The vertical side contains another spell, a drawing, a spell, and another drawing. There are thus three spells on the manuscript and four drawings.

Horizontal side

Fragment 1

(*to the right of the figure:*)
You spoke twenty-one times, from time to time: three times in the day, three times at night; the libation bowls being upon a brick; the libation bowl having oil—provide a certain amount of oil.

(*to the left of the figure:*)
[. . .] libation bowl . . . of glass . . . it being filled with grace . . . new; it is filled with flower water [. . .].

(*across the figure, in ring letters:*)
K E M O I
. . I O E O E
EA M M S

(*beneath the figure:*)
I invoke you today, Aknator the Ethiopian. I have inquired whether the offering of heaven is at the foot of the earth, whether he was bringing in those who are . . . in the hells.

I invoke you today so that you will come to me, N. child of N., at this place [where I] dwell, today, before my feet.

New pot with flower water in it. I will stop fasting and pour it upon it [. . .] every [night] and every day I will invoke you. [. . .]

Fragment 2

. . . your fasts. I shall sweeten your incenses. I shall eat your unleavened bread, and perform your orders [. . .] that you perform my heart's desire, this which my fortune desires.

Yea, it happens! Yea, it happens!

. . . which I cast under my feet. Therefore I shall perform your heart's desire. You complete the requests of my [. . .] in [. . .].

Fragment 3

[Go down to your father] Bethlolo.

[I will] decapitate him and I will cut off his head. I will even trample upon it with my feet, because I perform your heart's desire. I complete the request of your soul. Yours is. . . . If you come to us with your great power, I shall perform your fasts, [I shall] sweeten [your] incense, and I shall eat your [unleavened bread]. . . .

Fragments 4–5

[. . .] power of [your] name and your amulets and the place where you dwell, that you perform the things of my hands and complete the things of my mouth, in every place where I invoke your name. Do not [. . .], do not depart.

Yea, yea, at once, at once, at once!

[Akna]tor the Ethiopian †

COPTIC MUSEUM 4959, *fragments 4–5* (rearranged)

Fragment 6

(ring signs)

Fragment 7

(very fragmentary)

COPTIC MUSEUM 4960

120. Spell invoking the divine to accomplish whatever is requested

Text: Coptic Museum 4960

Description: papyrus, 18.5 x 13 cm, sixth–eighth century (?)

Bibliography: No edition of the Coptic has yet been published; see Aziz S. Atiya, ed., *The Coptic Encyclopedia*, 5.1502 (photograph)

Translator: Marvin Meyer

Coptic Museum 4960 includes three texts, two of papyrus and one set of parchment fragments, that present very similar spells and drawings of powers. One of these papyrus texts (the one conserved to the left) is translated here. Another such text is in the collection of the Beinecke Library of Yale University (see Theodore C. Petersen, A Collection of Papyri, 43; much of the actual invocation is paralleled in Cologne 10235 [text 103]). This text from Coptic Museum 4960 portrays three powers (decans? compare Cologne 10235, line 9) and presents an invocation (addressed to a single power) that asks for help for a variety of enumerated requests.

TEXT

(ring letters)

Archon   Abrak . . [ ]   Lamei

(drawing of power)   (drawing of power)   (drawing of power)

I	that you lis-	binding	(or)
adjure	ten to the	or	watching
you by	things of my	loosing,	well,
your	mouth and	whether killing	whether what
power	accomplish	or making	is hidden
of your	the things of	alive,	or what
name	my hand,	whether	is visible.
and	concerning	gathering	
your	everything	or scattering,	
figures	about which I	whether	
and	shall invoke	establishing	
your	you, whether	or overthrowing,	
amulets,	what is good		
	or what is	whether	
	[evil],	favor	
	whether	or	
		disgrace,	

121. Spell for a good singing voice

Text: Berlin 8318

Description: papyrus, 48 x 22.5 cm; eighth century (so Beltz)

Bibliography: Adolf Erman, *Aegyptische Urkunden aus dem Koeniglichen Museen zu Berlin*, 1.9–10; Walter Beltz, *Die koptischen Zauberpapyri*, 68–70; Angelicus M. Kropp, *Ausgewählte koptische Zaubertexte*, 2.109–13

Translator: Richard Smith

Just as the angels sing "Holy, holy, holy" before the lord of hosts, just as the tongue is sweetened by drinking honey, so the person casting this spell hopes to obtain a beautiful singing voice by invoking these comparisons. Although there is little information on professional singers from this period, we know that several entertainers were as lavishly rewarded in antiquity as they are in our day. Many hopefuls must have desired the fame and fortune that came to such stars, as there are several such spells for a good singing voice (see Yale 1791 [text 122] and London Oriental Manuscript 6794 [text 129]). The person with the pleasing voice could have sung in a theater, at private parties, or, probably, right on the street as a forerunner of the medieval minstrel. The economics of the Byzantine period are exposed by his requesting payment in commodities rather than coin: wheat, wine, oil, and clothing. Oil was especially useful, for cooking, illumination, and bodily ointments.

This spell is also helpful in showing us some of the actions that accompanied the invocation. The one using the spell invokes the trinity down into a chalice into which he has mixed the potion (recipe given), and then drinks it. And, while he is about the business of casting a spell, why not add a request for protection from "magic," and then, for good measure, throw in the final petition of the Lord's Prayer?

TEXT

> One holy father, [Amen]!
> One holy son, Amen!
> One holy spirit, Amen!
> Jesus, Amen! ' Savior, Amen! Sabaoth, Amen!

I invoke you (masc. sg.). Hear me in your mercy, ' O you who are the true god, god of the lights, god of heaven and earth,' lord god almighty, father of our lord Jesus Christ, the one before whom stand the ⁵ cherubim and seraphim, before whom everyone trembles, singing ' to him, praising him, and saying, Holy, holy, holy, ' lord Sabaoth, heaven and earth are full of your holy glory! ' Truly indeed, god almighty, heaven and earth are full of your ' glory.

Hear me today. I am the son of N. I invite ¹⁰ you down upon this wine and this honey that is mixed with water ' in this chalice that is before me, so that you might bless it ' with the blessing from heaven above, your holy dwelling place. And it might become ' for me a strong breath and most superior voice, and ' sweet as wild honey. And let my tongue be straight. ¹⁵ Let it sing beautifully in the presence of men and women and children ' all together, by your great holy name and also by the unutterable names ' upon it, namely ALAPHABE EPHOUAU SAENOUOPH ' KAAPHPHE KOPH! I adjure you by your names and your powers ' and your amulets, so that you might work your [20] powers upon it and perform for me a good thing without any evil, ' but good for me. When I drink from it, ' let my tongue become exalted like a sweet trumpet ' in my mouth, like raw honey. Let me obtain ' wheat and wine and oil and clothing. Let every [25] magical spell and every potion be destroyed in me for ever. And ' lead us not into temptation, but deliver us ' from evil. Let the holy spirit remain and stay among ' us for ever and ever, Amen. ' . . . in glory and [30] grace. Let them all happen this day of my life, let them happen, quickly, ' quickly!

This is the mixture in the chalice: 21 grape seeds; ' 12 grains wild mastic, with ' a little wild honey diluted with a little Tobe water ' [. . .] and grapes (?) and a torch that burns [35] three days; ' this bit of white wine with a . . . ' on a reed mat with clothing . . . ' at night while you eat bread . . . ' these . . . when . . . write in a book, [40] bind . . . another one, is bound to his mouth . . . ' is bound . . . drink it. '

23. Xanthios; 39. Sisinnios; ' 24. Priskos; 40. Aglaios.

122. Another spell for a good singing voice

Text: Yale 1791 (first text)
Description: papyrus, 37.3 x 25.4 cm, sixth or seventh century (so Petersen)
Bibliography: Theodore C. Petersen, A Collection of Papyri, 38–39 (no. 53), with a photograph (front only) showing an incorrect arrangement of the fragments prior to conservation
Translator: Stephen Emmel

At the top front of this document is a drawing, surrounded by short lines of text, of a winged angel blowing a trumpet. The angel is Harmozel, who is invoked in the spell as "the great ruler." Elsewhere he is often characterized as a trumpeter and as the leader of the heavenly *chorus of praise for god. Here his trumpet emits several strings of letters (probably O D D D and TH TH TH TH TH TH TH).*

The text surrounding the angel concerns the preparation of a chalice for ritual use. It prescribes the ingredients for making ink (lines 1–9), the manner of using the ink to inscribe certain signs on the chalice (lines 10–19, with the signs written on the papyrus to the right of lines 13–17), the ingredients to be mixed in the chalice (lines 20–22, perhaps also 23–24), and probably two ritual actions (lines 23–24). Two additional lines probably refer to a divining bowl and an offering (lines 27–28).

The spell to be recited over the chalice is written on the back of the document. It begins with a series of greetings to heavenly beings, followed by a prayer addressed to Harmozel, whom the practitioner entreats for a beautiful voice. Before reciting the incantation, the practitioner would first have presented the offering and prepared the chalice. Probably the purpose of the black bowl was to provide the angel with a medium in which to give a sign of his acquiescence to the prayer, at which point the practitioner would drink the contents of the chalice.

The text is edited for the first time in the Appendix, "Previously Unpublished Coptic Texts of Ritual Power in the Beinecke Library, Yale University."

TEXT

White dove's blood; ⁶ calamus extract; musk (?). ¹⁰ Writing (?): white reed (?). ¹³ Write these signs ¹⁵ on [the] base of the pristine chalice. . . . ¹⁸ Hang it from your neck. ²⁰

White honey; white wine; Tobe water (?). ²³ Offer greetings (?) 21 times (?), . . . 21 times (?). ²⁵ This is the preparation of the chalice. ²⁷

(drawing of a trumpeting angel; ring signs)

A black bowl, white housht. ³⁰
. . . the face of the father ' . . . .
Greetings, tabernacle of the father and the son and the
    spirit and ' those who dwell in it!
Greetings to the seven archangels ' who surround the glory
    of [the] father!
Greetings, principalities and ' authorities and forces on high!
Greetings, church ³⁵ of the firstborn and those who dwell
    in it! '

Greetings to the powers!

Greetings, cherubim!

Greetings, seraphim! '

Greetings to the twenty-four elders of the heavenly church '
and everyone who dwells in it! '

Greetings to paradise and everyone who dwells in it!

Greetings 40 to the shining sun!

Greetings to the twelve powers ' that surround it!

Greetings to the moon and all the stars!

Greetings, ' you twelve rulers in charge of the hours of the
night! '

Greetings, you twelve rulers in charge of the hours of the '
day!

Greetings, Harmozel, the great ruler, gathering together 45
the heavenly and earthly beings, whose voice the heads (?) hear '
and it sends them after (?) him!

Now I beg you today and ' I invoke you, Harmozel, you of
the sweet sound, ' pleasing like Philemon, you of the sweet voice,
so that ' you will come to me today, I, N. child of N., and stand
upon 50 this chalice that is placed before me, and fill it for me '
with a sweet, pleasing sound, [rising], falling, ' turning about like
a . . . , filled with every sweet melody, ' drawing like a wind, without hoarseness, without shortness of breath, ' without spittle.
Yea, yea, for I adjure you by the left hand 55 of the father, I adjure
you <by> the head of the son, ' I adjure you by the hair (?) of the
holy spirit, ' so that you will abandon wherever you are and '
come to me here in this place where I am, I, ' N. child of N., and
complete for me the will of my mind 60 and the spells of [my
tongue], immediately, immediately! ' Yea, for I swear <by> the
son's left hand, which ' rules the seven stars, with twelve ' stars
crowning his head.

123. Spell to bind or silence a dog

Text: London Oriental Manuscript 1013A

Description: papyrus, 23 x 35.5 cm, about the eighth century

Bibliography: Adolf Erman, "Zauberspruch für einen Hund";
Angelicus M. Kropp, *Ausgewählte koptische Zaubertexte*, 2.14–16; on the use
of cryptography see Frederik Wisse, "Language Mysticism."
Translator: Marvin Meyer

*This amulet contains a spell to bind a certain dog, probably a
watchdog guarding the property of "N., the son of the woman who is
his mother." Thus the amulet was to be used by a thief or someone else
who sought to bind a dog into silence, just as the person claims that he
binds all the earth. To accomplish this binding the person invokes the
great finger of god, Nathanael, as well as elements of the eucharist or
passover, the seven true names (including those of the four living creatures around the divine throne in Ezekiel 1 and Revelation 4), and
Apabathuel, the "true name of Sabaoth." The use of cryptographic writing (indicated by bold type) also highlights the secrecy of the spell.*

TEXT

TIKMARTIK KATHAKARA[. . .] this [. . .] ' written amulet
that Isis has written [. . .]. '

> I bind the sky,
> I bind the earth.
> I bind the [. . .],
> [I bind the four] ' foundations of the earth.
> I bind the sun in the [east . . .],⁵
> [I] bind the moon in the west,
> for I do not permit it to rise.
> I bind [. . .],
> [for I do not] ' permit it upon the earth.
> I bind the field on the earth,
> for I do not permit it [. . .].'
> I make the sky into bronze,
> I make the earth into iron [. . .].
> **[I] ' bind the dog of N., the son of the woman who [is]
> his mother.'**

Again, every bond is bound, unbreakable in this time
[. . .].¹⁰ Further, no family of all humankind that has existed in
the whole generation [of Adam and] ' the whole creation of Zoe
must be able to loosen the bonds that I have [bound and the] '

amulets that I have written against the dog of N., the son of **the woman who [is his mother]**, ' whether female magic or male magic. . . . ' No one must be able to loosen the magic and the amulets that I have [bound against the dog] [15] **of N., the son of the woman who is his mother.**

I place [you] under oath, ' I adjure you by the great finger, Nathanael, that . . . ' is bound with iron and unleavened bread and the blood of the lamb: ' Just as the iron and the stone are not loosened, so no [family] ' of all humankind <that> has existed in the whole generation of Adam and the [whole] creation [of] [20] Zoe must be able to loosen the bonds that I have bound and the amulets that I have [written] ' **against the dog of N., the son of the woman who <is his> mother.**

I adjure [you], ' I place you under oath, by the great finger, Nathanael: Bind, bind, bind, ' unbreakably!

> I beg, I invoke you, the seven true names . . . , '
> the eagle's face—Petagramata,
> the lion's face—Paramera-face,
> the ox's face—So[. . .], [25]
> the human face—Pemeriton,

Apabathuel, the great, true name of Sabaoth, ' the true fearful name: Bind, unbreakably!

124. Amulet with words and names of power

Text: Michigan 3023a

Description: papyrus, 23.8 x 3–5 cm; apparently rolled or folded to form an amulet

Bibliography: The text is published here for the first time

Translator: Paul Allan Mirecki

This amulet is typical of many brief texts of ritual power. It contains versions of several words and names of power for the strengthening of the one wearing it.

... this [5] amulet, [A'K]RAMMA'JAMARI ' AABLA'NAPH-
ANAL[10]BAA ... ' AXEE'EEEEE ' (ring signs and letters), ' Jesus,
Jesus, ' great mind [...], [15] Jesus, Jesus, ' ... ' Michael, ' Gabriel, '
... [20] [Pha]nuel.

125. Another amulet with names of power

Text: Michigan 3472

Description: papyrus, 5.8 x 11 cm; apparently folded; top portion of the
amulet survives

Bibliography: The text is published here for the first time

Translator: Paul Allan Mirecki

*The amulet, only the top part of which remains, contains several
names of angels (apparently including the seven archangels) and divine powers. It must have been used for protection, but we can only
guess.*

TEXT

Yao Sabaoth Adonai Eloai [...] ' Eloai Eloai Eloai ... '
Michael Gafriel Raphael Uriel Su[riel] ' Phanuel Manuel ... because ... [5] O god ... Sabao[th] ' ....

126. Collection of oracles

Text: Vatican Coptic Papyrus 1

Description: papyrus, 12 leaves, about 15.5 x 11.5 cm (the first fragmentary
leaf measures 11 x 2.5 cm); seventh–eighth century (so Émilien Sarti)

Bibliography: A. van Lantschoot, "Une collection sahidique de 'sortes
sanctorum'"

Translator: Marvin Meyer

The sortes sanctorum, *or "lots of the saints," are oracular statements collected together to provide the user a means to foretell the future. Since antiquity, people have consulted Homer, Vergil, and
Judeo-Christian, Muslim, and Chinese sources (compare the* I Ching)
*in order to gain a glimpse of what the future might hold. Frequently
given numerical designations, oracles could be selected by throwing lots,
dice, or knucklebones. This Coptic collection of oracles provides suitably
ambiguous statements about the future, as is typical of the oracular
answers from astrology and divination. For a similar Homeric oracle,
see Hans Dieter Betz,* The Greek Magical Papyri in Translation,
*112–19; in the present volume compare texts 30–35 (six oracular texts
written in Greek).*

TEXT

[21]. Do not [do] again ' [what is finished], ' or something
worse ' might happen to you. [Look, the] ' time has come
[for you to] ' experience compassion [through the peace] '
of the god of the [powers]. '

22. You are safe from [the] ' evil that has [left] ' you. [The lord]
' is with you, [keeping] ' you safe. '

23. What ' . . . '

[24. Now] do [what] you have been attempting [to ' do], and
hurry [to ' get] it finished. '

[25. Do not go] forth but ' [believe] in god: ' You will experience ' something good that you do [not] foresee. '

[26. Separate] yourself from this thing; ' do not hold onto it. '

[27]. A [good] reputation ' [awaits] you abroad. '

[28. . . .] what ' [. . .]. '

29. There [will] be [joy] ' for you at [once]. '

30. This will not happen ' now; rather, it will happen ' in a
little while. '

31. There is great ' danger in this matter. '

32. There will be a great ' opportunity for you [today], ' and
you will find rest ' in it and will be confident ' in the peace
of [Christ]. '

33. Walk in the [commandments ' of] renunciation, and ' [pre-
pare] for yourself a good ' path. '

[34]. Nothing bad will happen ' [to] you from this matter, ' for
[you are] safe. '

[35]. Reject this thing, ' for it is not advantageous. '

[36]. Reject [those who] advise ' you. Their ' counsel is empty and ' very bad. '

[37. Do not] do this thing [again]; ' it is not yet time. '

[38]. Do not do [this thing] again, ' because it is not right; ' it is not yet time. '

39. God will send ' his angel and it will [save you]. '

40. Do not hurry, [for] ' it is not the right moment. '

41. Hold onto ' what you have achieved. '

42. Abandon their ' counsel or you might be put [to shame]. '

[43. Set] your affairs in order at once, for [the] ' right moment is already past. '

[44]. Go out until someone ' will meet you. '

[45]. Remove yourself from this treacherous relationship ' and you will be safe. '

[46]. If you do this, things ' that are bad will happen to you and you ' will not understand them. '

[47. The] god of our fathers ' Abraham, Isaac, ' and Jacob will guide ' [you]. '

48. There is [benefit] ' in the path that you [are taking] ' . . . . '

49. Do not turn [back; ' do] what you have been attempting. '

50. The lord will lessen ' the ordeal that has come upon you. ' Only believe ' and you will be delivered from [it]. '

51. It is god who contends ' and he will repay [you]. '

52. There is great ' danger in this [matter]. '

[53. Do] not forsake ' [the] faith that is in your heart; it is ' of help to you. '

[54]. Do not be afraid of this ' thing. Look, its time ' [is] coming quickly. '

[55]. Do not follow those who ' advise you, and ' do not trust them. '

[56]. Set your heart on god; ' nothing bad will happen ' to you. '

[57]. . . . '

58. This will happen [to you] ' in a little while. '

59. Do not be afraid; no one [will be able] ' to trouble you. '

60. Do not attempt to do [this] ' thing, for it will be ' an obstacle and a [misfortune for you]. '

61. Do this joyfully. ' I shall send [my] ' angel, and it will guide [you] ' and make [your] ' way straight before you. '

[62. A] good reputation ' [awaits] you from afar, and ' [you will] rejoice greatly in ' this matter. '

[63]. The time has not yet come ' [for] you to seek this ' [thing]. If you do ' it, you will be like one who ' [has] been freed from a trap and has fallen ' into a hole. '

[64]. A little longer and you ' will get what you ' seek. '

65. He will give [to you according to] ' your [heart's] desire, ' [quickly], and you will glorify ' god because of [this]. '

66. Wait [very] patiently ' for now; [after] ' this, salvation will ' come to you with [gladness]. '

67. Wait patiently for the ' lord and he will save [you]. '

68. Do not seek ' what has passed [by, or] ' you might be harmed [because of it]. '

[69]. Do not give in ' [to someone who will] speak to you with ' the intention of deceiving you, ' but set your heart ' [on] god, for it is he ' [whose] way is straight. '

[70]. There is grief in this ' matter. '

[71]. Do this thing again. '

[72]. Do not bring an ordeal ' upon yourself alone, ' [for] you cannot ' [bear] it. '

. . .

153. Regarding [trial and] ' testimony. '

[154]. You will win [by going to] ' trial. '

155. What is lost ' will be found. '

156. Leave yourself a little ' time. '

157. The matter will be clear ' shortly. '

[158]. Great . . . '

[159. Let] this go. '

[160. Pay attention] to a [good] ' thing. '

[161]. Renounce this ' thing. '

[162]. It is good for you to do ' this thing. '

[163]. Do not do this. '

[164]. Remember your ' promise and keep it. '

. . .

166. Do not turn [to do] ' this thing. '

167. It is a good ' change. '

168. Great glory [will] ' bear witness on account of it ' . . . '

169. Turn away from ' this thing. '

170. If you do this, something ' very beneficial will happen ' [to] you. '

. . .

[173. It will] not happen. '

[174. Do] the thing; do not let ' [it] go. '

[175]. There will be a dispute; ' after that you will win. '

[176]. Repent; the thing ' will happen to you. '

[177]. You please people ' beyond measure. '

[178]. The matter is safe. '

 [179. It is] a good idea. '

  180. It is a good ' development. '

  181. Regarding something . . . '

  182. [The] carefree life ' is safe. '

  183. Do not tell anyone. '

  184. Do not accept this ' saying. '

  185. There is duplicity [in] ' this matter. '

[186]. . . . '

 [187. Let] this go. '

 [188. You] will be subject to another saying. '

 [189. It] is appropriate for you to benefit greatly. '

[190]. Peace awaits you ' [and] great joy ' comes to you. '

[191]. Look, your beliefs are ' good and they are right. '

[192]. You will win because of this ' saying. '

[193]. This will [not happen]. '

  194. . . . '

  195. What is lost ' will be found. '

  196. Do not be afraid; you [will win] ' in this matter. '

  197. It is appropriate for you to work [hard] ' at this thing. '

  198. The lord will ' finish ' what you have attempted. '

[199]. . . .

     . . .

 [202. Regarding] life and ' [safety]. '

 [203. It] cannot happen. '

[204]. It is you alone who ' trouble yourself. '

[205]. It is not yet time to ' attempt it. '

[206]. This will be found. '

[207]. He will delay its occurrence. '

[208]. Something hidden will [be] ' made clear. '

[209]. Regarding ' . . . '

  210. Let this go [from] ' you and you will live. '

  211. He has not yet done a great ' [thing]. '

  212. He will return . . . ' happen. '

[213]. A dispute ' will arise ' [because of] this matter. '

 [214. Something] good will [happen] ' to you. '

[215. It is] appropriate for you to bear up for ' [a] little while. '

[216]. (There is) mercy for a test. '

[217]. Regarding soundness ' [and] a good foundation. '

[218. Now] do [what] you have been attempting ' to do, ' quickly '

[219]. Do not . . .

PART 3

COPTIC HANDBOOKS
OF RITUAL POWER

9
CoLLECTIoNS
OF ReCIPES

INTRODUCTION BY DAVID FRANKFURTER

TRANSLATIONS BY DAVID FRANKFURTER

AND MARVIN MEYER

The following two texts, along with texts 129–35, represent a common late antique literary genre, the ritual handbook or *grimoire*. In fact, one should consider the first text, London Hay 10391 (text 127), in combination with the other texts in the Hay collection (texts 78–81), which repeat some of the same formulae and have been traced paleographically to the same scribal hand. The resulting cache of multiple leather pieces would thus have made a looseleaf handbook for a diversity of purposes. Both handbooks remind the historian of antiquity of that well-known cache of ritual texts, the Theban library collected by Giovanni Anastasi in the early nineteenth century, which included the London-Leiden Demotic Magical Papyrus and some of the larger texts among the *Papyri Graecae Magicae*.

In a world where ritual dominated the resolution of most crises in life, these handbooks seem to have been a prized component of private collections and the mainstay of temple libraries. Sources refer, for example, to occasional "purges" of such handbooks in as varied times and places as first-century Ephesus (Acts 19:19) and eastern Byzantium (Ammianus 29.2.4). In the broadest sense it would seem that the ritual handbook was a function of literacy itself and of the encyclopedism, the penchant for collecting and compiling, that characterized late antique religious literature.

The following texts belong to Egyptian culture, and it is proper to consider them in light of religious trends in Egypt itself. The catalogs of Egyptian temple libraries disclose substantial collections of spells for everything from festival processions to gynecological ailments (see Garth Fowden, *The Egyptian Hermes*, 57–68). Could such eclectic *grimoires*, as this and the next chapters contain, be regarded as a portable extension of such temple libraries, a digest of applied temple wisdom designed for the itinerant priest? We certainly see the importance and utility of such books of ritual in the fourth-century Egyptian countryside: When a village realizes its holy images are shortly to fall into the hands of abbot Shenoute and his monastic gang, the villagers "went and dug in the place that led to the village and buried some [magical] potions [that they had made] according to their books because they wanted to hinder him on the road" (Life of Shenoute 83, translated by David Bell).

But where the latter story wants to draw as dense a line as possible between the villagers' books and those being produced in the monasteries, the Coptic ritual texts in this chapter suggest a different situation. Not only the use of Egyptian traditions in these texts but also the mere fact of their writing may reflect continuity with Egyptian temple culture. As crude as it sometimes is, the writing of these spells still requires that their scribes, owners, and practitioners be literate and, moreover, be perceived as masters at the pen by clients. In Greco-Roman Egypt literacy in ritual texts was a skill that primarily distinguished the temple priesthood, and even when Pachomius sought to democratize literacy among monks, the scribe maintained a distinctive status. That the monastic scribes held a position in Coptic society similar to that of temple scribes can be seen in various amulets in this volume that place an exalted value upon the very letters themselves: an amulet composed of gospel *incipits* (text 62), a letter from Christ himself (text 61a), a Christian oracle (text 65), a prayer derived from contemporaneous liturgy (text 60), a general prayer for a monastic community (text 58). All of these amulets assume a continuity between monastic scribal culture and society at large, a creative effort to address local needs with the textual and liturgical discourse of the monasteries. We would expect in this context to find at the very least a reciprocity of influence, but perhaps also a continuity in the social role of scribe.

With so many Coptic monks having converted to Christianity as adults and still bearing names like Besa or Ammon, it may not be radical to assume that many of the monastic scribes actually learned their letters in a temple environment and carried with them the knowledge of practical rituals from the temple scriptoria. This hypothesis would, for example, explain the development of Coptic during the course of the Roman period from a language predominantly used for "magic" outside the monasteries to a distinctively Christian tongue within the monasteries. It would also explain the conscious syncretism of Christian, Jewish, and native Egyptian traditions in the spells themselves, for this phenomenon implies exchange among the literate elite of these different societies.

As examples of ritual handbooks the two texts in this chapter seem to show divergent tendencies in the rituals they record. The spells in the London Hay text (text 127) conform to a fairly regular spoken formula, invoking a power or series of powers to remove itself from its normal habitat and descend upon some named substance on an altar (water, oil, wool), after which the ingredients of the ritual are listed in a private shorthand. The emphasis on fairly extravagant invocations here contrasts with the ritual instructions in Cairo 45060 (text 128), which do not use shorthand for ingredients and which generally focus upon the concrete preparation of amulets or other substances. It is likely that the Hay text's "oral" versus the Cairo text's "written" tendency reflect the particular penchants of their owners or scribes. But this should not be taken to suggest that the Cairo text is somehow more medical or scientific than the Hay text. The "coefficient of weirdness" that anthropologist Bronislaw Malinowski observed as a dynamic element in the language of ritual power (*Coral Gardens and Their Magic*, 2.218–23) exists in both texts equally: In the Hay text it is the oral utterances, while the actual gestures in the ritual use fairly mundane oils and plants; in the Cairo text it is the exotic substances themselves—pieces of mummy, bat's blood, embalming salt, a fly—that may have provided this function.

Neither handbook depends overwhelmingly upon Christian traditions in contrast to, say, texts 60, 65, and 69 above. Hay

10391 makes brief use of eucharistic and trinitarian symbolism (1–6), demonstrates familiarity with Christ and the archangel Michael as names of power (103, 105), knows a story of Elijah as an *historiola* (60–64), but finds most value and power in the names of "the twenty-four elders" (78–94). None of these motifs would have required a familiarity with the New Testament as much as with the creative syntheses of Christianity that circulated in Coptic folklore. And it seems that, in the course of this folklore, the twenty-four elders of Revelation (4:4) had been interpreted as individual heavenly powers much like the thirty-six decans of Greco-Roman ritual spells.

Cairo 45060 also makes brief use of a trinitarian formula (11–12) and cites "Jesus Christ" and "god" in an arrangement of sacred names at the end of the text.

While this neglect of Christian traditions might suggest that the handbooks' owners worked independently from the monasteries, it may also reflect the type of language and symbolism that worked in the villages beyond the monasteries. For example, in adjuring heavenly powers to descend and transform ritual substances ("come down upon the chalice of water that is set before me [and] fill it with light for me"), the spells of the Hay text might suggest that the ritual model of transubstantiation had achieved a popularity and authority beyond the walls of monastic chapels.

127. The London Hay "cookbook"

Text: London Hay 10391

Description: leather, 64.5 x 19 cm, perhaps sixth or seventh century (so Walter E. Crum)

Bibliography: Angelicus M. Kropp, *Ausgewählte koptische Zaubertexte*, 1.55–62; 2.40–53

Translators: David Frankfurter and Marvin Meyer

London Hay 10391 is a text with spells and recipes for a wide variety of purposes. The document opens (1–6) with an invocation of the guardians (or watchers); this invocation seems to refer to the Christian trinity (that is, the almighty, the beloved son, and the holy spirit) and perhaps also to the eucharist ("the body and the blood . . . the remnant that lies upon the holy table of the son"). The powers invoked are asked to accomplish whatever the person using the spells might suggest. For example, they are to bring a woman to a man (12–19), give enlightenment and discernment of the mysteries (38–49, compare 50–57), cure sicknesses (for example, headaches, apparently foot and eye problems, bleeding, etc., 57–73), evict a person from a house (76–78), bring favor (78–79), cause the destruction of a dwelling (79–80), inflict derangement (80–82) or animosity between people (82–85) or breakdown (85–86), allow for the takeover of a business (86–89), instigate dispute (89–90) or recrimination (93–94) or defeat (94–95) or separation (perhaps divorce, 95–98), and curse a man's phallus (109–18). In the sections of the text offering remedies for sicknesses are references to Elijah crossing the Jordan River on dry ground (compare 2 Kings 2:8) and to Psalm 70:1.

David Frankfurter and Marvin Meyer were able to examine this document at the Department of Egyptian Antiquities of the British Museum during July and August 1989. The Department of Egyptian Antiquities also generously made available infrared photographs of London Hay 10391. For additional spells from the Hay collection see texts 78–81. On the guardians see particularly Hay 10122 (text 81).

TEXT

> † Amanou, Phourat, Phourani,
> > you three guardians, strong in your power, ¹
> > who guard the body and the blood of the almighty;

Beth, Betha, Betha, '
> you three guardians, strong in your power,
> who guard the body and the ' blood of the beloved
>> son;

Abiout, Karnabot, Karnabiel,
> you three guardians, [5] strong in your power,
> who guard the body and the blood of the holy spirit,
> and the ' remnant that lies upon the holy table of the
>> son,
> in the <place> of the lamb. ✝ '

Entreaty:
> I have invoked you and your names and your powers and
>> your figures ' and your amulets,
> that you leave all the places where you are '
> and come to me, to the place where I am—I, N. child of
> N.—
> and come upon my offering [10] that is set before me, N.
>> child of N., yea, yea, at once, at once!

How to perform it: black pigment; ' new white wine. Everything: storax; calamus extract; three days of fasting, while the
moon is full. ' Every sickness: mastic.

> I beg, I invoke you today—I myself—
> O ' great <one>, strong in your power,
> who is established over the iron bolts,
> calling out ' in this manner:
> You are the one who prepares your ears in . . .
> <I> went into Pellonida [15] through a door of iron.
> I found a beautiful woman, red with black eyes,
> sitting ' [upon] an exalted throne.
> I desired her and called out, saying,
> Come ' to me myself today.
> O great one, strong and mighty in your (masc.) heart,
> arise, go ' to N. daughter of N. and bring her to N. son of N.,
> at this moment, before she is finished—me, N. son of N.—
> that I may be ' with her, immediately, quickly!
> Yea, yea, for I adjure you today,
> by the three decans, strong [20] in their power,
> by whom I adjure you, that I may not disobey them,

whose names are ' Sak, Mesak, Shacha,
that I may accomplish the things of my mouth,
and you may fulfill the things of my hand,
and all the spells ' of my tongue.

He answered, saying,
What do you ask of me today?
I shall give it to you. '
If you ask stone of me, I shall split it;
if iron, I shall break it off;
if roots . . . , I [shall] ' destroy the foundations of the prison.
Miak, I press to ask these things of you . . . , 25
I ask, I invoke you,
that you leave all the places where you are
[and come] ' to this place where I am,
and come down upon the virgin [. . .] oil, '
that it may be for me a prescription for all the things
that I shall undertake, in order to do them—I, [N. child
        of N.]. '

Yea, yea, for I adjure you by your great names,
that I may accomplish the things of my mouth,
and you may [fulfill] ' the things of my hand,
and all the spells of my tongue,
whether good or bad, 30 immediately and quickly—me, N.
        child of N.
For I have observed your fasts and your purifications,
I have [. . .], '
I have offered incense to you with purity,
I have fulfilled your service [. . .], I, [N. child of N.].

[Yea, yea], ' for I adjure you today
by the one who sits upon the throne, this Satan,
[that I may] ' accomplish the things of [my hand],
and you may fulfill the things of my mouth,
and all the spells [of my tongue—me], ' N. child of N.—
for I [adjure] you today.

I adjure you, . . . , that at the moment that you incline
        (your) eye [upon my] right 35 [hand],
and the pad of lamb's wool, and the male . . . and . . . , '

they may be effective for the things that I shall
      undertake—I, N. child of N.—yea, yea, at once,
      at once! '

Mastic; censer of bronze; vine wood; virgin radish oil. '

[. . .]arararaf Chathtou Petakaththa,
I beg, I invoke ' [you], . . .ponros Anbersaou Araraf
      Kaththou Petakaththa Araraf [40] . . . ,
that you deem it worthy today
to leave every place ' where [you] are,
and come down upon the chalice of water that is set
      before ' me,
that you fill it with light for me,
like the sun and and moon, and sevenfold more,
that you ' adorn my eyes with divinity and discernment.
Rouse yourselves, that you may reveal ' all mysteries
that I shall seek through you.
Yea, yea, for [I adjure] [45] you by the great, true name of
      the father,
whose name is Aio Sabaoth [. . .], '
that you come to me today,
down upon the chalice of water that is set [before me], '
that you fill it with light for me,
like the sun and the moon, and sevenfold more,
that [you adorn] ' my eyes with discernment.
Rouse yourselves, and reveal to me [every mystery] '
that I shall seek.
Yea, yea, for I adjure you by your names.
      Spell [50]

Ertha Athrak Kouth Salpiel Tabithia Parek Chiao,
I adjure you [by] ' your names and your garments,
and your places where you are,
[that you] ' yield and come upon my right hand,
and establish your throne— '
the greatness that is in you sits upon it—
and widen the width . . . , '
and shine down upon it,
like the sun and the moon, and sevenfold more,

[and] [55] tell me everything that I seek from you, things hidden and things [revealed]. '

> Write the amulets. Bind them to your thumb. Utter the prayer.

> Off(ering): mas. . . ' maschaton or mela, Choras, Chemera, TH TH TH K (ring signs and letters).

The treatment:

A brain that hurts. ' A foot . . . salt and oil and wine and hot water ' . . . . An eye that is darkened, with kosht and water. Apply these. They will get better. [60] **(verso)**

✝ For a discharge or a flow of blood: As Elijah, about to cross the Jordan ' River on foot, raised his staff with commands ' that the Jordan be like dry land, so also, lord, you must ' drive the discharge from N. child of N., through (the) power of the one ' in whose hand are the keys of heaven, Lagar Gar Gar Aromarkar. [65]

> For everything destructive: an olive leaf,
> UBCHEULBCH (with rings) ASABIS
> SABARABA '

. . . Solkol. The head. Aknaelekou. A guard, Geoge ' . . . in the Psalm: God, give heed to my help; I have been saved through your ' right hand, ' Abracha Abrachao Abrachaoth.

For every spirit [70] of sickness, . . . our doctor: Write on his finger . . . ' and they heal every sickness . . . ' upon me alone (?), to dwell in N., through the letters of N., '

> (signs) '

I beg, I invoke you today, Marmariooth, the one who is seated over [75] all the authorities;

I invoke you today, and your form, which is ' a flame of fire; I invoke you.

A person you wish to leave ' his house: Recite the prayer over wild mustard. Cast it before the door ' of his house. He will flee.

A favor: Write the 24 elders. Bind them to your right forearm. ' It will bring favor.

A place you wish to be destroyed: Utter the prayer over ⁸⁰ wild mustard and salt water. Cast them at the door of his house.

Derangement: ' Write the 24 elders and their powers. Pronounce the prayer over them. Bury ' them by the altar of a place. He will be deranged.

Friends ' you wish to separate from each other: Write the 24 elders and their powers. ' [Pronounce the] prayer over wild mustard. Bury them at the place where they ordinarily come by ⁸⁵ [. . .].

Prostration: Write the 24 elders and their powers and the name of the person ' [. . . reed pen] from a growing plant. He will lie down.

A shop you wish to seize: water [. . .] ' 7 chains of salt. Pronounce over them. Cast them at the door.

A shop ' you wish to work: Write the elders and their powers . . . and ' . . . and . . . Bury them [at his] door.

A quarrel and an argument: ⁹⁰ . . . Bury them at the door of his house.

A . . . ' with wild thyme [and] a reed pen from a growing plant. Bury them at [. . .]. '

. . . give him understanding: Write the 24 elders and their powers. Bury [them . . .]. '

One who thinks evil against you: Write the 24 elders and their powers [. . . ' Bury] them at the door.

One whom you wish to destroy: Pronounce the 24 elders and their powers . . . ⁹⁵ over bathwater and wild mustard. Bury them at the door of his house.

A . . . ' love (?): Pronounce, over virgin oil, your name and hers. Prevail over her . . . ' like her parents, Ararab Thathou Petasjlu. Spell . . . ' the name of the man and the woman. They separate. '

Adonai Loei Marphoueb Atharkala Eloei Yaba ¹⁰⁰ Jerobathaei Meomermathchi Mebiob Emekphob ' . . . Kepri Moesis

Tmese Pekenneh Miacheani ' . . . Atonai Eloai Elomas Sabaoth
Meel ' [. . .] among the angels, holy Michael. '

A secret door; release it by means of the spell. [105]

(ring signs and letters)	For the woman (cross? ring signs) Yaoboth	Boubou, Christ Michaeel ' Aptisis ' Adini ' Marimam '	(drawing of three small standing figures in the praying position)

You who have restrained the heaven and have restrained [110]
    the earth,
who have restrained the sun in the east ' and have
    restrained the moon in the west,
who have restrained ' the store of [fire] in the midst ' of the
    heaven,
you must restrain [. . .] and make his head ' go to the
    place of his foot,
and make his male organ [115] become like an ant that is
    frozen ' in the winter, tiny and frozen,
like a spring ' of water in the winter,
    yea, yea, at once ' at once, 7 times! † (to the left:)

[. . .]bolo Bariana
[. . .]moun Minianto
. . . Barouch
Tupopsta El. . .
Banithe Ban.tal

(ring signs) _____

Mareupel (?)	Icho	. . . FTHFTHFTH
Chamachal (?)	Amachem	. . .
Amman (?)	Namer	. . .
Maiman (?)	Anael	
Subba (?)	. . .	
. . .		

128. A "cookbook" from Cairo

Text: Cairo 45060

Description: papyrus, 113 x 32.5 cm, found at Thebes, in a jar, buried in the floor of a monk's cell

Bibliography: Angelicus M. Kropp, *Ausgewählte koptische Zaubertexte*, 1.50–54; 2.31–40

Translator: Marvin Meyer

Cairo 45060 is another text with a variety of spells and recipes. The opening lines of the document (1–23) contain an invocation or prayer for divine power that includes angelic names, versions of well-known powerful utterances (for example, Ablanatha, Abra, Akramachamario, Semsemlam [compare Semesilam], Sesanke Barpharakes [compare Seseggen Barpharagges], Tameamnoues [compare Damnameneus], and an imperfect palindrome [10]), as well as a reference to the Christian trinity (11–12). This invocation is followed by a series of applications of the power to specific needs. Thus recipes are provided to treat a variety of diseases (including some sort of eye disease, 31–34), to obtain a favor (28–29) or an oracular response (38–40), to weaken a powerful person (40–45) or cause derangement (62–64), to drain a cistern (45–47), to strengthen or destroy a foundation (47–51), to locate or protect valuables or even buried treasure (52–61), to settle a quarrel (64–66), and to help a woman become pregnant (67–69). These recipes frequently include instructions for the precise day (or even time of day) to perform the ritual. The text closes with a reference to the "second spell" (75), along with another recipe, more powerful utterances, and drawings.

TEXT

✝ Athariel Eiphiel Sechrer Naltrothothr Yoranael Ne.ater ¹ Mimmechabatouthel Altheros Bunes Eknel Ekenel Kenel Gereel ¹ Bal Bael Chabrouel Erphanouel Xanael Anax Anael ¹ Eia Eieio Ananael Shanamael Gabriel—three times. ⁵

Then I adjure those of you on the right and on the left, ¹ Ablanatha Abra Akramachamario Sabaoth Atonai ¹ Etone Peloe Abrasax Xakourax Akouri Semsemlam ¹ Taor Salaper Michpeptaphos Athobar Ambaoueth ¹ Sesanke Barpharakes Tameamnoues Yaou Baphrenemon ¹⁰ ATHERARTHIKRAPHIAEUPHRICRAK-

RITHO Niomenelphab ' Oue Mennelphaboue Eieiaeiaei Ha Eieia, the father and ' the son, the holy spirit, Amen—seven times.
Aezouea ' Thariee—six times.
Nanaeiel—seventeen times. '

---

† Yatheael Xekunathanael Thaeie—seventeen times. 15
Chooch, the true name of god, who lives for ever, ' Amen—seven times.
Yea, listen to me in the power ' of Yageia Bathakakabatha-tharioumatha Bathabor ' Soko, thrice holy, for ever and ever, Amen—' seven times.

Listen to me, holy and glorious god, 20 and fulfill for me the request of my heart and the ' petition of my lips, for I am a descendent of Atamas ' Kanlahael Antanael Seblel.
Listen to me, Amen, '
Onototh Aoul, Amen—twelve times. '

---

† For a sickness . . . : Write the amulets on the twenty-fifth of the month. 25 Throw it into the oven of a bath.
For a hindrance: Utter ' the prayer three times over sulfur and pitch ' (and) oil of henna, and thus it will happen. You must prepare it on the fifteenth of ' the month.
For a favor: Write the amulets with the finger of a mummy ' on the tenth of the month.
For deception: Write the amulets 30 on a . . . They are written with bat blood on the sixth ' of the month.
For eye disease (?): (Take) a little aged vinegar, catch ' a sparrow, and write on it the first name of the ' prayer. Fill its eyes with aged vinegar, remove them, and let it go (?). ' You must prepare it on the eighth of the month.
For strain: 35 Take a bronze coin; catch a blue-green ' iridescent fly. Write with it the first name of the prayer. ' You must prepare it on the sixth of the month. Make it full of vinegar. Throw it into the oven ' of a bath.
For an oracle: Utter the prayer ' three times at the time when the morning star rises. 40 The matter will be revealed to you.
For a ruler, to make him impoverished: ' Take embalming salt . . . oil (?) . . . and a piece of ' bread and seven burned . . . and a fragment of a mummy, ' and mix them together. You

must utter the prayer ' over them three times at the time of the morning star, 45 and throw them into his house.

For a cistern, to suck it out: Write ' the amulets on a clay vessel. Throw it into the cistern. ' You must prepare it on the fourteenth of the month.

For a foundation, ' to lay it: Prepare a wax figure. Write the ' amulets on it. Bury it at that place on the eleventh <of> the month. 50 In order that it may be destroyed: Take embalming salt. Utter the prayer over it ' three times. Throw it into it on the twenty-third of the month. '

For something of value, to bring it up: Take hartshorn and essence ' of calamus extract and malakton and juice of the "panacea plant." ' When you recite the prayer, utter over these things, 55 "Flee, all you demons." Put on your head a wreath ' of thorns (?), bind around yourself a belt from fronds of a virgin palm. A ' branch of wild myrtle is to be in your right hand, a wand of . . . ' in your left hand. Write the amulets with ' blood of a white dove. Take hartshorn and put 60 it into it . . . away from you (?) in a cup (?) and do ' what you have in mind. You must prepare it on the second of the month. '

For leading someone astray: Take particles from his head, ' burn them, and throw them to the four winds. Put a little in ' your hand, throw it into the water. He will go to the desert.

If someone 65 quarrels with you: Utter it over oil. Anoint your head at the time ' when you sleep at night, and the argument will go away. '

To make a woman become pregnant: Utter it over dates of a virgin palm, and ' give them to her that she may eat them, and she will become pregnant. Utter it on the ' twenty-ninth of the month.

For a man . . . : 70 Fill your right hand with crystals of salt and present it ' before the sun. . . . Take a . . . , ' strike them on its head over honey water. Throw it into netting. ' Recite over it: '

Heart of a mouse, KELKEB (signs) OPHOOOPHOOPHOO
PETBE ATHE THOTHKK   PHOOPHOOPHOOO
OKNTHA 75

The second spell: ' seven days, when the moon is full; ' tar; juice of the "panacea plant"; ' hartshorn; storax; calamus extract; ' mastic. 80

† LAMON GI

OULAON B

EULAON A

EREKESIEPHTHIAB

RACHARAN

CHARANARARAEPHTHIERTHK

ARARAEIPHTHISIKERENBAR

CHAGSOUTOS

OUSMAHPE

† SIFHB HIPHRO

EFENH

(written on the larger rooster:)
Jesus Christ
god

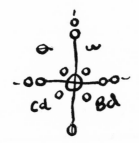 

(written within the ring signs:)
SABAOTH SABA AO

10

A PORTFOLIO OF SPELLS FROM THE BRITISH LIBRARY

INTRODUCTION BY RICHARD SMITH
TRANSLATIONS BY MARVIN MEYER
AND RICHARD SMITH

When Angelicus M. Kropp included the following spells from the British Library in his *Ausgewählte koptische Zaubertexte*, he separated them by genre: blessings, and legends about Christ and Mary. In spite of their diversity, it is more challenging to look at these spells as a group, which is the way their user regarded them. It is clear that they make up a single practitioner's portfolio. Not only is the handwriting the same on all seven pages of papyrus, but the several drawings of Jesus and King David employ the same artistic treatment of the heads, hands, and feet. Further, the first three spells name the user as "Severus son of (Jo)anna." That one man cast all these different spells gives us quite a complicated picture of a seventh-century personality.

London Oriental Manuscript 6794 (text 129) is a spell for obtaining a good singing voice (compare texts 121 and 122). The main power summoned is Davithe, originally one of the four lights of the Gnostics. He is conflated with King David of the Jewish Scriptures (also in text 70; compare text 113), the musician and legendary composer of numerous psalms. In the text and in the accompanying drawing, his hands hold bells and a kithara. The instrument depicted looks less like David's traditional zither or harp than a lute or guitar. The drawing also may depict his rather abstracted genitals, perhaps an allusion to David dancing naked in 2 Samuel 6. It makes sense that our hopeful singer would draw on the power of the Bible's most famous musician. The ring signs on and around Davithe's body convey the astrological character of the figure, and the text calls him "the great decan." The decans were thirty-six astronomical divinities, each of whom presided over ten degrees of the zodiac (although none of their names in this text match lists made by ancient astronomical writers). His "bed," therefore, is probably a constellation.

The text has several outrageous features. God the father has the Greek vowels tattooed across his chest. Lines 16–18 appropriate the language of the *epiklesis*, or invocation, of the eucharist, in which the deity is invoked into the elements and then consumed by the ritualist. Here, the word "grace" is invoked, as it was by the Valentinian Gnostic Marcus in his eucharistic invocation. At lines 23–24, the ritualist tries to coerce the divine powers by using some of Yahweh's old threats against Israel. But how can we resist the appeal of this ancient aspiring singer who sings his own praises at lines 29–39 with such exuberant egotism?

In Oriental Manuscript 6795 (text 130) Severus is pursuing a different goal. He wants to catch a big haul of fish in his nets, and the spell uses the common logic of the *historiola:* Just as the events in the well-known legend happened, so may my own similar desire happen, right now. Two famous biblical fish stories are used. The first is from the apocryphal book Tobit. In Tobit, the angel Raphael helps Tobias son of Tobit catch a fish in the Tigris River (not, as here, "the sea"). They eat the fish but use its innards in potions to heal the blind, drive out a demon, and get the girl. The other legend is from the final chapter of the Gospel of John, where after his resurrection Jesus instructs Peter to cast his net, and Peter hauls in 153 fish.

At the bottom of the spell is a drawing of Jesus, with pole and line, catching a big one. The ring letters across the drawing, "IS, IS, IS," are the abbreviation for his name. This is the figure, *zodion*, mentioned in line 21 together with the amulet, *phylakterion* (the roll of papyrus itself), and these were to be placed (but where? in the boat beside the nets?). If this is an amulet intended to draw fish to itself, the recipes alongside the figure are a problem. Because they call for a glass bowl, water, oil, a lamp, and an incense burner, they relate to a different kind of ritual practice. These items are usually used in bowl-gazing divination.

From the first two spells, what are we to imagine? There is a man named Severus who earns his living as a fisherman. But perhaps he never really wanted to be a fisherman; perhaps he wanted to be a famous singer. So, he is out in his boat, casting his net, and while he casts, he sings lustily, imagining himself surrounded by crowds of adoring fans. A little magic does not hurt the dream.

Although the lost ending of Oriental Manuscript 6796 (2), 6796 (3), 6796 (1) (text 131) may have contained a specific request, this spell appears to be a general protective amulet against the powers of evil. The added spell on the reverse of the papyrus also seems to be a generalized prayer for power and protection. In the first section, the ritualist uses the common self-predication formula "I am" to identify himself with Mary the mother of Jesus. In this exalted state, the ritualist calls on god and all the host of heaven to come to his defense. In the second section the predication is the actual person reciting the spell, Severus.

Other versions of this text are extant in Coptic, Ethiopic, and Arabic. The Ethiopic version claims that this is a prayer made by Mary at "Bartos" (Parthia? see Angelicus M. Kropp, *Ausgewählte koptische Zaubertexte*, 2.127–35). Our text expands in some interesting ways on these other texts. In another Coptic version, Mary has only Michael and Gabriel beside her. The text here, beginning at line 89, contains an elaborate angelic protection spell. Surrounding oneself with angels and deities is a widespread practice of ritual power. Examples exist from Babylonia, ancient Egypt, as well as in the Demotic and Greek magical papyri. A familiar example, still sung in many Christian churches, is the ancient *Lorica* or "Breastplate" of St. Patrick.

Sections of this text may be a "cup divination" (see notes for the translation problems). A cup would be filled with water with a little oil poured on the surface ("dew of heaven, fat of the land") and the deity would be descried in the suggestive patterns of the oil. Here, the deity would be Bathuriel, who is called on to "reveal yourself to me."

The last spell of this disparate collection, Oriental Manuscript 6796 (4), 6796 (text 132) is an exorcism. It describes the fantastic cosmic events that occurred at the time of the crucifixion and includes a drawing of the scene with the two thieves, named

Gestas and Demas (whose names are also found in apocryphal New Testament books). The power of the crucified Jesus is requested to "cast out every unclean spirit of the defiled aggressor."

Marvin Meyer and Richard Smith were able to examine this collection of manuscripts at the British Library during July 1991.

129–32 A portfolio of spells from the British Library

Texts: London Oriental Manuscript 6794; 6795; 6796 (2), (3), (1); 6796 (4), 6796

Description: seven papyrus leaves, of varying sizes, probably the work of a single scribe; "about the year 600" (so Walter E. Crum)

Bibliography: Angelicus M. Kropp, *Ausgewählte koptische Zaubertexte*, 1.29–49; 2.57–62, 89–101, 104–9, 135–43

Translators: Marvin Meyer (texts 131 verso, 132) and Richard Smith (texts 129, 130, 131 recto)

129. Spell to obtain a good singing voice
(London Oriental Manuscript 6794)

TEXT

† Iseosis and Diseos Afriukkekmaruk
Accomplish it, ' Uriel! Accomplish it, Michael!
I adjure you today, holy father ' of the breath of life which is in the height, the talk ' of the angels, the voice of the archangels, the gaze ⁵ of the heavenlies, the song of the father.

I adjure you ' today, Davithea, the one who reclines upon the bed of the tree of ' life, in whose right hand is the golden bell ' and in his left is the spiritual guitar, who ' gathers all the angels into the father's embrace. ¹⁰

I adjure you today, Davithea Eleleth, by the name ' of the 7 holy archangels, Michael, Gabriel, ' Suriel, Raphael, Asuel, Saraphuel, Abael, those who ' stand by the right arm of the father, who are ' prepared to complete his entire will, that you ¹⁵ obey everything I shall say with my mouth and ' perform the things of my hands, and descend upon this chalice ' that is placed before me, and fill it ' with grace and holy spirit, that it might become for me a new growth ' within me. I am N. child of N.

But if you ²⁰ do not obey my mouth or perform the things of my hands, I shall ' turn my face to the east and obstruct the sun in the east (and) the moon in the west. ' I shall fight with the creatures in heaven. ' I shall say to heaven, "Become bronze, do not send dew down ' upon the earth," and (to) the earth, "Become iron, do not bear ²⁵ fruit," until the father sitting on his throne casts beams ' and sends the great decan to me, ' mighty in his power, who is Davithea, ' and he arrives at the pure place in which I dwell ' —I, N. child of N—and he gives me a voice without hoarseness, 30 which does not crack, without roughness, which glides to the heights, as well as a tongue, ' breathily babbling, tagging along after each instrument, ' giving voice to music, which delights the crowd, ' in the middle of whom I sit. You must ' encourage and indulge me before my whole audience, 35 just as the voice of David the guitarist ' resides in the father's tabernacle singing to him. Do not ' let them watch me exit, but let them bring me back ' for a fine encore. Let them shut their shops ' and come to watch my show.

Yea, yea, for I adjure 40 you in the name of the 7 letters that ' are tattooed on the chest of the father, namely, ' A 7 (times), E 7 (times), E 7 (times), I 7 (times), O 7 (times), U 7 (times), O 7 (times), yea, yea, that you ' obey my mouth, at this moment, before it passes ' and another one comes in its place, and you appear to me 45 in a vision that is not frightening, through the power of the holy father. '

Yak Meiak Semiak, the three ' decans mighty in their power, who ' stand over the bed of the tree of life: Give ' sweetness to my throat.

I am Severus son of Anna. 50

Now, now, at once, at once, now, now, now! '

O(ffering) (?) to DAVITHEA RACHOCHI ADONIEL ' Thapsiorie . . . Thapsiorsth ' Thapsiorirar Thapsior Psior 55 Iriaathenneos.

At once, at once, now! '

You write the amulets with real honey, undiluted, unscorched, ' on an alabaster tablet. Wash them in white wine. ' White grapes—21. Wild mastic—21. ' Arabian gum, called "claw." A white robe. 60

Offering: wild frankincense; wild mastic; ' cassia.

Full up!

130. Spell for good fishing
(London Oriental Manuscript 6795)

TEXT

Greetings, father!

Greetings, son!

Greetings, holy spirit! '

Come to me today, O life breath ' of god almighty, from the '
four sides of the earth and the four corners 5 of the entire world.

O you who granted a ' collection to Tobias son of Tobit, ' who
appointed his archangel Raphael for him! ' He walked with him
upon the sea and caught ' a fish; its gall gave light to the 10 blind,
its liver cast out a demon. ' This is his name: Asmodeus.

O you who came to his ' apostles upon the sea! [Peter] said
to him, ' "Lord, we have labored a lot, yet nothing ' has shown
up." The lord said to him, "Cast 15 your nets to the right side of
the boat and you will ' find something." They cast them and discovered one hundred fifty- ' three.

You are the one whom I invoke today, ' I, Severus son of
Joanna.

So you must ordain ' Raphael the archangel for me, and he
must collect 20 every species of fish for me [to the place] where '
your figure and your amulet will [be], ' just as a shepherd collects '
his sheep [in] their sheepfold and blesses them, ' so they neither
become foul nor get lost, and grants favor 25 to them before the
entire race of Adam ' and all the children of Zoe. And strengthen '
the net, so it will not receive, it will not [catch], until ' it delivers
all of them to my hands.

I am [Severus] ' son of Joanna.

Yea, yea, for I adjure [you] 30 yourself.

I adjure you by the seven fiery [angels] ' within whom you
were hidden ' before you wanted to reveal that the universe had '
come into being.

Spell (?)

Yea, yea, for I adjure you by ' your true tabernacle, within
which you were hidden 35 before you created the universe.

Spell (?)

I adjure ' you by Yak Piak Sachorak Ph . . . . . . l ' Sablan Athanabla Achramach[ama]r[ioth]. ' These are the ones who brought you the clay, and you formed ' Adam.

Again, therefore, O god, we have named you [40] "Jesus." You ordained your holy apostles for yourself, ' and they served you. Ordain for me myself, today— ' me, Severus, son of Joanna— Raphael ' your archangel, and let him collect every species of fish for [me], ' from end to end of the [earth], [45] north, south, east, and west, to the place ' where your figure and your amulets will ' be.

At once, at once, at once,
now, now, now! '

(to the left of the drawing:)
A glass pot; ' flowing beneath it [50] immaterial water; ' a lamp; genuine (olive) oil. '
(to the right of the drawing:)
[Calamus] extract; ' wild mastic; ' frankincense; [55] clay censer; ' white charcoal ' . . . .

131. A prayer made by Mary and a prayer for power, with additions
(London Oriental Manuscript 6796 [2], [3], [1])

TEXT

Recto

. . . and said, it is with ' [this] holy prayer that she will re-quest, ' "By your hand, do it," for herself, so that ' every power of the devil, and all his operations, 5 and all his deceptions might be abolished.

Maria, who is ' in the presence of god the father, who dwells in [the heaven] ' of light, raised her eyes up to heaven ' to the compassionate god who resides in the holy [tabernacle], ' saying, "I praise [you. I glorify] 10 you. I invoke you today, O [god who is alive] ' for ever and ever, who is coming upon [the clouds] ' of heaven for the sake of the whole human race, Yao [Sabaoth], ' who is over all the aeons, [Adon]ai [Eloi, who is over] ' all kings, who resides over every power 15 even before heaven and earth had been revealed, ' so heaven will become a throne for him and ' the earth will become a footstool for his ' feet. Hear me today, by your ' holy and blessed name. Let all things 20 be subject to me, those of heaven and those of earth, and those that ' are beneath the earth.

I am Mary, I am ' Miriam, I am the mother of the life of the whole world, ' I am Mary. Let the stone [break], ' let the darkness break before me. [Let] the earth 25 break. Let the iron dissolve. Let the demons ' retreat before me. Let the [. . .] ' appear to me. Let the archangels ' and angels come and speak with me ' until the holy spirit clears my path. 30 Let the doors that are shut and fastened open for me. ' For your holy name shall become a helper for me, ' whether by day or by night. ' Adonel Ermarum Chobaoth Baracha ' Latem Chael Saphon, O true 35 hidden god, hear me today. The one who sits ' upon his exalted throne— ' every spirit of heaven and earth trembles before [him]. They ' fear [his holy name, which] ' is Yao Sabaoth Adonai Elo[i], 40 who, by his power, releases every one who is a prisoner. ' You must destroy every spirit and every power ' of the devil.

Yea, yea, by the power ' of the 24 elders, whose names are Beth Beth[a] ' Bethai Maruel Aruel Eriel Emael 45 Chobaoth

Chane Acham Omarima Sab[. . .] ' Ischosabael Yoel Emiel Sabacho[. . .] ' Latan Archimath Aloel Mu[. . . .] ' Siel Sedekie Bathuriel M . . . . ' Thus those who recline and those . . . [let them] ⁵⁰ tremble before me. ' [. . .] everyone who hates your [holy] name ' [must] fear and say that they have no lord ' to help. But let them say, ' "God our king dwells in ⁵⁵ heaven."

Amen, Amen, Amen!

Jesus Christ, ' who is coming on the day of Anabael Sorochat[a], ' who you are, Phaoba Bakthaniel, the one [born] ' in the mind of the father, Yao Sab[aoth] ' Adonai Eloi Garbael, who ⁶⁰ with his power destroys the bold!

Spell (?)

Amen, [Amen, ' Amen]!

Sanctus, Sanctus, Sanctus! You are holy, 3 (times), who [sits] ' upon the chariot of the [light]-cherubim. ' The four powerful creatures stand by you, ' with six wings. ⁶⁵ Bathuriel, the great fa-ther ' of those of heaven and those of earth, reveal yourself to me, ' you who, by your power, struck the sea ' and its waters <drew to themselves> ' through the power of the holy vowels. ⁷⁰ Sanctus! You are holy, 3 (times), who sits upon ' the seventh chariot of the [light]-cherubim. ' 4 great [creatures] draw it, ' each one of [them having] six wings. ' [Ba]thuriel, the great father of those of heaven and ⁷⁵ [those of earth], reveal yourself to me, Marmarimu ' Mar-mariu Marmar Marmar Marmar ' Marmar Marmar Mar[mar], who, by his power, split ' the sea and [its] churning [waters] drew to themselves. '

AAAAAAA EEEEEEE EEEE[E⁸⁰EE IIIIIII OOOOOOO] UU-UUUUU OOOOOOO

[True] god, ' [hear] me today—me, N. child of N. [. . .] ' and send the 7 ' [archangels to] me, who existed with you ' [before] you redeemed your image Adam, ⁸⁵ [Micha]el, Gabriel, Suriel, Raphael, ' R[ague]l, Asuel, Saraphuel, ' that they may be with me at [this hour]—me, N. child of N.— ' until I finish my invocation. '

[Let Mi]chael be on my right side, ⁹⁰
[Gabriel at] my left [side],
let Suriel ' [sound the trumpet before] me,
[let] Raphael ' [remain in] my heart,
let Raguel ' [crown] my head,
let Asuel give ' [power] and grace to me, ⁹⁵

let Saraphuel give [honor and] glory and grace to me.
I am Severus son of Joanna.

Sunsunges ' [Bar]ph[ara]ng[es be before me], fighting ' on
my behalf!
Yao Sabaoth be upon my head! '
[Adonai] Eloi be upon my heart, calling out 100 [before me]!

O perfect [and complete] power, ' [perform my] whole will,
the [name] of which is ' Akathama Chamaris ' [. . .].

Yea, yea, for I adjure you ' [by the] dew of heaven and the fat
of the land. I adjure 105 you by [the] cup of blessing ' that [is
placed before me . . .] until ' [. . . holy]. I [adjure] you ' [today
by] your very own [head] and your ' [holy tabernacle] and the
power of the [holy] vowels, 110 [which] are these: AAA OOO
MMM. ' [. . .] holy god, I invoke ' [you—I], Severus son of
Joanna—so that ' [you might send] the power of the holy [. . .]
to me, ' and it might come. . . .
(The rest is destroyed. About fifteen lines are missing.)

(London Oriental Manuscript 6796 [1] recto adds the following upside down:)

[. . .] my request ' [. . .]
Now, now! ' [. . .] 7 times.

(ring letters, drawings of small figures, etc.)

A A A A A A A
A A A A A A
A A A A A
A A A A
A A A
A A
A

Verso

✝ I call out to you today,
father 7 (times), Sanctus 7 (times), ' holy 7 (times),
the one who dwells in the holy place, '
fair one, god, invisible one, '
incomprehensible, ineffable,

lord ⁵ god almighty, god of gods,'

    [. . . .]elel 7 (times), Bel 7 (times), Achoubael

        Marmar'[. . .] Eriel Tatriel Miel Uriel'[. . .],

[without] blemish, undefiled,'

[. . .]

[I] invoke you . . . (today?), ¹⁰

    [. . .]oulach Marmaroulach,'[Jesus] Christ,

    [in] whose right hand is a [golden]'standard,

    who is clothed in Battin,'

    [in] whose mouth is drawn (?) the sharp two-edged'

        sword,

    whose entire creation is subject ¹⁵ to him,

        Yotael Yoel,

    who is seated'over the cherubim of light,

        Ab'bachiaox,

    who is seated over the serpent'that is in the abyss.

I entreat you today,'

    . . . l,

    who is seated over the Euphrates. ²⁰

[I] entreat you today,

    Iakiak.

I entreat'you today,

    Suriel Manuel,

    who'[is seated] over the two cherubim of'[light]

    [that are established], that are [glorious].

I entreat you today,'

    [. . . A]thanael,

    whom the ²⁵ [seraphim surround].

Lord god'almighty,

concerning all things that are'in heaven and earth and

    under [the]'earth,

give me power over them all,

    me,'Severus son of Joanna.

Yea, yea, I beg, I ³⁰ invoke you today,

send to me'from heaven the prayer of Koutha'Yao, god of

    the Hebrews,

who is'described in the heavens and upon'[the] whole

    earth as Alamouri Malamouri. ³⁵

[In the] power of Iakiak, Michael, Gabriel,'[Suriel],

    Raphael, Raguel, Asuel,'[Saraph]ael,

[. . . . A]thanael, Youlach, ' . . . . . . Eliach,
Marmarouach.
Sanctus, Sanctus 7 (times), ' lord Sabaoth,
heaven and earth 40 are full of your holy glory,
        holy, ' holy 7 (times).

All you angels of the lord, '
give aid to me today,
        me, Severus ' son of Joanna.
Let Michael stand at my ' right,
let Gabriel stand 45 at my left,
let Uriel sound the trumpet ' [before] me,
let Raphael set a crown ' upon my head,
let Uriel grant favor to ' my face,
let Anael wait upon my heart, '
let [Sara]phael bring grace upon me, 50
[. . .] go to him,
        before ' the whole world
        and the whole generation ' of Adam
        and all the children of Zoe.
[Ya]o ' Sabaoth be upon my head,
Adonaei [Eloei] ' upon my heart,
that they may give me glory [and . . .] 55 and favor and
        thanksgiving [and] excellent ' strength and good
        encounters. '
Come to me, holy immortal one, ' only begotten,
white grapevine ' that branches out upon the throne of the
        father 60 almighty.
Release the one ' who is proclaimed the father.
Unique one in the heavens ' [and upon] the earth,
        Doulaio Yao Sabaoth ' [Adon]aei E[lo]ei Elahar
                Azaba[k]d'[an]ei Ankraten, almighty, 65
who is seated over the four ' cherubim of light that are
        established, that are [glorious],
[stretch] ' out your right hand that is [. . .] ' exalted,
and your invisible, exalted ' arm,
and bless this water and this oil, 70 and seal them.
At the moment that N. child of N. ' will wash with it and
        anoint [himself] with ' this oil,
you must give him favor and ' glory and honor.

Yea, yea, for I adjure you by ' [your] great, true name,
    Adonai Ab.ami 75 . . laei Lamech Lousael [O]rp[h[a] '
        Authiouba Leuei Cherma Psobou. . ' Othiatha
        Sunthiatho Berbener[. . .] ' Latosiel Bel Mouis-
        ephthemel ' Amiel Ha[. . .] Kalou Kaloujal 80
        Lamna Yarech Enolchi Eno[. . . .] ' Toteleuei
        Baithiel Mouth[. . . . .]a ' Athanael,
            Amen!

Sanctus, [Sanctus, Sanctus], '
holy one, unique, Jesus [Christ],
[. . .] ' your father—
    who is beside him ?— 85
[. . .], '
who is extolled in the heavens [as] ' Sem Athanael:
Send me [your] ' holy spirit, healer, [life-giver], '
that it may come down upon this water and this oil.
At the 90 moment that [N. child of N. will] wash with this
    water ' and anoint himself with this oil,
you must give him [. . .]. '
        Spell (?)

In the power of Marimare Matho[. . . . .]'ouploupon
    Matouchamel [. . .], ' god of the Yamer
        Sar[. . . . . . .], 95
. . . all unclean spirits that [go around] ' and travel in the
    [course of the sun] ' and travel in the course [of
    the moon] ' and the stars and the earth and the
    mountains and [the] ' water and the abyss and
    the air.
[Send] 100 to me [. . .] from heaven,
that he may ' burn all [of them . . .],
    [now], ' now, at once, at once!

These are [the] instructions: Ethiopic ingredient; flesh of
a . . . (young animal?); ' storax; calamus extract; juice [of the
"panacea plant"]; 105 wild mastic.
The preparation of [the pot: . . .]: ' Tobe water. If you [. . .] '
in its water, . . . you drink it [. . .]. ' Put it on the ground. Incense: wood of [Abraham]; ' wild myrtle—7; sarapoi—7; [genuine

(olive)] oil [110] for a [lamp] . . . ; wool wick . . . ; ' linen . . . ; '
. . . in the small silver flask in [its dust (?)].

You write [the amulets] ' with blood of a white dove and
[myrtle] ' and white wine; charcoal from white [wood; [115] clay]
censer.

(written alongside:)

Jesus   [Christ]
  A   O

(London Oriental Manuscript 6796 [1] verso adds the following:)

K . . . CHCHEEE † (with rings)

† I call out to you today, '
ABBA ABBA ABBA ABBA ABB[A] ABBA A[. . . , '
    . . .]BBARACH . . . IOURI . . . , '
god of Israel, Jesus, god [. . .], [5]
[who] shatters the counsel [of . . .], '
[. . . stand in] the counsel of [. . .], '
since he grants [favor] and power [. . .], '
[. . .] living god [. . .]. [10]

O(ffering): [frankincense . . .]; ' cassia [. . .]; ' wood of
[Abraham . . .]; ' pot [. . .]. ' The preparation [of the pot . . .]: [15]
laurel [. . .]; ' genuine (olive) oil [. . .] ' purity ' [. . .]; ' cassia
[. . .]; [20] censer [. . .]; ' linen [. . . ' sandals . . .].

132 Spell to cast out every unclean spirit
(London Oriental Manuscript 6796 [4], 6796)

TEXT

[† Sanctus, Sanctus], Sanctus!

The prayer of Jesus Christ that he uttered ' [upon] the cross, calling out (and) saying, "Eloi [Eloei ' La]m[a Saba]ktani Marmarimari," that is ' "God, my god, why have you abandoned me?" Some of them ⁵ said, "Elias," others, "Jeremias." One ' of them took a sponge and dipped it in vinegar, and he (that is, Jesus) took a taste. ' He said, "My father, all things have been completed," and at once he gave up ' the spirit. The heaven opened, the earth quaked, and the bones of those who had ' died arose. In their bodies they went to Jerusalem, and they went (back) ¹⁰ into the tomb.

I am Jesus Christ. I took to myself a ' chalice of water in my hand and gave an invocation over it in ' the name of Marmaroi, the force standing before ' the father, the great power of Barbaraoth, the right ' forearm of Baraba, the cloud of light standing ¹⁵ before Yao Sabaoth. So I poured my chalice ' of water down into the sea, and it divided in the middle. I looked ' down and saw a unicorn lying on a golden ' field, that is named Sappathai.

He spoke ' to me, saying, "Who are you? If thus you stand ²⁰ in this body or this flesh, you have not been given into my hand."

I spoke ' to him, saying, "I am Israel El, the force of ' Yao Sabaoth, the great power of Barbaraoth."

So he ' hid himself from before me.

In the power of the six other names that ' the father uttered over the head of his beloved son when he was hanged ²⁵ upon the cross, saying, "My true name is Pharmen ' Eiboubar Sich Tach Saba Chirinou."

In the power ' of Heretimos, in the power of Hikousad, in the power of Harmichousad, ' in the power of Pharmen, the messenger of the father, in the power ' of Senkeber Kankitha, in the power of Orphaneute and the power ³⁰ of Orphamiel, the great finger of the right hand of the father! '

Arouse yourself, father, in the seventh heaven and the fourteenth ' firmament, and send me Jesus Christ, your only begotten son, ' that he may seal my body and this bowl, for what you will bless ' will be under the blessing, that he may cast out every [35] unclean spirit of the defiled aggressor, from a hundred years ' downward and twenty-one miles around, whether ' a male demon or a female demon, whether a male ' potion or a female ' spell, or a demon that is empty, ignorant, [40] defiled.

I adjure you, father, by Orpha, that is ' your entire body, and Orphamiel, that is the great finger ' of your right hand, that you send me Jesus Christ ' and the seven archangels, whose names are ' Michael, Gabriel, Suriel, Asuel, Raguel, [45] Raphael, Saraphuel. '

O(ffering): charcoal from olive wood; ' censer of white clay; genuine (olive) oil for a lamp; wild frankincense; ' wild mastic; gourd; storax; calamus extract. '

The preparation of the pot: myrtle—7; bay leaves—7; [50] purple mint (?); baked (safflower?) mint; thorns (?)—7; virgin ' palm leaves—7; wood of Abraham—7; garland of artemisia ' upon the pot. '

JESUS CHRIST ' BETH BETHA [55] BETHA YAO SABAOTH
ADONAI ' ELOEIU MICHAEL GABRIEL RAPHAEL SURIEL
ASUEL RAGUEL SARAPHUEL (with rings)

(drawing of crucifixion)

(title on the cross:)

The king

(on the crown:)

AEE
(names of the thieves:)

Gestas   Demas

Troglodytic myrrh.

Draw two figures, | one for the pot, one | for your neck.

Bricks: three, | under the pot without handles. Purity. Put |
royal salt round about you.

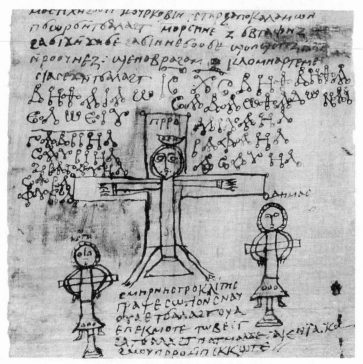

11

THE CoPTIC HoARD oF SPeLLS FRoM THE UNiVERSiTY oF MiCHIGAN

INTRODUCTION AND TRANSLATION
BY PAUL ALLAN MIRECKI

Within the large collection of ancient manuscripts at the University of Michigan there is a group of Coptic papyri which appears to have been a hoard or library of texts of ritual power produced by at least five copyists sometime in the fourth through sixth centuries. Originating from an unknown location in Egypt, the collection was brought to the British Museum by Sir E. A. Wallis Budge in February 1921, examined by the Coptic lexicographer Walter E. Crum in August of that year, and later acquired by the University of Michigan.

Apart from the importance of the texts for the study of Coptic ritual power and related fields, the "wizard's hoard" provides researchers with a rare glimpse into the activities and literary production of a workshop in which several individuals, perhaps working together, produced a written collection of texts of ritual power in scroll, book, and loose-leaf form, including at least one folded amulet (Michigan 1294). Thus, we shall examine the character of this collection rather carefully.

ONE UNANSWERED QUESTION, crucial to an understanding of the nature and original function of the collection, is whether or not some manuscripts have been lost or displaced from the collection. There is no internal textual evidence, such as an index or other indicators of cross-referencing among the texts, which would suggest that the collection as it now exists is either complete or incomplete. Except for the lost opening lines of the two texts copied onto the two smaller scrolls (Michigan 600 and 601), all of the texts that have been copied are complete, and even where a text is copied two or three times within the collection, each of those copies is complete, giving no reason to suppose that a significant portion of the collection is now lost.

Although the collection as it now exists may be intact and in its originally complete form, it has suffered some dismemberment in the modern period since its discovery. William H. Worrell published in 1930 a brief description of the collection along with a partial transcription and translation of one of its texts ("A Coptic Wizard's Hoard"). In that study Worrell noted that the collection consists of eleven manuscripts, and he assumed that it was complete. But while perusing the large collection of Coptic manuscripts in the Michigan collection in the fall of 1986, Paul Allan Mirecki came across twenty-seven fragments of what proved to be the damaged and partial remains of a folded papyrus amulet (Michigan 1294), conserved it, and later identified it as part of the wizard's hoard, thus raising the number of extant manuscripts to twelve. The inventory files for the papyrus collection at the University of Michigan, which quote from Crum's notes (dated August 1921), refer only to the eleven manuscripts numbered from 593 to 603, and state that all manuscripts related to the collection were conserved by C. T. Lamacraft at the British Museum. This suggests that both Crum and Lamacraft knew of only eleven manuscripts. There is thus the possibility that some manuscripts, like the displaced and only recently identified and conserved amulet, had been unknowingly separated from the collection or even lost before they reached the British Museum. In addition, the haphazard inventory numbering system by which the twelve manuscripts are identified (Michigan 593–603 and 1294) exhibits no knowledge of the inner logic of the collection.

Given these limitations on our knowledge of the size of the collection at the time of its discovery, researchers need not assume that it originally comprised a rigid canon of only eight texts on twelve manuscripts. Rather, the contents of the collection probably expanded and contracted as the ritualists, working alone or together, found some texts to be useful (which were then added or retained) and other texts to be no longer useful (which were then removed from the collection). Thus, even if researchers suppose that the collection is complete in its present form, it may represent no more than the complete contents of the collection at only one particular moment, probably the final moment, of its evolution.

THE COLLECTION CONSISTS of twelve manuscripts containing as many as eight texts written by at least five scribes. Some of the texts were copied two and three times by the scribes. Three of the hands are practiced, with one (scribe three) tending toward a "bookish" style, and together they copied a single lengthy text onto a twenty-page codex (Michigan 593). A fourth hand, also practiced but exhibiting a pronounced fluidity in style and varying considerably in size, copied as many as four texts onto a large scroll (Michigan 602), as well as another text onto a now fragmentary scroll (Michigan 600), and yet another text onto a final and now fragmentary scroll (Michigan 601). The fifth hand is clearly unpracticed, demonstrates little physical control over the writing instruments and materials, and copied as many as five texts onto a diverse set of eight papyrus sheets (Michigan 594, 595, 596, 597, 598, 599, 603, and 1294).

It is not yet clear whether the collection was made at one time by the five scribes or whether it gradually grew over a period of time in the hands of several copyist owners. It appears that perhaps parts of two independent and separate collections, one in a single codex format and one in a triple scroll format, were secondarily edited together onto scrap papyrus sheets by a person who had little writing ability. The three scribes who copied the lengthy text onto the codex apparently shared no texts with scribe four, while scribe five copied texts from each of the four other scribes, that is, from the two earlier collections. Worrell has suggested that the three scribes of the codex and scribe five were mutually dependent on a now lost common manuscript, but this issue of the intertextual and literary relationships among the texts cannot be resolved until a detailed philological analysis is completed. Two of the most striking common features among the manuscripts is that none appears to have any significant signs of wear (from practical use) or textual alterations by later hands, suggesting that the collection was used little, if at all.

The amulet (Michigan 1294) provides internal evidence that the large scroll (Michigan 602), or Worrell's proposed lost common source, was used as the sourcebook from which individual amulets were written, suggesting that the other two rolls (of scribe four) and the codex were also used as sourcebooks. The difficult question is why this particular amulet remained with the collection, unless we are to assume that it had not yet been given to a client or that it was personally used by one of the five scribes.

THE CODEX ITSELF is constructed of four papyrus sheets which were cut from a blank roll, stacked, and then folded together to form a standard fourfold quire of eight leaves or sixteen pages (pages 1–16), to which was added a single-sheet quire of two leaves or four pages (pages 17–20). The two quires were then bound together by mere threads which pierced through two small holes in each quire. The fragile codex was then apparently wrapped in two blank codex sheets and secured with braided cord, forming a nearly square twenty-page codex measuring 15.3–16 cm (vertical) and 15.3–17.3 cm (horizontal).

The book of ritual power contains the longest text in the collection, filling the codex of twenty pages with 338 lines (about twenty-two letters per line). It may be outlined as follows:

I. The prayer, invocations, credentials, and requests (1.1–4.14a)
    A. Invocation to the highest deity (1.1–11)
    B. Request ("grant me everything") (1.12–13)
    C. Invocation to the seven archangels (1.14–16a)
    D. Request ("act on my behalf") (1.16b)
    E. The ritualist's credentials ("I am Seth") (1.16c–2.2)
    F. The secret Hebraic names of the twenty-one powers (2.3–9a)
    G. Description of the twenty-one powers (2.9b–15a)
    H. Request and description (2.15b–3.10)
    I. Credentials ("I am Seth") (3.11–17a)
    J. Editorial comment on ritual purity (3.17b–4.1a)
    K. Credentials ("I am Seth") (4.1b–4.8a)
    L. Editorial comment on ritual purity (4.8b–14a)

The text appears to be a compilation of traditional materials from a variety of sources. It opens with a lengthy prayer (1.1–4.14a) that includes the standard elements of invocation, credentials, and requests. The invocations are directed to an unnamed highest deity (1.1–11) and the seven archangels (1.14–16a), the credentials are those of the practitioner (1.16c–2.2; 3.11–17a; 4.1b–8a), and his requests are of a nonspecific nature (1.12–13, 16b; 2.15b–3.10). The prayer includes a traditional list of twenty-one angels with Hebraic names followed by a description of their functions (2.3–9a, 9b–15a), and two editorial comments, or glosses, concerning ritual purity (3.17b–4.1a; 4.8b–14a). The prayer is referred to objectively, is called "a prayer" (1.12; 3.8b–9a; 4.5b–6a [plural]; 11.13), is variously described as powerful (3.13; 4.14b), as capable of "action" (3.15; 4.4; 4.17), as something performed (3.17; 4.9; as a "response" or "request" in 5.8–9), as something "recited" (4.14), as something highly honorable and of great virtue (5.9–10), as efficacious (5.11–19a), as something recited only in ritual purity (3.10–12; 3.17b–4.1a; 4.8b–9; 5.3–8; 11.15b–12.1–5) and in conjunction with specific ritual actions (1.12–13; 4.13–16; 5.19b–11.12a), as containing secret names (4.6, 10–11) and Hebrew names (3.6–7) and Hebrew words (3.14) that are in the language of heaven (that is, Hebrew; 3.7).

The prayer is followed by a series of ritual instructions and promises (4.14b–5.19a) that includes a ritual involving the ingestion of a hawk's egg fried over honey. These ritual instructions are followed by a traditional list of thirty-two prescriptions (4.19b–11.12a), further instructions, promises, and ritual preparations (11.12b–12.5). The text then apparently concludes with nine lines of words of power (12.6–14).

Added to the text is a lengthy invocational prayer (13.1–15.7) that assumes a different mythological structure than the preceding materials. This invocation does not appear to be originally part of the preceding text and may have been added by a redactor. The invocation is then followed by a lengthy section of words of power in ninety-five lines (15.8–20.18).

THE MAJORITY OF the prescriptions involve reciting the prayer (items 1–17, 19–24, 28–32) or copying it onto papyrus amulets (items 18, 25–26). The prayer most often is to be recited over the specifically prescribed sympathetic elements (for example, oil or water), in order to enchant them, after which those elements are to be applied in various fashions (for example, anoint, wash, or drink).

The thirty-two items in the list cover a broad variety of concerns including cures for physical and psychological ailments (1–11, 13–19, 23, 28–29, 32), guarantees for success in a variety of social relationships (12, 20–21, 26, 28–29) and business endeavors (24–25), guarantees for the protection of property (22, 30) and protection from evil (30–31), and a single guarantee for personal revelations through dreams (27).

Several of the healing prescriptions contain reference to the use of sympathetic elements, or concoctions of such elements, which are either ingested (items 1–3 and 32, sometimes including washing) or applied topically as enchanted ointments (items 5, 6, 8, 14–16, and 23). Some of these topical applications may be ritual anointings or placebos with no medicinal benefit, but others may reflect a more scientific approach to the topical application of healing balms and medicaments (items 14–16 and 23). In any case, there seems to be no knowledge of the healing methods from the learned medical profession that one finds, for example, in the tradition of Galen.

We can also note a marked absence of exorcism as a cure for physical and psychological ailments. Except for an obscure reference to protection "from every (evil) thing" (5.17), the text's only possible exorcistic feature is contained in the prayer itself: "extinguish this chaos and this great dragon and all his forms and all his threats" (13.5–7). However, some of the prescriptions in the thirty-two-part list probably suggest that their purpose is to keep away evil spirits by sprinkling an area with enchanted water (items 11, 21–22, 24, and 30).

The thirty-two-part list of prescriptions is loosely constructed according to thematic and catchword associations. The first nineteen prescriptions concern physical and psychological problems, suggesting the first nineteen items may have comprised one of the primary sources used in the compilation of the larger list. The notable exception is item 12, which does not refer to a physical or psychological problem, but is included at this point through a catchword association ("sleep") with the preceding item and so might be a secondary interpolation into an earlier source list. This proposed earlier list of eighteen items is loosely arranged according to the part of the body affected. Items 4 and 5 refer to abdominal problems, while items 6 through 9 apparently refer to problems believed to be related to the head. Items 10 and 11 are related to psychological and behavioral problems related to the dark evening hours (fear of dark and irregular sleep) to which is interpolated item 12, as noted above. Items 14 and 15 apparently refer to breathing problems, while items 17 and 18 apparently refer to perceived mental disorders affecting motor control.

At this point the list moves beyond concerns for physical and psychological problems. Items 20 and 21 refer to social conflict, while item 22 refers to the protection of one's house, sheep enclosures, and property and is probably thematically related to the preceding item (21), which refers to protection against one's enemies. Items 21 and 22 appear to have been conflated in item 30.

Items 24 and 25 refer to concerns for merchants (guarantees for financial profit and safety in water transport). Item 26, which guarantees political favor, is also related to the travelling merchant's concerns for political safety while travelling abroad.

Items 27 through 32 seem to be a concluding set of loosely related medical prescriptions which deal with personal revelations given through dreams (27), a concern for love (28), general concerns for "your men and the men of your village" (29), protection of one's house and walkways (30; compare 21 and 22), protection from the evil eye (31), and healing for "a woman whose milk does not flow" (32). Items 30 and 31 are related through the catchword of the "evil eye" in both humans (30) and animals (31). Although not clustered together, items 32 and 23 are both concerned with female medical problems (menstruation, or hemorrhage, and lactation; women are also specifically mentioned in item 12). It is striking that women are mentioned only in relation to their functions as sleeping partners (12) and to their reproductive capacities (23 and 32).

The thirty-two items are also interrelated according to the sympathetic elements employed (water, oil, vinegar, mint, figs, wine, ibis blood, rocksalt, candy) and the associated activity (wash, drink, anoint, pour, bind, wear, eat). Items 2 and 3 refer to drinking and then washing in "laurel water" (2) and "Tobe water" (3). Items 5 through 9 employ oil which is used to anoint (items 5 and 6 refer simply to "oil," while items 8 and 9 refer specifically to "first-pressed oil"). Items 10 and 11 refer to washing in "rainwater" (10) and, simply, "water" (11). Items 17 and 18 refer to anointing with "oil" (17) and "genuine (olive) oil" (18). Items 21 and 22 (compare 30) refer to the sprinkling with water of "your house and every one of your walkways" (21) and "your house and every place that belongs to you" (22). Items 25 and 26 refer to the manufacture of papyrus amulets that contain the text of the spell: "write it on a clean papyrus sheet and tie it to the tip of the mast" (25), and "make it into an amulet, and tie it to your right arm" (26; compare the papyrus amulet employed in item 18).

The preceding observations on the thematic and catchword arrangement of the thirty-two-part list suggest that the list is a conflation of earlier source material. The first nineteen items (perhaps without the later interpolated item 12) possibly derived from an already integrated source that was primarily concerned with physical and psychological problems. Then follows a series of thirteen diverse items (20 through 32) that show specialized concerns for a variety of social and political relationships, business concerns, the protection of property, and protection from evil, including a single item for personal revelation, and two items reflecting medical concerns specific to women. This concluding series of thirteen diverse items represents a clustering of traditional units according to themes and catchwords and may have been secondarily added to the preceding nineteen items that derived from the proposed earlier source dealing with physical and psychological concerns.

THE OPENING INVOCATIONS in the text suggest some of the basic features of the orderly cosmological myth assumed by its author. The author is certainly familiar with numerical symbolism common in religious texts from antiquity. The numbers employed typically serve to create order in the human experience of the space-time environment. There is one highest deity, the almighty; there are twenty-one angelic powers (in three groups of seven, six, and eight); the ritualist purifies himself for a period of forty days; the prayer is initially recited over honey and licorice root seven times; and the god comes "out of the four winds, the four corners." This orderliness of the human and divine environment reflected in numerical symbols is coupled with a theory of purity and impurity which further serves to order human experience. The requirement for ritual purity is repeatedly stressed and its fulfillment is crucial to the efficacy of the prayer. The concern for order in human experience is especially reinforced by the rebuke of "chaos" in the opening lines of the second prayer.

The orderly cosmos is divided into two levels, that of the unclean world below in which the human drama is played out (the locus of the ritualist and his client), and that of the spiritual world "in the height" populated by the "aeons of light" and the almighty. The "one who activates the prayer" (the only self-designation of the ritualist in the text) invokes the almighty in order that his requests will be answered. The almighty is surrounded by the twenty-one angelic powers or "great ones" who are appointed over his work and service, and so carry out his will in response to the request of the practitioner, now divinized as the authoritative and heavenly Seth, son of Adam (see Paul Allan Mirecki, "The Figure of Seth in a Coptic Magical Text").

The twenty-one powers are comprised of three levels of angelic beings: the seven archangels, the eight ministrants, and the six authorities. The "one who activates the prayer" three times identifies himself with the heavenly Seth, son of Adam, and so has authority over the seven archangels and the other fourteen powers, so that they will "bring to pass" everything which the almighty has granted to the practitioner as he makes his request known, "performs the ritual in purity," and recites the efficacious prayer.

Because the ritualist identifies with Seth, son of Adam, he has access to "the virtues and the mysteries" that Seth received from his father Adam. The prayer that the ritualist possesses in this text also contains "secret names . . . Hebrew names . . . Hebrew words," which are in "Hebrew, the language of heaven." According to the myth, the ritualist's claim that he could effectively communicate with angels in their heavenly language, that he knew and could pronounce their "secret names," and that he had access to the revelations given to biblical Seth from his father Adam, provided the ritualist with the necessary "authority over" the twenty-one angelic powers to expect that they would carry out the work that the almighty has granted to the ritualist. The ultimate promise of the prayer for the ritualist who activates it and for his client is that the problematic human condition, plagued by social dysfunction and physical and psychological maladies, can be overcome by direct access through the ritualist to the highest heavenly being, the "god, lord lord, almighty" of the text's opening lines.

ONE CAN ISOLATE well-known words and names of power in the 104 lines of powerful utterances, derivations thereof, and many new forms. (See the glossary, below, for a few of the common words and palindromes.) Here a few additional words may be noted. The two biblically significant place names of Nazareth and Samaria were apparently used to create NARARAZOTH (16.14) and SOUMARIA (18.7). The names of letters in the Hebrew alphabet are similarly employed in ALETH (for Hebrew "Aleph"? 18.7) and BETH (Hebrew "Beth" occurs twice: 16.5, 10). ASLAM (20.15) might be based on the consonantal triad "SLM" which is shared by the Hebrew "Shalom" and the Arabic "Salam" and "Islam." Greek words are possibly seen in SALPSOLAMPSO (18.2–3; a corrupted and mnemonic form of "trumpet-lamp" or "shining-trumpet"?), PITHAE (18.14; for "Pythia," the famous oracular priestess at Delphi?), PSEE (18.17; for Psi, the twenty-third letter of the Greek alphabet?), or the Copticized form ṆAGGELOS (19.8; "the angels").

This translation of the Coptic text is by Mirecki, who adds words in parentheses to clarify the intent of the often obscure Coptic sentences, and adds numbers in parentheses to designate items in the thirty-two-part list. The translation presented here is based on Mirecki's transcription of the text found in the codex rather than on his transcription of the nearly identical text found on the scrap papyrus sheets. This contrasts with Worrell's "reconstructed" Coptic text, which is a collation of the two complete but slightly varying versions of this text. Worrell's reconstructed text does not exist in any of the manuscripts (note his comments in "A Coptic Wizard's Hoard," 241). Mirecki's selection of the text in the codex, rather than the text on the scrap sheets, is not meant to imply that the text in the codex preserves a better form of the text. For the English reader of this study, the differences between the two versions are minimal.

Through the generosity of Ludwig Koenen and Traianos Gagos, Mirecki has had access to both the papyrus collection and the research library at the University of Michigan since 1986. This access has provided the basis for the work that is published here.

133. The Coptic hoard of spells from the University of Michigan

Text: Michigan 593
Description: papyrus codex consisting of twenty pages bound together by
threads; 15.3–16 x 15.3–17.3 cm; fourth–sixth century
Bibliography: William H. Worrell, "A Coptic Wizard's Hoard"
Translator: Paul Allan Mirecki

TEXT

God, lord lord, ' almighty, whose body has ' the appearance
of fire that is light ' in the hidden things! The one [5] who is born of
flesh does not know your name, ' but only you yourself (know it),
the entire way ' of wisdom who alone is ' from the aeons of light,
who is unknowable ' (and) is surrounded by all of the powers [10]
who are each appointed over your ' work and your service. ' Grant
me everything related to this prayer and ' (to) every (ritual) action
that I perform. '

You seven angels, each [15] appointed over his work and his '
service, act on my behalf. (For) I am Seth, (page 2) the son of
Adam, the first revelation ' of the unformed hands. ' Michael,
Gabriel, Raphael, Uriel, ' Saraphael, Suriel, Anael, and also [5] his
other ministrants, Amoel, Anathael, ' Ananael, Anael, Phiel,
Thriel, ' Apiel, Israel, and the other authorities, ' Mosul, Osul,
Phael, Yoel, Arphael, ' Tremael!

All of these great ones are the [10] powers who are in the presence of ' this unseeable light ' (and are) the angels who are in the
height, those of the night ' and those of the day, each of whom ' is
appointed over his work and the [15] service.

Hear our ' authority that is over you, all of his ministrants
(page 3) who are called (by name) by ' those above them, even
you great archangels ' who are strong in your power, you whose '
names were first given to you, [5] that is, (you) angels who call all
of the special names ' that are written (here) in Hebrew, ' the language of heaven, in order that they might hear the ' one who will
activate this prayer ' (and that) they might bring to pass for him
everything that he will perform [10] in purity and chastity of ritual. '

I am Seth, the son of Adam. ' I have purified myself forty days
' until its power is revealed ' and the power of its Hebrew (lan-

guage) [15] and all of its manipulations, so that it can [assist in every action that I [perform. Perform it while you (**page 4**) are pure and in awe.

I am [Seth, the son of Adam, to whom have been [revealed the virtues and the mysteries, [and its manipulations, and the power of these [5] arts, which are honored more than the other [prayers that are concerned with these secret names and [all the rest, for I am in agreement with its [operations.

No person can perform [it except (one) who is sufficiently pure, [10] who is perfected in [all of its secret names and its powers, [for this (prayer) causes a spirit to rest [upon him and (gives him a measure of) wisdom more than [any person.

You are to recite it seven [15] times over some honey and some [licorice root. It sets a reminder [within you, for ever and ever, [in your mind and spirit. Take (**page 5**) a hawk's egg and fry [it, then eat it over the [honey, purifying yourself for forty [days until its mind appears [5] to you, in cleanliness and purity [for forty days, before you begin (the ritual, with) [your garments [cleansed. Perform it as a [response, for it is highly honorable, (and) [10] a great grace is in it. [For it removes the anger [of every married man (and) [it heals the bites of beasts [and reptiles. Do not despise [15] it because of these great secret names, [for its powers are great. [It causes every (evil) thing to disappear. [It saves you from those who hate and [from every curse.

(1.) Concerning the bite (**page 6**) of a reptile: Recite it over some water [and have him drink it.

(2.) For jaundice: Recite [it over some water that has some laurel [in it, and have him drink it and then wash him (with it). [5]

(3.) For one who is swollen: Recite it over [some Tobe water, and have him drink it and then [wash him (with it).

(4.) For ribs that are [in pain: Recite it over some figs (and) [bind them on him.

(5.) For the spleen: Recite it [10] over some oil and anoint it.

(6.) For the [headache: Recite it over some oil and anoint [his temples.

(7.) For one who has been troubled: [(Recite it) over some oil of hiktanos, over some oil of [spanon, with some frankincense, and anoint him. [15]

(8.) For one who has fever: Recite it over some ' first-pressed oil and anoint him.

(9.) For one ' who suffers vertigo: Recite it over some first-pressed **(page 7)** (oil) and anoint him.

(10.) For one who fears ' the night: Recite it over some rain-water ' and wash him (with it).

(11.) For one who does not (regularly) sleep: ' Recite it over some water and wash the 5 area around his bed (with it).

(12.) For one ' who does not usually sleep with (a) woman: Recite it ' over some wine and have him drink it.

(13.) For one ' in whom there is a worm: Recite it ' over some mint and make it into 10 a wreath for him.

(14.) For the illness of ' burning (lungs): Recite it over some ' wine, and have him inhale it(s fumes).

(15.) For ' strep throat: Recite it over some water ' and sprinkle it down (his throat).

(16.) For the one who 15 is gouty in the joints: Recite ' it over some ibis blood and ' some wine, and smear them (with it).

(17.) For one ' who has a seizure: Recite it over some oil **(page 8)** and anoint him.

(18.) For one who is slow: ' Recite it over some genuine (olive) oil and anoint him, ' and write it on a clean papyrus sheet ' and tie it to him.

(19.) For a hemorrhage: 5 To stop it, recite it over some vinegar ' and pour it over his head.

(20.) For those who ' are estranged from one another: Recite it ' over some oil and anoint the face of one ' of them. Let them look into the face of one 10 another so that they (both agree to) accept what you ' say, (and then) recite it over some rose oil ' and anoint your face.

(21.) For ' your enemies, that they (may) not prevail over you: ' Recite it over some water, adjuring 15 him, and sprinkle your house and ' every one of your (walk)ways.

(22.) For your house, ' and your sheep enclosures, and all that belongs to you: ' Recite it over some water **(page 9)** and sprinkle your house and every place ' that belongs to you, (and) no evil will overtake you. '

(23.) For a woman with an issue of blood: ' Recite it over some vinegar and pour it ⁵ over her head. Recite it over some oil ' of spanon and anoint her abdomen ' and genitals.

(24.) For a merchant to profit: ' Recite it over some first-pressed oil ' and sprinkle some merchandise, (and) let ¹⁰ him take it with him abroad. '

(25.) For the safety of ships at ' sea or on the ocean ' with everything (on board): Write it on a clean papyrus ' sheet and tie it ¹⁵ to the tip of the mast.

(26.) For a ' ruler to spare you ' or (at least) not to spurn you: Write it (**page 10**) on a papyrus sheet and make it into an ' amulet, and tie it to your right ' arm, and you will be spared. '

(27.) To cause a revelation to be given to you ⁵ in a dream: Take some rocksalt ' and place it under your head ' as you are about to sleep, and you will be ' informed about everything (concerning your inquiry).

(28.) To cause someone ' to desire you: Recite it over some ¹⁰ newly pressed wine and give it to the person ' to drink.

(29.) For your men ' and the men of your village: ' Recite it over some oil and ' anoint your face in their presence. ¹⁵

(30.) For the safety of your house ' and the walkways by your door: ' Recite it over some torrential water ' and sprinkle your house and the (**page 11**) walkways by your door, and it will guard ' you from every potion, and (will) ' heal every disease, and (guard you from) every demon ' and every evil eye; and it ⁵ also will not allow estrangement to occur in your house, ' nor (any) trouble (at all).

(31.) For the evil eye ' that is among domestic animals: Recite it over some ' oil and anoint them.

(32.) For a ' woman whose milk does not flow: ¹⁰ Recite it over something sweet, let ' her eat it when she comes out ' of the bath.

You shall keep the ' prayer in your mouth at all times, (and) no ' obstacle will come ¹⁵ near you.

Before you use it (**page 12**) at any time, you must wash yourself with some laurel water, ' be free from every defilement, ' and (only) eat food that is clean, ' (then) wash your mouth with some rocksalt ⁵ and some clean wine. '

> >

✝ ✝ ✝ ✝ ✝ ✝ ✝ FTHP FTHP OTHTHSA ' TINOU MA CHHXLPS
ML CHECH ' PHRLOCHNB XKEX PSLEELEI ' NURSXENFX
HNPSCH XXKEU 10 OKEPS EHOS FKEISNDX ' PSEOXS KFOP-
SNTH CHEURA ' EFKHK SHB[?]RS OTHOOAA ' THXBN
HTHXBN HTHXBN ' HTHXBN

> (page 13)

✝ Come out of the four ' winds of heaven, or (out of) the
four corners, ' with the spirits (who ride) the ' breath-chariots of
this great spirit. Extinguish 5 this chaos and this great ' dragon and
all his forms ' and all his threats, the one ' who attacks this being
of light, (and) ' whose gates and windows 10 exist through him, '
as well as his chambers, countless as they are. '

> You cause the ordinances of this ' great fiery servant ' to
> guard everything.
> You are protected 15 by these great (page 14) angelic
> authorities.
> You, ' whose beginning is first to leap ' into the river of the
> ocean, shining ' until the end through the
> burning of the trees 5 that are in all the world!
> You, the ' heat of whose strength results from ' the long-
> suffering of the father, ' (who is) the father of all
> the angels and archangels, ' and all the powers, 10
> the father of heavenly and ' earthly things, the fa-
> ther of all that exist, ' the father of all the praises,
> ' the father of all the thrones ' and their glory, the
> father of all 15 lordships, the father of ' those
> who are in the abyss, the father of the ' holy
> majesties, the father of ' those who surround all
> humankind, (page 15) the father of the judges,
> the father ' of all the exalted powers, ' the judge
> of people!
> You, before ' whose name one trembles and fears! 5
> You, whom the ones in the heavens and on ' earth adore!
> You, who founded ' the crowns of the firmament! '

MAR MARAK LOUAK KLOUAK ' AMARIAK MARMAROUAK
BATHI 10 ORAK LOAK ANOAK MARMA ' RATHAK MAR-
MAOCH MARAMATH ' MASA AXA SALOA AMARE ' THAMIA
CHAOAAMACHO AOPHI ' AMABARBES SALA OXA MA 15
RISEL BEL MARMA RAB IAO ' ABRACHA ABRASAK PHNOUN '
ABOUEL IAOTH BAPHRA NEMOUN (page 16) OUTHILORI
KEIPHIA EUE AIIPHIR ' KIA LITHOU NAOMEN EBRAPHA '
ERPHABOIAI DISIOS AKRAKATH ' ECHOI CHOUCHO
CHEOCHCHATHIE 5 EIE IE AI IE BETH ELELAE ' IE ETHO
ETHA LELMA LAEI NAM ' PTOE NATIS MOUISRO SARACHA '
AEIE ZEIOK KAPH KANIPH KA ' KRIS ROM BIOROU MEN
ZETH 10 ZETH BETH ZOCHE LETH COU MAU ' AZAE BO-
CHOEI SABAE METHA ' THONOUN THATHOUM EREBOEL '
EREBOEL MARALOE AMALOEITH ' ACHA KASLOEI NARARA-
ZOTH 15 ENAEIBAOTH ZETH THALA LAIMA ' ACHARMATH
NEBABAIN BAERA ' AKRA CHAR KARCHORE EXHORA (page
17) GRAMA AKRAMETH KRAMARAM ' AMAMAM MAM
KALEU LOECHE ' EUEU EMARAM MARTHAO THAOTH '
AOTH ADONE ELOAEI ELOAEI 5 ELOAEI AMARACHO
EBLAMABLAM ' ATHANAMA NATHA ALBA NATHAN ' ABRI-
OCH OCHOCH CHIOCHA IO ' CHAE KLASEU MAOTH CHIE
XROU ' THOA THOUTHOTH ROUTH THAPSAE 10 PSAROUEL
IAEL IOEL MARMA ' ROTHOAN ANAEL ATHANAEL ' NAEL
NACHOIOTH NENA THARA ' EL THARIEL CHOA ARICHO
RACHOE ' AMALARIA BASEM BACEMA 15 ADONAEI ELOAEI
SAOTHBA ' SABAOTH AO AOABRAOA ' CHEIMARMEN AE
CHARARAR (page 18) CHARARAN LAROUTH ROUROUTH
OUTH ' ETHITH CHOCHOO ISIO SALPSO ' LAMPSO
ROTHERI ELEILAM EIELA ' EIALATH KAKI MACHARIMA ELTH
5 ELTH EITHINALAM EUE THALASOU ' THOUR MICHIKL
MICHTHAM ELTHA IEE ' LAMNEU ALETH SOUMARIA
SOUTHA ' EU SOULOTHIA THOPHONIA DREM ' PHANAEL
ABRATHA MARMAREL 10 THANAEL AKOL IA EO IA EA '
IOPOTHEN ATHAMAO ATHIE IO ' IOLA PHILATHE CHO
CHO CHO ' CHO SATHEA IAEL EA PALAK ' PALAMETH PITH
PITHAE PICHORA 15 SOTHAE PITHOTH EIALAEL LOUAM '
ETHALAETHA ETHAL THALOEOU ' TEUE EUE PSEE DROATH
THAEIETH (page 19) ELEIL IAKNEU ITHOA TREMOUTH '
EABRATH ABRATH IATHOTH SESEKIN ' BARPHAKES AR-
BELEOADONAI ' ONB ABRACHOTHA ABRACENATHOTHO 5

ABBIA ELOA MARITHCHARI IOTH EEA ' PHOROU LOAM
ELEA E LOL IEL EBRE ' BAEL REM PHANOUEL PEBRESTER '
NAGGELOS PHANOUEL MICHAEL CHILATH ' IAO AE PLE
OA IEL ELEMOUR 10 RIEL RIEL LALA AO LOLAM ' ELSEL
LABOTHIAEL AOTHA AEL EAE ' IATH ITHE IAO OTH
KEENATH GENEEN ' AEL MARIAO MIRIO MARITHIOTH EOA
' THALEATH MARMARIARIOTH ARIOA 15 EUARIA RARA
ERIKEM PHTHEARA CHARA ' RAE PHTHESEKERE ABRA-
NATHAN (page 20) ALBA ALAO ALAO ALAMARI MARI '
ACHEL NEEL SEMESI EMIEUEAI ' ILAM SEMESI LAM
ABRASAK ' ABRAMACHAMARI MAMNA CHAMARI 5 AKRA-
CHARAN EL EL CHAEL PHANAEL ' PHANOUEL AKRAEL
MARI SOUMENZETH ' ZOUCHELETH LETH THA-
LATHAAKOTHBI ' LETH DINAMIEEL EENM BIBTOU ' ANAEL
LATH AINATHA EPHIEPHIEPH 10 KOTHOOTH CHOTH
ELEAPH APHERA ' LATHKILOCH PHENEMOUN ' OTHIOR-
ITHE LAO OASMOUTH PHABOUEA ' BOEASIELOAEISAM-
ABRACHTHES ALAOXA ' PHREXO ENEUOTH RISO ISATH
KALATH 15 ACHATH THERAM ASLAM PECHOR MOR-
PHEOTH ' MOUPHIATH MORPHILAB MORPHILAB ROTH
PHIL ' OPHILATHOTH EEE EO PHILA EEO PHANOEO ANOL-
BIBA † † †

12

THE CoPTIC BOOK oF RITuAL PoWER FRoM LEiDEN

INTRODUCTION AND TRANSLATION
BY RICHARD SMITH

This sixteen-page papyrus codex from Leiden is a seemingly disparate collection of texts, yet they are unified in their common apotropaic purpose. All the texts are for protection and the aversion of harm. The first two texts are prayers attributed to Gregory, the following three are letters between Jesus and King Abgar, and the last three are name lists and short biblical texts commonly used as amulets.

The prayer and exorcism of Gregory (1) is an all-encompassing charm for protection of person and property. It invokes god the father and his "powers," the archangels, to protect the user from all sorts of harmful threats, including sorcery. The charm can be employed as an amulet in several ways, apparently, by reciting it, wearing it, or depositing it in a sacred place. The prayer of St. Gregory (2) invokes the astrological constellations to exorcise the power of the devil. It is unclear whether this is Gregory of Nazianzus (329–89), or Gregory Thaumaturgus (ca. 212–ca. 270), the "wonder-worker." The theological vocabulary toward the end of the opening prayer probably postdates both of these figures. The Greek words *hypostasis . . . prosopon*, "realization . . . person," were prominent terms in the Nestorian controversy, which raged between 428 and 451. The phrase "one *prosopon* and one *hyposta-*

sis" also appears in a fragment of Theodore of Mopsuestia (died 428).

The following three texts (3, 4, 5) are an expansion of the pseudepigraphical correspondence between Jesus and Abgar, king of the city of Edessa (modern Urfa in Turkey) (compare text 61). The letters are first found in the fourth-century Ecclesiastical History of Eusebius, who says he discovered them in the Edessan archives and translated them from the Syriac. Because the subject of the correspondence is healing, the reply of Jesus to Abgar was much used in antiquity as an amulet. It was employed in various forms as a protective charm, and at Ephesus it was inscribed on the lintel of a door. The version here (4) is quite expanded from the letter quoted by Eusebius, which contains three brief statements: Jesus praises Abgar for believing without having seen (John 20:29), he explains that he is too busy to come, but after he is taken up he will send one of his disciples to perform the cure. "It is only a few lines long," as Eusebius says, "but it is very powerful (*polydynamos*)." Not powerful enough, apparently, as our version is much improved. In addition, we have a second letter said to be from Jesus (5), which was not even mentioned by Eusebius. The letter patches together a "Hebrew" prayer and part of the legend of St. Helena's discovery of the true cross (for which there are Greek parallels).

The next two texts are name lists. The seven sleepers of Ephesus (6) were Christian young men who took refuge in a cave during the Decian persecution (ca. 250). The cave was walled up, but under the Emperor Theodosius II (died 450) they awoke as proof of the resurrection of the dead. By the following century their tomb had become a popular pilgrimage site. The seven sleepers continued into Islamic tradition (Quran, sura 18), along with their pet dog named Kitmir.

The second list of names (7) is that of the forty Christian soldiers of the "Thundering Legion," *Legio XII Fulminata*, who were martyred at Sebaste in Lesser Armenia during the Licinian persecution (ca. 320) by being left naked on the ice of a frozen pond. Their story is told near the end of the century by Basil of Caesarea and Gregory of Nyssa. The "Thundering Legion" had been known since the time of Marcus Aurelius for its Christian component.

The final text (8) contains the opening words of the four gospels and Psalm 90 (Psalm 91 according to the numbering system in the Hebrew Bible). Psalm 90 is the most frequently used psalm on early Christian amulets, appearing on papyrus and parchment as well as on pieces of jewelry. It is, as here, often found in conjunction with the *incipits* of the gospels, to be worn as an amulet.

134. The Coptic book of ritual power from Leiden

Text: Leiden, Anastasi No. 9

Description: papyrus codex of sixteen pages, recto and verso

Bibliography: W. Pleyte and P. A. A. Boeser, *Manuscrits coptes du musée d'antiquités des Pays-Bas à Leide*, 441–79; Angelicus M. Kropp, *Ausgewählte koptische Zaubertexte*, 2.72–79, 81–85, 161–75, 220–21; 3.210

Translator: Richard Smith

TEXT

(1) A prayer and exorcism ' that I wrote, I, Gregory, ' the servant of the living god, ' to become ⁵ an amulet for every one ' who will receive and read it, ' making it destroy every operation ' that comes about by ' villainous people, ¹⁰ whether sorcery, ' or incantations, or ' binding of people ' by various diseases, ' or jealousy, ¹⁵ or envy, or ' lack of success, that is, ' one does not find a task to perform— ' in general, every [task] ' for which we are skilled ²⁰ and those for which we are not skilled, ' and [every] task [that] ' comes about due to ' meddling [people] or crooked ' [people or through] ²⁵ villainy.

I [invoke] ' you, [lord god] almighty, I, Gregory, (**page 1, recto**) the servant <of the living god>. And I beg ' you, father of our lord ' Jesus Christ, god of ' gods, king of all kings, ⁵ incorruptible, undefiled, ' uncreated, ' untouchable, morning star, ' mighty hand, ' Adonai Eloei Elemas ¹⁰ Sabaoth, god of ' gods, the king who is mighty ' in all things, who is glorious, ' father of truth, ' great in his mercies, ¹⁵ who rules alone ' over all flesh and over ' all authorities, father of ' [our] lord Jesus Christ. You must ' [enliven] every one who will ²⁰ [recite] this prayer or ' [who will] put it on himself as an [amulet]. '

I invoke ' you, lord god ' almighty: ²⁵ [You must give] salvation and ' [healing] and purification ' at [the place] where this ' [prayer] is deposited, whether (**page 1, verso**) (to) man or woman, ' free or slave, ' little children or those at the ' breast, or even all the livestock. ⁵ You must guard the ' entrance and the exit, ' and all his dwelling places, ' and his windows, ' and his courtyards, and ¹⁰ his bedrooms, and his ' open rooms, and ' the lands which belong ' to him, and his foundations, and ' his orchards, and his wells, ¹⁵ and his trees that bear fruit, ' and those that do not bear ' fruit.

I invoke ' you, god of ' gods, king of all powers, [20] the one who sits ' over the cherubim [and] ' the seraphim, that you do ' away with all violent deeds [that] ' are directed against [every] place [25] where this prayer will be uttered, ' either [that] have ' not yet happened or that **(page 2, recto)** are destined to happen, or if ' someone has bound a place by having ' put bonds of ' deceit in it, hidden in its [5] foundations, or in its open ' places, or at its ' entrance, or at its ' exit, or by the door, or by the ' window, or in the sleeping room, [10] or in the livestock pen, or in ' the dining room, or in the ' central courtyard, or in the ' field, or with the fruit, ' or in the orchards, or in a [15] garment, or two or three, ' or in <trees with fruit>, or in trees without ' fruit, or in the waters ' in the rivers, ' or in the fields, or in the gardens, or [20] in any place.

You violent deeds, ' all that have happened ' or are destined to happen, ' [I] adjure you, I, ' Gregory, the servant of Jesus [25] [Christ], (by) the great name that ' . . . and full of ' trembling and terror, that **(page 2, verso)** is glorious, honorable, ' worthy of worship, ' the unproclaimable, unencounterable, ' holy and [5] blessed name, Adonai ' Eloei Elemas Sabaoth, ' that you be undone ' and withdraw ' from every one near whom [10] this prayer shall be recited, ' or every place where ' it will be deposited and ' all those who belong to it, and ' each of you descend [15] upon the head of ' the one who sent you ' to perform these abominations and ' upon the head of those who consent ' with them, whether the person is a [20] stranger or a boss ' of those belonging to him, or is one ' who leads, or is a ' servant, or is a free person, ' or is a magician or a [25] female magician, or is a ' male Persian ' or a female Persian, **(page 3, recto)** or is a Chaldean or a ' female Chaldean, or is a ' Hebrew or a female Hebrew, ' or is an [5] Egyptian or a female Egyptian, ' in general, ' whoever it is.

Let ' all violence be destroyed ' through this exorcism [10] and through the holy seal ' of the one who is coming to ' judge the living and the ' dead, namely, ' the king and god [15] who was crucified for us. '

Michael, Gabriel, ' Raphael, Uriel, the ' holy angels who stand ' before [20] him who dwells in the ' heavens, the holy ' and exalted one: Guard ' all the limbs of those ' who possess [25] this prayer, who ' not only recite it ' but also use it **(page 3, verso)** as an amulet. ' Save them from ' every wicked and ' every evil thing.

Once again [5] I adjure all you violent deeds, ' by the great glorious name (of) ' god ' almighty, who ' brought his people out [10] of the land of Egypt with a ' strong hand and a raised arm, ' who ' struck Pharaoh and his ' entire force, who [15] spoke with Moses on ' Mount Sinai, who gave ' his law and his ' commandments to the children ' of Israel and made <them> [20] eat manna, ' that you flee ' far away and not ' at all continue ' to stay [25] in the place where ' this prayer is deposited. '

The cause:

I am Gregory, **(page 4, recto)** the servant of the living god. ' I invoke all you ' violent deeds, ' by the great fearful name [5] of the father of our ' lord Jesus Christ, the god ' of Abraham and Isaac and ' Jacob, all ' at once, whether [10] they be magic, or ' idols, or they be in places of worship, ' or in any places to which ' you have been sent ' to produce [15] terror and ' convulsions and ' dumbness and deafness ' and speechlessness ' and disgrace [20] and pains of every kind. ' And whether you are nearby ' or you are far ' away, be afraid ' of the name of the lord, and [25] retreat from ' wherever ' this prayer shall be read **(page 4, verso)** or deposited ' and from all those who belong there. ' But each one of you descend ' upon the head [5] of any one who is like ' you, or whoever sends ' you, upon them ' and those who consent ' with them.

God is [10] peace, god is ' health, god is ' justice, god ' is light, lord ' god of the powers: [15]

Michael is usually translated ' as "peace," that is, the ' god of light,

Gabriel, ' "god and man," '
Raphael, "health," [20]
Uriel, "power," '
Sedekiel, "justice," '
Anael, "obedience," '
Azael, "mercy." '

All of these are [25] the names of god, and ' all of these are the archangels' names, ' and **(page 5, recto)** every one who has them, ' who bears ' them, has ' a great helper, filled [5] with every good, because ' god is with us.

Obey ' me to the end of the earth: ' God is with us. ' For whenever you are [10] strong, you ' shall be defeated again, for god ' is with us. And the plot ' that you are contemplating the ' lord will hinder, [15] and the words that you shall ' speak will not remain in you, ' for god is with us. ' Let not an obstacle stone or a ' stumbling block [20] dare to ' be near those who have ' this prayer, ' for god is with us. ' For every one who [25] shall take this prayer ' to the place ' where this prayer is deposited ' shall not be afraid. **(page 5, verso)** They shall be neither afraid ' nor disturbed, for god ' is with us.

But you ' yourselves, every one [5] who has ' the request of this ' prayer, the lord ' god purifies it in ' you (pl.), and it will become [10] a guardian with us ' and it will heal all our fears ' of the enemy and ' his demonic operations, ' and if we [15] trust in our whole heart, ' the lord god ' will become a purification for us, ' for god is with ' us. Therefore we shall [20] say the word of the lord: ' Look, I and ' the children whom ' god gave to me. . . . The people ' who dwell in the darkness [25] have seen a great light, ' for god is with us. ' Christ Jesus is with us, ' about whom it was written, **(page 6, recto)** His name will be called ' the angel of the ' great counsel, the mighty god, ' god of [5] the great amazing counsel. ' Let us raise our eyes up ' to heaven and praise ' him with a joyful soul, ' calling out and saying, [10] Glory and worship ' and greatness ' distinguish you. The father and the ' son and the holy spirit ' are unified, [15] and unity is a ' trinity. It is a single divinity ' with three ' realizations, with a ' single lordship and [20] a single rule and a ' single power, and a ' single activity with ' every authority, and a ' single person, and [25] a single baptism, ' a single lord, a ' single god, the father ' and the son and the spirit. **(page 6, verso)**

A thought of slander, ' a thought of envy and hatred ' and hostility and ' arrogance and pride [5] and disobedience and ' lack of restraint and ' money-loving, the root of ' all evil, and ' bragging, and every slander, [10] and every dirty thought, ' and every bitterness: '

Holy trinity, spare ' every one. The holy trinity ' purifies the person [15] within and without. ' It leads us out of every ' painful temptation ' from them as well as every operation ' of the devil,[20] and every operation of the ' evil one, and every plot ' of evil people. '

Holy trinity, ' spare every one who [25] has this ' seal, and those who ' have this ' prayer, and every place ' in which it is published **(page 8 [sic], read 7, recto)**, and become for them an ' amulet and ' aid, a cure-all ' for every pain of any sort. [5] The holy trinity must ' be with us. Glory ' and honor and greatness ' and power ' to the holy, consubstantial, [10] and enlivening trinity, now ' and at all times, for ever ' and ever, Amen. '

(2) Prayer of Saint Gregory. '
O creatures who are rising [15] with the moon, come to me. ' Hear my exorcism, ' you whose great names are ' Aram Aram Arimatha ' Aioutha Athael.

O great [20] shining cherubim ' who are rising with the sun, ' come to me. Hear ' my exorcism, Aracha ' Aracha Arachael.

O creatures [25] who are rising with ' the stars of heaven toward **(page 8, verso)** the east, come ' to me today. Hear ' my exorcism, ' Arael Arael Aratachael [5] Uriel Arachael. '

O creatures who are rising ' with the light, come ' to me. Hear my ' exorcism, Amanael [10] Amarael Nanoel ' Anael Ananiel.

O creatures ' who are rising with the ' sun, come. Hear my ' exorcism, Atha Atha [15] Athael.

O creatures who ' are coming with the great star, ' come to me. Hear ' my exorcism, Er ' Er Er Er Er Er Er.

O [20] creatures who are rising, who ' serve the seven ' archangels, come ' to me. Hear my ' exorcism, Arimatha [25] Marinthael S[e]dekiel. '

O creatures who . . . in heaven, ' who . . . under the authority **(page 9, recto)** of the father, hear my ' exorcism, Manuel ' Manuel Semanuel ' Manuel.

The four gates [5] of the heavenly Jerusalem, ' come to me today. ' Hear my exorcism. '

I adjure you (pl.) by the first ' gate of heaven, the [10] northern, with all the creatures ' who stand ' and who confess the name of ' the lord, the father of the ' whole world, Adonai [15] Eloei Elemas Sabaoth. ' These are their names: Er Er Er ' Er Er Er Er.

O creatures who ' are entering the gate of the south, ' come to me with my [20] exorcism, Maroutha ' Maroutha Marouthael. '

O creatures who are rising ' at the gate of the east, ' come to me today. [25] Hear my smallest speech, ' Aratha Aratha ' Arathael Anatel ' Manuel [S]edekiel.

O creatures ' who are rising at the **(page 9, verso)** gate of the west, ' come to me. Hear ' my smallest speech, ' Achael Ael Manuel [5] [S]edekiel Sntael ' Cheroubin Cherinael Sarinael ' Arinatael.

O ' cherubim and seraphim ' who stand below the [10] face of Christ, come to ' me today. Hear my ' exorcism, O creatures ' of the archangels, ' Michael, Gabriel, Raphael, [15] Uriel, Sedekiel, ' Anael, Setel, Azael, ' who stand opposite the presence ' of the one who dwells in the ' heavens, the seven names [20] worthy of being heard. ' If every one of the ' angels and all his creatures ' name them, ' the earth trembles [25] and the mountains shake, and the ' waters rejoice over the ' great light of his name. ' Adonai Eloei Miel Alpha is (**page 10, recto**) his great name and his ' true name.

I adjure you (pl.) ' by his great name, ' every creature who shall be named [5] by this exorcism, that ' you cancel the entire power ' of the devil ' and release all the bonds ' as well as violent deeds that exist [10] due to them. Let my ' demand be fulfilled, ' my exorcism be called, ' before an hour passes. ' Afterwards, moreover, let me [15] tear the roots of Satan ' and all the bonds ' of the devil, and let my ' request be fulfilled through ' your name, O lord Sabaoth [20] Eloei Eloei ' Eloei Yao Eiaoheiao ' Sabaoth Rhabounei, ' which is translated ' "teacher," the one in whom [25] all the creatures, ' angels, and archangels ' rejoice, ' saying, "Holy, holy (**page 10, verso**) holy, lord of hosts! ' The heavens and the earth are full ' of your glory and your ' blessing!" Rejoice, all you creatures, [5] for the lord has ' risen from the ' dead on the third ' day and freed ' the whole race of Adam. [10] He has destroyed the Jews who were ' ashamed on account of what they ' did. He met his ' disciples and gave them the ' good news, the great Alpha [15] that is stronger than ' anything. I invoke ' you to stand ' with me ' today and fulfill [20] the good things ' in my heart. Let those who ' love the devil be ashamed, ' and let them fall ' beneath this prayer. [25]

All evil spirits, ' all filthy spirits, ' all magic, all wickedness, ' retreat. Christ ' Jesus expels (**page 11, recto**) you. The blood of ' Christ protects every one who ' wears this prayer. ' The holy trinity [5] be with us all.

Amen. '

(3) Abgar, the king of the city of Edessa, ' writing to the ' great king, the son of the ' living god, Jesus Christ: Greetings! [10] Some people, honored ' and worthy of faith, ' have related about you to me ' that the world has been ' very worthy, in our time, [15] of your good visit ' through your ' manifestation. This, ' our inferior race, ' among whom you visited, [20] is completely saved ' by means of your love of humankind, ' which is from the ages. ' So when I heard these things, ' I firmly believed [25] without doubt. And at the

same time ' they said that you perform ' great healings without (**page 11, verso**) medicines or herbs, and ' they have lasted for a ' while. The blind, and ' the disabled, and the mute, 5 and the hearing impaired, and those who are lepers, ' you truly cleanse by ' the word of your mouth. ' And the demons are ' departing in fear and 10 trembling, acknowledging ' your glorious name ' publicly. And you ' authoritatively command ' the dead: They are leaving 15 the graves ' after having been buried. ' These deeds reveal you, ' causing all flesh to know ' you, for you are the 20 only begotten son of ' god, and there is no other except ' you.

Therefore I have requested ' of you, lord, in ' writing, that you remember 25 Edessa also in ' the concern of your divinity ' and your humanity. (**page 12, recto**) Certainly all the races ' are your concern, ' and no one is able ' to flee from you. We 5 beg you, therefore, I and ' the people worshiping ' you, that you trouble ' yourself and come to us for the sake of ' our wholeness and 10 the health of our numerous illnesses, ' and that your name may be proclaimed ' over us, ' O lord, and the city ' will serve as 15 your throne all the days ' of its life.

I have ' heard that your race ' rejected your lordship. ' They live wickedly 20 and enviously, ' and they prosecute you, ' not wanting ' you to reign over them. ' They are ignorant of this, 25 that you are the king of those ' in the heavens and those who are ' upon the earth, (you) who gives life (**page 12, verso**) to every one. What, ' however, is the people of Israel? ' A dead dog, since ' they reject the living god. 5 For surely ' they are unworthy of your holy gift. ' But I tell ' you, my lord, that ' whenever we request 10 that you bother to come to ' me, to the small city that I ' rule, it is enough for us— ' together in love ' without envy or jealousy—15 that you be a king ' over us. I and the people ' shall sing beneath you, ' worshiping the footstool ' of your feet and 20 serving your holy throne. ' Glory to you! ' Glory to your invisible ' father, who sent ' you to us! Glory to the 25 holy spirit, who is ' powerful for ever! Amen. (**page 13, recto**)

(4) The letter of Jesus Christ our ' lord, to Abgar. Amen. '

The copy of the letter ' of Jesus Christ, the son 5 of the living god, ' writing to Abgar, the king ' of Edessa:

Greetings! ' You are blessed, and goodness ' will come about for you, 10 and blessed is your city, ' its name being ' Edessa. Since you have not ' seen but have believed, you will ' receive according to your faith ¹⁵ and according to your ' good policy. Your ' diseases will be healed, ' and if you have committed many sins ' as a human being, they will be forgiven ²⁰ you. And Edessa ' will become blessed ' for ever. And the glory ' of god will multiply among ' your people, and faith ²⁵ and love will ' shine in its streets. '

I am Jesus, I am the one who commands, ' and I am the one who speaks. ' Because you love so much, (**page 13, verso**) I shall set your name as an ' eternal remembrance and ' an honor and a blessing ' among the races who are coming ⁵ after you through all your descendants, ' and they will hear ' it to the end of the ' earth. I am Jesus, who writes ' this letter with ¹⁰ my very own hand. At the ' place where ' this manuscript ' will be affixed, ' no power of the adversary ¹⁵ or unclean spirit ' will be able to ' approach or to ' reach into that place, ' for ever. ²⁰

Hail in peace! ' Amen. '

(5) The letter of our lord ' Jesus Christ to Abgar. Amen. '

He raised up his voice in ²⁵ Hebrew, and prayed ' thus, saying, ' Akrabi Akrabei Milas ' Phinadon Aeir Eloei (**page 14, recto**) Aamektol Azasel Borao ' Abraxio Atheal ' Barouch Ziamour Mlmouth ' Achle Biroba Ermou ⁵ Kathajo Davla Melmon ' Sesen Gemnan Ilem ' Iel, Amen. This is ' their interpretation: It is god who ' is seated above the cherubim, ¹⁰ with the four living creatures ' beneath him, and they are those who ' have flown forth fearfully from the course ' of the air.

God, ' who is in the limitless light: ¹⁵ Whoever is without human nature ' shall be able to dwell ' there. For it is you, you, who have ' created them for yourself as ' attendants for you, four ²⁰ living creatures from four lives (?), ' who always serve, ' calling out in an ' unmuted voice, ' "Holy, holy, holy!" ²⁵ But two are entrusted ' to paradise, ' to guard paradise ' and to guard the (**page 14, verso**) tree of life. These are ' called "seraphim." ' For you are lord ' over everyone. We ⁵ are the ones who are yours, and your ' creation, god, ' who handed over the ' angels that went down ' to the depth of the underworld, ¹⁰ and they are the ones who ' are guarded by the bolts ' of Hades, as a chastisement ' to them for ever.

If ' this is your will, ¹⁵ that the son ' of Mary the true dove ' will reign, this one whom you ' sent from yourself, ' that he might manifest your [20] wonders, I know, lord, ' that unless he had ' come from you, ' he would not have been able to perform these ' wonders. And unless [25] he was your beloved son, ' he would not have arisen ' from the dead. **(page 15, recto)**

So perform your signs. ' Show them, lord, ' and in the way that you listened ' to your servant Moses [5] and showed him the bones ' of our brother Joseph, ' so now, lord, show ' the location where ' the cross of Christ is placed. [10] And command that ' smoke come forth, ' so that I shall believe ' in the cross of Christ, ' {and command that smoke [15] come forth, so that ' I shall believe in ' the cross of Christ}. For ' you are the king of Israel ' and the salvation of the world [20] and Jerusalem, for ever ' and ever. Amen. '

(6) These are the names of the seven ' children of Ephesus: ' Archillitos, Diometos, [25] Allatios, Probatios, ' Stephanos, Kyriakos, ' Sabbatios. **(page 15, verso)**

(7) The forty martyrs of ' the city of Sebaste: ' Domedianos, Onalles, ' Esechios, Smaraktos, [5] Sisinnios, Seuepianos, ' Philoktemon, Elaklios, ' Kyrion, Alexandros, ' Onallerios, Eutechios, ' Bebianos, Lesimachos, [10] Kyrillos, Eutychios, ' Eunoeikos, Phaueios, ' Xanthias, Leontios, ' Meton, Egias, ' Ekdikaios, Akakios, [15] Aedios, Nikolaos, ' Johannes, Choudion, ' Kaios, Klandios, ' Ulitomnos, Athanasios, ' Priskos, Kantitos, [20] Sakerton, Korkonios, ' Theodoulos, Theophilos, ' Tomnos, Aklaeikos. '

(8) This is the order of the opening ' of the four gospels. [25]
Matthew Gospel: ' The book of the generation ' of Jesus Christ, the son of ' David, the son of ' Abraham. **(page 16, recto)**
The Gospel according to ' Mark: ' The beginning of the gospel ' of Jesus Christ, the son of [5] the living god, as it is ' written in Isaiah the ' prophet. '
The Gospel according to ' Luke: [10] Inasmuch as many undertake ' to write the stories ' about the deeds that have been ' agreed to among us . . . '
The Gospel according to [15] John: ' In the beginning was ' the Word, and the ' Word was with ' god, and [20] god was the Word. '
Psalm 90, of the song(s) of David: ' One who dwells in the shelter ' of the exalted will ' live in the shadow of the [25] god of heaven. He shall ' say to the lord, ' You are my guardian ' and my refuge.

13

A CoPTIC BOOK oF RITuAL PoWER FRoM HEiDELBeRG

INTRODUCTION AND TRANSLATION
BY MARVIN MEYER

For a very long time Heidelberg has been famous for its ancient and late antique texts, and among these texts is a substantial
number of Greek and Coptic texts of ritual power. Several texts
published in the present volume derive from the Heidelberg collection: the Greek list of biblical names and their translations
(Heidelberg G 1359 [text 37]), a Coptic amulet against fever (Heidelberg Kopt. 564 [text 53]), an amulet to heal Ahmed from fever,
the evil eye, and other problems (Heidelberg Kopt. 544 [text 54]),
the erotic spell of Cyprian of Antioch (Heidelberg Kopt. 684 [text
73]), an erotic spell to attract a woman (Heidelberg Kopt. 518
[text 77]), one of the sexual curses to leave a man impotent (Heidelberg Kopt. 682 [text 86]), a curse against a woman's face and
work (Heidelberg Kopt. 681 [text 105]), a curse to harm a person
through the use of wax dolls (Heidelberg Kopt. 679 [text 110]),
and the Coptic handbook of ritual power translated in this chapter. Some of these texts are published in Friedrich Bilabel and
Adolf Grohmann, *Griechische, koptische und arabische texte*, a work
that was published in Heidelberg by the Verlag der Universitätsbibliothek and that contains other Greek, Coptic, and Arabic
spells of ritual power.

On page 392 of this German book Bilabel refers in passing to two parchment books of ritual power from Heidelberg, both palimpsests and both to be dated, according to Bilabel, to around the second half of the tenth century. These books were assigned the inventory numbers Heidelberg Kopt. 685 and Heidelberg Kopt. 686. Heidelberg Kopt. 685 has not yet been published, though Hans Quecke has given some limited attention to the first text on the parchment, a Coptic liturgical text (a lectionary), in his article "Palimpsestfragmente eines koptischen Lektionars (P. Heid. Kopt. Nr. 685)." Marvin Meyer has briefly examined photographs of this text of ritual power, thanks to the generosity of the Institut für Papyrologie of Heidelberg. The text occupies seventeen pages of the twenty-page book (on the other three pages and the portions of pages not used for the text of ritual power the first text is clearly visible). It opens with the twenty-first prayer that the virgin Mary uttered, a prayer that shows clear similarities to the prayer of Mary in London Oriental Manuscript 6796 (2); 6796 (3); 6796 (1) (text 131). The present text maintains that the prayer can provide cures for all diseases and sicknesses. Among the powers invoked the text names nine guardians in a manner reminiscent of the opening of the London Hay "cookbook" (text 127). The text is well illustrated, with drawings of the nine guardians (compare London Hay 10122 [text 81]), the three young men in the fiery furnace (Ananias, Azarias, and Misael), and Jesus (perhaps also an exalted Mary). The ritual interpretation of Jesus as one through whose life and death power for healing and protection comes to expression recalls the presentation of Jesus in the other Coptic book of ritual power originally from Heidelberg, Heidelberg Kopt. 686, which is translated below.

Heidelberg Kopt. 686 is more properly referred to by the title provided in the manuscript: "The Praise of Michael the Archangel." The parchment text itself unfortunately was lost during World War II, and what remains to provide access to the text is the published edition of Angelicus M. Kropp, Der Lobpreis des Erzengels Michael, and Kropp's own transcription of the Coptic text (made available in the form of photocopies from the publisher, Fondation égyptologique reine Élisabeth, according to the wishes of Kropp himself). According to Michel Pezin, "Les manuscrits coptes inédits du Collège de France," 24–25, another edition (currently unpublished) of this text has been identified in the manuscript collection of the Collège de France. The Heidelberg text contained drawings near the end of the document; these drawings are not now available, of course, but they are mentioned in the prescriptions at the close of the text.

"The Praise of Michael the Archangel" opens with the hymn of greeting and praise directed to god the father, son, and holy spirit. Michael is described as a winged angel who rides in a chariot and wields a wand of power. The words of praise include an unusual interpretation of the creation account at the opening of Genesis (34–42; note also the lines that follow and compare the account of Sanatael/Satanael in the Questions of Bartholomew). On the basis of this a request is directed to god: "Have mercy upon your likeness and your image (compare Genesis 1:26–27) and listen to my cry, and take away all the suffering from N. child of N." (53–54). Additional summons follow, including summons of god by his names, throne, sandals, clothing, great sealed book, and even his exalted body (86–107). The parts of the divine body are named as divine powers; as is common in texts of ritual power, Orphamiel is named as the finger of god's right hand. Among the other powers that are summoned are the four creatures that draw the divine Merkabah, or throne-chariot (112–14), the six seraphim who cover themselves in modesty and chant the trisagion (115–19), and the twenty-four elders (120–27). Thereafter (171–213) a ritual "life of Jesus" is presented in the form of a series of summons through the powers identified with the moments of Jesus' life, death, and resurrection. The powers of the initial word of god, the conception of Jesus and pregnancy of Mary, her labor pains, the "signs and wonders" worked by Jesus, the tear of the divine father of the crucified Jesus, and the crown of thorns, five nails, spear thrust, and three last breaths of Jesus all are invoked by name in order to enable the healing presence of the divine to come upon the person using the spell. The person requests that the lord Jesus Christ come (with the power of the father and the holy spirit), in the flesh, to bless and empower the water and the oil employed in the healing ritual. At the end of the document are twenty-one numbered prescriptions for such problems as demon possession, imprisonment, domestic quarrels and violence, male impotence, a wife's unfaithfulness, infant death, insomnia, and issues related to villages, workplaces, and herds of cattle. To the prescriptions are attached instructions for the use of the spell and the preparation of an amulet.

135. The Praise of Michael the Archangel

Text: Heidelberg Kopt. 686
Description: parchment book of sixteen pages, lost during World War II; around the second half of the tenth century (so Friedrich Bilabel)
Bibliography: Angelicus M. Kropp, *Der Lobpreis der Erzengels Michael*
Translator: Marvin Meyer

TEXT

The Praise of Michael the Archangel

Michael offered adoration at the feet of the good father. ' He stood there, set his wand in place before him, ' put his chariot behind him, ' stretched out his wings of light, 5 and called out, saying, '

> Greetings, father, greetings, beloved son, greetings, holy
>   spirit. '
> Greetings, you who created the sky. '
> Greetings, you who established the foundations of the
>   earth upon the waters. '
> Greetings, you who spread out the 7 heavens and the 14
>   firmaments. 10
> Greetings, you who created the sun and gave it its heat. '
> Greetings, you who created the moon and gave it its light. '
> Greetings, you who created the stars and gave them names. '
> Greetings, you who created the angels and gave them spirit. '
> Greetings, you who arranged the archangels. 15
> Greetings, you who created the cherubim and the seraphim '
>   and gave each of them 6 wings. '
> Greetings, you who arranged the holy powers. '
> Greetings, you who (**page 2**) created us and gave us spirit. '
>
> I praise you today, you who gave me intellect. 20
> Give honor, you angels on high, come;
> praise the father with me today. '
> You cherubim on high, come;
> glorify the son with me today. '
> You powers on high, come;
> dance to the holy spirit with me today. '

Let the sun and the moon and all the stars stand with me
    today, '
so that I may sing the glory of the father and the son and
    the holy spirit. 25
You singers to the father, sing to the father with me today. '
Let the earth open its mouth and burst forth against the
    devil and all his forces. '
Let the gates of heaven open and the angels of light come
    to me, '
so that I may complete the holy praise. '

Listen to me today, father of light. 30 I am Michael; my name
is god and humankind. ' Give ear to me today, king of kings. ' I am
Michael; I am also the one who is placed over the 7 mysteries '
that are hidden in the heart of the father, that he made on the day
when he created humankind in his likeness and his image, after
he created Phausiel. Yea! '

I, Michael, with all those who follow me, 35 offered adoration to Atoran, who is the work of his hands. ' When we offered
adoration to Aromachrim (**page 3**), who is Adam, ' Sanatael was
disobedient to you. ' You deprived the first formed one of your
holy glory, ' you deprived the son of perdition of your holy glory.
40 You overturned his foundations. ' He brought upon them (that
is, humankind) a great illness so that they did his will. ' After that
he mistreated the people whom you created; after that you would
save them. '

So now, my lord, have mercy upon your likeness and your
image, ' and grant healing to every person who will take up this
holy praise with awe for 60 months, month by month.
    Yea, yea, at once! 45

I adjure you today,
that you hear me today, ' O ruler of what is in heaven and
    what is on earth, '
(by) the chalice that the father has blessed, '
from which the angels have drunk,
so that they have received holy spirit. '

I adjure you today
by the seven words that you exchanged between you and
    your beloved son Jesus Christ, 50
at the time when he came to the world,
on the day when he created Adam. '

I adjure you today
by the great name which you have taught the angels, '
so that they have glorified you through it,
which is Methemon, the great name of the lord Sabaoth. '

So now, my lord, have mercy **(page 4)** upon your likeness
and your image ' and listen to my cry, and take away all the suffering from N. child of N., 55 whether it is a severe illness or an attack of a demon. ' Let them come out of him at the moment that
he is washed with this water and is anointed with this oil. '

I adjure you today
by the seven foundations of the earth and the seven gates '
    upon which the one hundred forty-five thousand
    angels sit. '

I adjure you today
by the 7 rays of the sun and the moon. 60

I adjure you today by the chorus of the stars of heaven, '
that you send me the archangel Michael ' upon this water
    and this oil that are placed before me, '
and he bless them and consecrate them, '
so that if they are poured upon the body of N. child
    of N., 65
all the suffering that is in his body may be taken away
    from him. '

You must obliterate all the power of the adversary, '
and make all his power become like the power of a gnat,
    when I stretch out my wings. '

I adjure you today
by all the ranks of the whole angelic realm of the heavens, '
which came and offered adoration to Adam on the day
    when you created him. 70

I adjure you today
by your names and your powers and your figures and your
    amulets, '
which are written in heaven,
which (**page 5**) terrify the authorities of darkness, '
that you send them upon the water and the oil,
and bless them and consecrate them, '
so that if they are poured upon N. child of N.,
all the suffering that is in his body may come out of him,
and he may be filled with strength and power, '
and may flourish like the tree of life growing in the middle
    of paradise. 75

I adjure you today
by the seven angels who stand over the seven baths of the
    church of the firstborn that is in the heavens, '
whose names are Yao, Yak, Piak, Siak, Artole, Artolan,
    Artolar. '

I adjure you today
by the first offering that was lifted up to you within it, ' and
    the altar that stands in the middle of it. '

I (adjure you) today
by the 4 pillars that hold it up,
the names of which are Ekterisan, Santas, Santal, Talias. 80

I adjure you today
by the blood of the firstborn which was poured out
    violently, '
that you bring me today—me, N. child of N.— ' the
    firstborn,
before whom there submit one hundred forty-five thousand
    in number. '

Come in a marvelous way,
come upon this water and this oil,
breathe upon them and fill them with holy spirit, '
so that if they are poured upon N. child of N.,
all the suffering that is in his body may come out of him. 85
Let the devil be ashamed, and all his power,

and become like the power of a (**page 6**) gnat.
Yea, yea! '

I adjure you today
by the 3 holy names that you have revealed to the world, '
that you may be known, the only true god,
who is the father and the son and the holy spirit, '
the haven of salvation,
the father of the seal that is for the glory of the father, '
the ruin and the destruction of all the power of the devil,
the father and the son and the holy spirit. 90

I adjure you today
by the great golden base upon which your throne is
situated. '

I adjure you today
by the golden sandals that are on your feet,
the name of which is Batha. '

I adjure you today
by the golden support (?) which is above your throne,
which is Thiel. '

I adjure you today
by the beautiful (?) purple covering,
the name of which is Mariel. '

I adjure you today
by the garment of light that clothes you,
the name of which is Thoel. 95

I adjure you today
by the great book that is in your hand,
upon which are 7 seals,
in which is written the destiny of what is in heaven and
what is on earth. '

I adjure you today
by your exalted arm that grasps the foundations of the
earth and the gates of heaven. '

I adjure you today
by the stars of light,
by your two eyes, Thol and Thoran. ' (page 7).

I adjure you today
by the breath of life that comes from your nostrils,
the name of which is Stoel. '

I adjure you today
by Ephemeranion,
which is your tongue. 100

I adjure you today
by Tekauriel,
which is your mouth. '

I adjure you today
by your teeth,
which are Oriskos. '

I adjure you today
by your head,
which is Orasiel.

I adjure you today
by the image of the cross of light that is over your head,
which is Sitoriel. '

I adjure you today
by the crown of light that is about your neck,
the name of which is Lelael. '

I adjure you today
by Orphamiel,
which is the (?) finger of your right hand. 105

I adjure you today
by your two hands,
Anramuel, your right hand,
Antrakuel, your left hand. '

I adjure you today
(by) your two feet, Thaoth, Thaotha. '

I adjure you today
by the throne of light upon which you sit,
giving judgment over the whole creation that you have
    made. '

I adjure you today
by the great power who stands over your head,
whose name is Meruel,
who places upon you the crown of shoots from the tree of
    life, Asaf, Asama, Asamlol. '

I adjure you today
by your great powers, who add up to thirty times fifteen
    and thirty, [110]
one on your right, another on your left, '
with swords of fire in their hands,
ready to do your command. '

I adjure you today
by your 4 creatures that (**page 8**) draw your throne,
whose names are Meliton, Akramata, Psourouthioun,
    Paramera, '
who praise you day and night, saying,
Holy, holy, holy, lord Sabaoth, '
what is in heaven and what is on earth are full of your holy
    glory. [115]

I adjure you today
by the 2 seraphim who cover their faces,
whose names are Phoraeim, Olalborim. '

I adjure you today
(by) the other two who cover their feet,
whose names are Solomon, Torothora. '

I adjure you today
by the two who cover their bodies,
whose names are Sochot, Achorbou, '
whose way of speaking is,
Holy, holy, holy, lord Sabaoth, '
heaven and earth are full of your holy glory. [120]

I adjure you today
by the 24 elders who are under your supervision, '
whom you established on the day when you created them
        from Alpha to Omega. '

I adjure you today
by the great hand that you laid upon them. '

I adjure you today
by the 24 thrones upon which they sit, '
and their golden diadems upon their heads, 125
and the crowns that are on their necks,
and their golden bowls that are (in) their hands, '
and the incense that rises ' up to the face of the father and
        the son and the holy spirit. '

Listen to me today, O elders, listen, hear my voice, O elders, hear my voice. ' Let my prayer come to you and my voice come up to [your] throne, 130 that you may have mercy upon your likeness and your image. ' Take my spell from my hand, O my lord, ' and come upon the water and (page 9) the oil through which you pour out your holy spirit, and bless them ' and consecrate them, and fill them with all healing, ' so that at the moment that I pour the water upon N. child of N., 135 every illness that is in the body of N. child of N. may come out of him. Yea! ' Whether it is a severe illness or an attack (of) a demon or a force ' or sorcery, let them depart, whether shameful sorcery or injury ' or any demonic craft or defilement or female force ' or enchantment or evil power, whether of the air 140 or what is dry (or) what is flooding, whether male magic ' or female magic, let them come out of N. child of N. ' The curse that comes out of the mouth of the father and the son and the holy spirit ' must come upon you and destroy you.
        Yea, at once! '

I adjure you today
by the three breaths that you blew into the face of Adam 145
        on the day when you created him,
so that he received the holy spirit, '
that you listen today to my spells and my complaints, '
and come down upon this water and this oil.

Come in a marvelous way, '
come upon the wings of Asaroth, the great cherub of the
     air (?), '
with forty-five thousand angels and archangels proceeding
     before him, 150
as once you pursued (**page 10**) Adam in paradise
when the serpent deceived him. '
They call out, saying,
Glory to you, king, Christ, almighty, '
heaven and earth are full of your holy glory. '

Come in a marvelous way, come,
with the seven firmaments proceeding before you, '
the sun and the moon and the stars giving you light, 155
all the great powers of heaven and earth standing there, '
the trumpet proceeding before you, announcing,
You who are dead, arise. '

May this be the way you lead (?),
standing over this water and this oil. . . . '
If they are poured upon N. child of N.,
may they come out,
     Yeh, Hak, Hak. '

So now, my lord, have mercy upon your likeness and your
image. 160 Do not allow the work of your hands to fall into ruin.'

I adjure you today
by the first bath that you took
in the spring of living water in the middle of paradise. '

I adjure you today
by the power whose name is Parbiona, '
the second whose name is Timesrokhatheari,
the third whose name is Tirachael, '
the fourth whose name is Talloei,
the fifth whose name is Ouanon, 165
the sixth whose name is Sariel,
the seventh whose name is Tauriel. '

I adjure you today
by the grasp of your great, exalted arm, '

that you send me the holy powers down upon this water
and oil, ' **(page 11)**
and they fill it with all healing.
If it is poured upon N. child of N., '
may all the suffering that is in his body come out of
him, 170
and may he flourish like the tree of life that is in the
middle of paradise.
Yea, at once! '

I adjure you today
by the first word that came out of your heart
and became for you an only begotten son,
who is Jesus Christ. '

I adjure you today
by the peace that you gave to him
when he came down to the world '
and dwelled in the belly of a woman,
Mary, Mariham. '
You revealed your name in the world,
which is Manuel. 175

I adjure you today
by the 9 months that you spent in the womb of Mary
your mother. '

I adjure you today
by the 3 strong powers who guard her, '
whose names are Garmaniel, Exiel, Louloukaksa. '

I adjure you today
by the first labor pain that she had with your only
begotten son on the day when she gave birth to
him,
the name of which is Choroei;
the second labor pain is Abko,
the third labor pain is Hanautos. '

I adjure you today
by the signs and wonders that he worked in the middle of
the whole inhabited world,
in the name of Jesus. 180

The dead arise in the name of Jesus. '
The demons come out of a person in the name of Jesus. '
The lepers are cleansed in the name of Jesus. '
The blind can see in the name (**page 12**) of Jesus. '
The lame can walk in the name of Jesus. 185
The one who is paralyzed can arise, his foot can move, in
        the name of Jesus. '
Those who do not talk can speak in the name of Jesus. '
Fire is extinguished, water is dried up, in the name of Jesus. '
Rocks are split in the name of Jesus Christ. '
All the suffering comes out of the body of N. child of N., 190
        and his body flourishes like the tree of life in the
        middle of paradise. '

I adjure you today
by the image of the cross upon which you were lifted up for
        the salvation of the whole race of humankind, '
which is what has obliterated all the power of the devil and
        all demons, '
who attack the children of humankind. '

I adjure you today
by the first tear that came forth from the eyes of the
        father, 195
and came down over the head of your holy son Jesus
        Christ, '
at the time when he was hanged on the cross for the
        salvation of all humankind. '

I adjure you today
by the crown of thorns that was placed upon your head, '
and the 5 nails that were driven into your body, '
and the spear thrust that pierced his side, 200
and his blood and water that came forth from him upon
        the cross. '

I adjure you today
by the 3 breaths that you blew into the hands of your
        father upon the cross,
which are Eloei Elemas Abaktani Sabaoth. '

I adjure you today
by the 3 days that he spent in the tomb,ˈ
and his resurrection from the dead,ˈ
and the cloth with which he was covered, Jesus Christ, the
    son of god in truth. 205

I adjure you today
by your holy resurrection,ˈ
and the three breaths of life that you blew into the face(s)
    of your holy apostles.ˈ

Come to me today, O lord Jesus Christ,
in the flesh (**page 13**) that you have borne,ˈ
and bless the water and the oil that are before me,ˈ
and breathe down on them,
filling them with the holy spirit, 210
so that all the suffering that is (in) his body may come out
    of N. child of N.,ˈ
if he is washed with it.

Come in a marvelous way,ˈ
come with the power of your good father accompanying
    you,ˈ
and the overshadowing of the holy spirit upon you.ˈ

I adjure you today
by the 6 days that you spent working on heaven and
    earth, 215
and you rested on the seventh day.ˈ

I adjure you today
by your own head and my standpoint toward you,ˈ
and my 7 commanders,
whose names are Gabriel, Raphael, Suriel, Setekiel,
    Salathiel, Anael.ˈ

I adjure you today:ˈ
Gabriel, bearer of good news, come to me so that I may
    complete the holy praise; 220
Raphael, angel (of) gladness, come to me today so that I
    may complete the holy praise;ˈ
Suriel, angel of the powers, come to me so that I may
    complete the holy praise;ˈ

Salathiel, angel, come to me and glorify the father with me
today; '
Setekiel, angel of righteousness, come, glorify the son with
me today; '
Anael and the grace in whose womb the grace of the father
is hidden (?), 225 come, dance with me for the
holy spirit— '
those standing there on the day when you created Adam—'
that they come to me today with their swords of fire in
their hands, '
and stand over this water and this oil, '
and pursue all the authorities, 230
so that they may withdraw from N. child of N.
Yea, yea, at once, at once! '

I adjure you today
by the thousands of thousands and the ten thousands of
ten thousands '
who fly down from the air
and chase after all the authorities of darkness: '
Come forth before the father,
so that he may come and stand over this water and this
(page 14) oil,
and fill them with power and healing, '
so that if it is poured upon N. child of N.,
all the suffering in his body may come out of him. 235

If this water is poured upon a tree that is rotten, it
flourishes. '
If it is poured upon iron, it dissolves and becomes water. '
If it is poured upon rock, it breaks and lets water stream
out. '
If it is poured upon the dead in faith, they will arise. '
It is the mouth of the lord Jesus Christ Sabaoth that has
said these things. 240

I praise you with all the creatures that you have created,
and all beasts of the earth,
and the birds of heaven, '
who praise you,
Aram, Aram, Aram, Anphou, '

hidden god, listen to me.
I am Michael the archangel. '
Let my praise enter in before your greatness, '
let my repentance attain to your holy throne. 245

So now, my lord, have mercy upon your likeness and your image, ' and grant healing to anyone who will take up this praise, especially N. child of N., ' and take away from him every sickness and every disturbance and every attack, ' for you are the one to whom all glory is due, ' the father and the son and the holy spirit, for ever and ever,
Amen, Amen, Amen! 250

1. A person whom a demon is afflicting: ' Utter the prayer over a flask of rose water. Pour it over him. He will get better. Off(ering): mastic. '

2. A person who is in prison: Copy the power on sherds (?) of a new jar. Throw them to him. They will force him out onto the street, by the will of god. Off(ering): mastic, alouth, koush. '

3. A favor: Copy the figure with blood of a white dove. Bind it upon you. Off(ering): muscatel. ' **(page 15)**

4. A person who . . . : Copy the figure with blood of a vulture. Bind it upon him. They will get better, (by) the will of god. Mastic. 255

5. A person who is experiencing hostility between him and his wife: Utter the prayer over oil, and let her anoint her face, for the sake of peace. Frankincense. '

6. A person who is bound so that he is unable to have sex with his wife: Utter the prayer over virgin oil. A pot of water. Pour it over him. He will be released, in a marvelous way. Off(ering): koush and storax. '

7. A person who has been given a chalice: Utter the prayer 3 times over a glass flask filled with rose water and water of charlock. Give it to him to drink. Funerary incense. Incense. Off(ering): white koush. '

8. A person who has pain: Utter the prayer over virgin oil. Give it to him to drink. Frank(incense). He will get better. Off(ering): bitumen. '

9. A person who is going on a mountain: At sunrise visit him. Bind the figure on his hand. Surely no robber or beast will be able to touch him. Alouas. 260

10. A person who is irate because his wife is sinning against him: Copy the figure. Wash them with oil. Disperse fragrance on it. No one will be able to sleep with her. Let (him) anoint her with oil. Mastic. '

11. A woman whose husband is violent with her: Copy the figure on a shell. Fill it with oil. Disperse fragrance. Recite the prayer over it. Anoint her face, for the sake of peace for her. Off(ering): mastic, alouth. '

12. A person who is hastening toward ruin: Copy the figure. Bind it to him. No person will recognize him. Off(ering): storax. '

13. A person who cannot find rest for himself: Copy the figure. Put it on him. He will sleep. Off(ering): mastic. '

14. An authority whom you are approaching: Copy the power that is on the right side. Bind it upon him. Approach. Do not speak. No sorcery will deprive (you) of well-being (?). 265

15. A village that you want to be inhabited: Copy the figure. Bury it at a crossroads. Surely it will be inhabited. Muscatel. '

16. A workplace that is deserted when a flow of water streams in: Utter the prayer over it 7 times. Take a broken basin (of water) and let it stream out behind you so that you make it flow through the door of the house. Off(ering): chabani. (page 16) '

17. Unresponsiveness that you can bring upon a person: Utter the prayer over water. Throw it over him. He will become like a dead person. Frankincense. '

18. A person who is at odds with you: Take a rag of yours. Copy the figure. Bind it along with the entrails of a swallow-sparrow. Cast it away. Completion: 3 days. Wherever the person is, he will come with the swallow-sparrow. [1]

19. A person who is chasing after a woman: Copy the figure. Let the woman bury it in her house. Surely he will no longer pursue a strange woman. Off(ering): mastic, alouth. 270

20. A herd of cattle, when sorcery has been performed against you: Copy the power with the head of a bird. Hide it in it. It will be released, in a marvelous way. Off(ering): mastic. [1]

21. A woman who has children who have died: Copy the 7 powers on a sheet. Bind it to her right arm. Bind another one to her left arm. Her child will not die. Off(ering): mastic. [1]

Procedure: First copy the sheet. Bind it to yourself. For its release (?): names. Mastic. Alouth.

A pot: up to 3 measures of barley (?). Hidden water. Incense. 7 virgin palm leaves. Without leaven, until evening. The one who is ill: fasting.

(drawing of a power)

(drawing of a power)

The power[1]

The power[1]

(drawing of Michael)

Michael, Gabriel, Raphael, Suriel, Set[ekiel . . .]

APPENDIX

Previously Unpublished Coptic Texts
of Ritual Power in the Beinecke Library,
Yale University

STEPHEN EMMEL

The Yale Papyrus Collection of the Beinecke Rare Book and Manuscript Library includes at least fifteen texts of ritual power in Coptic: P.CtYBR inv. 846 (second text), 882, 1781 (second text) qua, 1791 (first text) fol, 1791 (second text) fol, 1792 qua, 1793, 1794 qua, 1796 (A) qua, 1796 (B) qua, 1800 qua, 1801 qua, 2099, 2124, and 3549; and perhaps also 1844 and 2258. One of these texts has been published already (P.CtYBR inv. 1792 qua [= text 55 above]), and five others are published here, with the permission of the Beinecke Rare Book and Manuscript Library.

The manuscripts published here are each mounted in an acrylic plastic frame. For the purposes of description, the "front" and "back" of a manuscript are distinguished by the inventory number label that is mounted inside the frame. The library designates front and back by *A* and *B* respectively. The designations *first text* and *second text* are used to distinguish two texts written on a single sheet when the two texts are not restricted one to each side; these designations do not necessarily imply chronological sequence (in the case of P.CtYBR inv. 1791 fol, however, I believe that the "first text" was inscribed before the "second text").

In keeping with the editorial tradition toward Coptic texts of ritual power, I have tried not to alter the text except to introduce spacing and to simplify the representation of superlinear strokes with regard to length and position. Problematic passages, including passages where a different editorial policy would dictate emendation, are glossed in the notes. However, generally I have refrained from commenting on passages where unusual orthography is relatively transparent, or at least is made so by my translations, which appear earlier in this volume. The few relevant bibliographical citations accompany the translations and are not repeated here. Elsewhere in this volume, the abbreviation "Yale" is used as a replacement for "Beinecke Library, P.CtYBR inv."

I acknowledge gratefully that I have received helpful comments on several obscure passages in these texts from Leo Depuydt, Howard M. Jackson, Paul Allan Mirecki, and Stephen H. Skiles.

1. P.CtYBR inv. 882 (A)

Papyrus, 9.1 x 15.9 cm, sixth or seventh century (so Birger A. Pearson); purchased from Phocion J. Tano in Cairo, early in 1931. The text on the front is written across the fibers. A second text of ritual power nine lines in length (P.CtYBR inv. 882 [B]) was written on the back of this document (also across the fibers, perpendicular to the text on the front), but almost all of it is now blotted out with heavily smeared ink, perhaps an intentional erasure. Enough of the first line is legible to show that the text began ⲦⲒⲰⲢⲔ̣ ⲈⲢⲞⲔ, *"I adjure you. . . ." The handwriting of both of these texts is so much like that of Cologne 1470 (Manfred Weber, "Ein koptischer Liebeszauber," pl. 35) and P.CtYBR inv. 3549 that probably all four can be identified as the work of a single scribe (whose handwriting Weber dates to the seventh century).*

A translation appears as text 107 above.

TEXT

```
   † ⲀⲘⲞⲨ ⲚⲀⲒ ⲠⲞⲞⲨ ⲠⲀⲰⲢⲈ ⲈⲚⲦⲈⲨⲄⲞⲘ
2  ⲘⲀⲨⲢⲒⲎⲀ ⲠⲀⲚⲄⲈⲀⲞⲤ ⲦⲀⲨ [........]
   ⲘⲒⲨⲒ̈ ⲠⲞⲞⲨ ⲘⲀⲦⲈⲨⲂⲒⲦⲈⲨⲈⲒ̈ⲢⲎⲚⲎ
4  ⲈⲂⲞⲀ ⲈⲒ̈ⲒⲞⲨ ⲦⲒⲤⲞⲠⲤ ⲀⲨⲰ ⲦⲒⲠⲀⲢⲀⲔⲀⲀⲈ
   ⲘⲞⲔ ⲀⲚⲞⲔ ⲚⲒⲘ
6  ⲀⲈⲔⲀⲀⲤ ⲈⲄⲈⲈⲒ̈ ⲚⲀⲒ̈ ⲠⲈⲢⲞⲞⲨ ⲚⲚⲒⲘ
```

NOTES

1 A point, probably unintentional, appears above Ⲩ in ⲀⲘⲞⲨ.

2 ⲦⲀⲨ: that is, ⲚⲦⲀⲨ? At the end of the line, eight letters or more are blotted out with heavily smeared ink (as on the back of the document); if the text was erased intentionally, then probably the three preceding letters (ⲦⲀⲨ) should have been included in the erasure.

3 ⲘⲒⲨⲒ̈: that is, ⲘⲒⲂⲈ? If so, the usage here might be similar in meaning to ⲔⲒⲘ Ⲛ̄ⲘⲞⲔ in Sergio Pernigotti, "Il codice copto," 33 (II.7, 9, 11). ⲘⲀⲦⲈⲨⲂⲒ: that is, ⲘⲀⲚⲦⲈⲨⲨⲒ.

4 ⲈⲒ̈Ⲓ̈ⲞⲨ: that is, Ⲉ ⲒⲰⲰⲨ; the two tremas are expressed with only three points.

6 ⲈⲄⲈ: that is, ⲈⲔⲈ. ⲠⲈⲢⲞⲞⲨ: that is, ⲠⲈⲈ ⲢⲞⲞⲨ; in Cologne 1470 (Manfred Weber, "Ein koptischer Liebeszauber," 117), the same scribe omits Ⲉ in ⲈⲀⲞⲄ (line 3) and in ⲘⲀⲈⲞⲨ ("fill them," line 4). An eight-pointed star and a triangle are drawn below this line.

2. P.CtYBR inv. 1791 (first text) fol

Papyrus, 37.3 x 25.4 cm, sixth or seventh century (so Theodore C. Petersen); purchased from Hans P. Kraus in New York, spring 1964. As viewed from the back, a kollesis *runs across the sheet horizontally between lines 40 and 41 of the first text (stepping up from top to bottom). Part of the top of the sheet has broken away, with the loss of some text at least on the back. At one time, the sheet was folded eight times (or more) from bottom to top and vertically in half. The first text occupies the upper portion of the front (along the fibers) and, when the sheet is turned over side to side, the upper portion of the back (across the fibers). The second text, in a different handwriting, begins on the lower portion of the front (along the fibers) and, when the sheet is turned over top to bottom, ends on the back in the space left blank at the end of the first text (across the fibers, but upside-down in relation to the first text).*

The present transcription of the first text only partly reflects its actual layout on the papyrus. Lines 1–12 are written in a narrow column to the left of a drawing of a trumpeting angel, lines 13–17 and 20–26 in a narrow column to the right. Lines 18–19 are written to the right of lines 15–17, thus serving partly to frame a group of signs (not reproduced here) to the right of lines 13–15. Lines 27–28 are written to the right of lines 20–21, but upside-down in relation to the rest of the text. The handwriting of these two lines (which are accompanied by another group of signs not reproduced here, to the right of lines 22–26) is more like the second text than the first, but I associate them with the first text both because of their position on the sheet, and because they seem to prescribe an offering, which would be redundant if associated with the second text. Lines 29–63 are written on the back. Whereas very little text, if any, seems to have been lost above lines 1 and 13, it seems likely that several lines are missing between lines 28 and 29, as are the beginnings of lines 29–31.

The handwriting and orthography of the first text are particularly atrocious. A translation appears as text 122 above.

TEXT

	CHNOϥ		ЄKCΔI ЄN
2	ЄNGЄ	14	NΔI
	ροπЄ		ЄNⲍЄN [T]
4	ЄNⲗЄ	16	BΔCIC ЄMⲡⲁ
	ⲧKⲱN		ⲁⲡOT NⲁTTⲱЄⳛЄM

6 ⲥⲧⲏⲣⲉⲍ
    ⲛⲁⲡⲟⲩⲕⲁ

8 ⲗⲁⲙⲱⲛ
    ⲙⲁⲥⲭⲉ

10 ⲡⲥⲉⲓ.
    ⲕⲟⲱ

12 ⲗⲉⲩⲕⲱⲛ

18 ⲁⲱⲧⲟⲩ ⲉⲡⲉⲕ
    ⲙⲟⲧⲉ

20 ⲉⲩⲓⲱ ⲗⲟⲩⲕⲱⲛ
    ⲉⲣⲉⲡⲗⲉⲕⲱⲛ

22 ⲙⲟⲩⲧⲱⲃ
    ⲭⲁⲓⲣⲉ ⲕⲁ

24 ⲅⲉⲙⲟⲩ ⲕⲁ
    ⲡⲁⲓ ⲡⲉ ⲅⲱⲣⲉⲍ

26 ⲉⲛⲡⲁⲡⲟⲧ

    ⲟⲩⲫⲓⲁⲗⲉ ⲛ̄ⲕⲁⲙⲉ,
    ⲕⲟⲩⲱⲧ

28 ⲛⲁⲗⲁⲩ

[   ]....ⲟⲩⲙⲉⲛⲟⲥ ⲉⲙ

30 [   ].[.....].ⲟ ⲙ̄ⲫⲟ ⲉⲙⲡⲓⲱⲧ
[......].ⲛⲁⲓⲟⲩⲛⲏ ⲭⲉⲣⲉ ⲧⲏⲥⲕⲩⲛⲏ ⲉⲙⲡⲓⲱⲧ
    ⲙⲛⲡⲱⲏⲣⲉ ⲙⲛⲡⲛⲉⲙⲁⲧⲓ ⲙⲛ

32 ⲛⲩⲧⲱⲟⲟⲡ ⲉⲛⲡ̄ⲧⲥⲉ ⲭⲉⲣⲉ ⲉⲥⲱⲁⲩⲉ
    ⲛⲛⲁⲣⲭⲏⲁⲅⲅⲉⲗⲟⲥ
    ⲉⲧⲧⲁⲅⲉⲣⲁⲧⲟⲩ ⲉⲡⲉⲟⲟⲩ ⲉⲙ[ⲡ]ⲓ̈ⲱⲧ ⲭⲉⲣⲉ ⲛⲁⲣⲭⲏ
    ⲙⲛ

34 ⲛⲏⲕⲍⲟⲥⲓⲁ ⲙⲛⲉⲛⲅⲟⲙ [ⲉ]ⲧⲅⲉⲙⲡⲍ̄ⲓ̈ⲥⲉ ⲭⲉⲣⲉ ⲧⲩⲕ
    ⲗⲉⲥⲓⲁ ⲛ̄ⲛⲉⲱⲉⲣⲉⲡⲙⲉⲥ[ⲉ] ⲙ̇ⲛⲛⲉⲧⲱⲟⲟⲡ ⲉⲛⲡ̄ⲧⲥⲉ

36 ⲭⲉⲣⲉ ⲉⲛⲧⲩⲛⲁⲙⲉⲥ ⲭⲉⲣⲉ ⲛⲩⲭⲉⲣⲟⲩⲃⲉⲛ ⲭⲉⲣⲉ
    ⲉⲛⲥⲟⲩⲣⲁ
    ⲡⲫⲉⲛ ⲭⲉⲣⲉ ⲉⲡⲍⲟⲩⲧⲁⲃⲧⲉ ⲙ̄ⲡⲣⲉⲥⲃⲏⲧⲏⲣⲟⲥ
    ⲉⲛⲧⲩⲕ

38 ⲗⲟⲥⲓⲁ ⲧ̄ⲅⲉⲛⲛⲏⲡⲉⲩⲉ ⲙⲛⲛⲟⲩⲟⲛ ⲛⲓⲙ ⲉⲧⲱⲟⲟⲡ
    ⲉⲛⲡⲏⲧⲉⲥ
    ⲭⲉⲣⲉ ⲉⲧⲡⲁⲣⲁⲍⲓⲥⲱⲥ ⲙⲛⲛⲟⲩⲟ̇ⲛ ⲛⲓⲙ ⲉⲧⲱⲟⲟⲡ
    ⲛ̄ⲡ̄ⲏⲧⲥ̄ ⲭⲉⲣⲉ̇

40 ⲉⲡⲡⲣⲏ ⲉⲧⲧⲉⲣⲟⲩⲉⲓⲛ ⲭⲉⲣⲉ ⲉⲧⲙⲏⲧⲥⲩⲛⲟⲟⲥ
    ⲉⲛⲧⲏⲛⲁ
    ⲙⲓ̈ⲥ ⲧ̄ⲕⲱⲧⲉ ⲉⲣⲟⲩ ⲭⲉⲣⲉ ⲉⲡⲟⲡⲉ ⲙⲛⲛⲏⲥⲓⲟⲩ
    ⲧⲏⲣⲟⲩ ⲭⲉⲣⲉ

42 ⲡⲙⲏⲧⲥⲩⲛⲟⲟⲥ ⲉⲛⲁⲣⲭⲱⲛ ⲉⲧⲧⲏⲱ ⲛ̄ⲉⲧⲩⲛⲟⲟⲩⲉ
    ⲛ̄ⲧⲩⲱⲏ
    ⲭⲉⲣⲉ ⲡⲙⲏⲧⲥⲩⲛⲟⲟⲥ ⲉⲛⲁⲣⲭⲱⲛ ⲉⲧⲧⲏⲱ
    ⲉⲛⲛⲉⲧⲛⲟⲩⲉ ⲙ̄ⲡⲉ

44 ϩ ⲟⲟⲩ ⲭⲉⲣⲉ ϩⲱⲣⲙⲟⲥⲉ ⲏ ⲁ ⲡⲛⲟ ⲉ ⲉⲛ ⲁⲣⲭⲱⲛ ⲉ ⲩⲥ ⲱⲧ ϩ ⲉ ⲉ ⲛ

ⲛ ⲁ ⲧⲡⲉ ⲙ ⲛ ⲛ ⲁ ⲡⲕ ⲁ ϩ ⲡ ⲁ ⲓ ⲉ ⳃ ⲁ ⲣⲉⲛ ⲁ ⲡⲉⲩ ⲥ ⲱⲧ ⲉⲙ ⲉ ⲧⲉⲩⲥⲉⲙ ⲏ

46 ⲥ ⲩ ⲏ ⲧⲟⲩ ⲛ ⲙⲉⲛ ⲥ ⲱ ⳃ ⲧ ⲓ ⲛ ⲟⲩ ⲧ ⲉ ⲥⲟ ⲡⲥ‾ ⲙ‾ⲙⲟⲕ ⲙ‾ⲡ ⲟⲟⲩ ⲁⲩ ⲱ

ⲧ ⲓ ⲡ ⲁ ⲣ ⲁ ⲅ ⲁ ⲗⲉ ⲉⲙⲟⲕ ϩ ⲟⲣⲙⲟⲥⲉⲏ ⲁ ⲡ ⲁ ⲡ ⲓ ϩ ⲣⲟⲟⲩ ⲉ ⲧ ϩ ⲟ ⲗⲉ ⳃ

48 ⲉⲧⲛⲟⲧⲉⲙ ⲉⲛ ⲑ ⲉ ⲙ ⳁ ⲓ ⲗ ⲉ ⲙ ⲟⲛ ⲡ ⲁ ⲧ ⲉⲥ ⲙ ⲏ ⲉ ⲧ ϩ ⲟ ⲗⲟ ⳃ ⳅ ⲉⲕ ⲁ ⲁ ⲥ

ⲉ ⲕ ⲁ ⲉ ⳧ ⳃ ⲁ ⲣ ⲟ ⲓ ⲉⲙⲡⲟⲟⲩ ⲁ ⲛⲟⲕ ⳅ ⳅ ⲛ‾ⲉ ⲅ ⲁ ϩ ⲉⲣ ⲁ ⲧ ϩ ⲉ ⳅ ⲉ

50 ⲛ ⲡ ⲓ ⲁ ⲡⲟⲧ ⲉ ⲧ ⲕ ⲏ ⲉⲣ ⲁ ⲓ ⲉⲙⲡ ⲁ ⲙⲧⲟⲩ ⲉⲃⲟ ⲗ ⲛⲉ ⲅ ⲙ ⲁ ϩ ⲉ ⳃ ⲛ ⲁ ⳧

ⲉ ⲛ ϩ ⲉ ⲣ ⲟⲟⲩ ⲉ ⳃ ϩ ⲟ ⲗⲉ ⳃ ⲉ ⳃ ⲛⲟⲧⲉ[ⲙ] ⲉ ⳃ ⲃ [ⲏⲕ] ⲉ ⲣ ⲁ ⲓ ⲉ ⳃ ⲛ ⲏⲩ ⲉ ⲡⲉ

52 ⲥ ⲏⲧ ⲉ ⳃ ⲕ ⲱ ⲧ ⲉ ⲛ‾ ⲑ ⲉ ⲛ ⲟⲩ ⲧ ⲣ..ⲟ ⲥ ⲉ ⳃ ⲙ ⲏ ϩ ⲉ ⲛⲛⲟⲩ ⲉ ⲗ ⲁ ⲗ ⲉ ⲛ ⲓ ⲙ

ⲉ ⳃ ϩ ⲟ ⲗⲉ ⳃ ⲉ ⳃ ⲥ ⲱⲕ ⲑ ⲉ ⲛ ⲟⲩ ⲧ ⲏ ⲩ̄ ⲛ ⲁ ⲧ ⲑ ⲟ ⲗ ⲛ ⲁ ⲧ ⲑ ⲉⲙ ⲛ ⲉ ⳃ ⲉ

54 ⲛ ⲁ ⲧⲛⲉ ⳅ ⲑ ⲁ ⲃ ⲉⲃⲟ ⲗ ϩ ⲁ ⲉ ⲓ ⲟ ϩ ⲁ ⲉ ⲓ ⳅ ⲧⲉⲱ ⲣ ⲉ ⲕ ⲉⲣ ⲟ ⲕ ⲛ‾ⲧ ⲟⲩ

ⲛ ⲁ ⲙ ⲙ‾ⲡ ⲓ ⲱⲧ ⲧ ⲓ ⲱ ⳃ ⲣ ⲉ ⲕ ⲉⲣ ⲟ ⲕ ⲧ ⲁ ⲡ ⲉ ⲉⲙⲡ ⳃ ⲏ ⲣ ⲉ

56 ⲧ ⲓ ⲱ ⲣ ⲉ ⲉⲣ ⲟ ⲕ ⲉⲙ ⲧ ⲉⲃ ⲟ ⲉⲙ ⲡ ⲉⲛⲉⲩ ⲙ ⲁ ⲉ ⲧ ⲟ ⲩ ⲁ ⲁ ⲃ ⳅ ⲉ ⳅ ⲕ ⲁ ⲁ ⲥ ⲉ ⲕ ⲩ ⲕ ⲱ ⲉⲛ ⲥ ⲱⲕ ⲛ‾ⲧ ⲟ ⲡ ⲟⲥ ⲛ ⲓ ⲙ ⲉ ⲛ‾ⲛ ⲉ

58 ⲕ ⲕ ⲉ ⳃ ⲁ ⲣ ⲟ ⲓ ⲉ ⲡⲉ ⲧ ⲟ ⲡ ⲟ ⲥ ⲡ ⲁ ⲓ ⲉ ⲓ ⳃ ⲟ ⲟ ⲡ ⲉⲛ ϩ ⲏⲧ ⳃ̄ ⲁ ⲛⲟⲕ

ⳅ ⳅ ⲛⲉⲕ ⳅ ⲱⲕ ⲛ ⲁ ⲓ ⲉⲃ [ⲟ] ⳑ ⲉ ⲙ ⲡⲟⲩ ⲟ ⳃ ⳃ ⲉⲙⲡ ⲁ ϩ ⲏⲧ

60 ⲙ ⲛ ⲛ ⲁ ⲡ ⲟⲩ ⲗⲉ ⲁ ⲅ ⲓ ⲁ ⲉ ⲛ ⲡ [ⲁ] ⳑ [ⲁ] ⲥ ϩ ⲛ‾ⲟ ⲩ ⲧ ⲁ ⲭ ⲏ ⲧ ⲁ ⲭ ⲏ

ϩ ⲁ ⲉ ⲓ ⲟ ⳅ ⲉ ⲧ ⲓ ⲱ ⲣ ⲉ ⲕ ⲧ ⲟⲩ ⲛ ⲁ ⲙ ⲉⲙⲡ ⳃ ⲏ ⲣ ⲉ ⲧ ⲁ ⲓ ⲉⲧ

62 ⲧ ⲁ ⲙ ⲁ ϩ ⲧ ⲉ ⲉⲙ ⲡⲥ ⲁ ⳃ ⲉ ⳃ ⲉⲛ ⲥ ⲓ ⲟⲩ ⲉ ⲉⲣⲉⲙ ⲏⲧⲥ ⲏⲛ ⲟ ⲟ ⲥ ⲉⲛ ⲥ ⲓ ⲟⲩ ⲟ ⲛ ⲛ ⲟⲩ ⲕ ⲗ ⲟ ⲙ ⲉⲛ ⳅ ⲉ ⲛ ⲧ ⲉ ⳃ ⲁ ⲡ ⲉ

NOTES

1–3 That is, ⲥⲛⲟⳃ ⲛ‾ⲑ ⲣⲟⲟⲙⲡⲉ.

6 ⲥ ⲧ ⲏ ⲣ ⲉ Ⳝ : that is, στύραξ.

7–8 ⲁ ⲡⲟⲩ ⲕ ⲁ ⲗ ⲁ ⲙ ⲱⲛ : that is, ὁποκάλαμος.

9 ⲙ ⲁ ⲥ ⲭ ⲉ : that is, μόσχος, or perhaps μοσχάτων (compare Walter E. Crum, "Magical Texts in Coptic," 196, verso line 17) or μαστίχη.

10–12 The unread letter is ⲧ, ⳙ, or ⲩ. The syntax is not clear, but probably the first two lexemes are ⲥϩⲁⲓ̈ and ⲕⲁⳙ (compare Crum, "Magical Texts in Coptic," 199:11 ⲕⲟⳙ ⲛⲗⲉⲩⲕⲟⲛ).

13 ⲥⲁⲓ: that is, ⲥϩⲁⲓ̈.

15–17 That is, ⲉⳅⲛ̅ⲧⲃⲁⲥⲓⲥ ⲙ̅ⲡⲁⲡⲟⲧ.

17 ⲛⲁⲧⲧⲱⲉⳙⲉⲙ: that is, ⲛ̅ⲁⲧⲱⳙⲙ̅, used here in a sense that is obscure (for other relevant examples, see Crum, *A Coptic Dictionary*, 39a 1–5, 69a 8–9, though in none of these cases is the topic a vessel); my translation ("pristine") is hypothetical, based on an assumption that the opposite meaning, that is, what it means to ⲱⳙⲙ̅ a vessel, is to use it, either simply by filling it with something, or by cooking in it.

18 ⲁⳙⲧⲟϥ: that is, ⲁⳙⲧϥ.

20 ⲉϥⲓⲱ ⲗⲟⲩⲕⲱⲛ: that is, ⲉⲃⲓⲱ ⲛ̅ⲗⲉⲩⲕⲟⲛ.

22 ⲙⲟⲩⲧⲱⲃ: that is, ⲙⲟⲟⲩ ⲛ̅ⲧⲱⲃⲉ?

23–24 ⲭⲁⲓⲣⲉ: or ⲕⲁⲓⲣⲉ. I adopt the former reading because the incantation begins with a series of at least sixteen "greetings" (ⲭⲉⲣⲉ = ⲭⲁⲓⲣⲉ), with the possibility that five more are lost before line 29, for a total of twenty-one (ⲕⲁ). But in any case the direction could mean rather to offer the entire series of however many greetings twenty-one times. Compare Angelicus M. Kropp, *Ausgewählte koptische Zaubertexte* 1.22–28 (text D), where ⲕⲁ occurs repeatedly, sometimes in the phrase ⲕⲁ ⲛⲥⲟⲡ, "twenty-one times"; or 1.50–51 (text K:1–23), where the ritualist is directed to recite certain passages a specified number of times. If this interpretation is correct, probably ⲅⲉⲙⲟϥ is also a verb (possibly with masc. sg. direct object), but I cannot identify the lexeme. On the other hand, ⲕⲁⲓⲣⲉ occurs as a substance in measured quantities in alchemical formulas (Ludwig Stern, "Fragment eines koptischen Tractates über Alchimie," 110 [Coptic p. 11:12–13], 113 [Coptic p. 15:3]), and for ⲕⲁ probably meaning "twenty-one" in a list of ingredients, see Kropp, 1.31 (text E:57).

25 That is, ⲡⲁⲓ̈ ⲡⲉ ⲡⲅⲱⲣⲅ; compare Adolf Erman, *Aegyptische Urkunden aus den Koeniglichen Museen zu Berlin: Koptische Urkunden* I, text 8:31.

27 What appears to be an incomplete ⲏ is written between ⲙ and ⲉ in ⲕⲁⲙⲉ.

31 ⲭⲉⲣⲉ: that is (here and passim), ⲭⲁⲓⲣⲉ. ⲧⲏⲥⲕⲩⲛⲏ: that is, ⲧⲉⲥⲕⲏⲛⲏ. ⲙⲛⲡⳙⲏⲣⲉ ⲙⲛⲡⲛⲉⲙⲁⲧⲓ (that is, ⲙⲛ̅ⲡⲉⲡⲛⲉⲩⲙⲁ) is written between lines 31 and 32.

32 ⲛⲩⲧ: that is, ⲛⲉⲧ. ⲉⲛϩϩⲧⲥⲉ: that is (here and in line 35), ⲛ̅ϩⲏⲧⲥ. ⲉⲥⳙⲁϥⲉ ⲛⲛ: that is, ⲉⲡⲥⲁⳙϥ ⲛ̅.

33 ⲉⲧⲧ: that is, ⲉⲧ; note the same duplication of ⲧ in lines 40 (here also the duplication of ⲡ) and 61–62.

36 ⲛⲩ: that is, ⲛⲉ.

38 ⲧ̅ϩⲉⲛⲛⲏⲡⲉⲧⲉ: that is, ⲉⲧϩⲛ̅ⲙ̅ⲡⲏⲩⲉ.

40 ⲙⲏⲧⲥⲩⲛⲟⲟⲥ: that is (here and in lines 42 and 43), ⲙ̅ⲛ̅ⲧⲥⲛⲟⲟⲩⲥ.

42 Perhaps a letter (ⲉ?) erased at the beginning of the line. ⲧⲏⳙ: ⳙ is formed like ϥ, but compare line 43. ⲛ̅ⲉⲩⲛⲟⲟⲩⲉ: that is, ⲉⲛ̅ⲟⲩⲛⲟⲟⲩⲉ.

43 ⲉⲛⲛⲉⲩⲛⲟⲟⲩⲉ: that is, ⲉⲛ̅ⲟⲩⲛⲟⲟⲩⲉ.

44 ⲥⲱⲧⲅⲉ: that is, ⲥⲱⲟⲧⲅ (for ⲥⲱⲟⲧⲅ ⲉⲅⲟⲩⲛ; compare Crum, "Magical Texts in Coptic," 198, recto lines 14–17 ⲅⲱⲣⲙⲟⲥⲓⲏⲁ ⲡⲁⲅⲅⲉⲗⲟⲥ ⲡⲁⲓ ⲉⲧⲉⲣⲉⲧⲍⲁⲗⲡⲓⲍ ⲛⲧⲟⲧⲏ ⲉⲩⲥⲱⲟⲧⲅ ⲉⲅⲟⲩⲛ ⲛ<ⲛ>ⲁⲅⲅⲉⲗⲟⲥ ⲉⲡⲁⲥⲡⲁⲥⲙⲟⲥ ⲛⲡⲓⲱⲧ, "Harmozel the angel, with the trumpet in his hand, gathering together the angels for the salutation of the father"—London Hay 10122 [text 81 above]).

45 ⲛⲁⲧⲡⲉ: ⲧ inserted (erroneously between ⲛ and ⲁ).

45–46 ⲡⲁⲓ ⲉϣⲁⲣⲉⲛⲁⲡⲉⲩ ⲥⲱⲧⲉⲙ ⲉⲧⲉⲩⲥⲉⲙⲏ ⲥⲩⲏⲧⲟⲩⲛ-ⲙⲉⲛⲥⲱⲩ: The meanings of ⲛⲁⲡⲉⲩ and ⲥⲩⲏⲧⲟⲩⲛⲙⲉⲛⲥⲱⲩ are not clear. Perhaps the former is for ⲛ̄ⲁⲡⲏⲩⲉ, "the heads." By ⲥⲩⲏⲧⲟⲩⲛⲙⲉⲛⲥⲱⲩ perhaps ⲛ̄ⲥⲟⲩⲁⲁⲧⲟⲩ ⲙⲛ̄ⲛ̄ⲥⲱⲩ (for ⲛ̄ⲥⲱⲩ?) is meant ("and it [that is, Harmozel's voice] sends them after him [that is, Harmozel]"). This passage may be compared with L. Saint-Paul Girard, "Un fragment de liturgie magique copte sur ostrakon," 64, lines 25–27 ⲛϣⲁⲩⲥⲱⲧⲙ ⲉⲣⲱ (that is, ⲉⲣⲟⲩ, referring to Harmozel, line 23) <ⲛ>ⲅⲓⲡⲁ.ⲉ (so Girard, but perhaps read <ⲛ>ⲅⲓⲛⲁⲡⲉ[ⲩ] or the like) ⲛⲉⲧ<ⲙ>ⲡⲅⲟⲩⲛ <ⲙ>ⲡⲙⲉⲧⲥⲛⲱⲩⲥ <ⲛ>ⲕⲱⲥⲙⲱⲥ ⲡⲉⲩⲛⲟⲃ (was ⲛⲥⲉⲟⲩⲛⲟⲩ intended?) ⲛⲥⲉⲩⲱⲅⲉⲙ ⲥⲱⲃ (that is, ⲛⲥⲱⲩ) ⲍⲉ etc., "the heads (?) within the twelve worlds hear him (that is, Harmozel, singing psalms inside the curtain veiling the father, lines 23–24) and rejoice and respond to him, saying. . . ." (Cairo 49547 [text 113 above]).

46 ⲧⲉ: that is, ⲧ (for the spelling, compare line 54).

47 ⲅⲣⲟⲟⲩ: ⲅ inserted.

48 ⲛⲟⲧⲉⲙ ⲉⲛⲑⲉ: ⲉⲛ written above ⲉⲙ.

49 ⲉⲕⲁ: that is, ⲉⲕⲉ. ⲛ̄ⲉⲅⲁⲅⲉⲣⲁⲧ: that is, ⲛ̄ⲧⲁⲅⲉⲣⲁⲧⲕ.

50 ⲉⲣⲁⲓ: that is, ⲉⲅⲣⲁⲓ̈.

51 ⲉⲣⲁⲓ (that is, ⲉⲅⲣⲁⲓ̈): for the reading, compare line 50.

52 ⲧⲣ..ⲟ̣ⲥ̣: The first letter is almost certainly ⲧ, but it appears to be deformed; the first unread trace is probably from ⲁ, ⲉ, ⲑ, ⲟ, ⲥ, ⲱ, ϣ, ⲅ, or ⲅ; the second unread trace is probably from ⲁ, ⲉ, ⲍ, ⲕ, ⲗ, ⲙ, ⲥ, ⲧ, ⲭ, or ⲅ; ⲟ̣ could also be ⲅ; the last letter is almost certainly ⲥ, but it appears to be deformed. ⲉⲛⲛⲟⲩⲉⲗⲁⲉ: that is, ⲛ̄ⲟⲩⲁⲗⲉ.

53 ⲑⲉ: that is, ⲛ̄ⲑⲉ. ⲛⲁⲧⲑⲟⲗ: that is, ⲛ̄ⲁⲧⲅⲱⲗ. ⲛⲁⲧⲑⲉⲙⲛⲉⲩⲉ: that is, ⲛ̄ⲁⲧⲅⲙ̄ⲛⲓⲩⲉ.

54 ⲑⲁⲃ: that is, ⲧⲁⲩ (Bohairic ⲑⲁⲩ). ⲅⲁⲉⲓ ⲍⲧⲉ: that is, ⲅⲁⲉⲓⲟ ⲍⲉⲧ (compare lines 61 and 46). ⲱⲣⲉⲕ ⲉⲣⲟⲕ: ⲉⲣⲟⲕ written above ⲱⲣⲉⲕ.

55 ⲧⲁⲡⲉ: that is, ⲛ̄ⲧⲁⲡⲉ; compare lines 54 and 56, and note also that the object of ⲱⲣⲕ here does not agree in gender with ⲧⲁⲡⲉ.

56 ⲱⲣⲉ: that is, ⲱⲣⲕ. ⲉⲙⲧⲉⲃⲟ: that is, ⲙ̄ⲡⲩⲱ (?). ⲡⲉⲛⲉⲩⲙⲁ: that is, ⲡⲉⲡⲛⲉⲩⲙⲁ.

57 ⲍⲉⲍⲕⲁⲁⲥ ⲉⲕⲩ: that is, ⲍⲉⲕⲁⲁⲥ ⲉⲕⲉ.

57–58 ⲉⲛ̄ⲛⲉⲕⲕⲉ: that is, ⲛ̄ⲧⲉⲓ.

58 ⲉⲓ: ⲉⲧ is expected.

59 ⲛⲉⲕ: that is, ⲛ̄ⲧ.

60 ⲁⲡⲟⲩⲗⲉⲅⲓⲁ: that is, ⲁⲡⲟⲗⲟⲅⲓⲁ. ⲡ[ⲁ]ⲗ̣[ⲁ]ⲥ: Compare Crum, "A Coptic Palimpsest," 214:3–4, 20–21 (and p. 217 n. 1); Kropp, 1.56–57 (text M:21–22, 28–29, 33); etc.

61 **ⲧⲟⲩⲛⲁⲙ**: that is, **ⲛ̄ⲧⲟⲩⲛⲁⲙ**, or perhaps **ⲉⲣⲟⲕ ⲛ̄ⲧⲟⲩⲛⲁⲙ**; see lines 54 and 56 (compare note on line 55).

62 **ⲙⲏⲧⲥⲏⲛⲟⲟⲥ**: that is, **ⲙⲛ̄ⲧⲥⲛⲟⲟⲩⲥ**.

63 **ⲛⲛ**: that is, **ⲛ̄**; the expression ⲟ **ⲛ̄-ⲟⲩ-** (rather than ⲟ **ⲛ̄-∅-**), though rare, is attested elsewhere (Gospel of Truth [NHC I,2] 19:20, 20:38, 23:23–24, 29:2, 31:28).

3. P.CtYBR inv. 1791 (second text) fol

Papyrus, 37.3 x 25.4 cm, sixth or seventh century (so Theodore C. Petersen); purchased from Hans P. Kraus in New York, spring 1964. For a description of the manuscript, see the preceding text. Lines 1–15 are written on the front (along the fibers), lines 16–18 on the back (across the fibers). Many of the superlinear strokes are very short, often no more than points. Between lines 4 and 5 are strings of letters and signs (not reproduced here).

A translation appears as text 74 above.

TEXT

```
   ⲉⲧⲃⲉⲟⲩⲙⲏ ⲛ̄ⲥϩⲓⲙⲉ ⲟⲩⲇⲏⲣⲁⲛⲟⲥ ⲉϥⲛ̄ϣ̄ⲧ
   ⲕⲁⲗⲱⲥ̄·
2  ⲉⲕⲥϩⲁⲓ̄ ⲛ̄ⲛⲁⲓ̄ ⲉⲩⲡⲉⲧⲁⲗⲱⲛ̄ ⲛ̄ⲕⲁⲥⲓ̄ⲧⲏⲣⲛ̄·
   ⲑⲩ . ⲁⲥⲡⲁⲣⲧⲟⲛ
   ⲟⲩⲥⲃⲏⲧⲉ ⲛ̄ⲧⲉⲣⲱϥ ⲛⲟⲩϩⲧⲟ ⲛ̄ⲕⲁⲙⲏ ⲧⲏⲣϥ̄·
   ⲙ̄ⲛⲟⲩϭⲓⲛϭⲁⲱ ⲉⲕ
4  ⲧⲱⲙⲉⲥ̄ ⲙ̄ⲙⲟⲥ ⲉⲡⲣⲟ ⲛ̄ⲧⲉⲥⲓ̄ⲙⲉ ⲕⲛⲁⲛⲁⲩ
   ⲉⲧⲉϥϭⲟⲙ ϩⲛⲟⲩⲧⲁⲭⲏ
   ⲧⲓ̄ⲱⲣⲕ ⲉⲣⲱⲧⲛ̄ ⲛ̄ⲛⲉⲧⲛ̄ⲣⲁⲛ ⲉⲧⲟⲩⲁⲁⲃ ⲧⲏⲣⲟⲩ
   ⲙ̄ⲛⲛⲉⲧⲛ̄ⲑⲉⲥⲓⲁ
6  ⲙⲛⲛⲉⲧⲛ̄ⲫⲏⲗⲁⲕⲧⲏⲣⲓ̄ⲟⲛ ⲙ̄ⲛⲛⲉⲧⲛ̣̄ⲑ̣ⲣⲟⲛⲟⲥ
   ⲉⲧⲉⲧⲛ̄ϩⲙⲟⲟⲥ̣
   ϩⲓ̄ⲁⲟⲟⲩ̄ ⲙ̄ⲛⲛⲉⲧⲛ̄ⲥⲧⲱⲁⲏ ⲉⲧϭⲟⲗⲉ ⲙ̄ⲙⲱⲧⲛ̄
   ⲙ̄ⲛⲛⲉⲧⲛ̄
8  ⲥⲧⲏⲗⲏ ⲉⲧⲁⲭⲏⲕ ⲉⲃⲟⲗ [ⲙ̄ⲛⲛⲉⲧⲛ]ⲧⲟⲡⲟⲥ
   ⲉⲧⲛ̄ⲧⲛ̄ϣⲟⲟⲡ ⲛ̄ϩⲏⲧⲟⲩ
   ⲧⲓ̄ⲱⲣ̄ⲕ ⲉⲣⲱⲧⲛ ⲛ̄ⲛⲁⲓ̄ ⲧⲏⲣⲟⲩ ⲉⲧⲃⲉⲟⲩⲙⲏ ⲛ̄ϩⲏⲧ
   ⲙ̄ⲛⲟⲩⲗⲏⲡⲉ̣
```

10 Ⲙ̄ⲚⲞⲨⲀⲒⲂⲈ ⲚϨⲎⲦ ϨⲚ̄ⲠϨ[Ⲏ]Ⲧ ⲚⲀⲀ ϨⲚ̄ⲞⲨⲦⲀⲬⲎ
    ⲦⲒ̄ⲰⲠⲔ̄ Ⲛ̄ⲚⲈ
    ⲦⲚ̄ⲦⲚⲞϬ ⲚϬⲞⲘ Ⲛ̄ⲦⲈⲂ[Ⲉ]ⲣⲤⲈⲂⲞⲨⲣ ⲠⲣⲢⲰ
    Ⲛ̄ⲚⲀϨⲘⲞⲚⲒⲞⲚ̣

12 .[..].ⲞⲨⲀⲀⲒ̄ Ⲛ̄.ⲞⲨ....Ⲙ̣Ⲛ̣ⲦⲣⲘ̣Ⲛ̣ϨⲎⲦ ⲦⲒ̄ⲰⲠⲔ ⲈⲣⲰⲦⲚ̄
    ⲚⲚⲀⲒ ⲦⲎⲢⲞⲨ Ⲙ̄ⲠⲈⲣⲔⲀⲀⲤ ⲈⲞⲨⲰⲘ̄ ⲞⲨⲀⲈ [Ⲥ̄Ⲱ
    ⲞⲨⲀⲈ ....]

14 ⲞⲨⲀⲈ ϨⲘⲞⲞⲤ ϢⲀⲚ̄ⲦⲈⲤⲈⲢⲐⲈ Ⲛ̄ⲚⲒⲞⲨϨⲰⲰⲣ ⲚⲔ[....]
    ⲈⲦⲀⲞⲂⲈ Ⲛ̄ⲤⲀⲚ̄ⲈⲨϢⲎⲣⲈ ⲀⲨⲰ Ⲛ̄ⲐⲈ ⲚⲞⲨⲦⲈⲀⲦⲒ̄Ⲁ̣[Ⲉ]

16 Ⲙ̄ⲘⲞⲞⲨ ⲈⲤⲀϢⲈ Ⲛ̄ⲤⲀⲞⲨⲔⲀⲦⲞⲤ Ⲛ̄ⲐⲈ ⲚⲞⲨϨⲞϤ
    ⲈⲤⲀϢⲈ Ⲛ̄[ⲤⲀⲦⲈ]
    ⲮⲨⲬⲎ ⲚⲀⲀ ϢⲀⲚ̄ⲦⲈⲤⲈⲒ ϢⲀⲚⲦⲘ̄ Ⲁ ϨⲚ̄ⲞⲨⲦⲀⲬⲎ
    ...[...]

18 *vacat*   ⲦⲈⲐⲎⲘⲒⲤⲈⲐ[...].[......]Ⲁ̣[.]

NOTES

1 ⲘⲎ: that is (here and in line 9), ⲘⲈ. ⲀⲎⲣⲀⲚⲞⲤ: meaning not clear; perhaps for τύραννος (as in Angelicus M. Kropp, "Oratio Mariae ad Bartos," 152 [III.3], where, however, this interpretation makes good sense), but if so the usage seems extraordinary. Ⲛ̄ϢⲦ̄: that is, Ⲛ̄ϢⲞⲦ.

2 ⲔⲀⲤⲒ̄ⲦⲎⲢⲚ̄: that is, κασσίτερος. ⲐⲨ: that is, ⲐⲨⲤⲒⲀ. ⲀⲤⲠⲀⲣⲦⲞⲚ: Compare Walter E. Crum, "Magical Texts in Coptic," 199 with n. 2. It is probable that after the abbreviation ⲐⲨ, a sign resembling a tall cursive Greek Gamma does not simply mark the abbreviation, but rather is itself an abbreviation for some word that is modified by ⲀⲤⲠⲀⲣⲦⲞⲚ (compare Friedrich Bilabel and Adolf Grohmann, *Griechische, koptische und arabische Texte*, text 142:23, where this seems certainly to be the case: ⲐⲨ: γ ⲈⲐⲞⲞⲨ). It is also possible that ⲀⲤⲠⲀⲣⲦⲞⲚ is for ⲀⲤⲠⲀⲣⲒⲦⲞⲚ (= ἀσφαλτος; compare Émile Chassinat, *Le manuscrit magique copte*, 58–74).

4 ⲤⲒ̄ⲘⲈ: that is, ⲤϨⲒⲘⲈ.

5 ⲐⲈⲤⲒⲀ (that is, ⲐⲨⲤⲒⲀ): Ⲁ written above Ⲓ at the edge of the sheet.

8 ⲈⲦⲚ̄ⲦⲚ̄: that is, ⲈⲦⲈⲦⲚ̄.

9 ⲀⲎⲠⲈ: that is, ⲀⲨⲠⲎ.

10–11 Ⲛ̄ⲚⲈⲦⲚ̄ⲦⲚⲞϬ: Ⲧ² inserted, requiring deletion of the possessive article, that is, emendation to Ⲛ̄ⲦⲚⲞϬ.

13 [Ⲥ̄Ⲱ ⲞⲨⲀⲈ ....]: For the restoration, compare Bilabel and Grohmann, *Griechische, koptische und arabische Texte*, text 122:99–101 (ⲞⲨⲰⲘ...Ⲥ̄Ⲱ... ⲚⲔⲀⲦ...ϨⲒⲚⲎⲂ), 131:12–13 (ⲞⲨⲰⲘ...Ⲥ̄Ⲱ...ϬⲰ ϨⲚⲀⲀⲀⲨ Ⲙ̄ⲘⲀ); the restoration could be completed, for example, by ⲚⲔⲞⲦⲔ (compare Paul C. Smither, "A Coptic Love-Charm," 173, lines 9–10 ⲀϨⲈ...ϨⲘⲞⲤ...ⲚⲔⲞⲦⲔ).

14 Ⲕ[....]: possibly Ⲕ[ⲀⲘⲈ] (compare Adolf Erman, *Aegyptische Urkunden aus den Koeniglichen Museen zu Berlin: Koptische Urkunden* I, text 3:8).

15–17 The first Ⲛ̄ⲐⲈ clause is a premodification of the second ⲀϢⲈ, not a continuation of ⲈⲣⲐⲈ in line 14; the second Ⲛ̄ⲐⲈ clause modifies the first ⲀϢⲈ.

On the image evoked, see Petr V. Ernštedt, "Graeco-Coptica," 125–27; Hans J. Polotsky, "Zu einigen Heidelberger koptischen Zaubertexten," 418–19; Ernštedt, *Koptskie teksty Gosudarstvennogo Èrmitaža*, 159–62. According to my understanding, however, the parallel is always drawn between the drop of water, as an object of desire to a thirsty person, and the beloved, never between the drop and the lover (nor between the jar and the beloved). Here and in the other love charms where it occurs, "the beloved" in this comparison is the ritualist, who seeks to become an object of desire to the ritually aroused "lover." The repetition of ⲁϣⲉ in four out of six examples of the comparison probably is a conscious play on words, but it is not significant for the meaning of the comparison: There is no parallel to be drawn between the relationship of lover to beloved on the one hand, and drop to jar on the other, even though it happens that the same verb (ⲁϣⲉ) can be used to describe both relationships. See above, text 73, lines 120–25 (and the note), etc.

18 The meaning of the remains of this line is not clear.

4. P.CtYBR inv. 1800 qua

Papyrus, 32.4 x 24.1 cm, sixth or seventh century (so Theodore C. Petersen [with hesitation], Birger A. Pearson); purchased from Hans P. Kraus in New York, spring 1964. At one time, the sheet was folded eight times from bottom to top and vertically in half. A kollesis runs across the sheet horizontally between lines 14 and 15 (stepping up from top to bottom). The text on the front is written across the fibers. The back is blank.

A translation appears as text 106 above.

TEXT

```
   [.].[..].[.]..ⲛⲁⲥ ⲡⲥⲁⲧⲁⲛⲁ ⲧⲓⲱⲣⲕ ⲉⲣⲟⲕ ⲉⲛⲛⲁⲏⲁ
2  ⲡⲁⲓ ⲉⲧⲉ]ⲣⲉⲧⲉϥⲟⲩⲛⲁⲙ ⲧⲁⲗⲏⲩ ⲉϩⲣⲁⲓ
   ⲉϫⲉⲛⲫⲁⲣⲙⲁ
   ⲉⲛⲡⲓⲱⲧ ⲉⲧⲟⲩⲁⲁⲃ ⲙⲉⲛⲁⲥⲁⲣⲱⲑ ⲡⲛⲟϭ
   ⲉⲛⲭ[ⲉ]ⲣⲟⲩⲃⲓⲛ
4  ⲡⲁⲓ ⲉⲧⲣⲟⲉⲓⲥ ⲉⲧⲉⲥⲕⲩⲛⲏ ⲉⲛⲡⲓⲱⲧ
   ⲡⲡⲁⲛⲧⲱⲕⲣⲁⲧⲱⲣ
   ⲧⲓⲱⲣⲉⲕ ⲉⲛⲡ[ⲟ]ⲟⲩ ⲡⲁⲅⲅⲉⲗⲟⲥ
   ⲉⲛⲡⲉⲑⲏⲥⲓⲁⲥⲧⲏⲣⲓⲟⲛ ⲉⲧⲟⲩⲁⲁⲃ
6  ϫⲉⲛⲕⲟ ⲛⲣⲉⲙϩⲉ ⲁⲛ ⲟⲩⲇⲉ ⲛⲉⲧⲃⲏⲁ ⲉⲃⲟⲁ ⲉⲃⲱⲕ
   ⲉϩⲣⲁⲓ ϣⲁⲡⲛⲟⲩ[ⲧⲉ]
```

ⲞⲨⲆⲈ ⲦⲈⲔⲐⲎⲤⲒⲀ ⲈⲨⲢⲀⲒ Ⲏ ⲈⲞⲨⲰϢⲈⲦ
ⲈⲚⲠⲈⲔⲢⲒⲦⲎⲤ ⲈⲘⲘⲎ[Ⲧ]

8 ⲞⲨⲆⲈ ⲈⲀⲠⲀⲚⲦⲀ ⲈⲠϪⲞⲈⲒⲤ ⲈⲚⲠⲈⲔⲀϨⲈⲢⲀⲦⲈⲔ
ⲈⲨⲢⲀⲒ ⲈϪⲈⲚ

ⲠⳊⲰⲘ[Ⲁ] ϪⲆ ⲚⲈⲦⲈⲒⲚⲈ ⲈⲨⲢⲀⲒ [Ⲉ]ϪⲰϤ ⲈⲚⲞⲨϨⲒⳤ
ⲘⲈⲚⲞⲨϢⲰ[ⲚⲈ]

10 ⲘⲈⲚⲞⲨⲖⲞϨⲖⲈϬ ⲘⲈⲚⲞⲨϨⲢⲈⲨⲘⲀ ⲘⲈⲚⲞⲨⲀⲤⲒⲔ
ⲘⲈⲚⲞⲨⲦⲔⲀⲤ

ⲘⲈⲚⲞⲨϨⲖⲞⲠⲖⲈⲠ ⲘⲈⲚⲞⲨⲘⲈⲦⲔⲞⲨⲒ ⲈⲚϨⲎⲦ
ⲘⲈⲚⲞⲨⲈⲢⲘⲞ

12 ⲈⲦ ⲘⲈⲚⲞⲨϢⲈⲂⲈ ⲘⲈⲚⲞ[ⲨⲦ]ⲈⲘⲞⲚⲒⲞⲚ ⲈⲚⲀⲒⲂⲈ ⲘⲈⲚ
ϢⲂⲈ ⲈⲚⳊⲒ ⲈⲚϢⲰⲚⲈ ⲈⲢ[ⲈⲚⲀⲒ] ϢⲞⲂⲈ ⲈⲨⲈⲒ
ⲈⲚⲔⲈⲚⲦⲞⲨ ⲈⲨⲢⲀⲒ

14 ⲈϪⲈⲚⲠ[Ⳝⲱ]ⲘⲀ ϪⲆ ⲈⲚⲚ[Ⲉ]ϨⲞ̣Ọ̣Ⲩ ⲦⲎⲢⲞⲨ
ⲈⲚⲠⲈϤⲰⲚⲈϨ

ϪⲈⲚⲈⲘⲀⲔⲞⲤ ⲈⲚϨⲞⲞⲨⲦ ⲞⲨⲆⲈ ⲪⲀⲢⲘⲀⳀⲞⲤ
ⲈⲚⲤϨⲒⲘⲈ ⲈϢⲚⲀ

16 ⲚⲀϤ ⲞⲨⲆⲈ ⲈⲢⲠⲀϨⲢⲈ ⲈⲢⲞϤ ⲈⲂⲞⲖ ϨⲈⲚⲚⲀϬⲒϪ
ⲀⲚⲞⲔ ϪⲆ ϢⲀⲚ

ⲦⲒⲚⲀ ⲚⲀϤ ⲈⲒⲢⲈ ⲀⲨⲰ ⲚⲈⳀϪⲰⲔ ⲚⲀⲒ ⲈⲂⲞⲖ
ⲈⲚⲠⲞⲨⲰϢ ⲦⲎⲢⲈϤ

18 ⲈⲚⲠⲀϨⲎⲦ ⲠⲈⲦⲈⲘⲀ ⲈⲚⲦⲀⲮⲨⲬⲎ ϨⲈⲚⲦⲈⲔⲚⲞϬ
ⲈⲚϬⲞⲘ ⲀⲤ

ⲘⲞⲦⲈⲞⲤ ⲦⲈⲘⲞⲚⲒⲀⲔⲞⲤ ⲀⲒ[Ⲟ ⲀⲒ]Ọ ⲦⲀⲬⲎ ⲦⲀⲬⲎ
. . . [͞.] ͞. [͞.]Ⲑ̄

20 Φ̄Ⲉ̄Ⲗ̄Ⲗ̄Ⲱ̄Ⲑ̄ Ⲁ̄Ⲑ̄Ⲉ̄Ⲥ̄ ⲦⲀⲬⲎ Ⲧ[ⲀⲬⲎ   *vacat?*   ]

NOTES

1 There is a lacuna over this line through ⲠⳔⲀⲦ, the superlinear stroke over these four letters being restored. The first extant trace is probably from Ⲓ, Ⲕ, Ⲧ, or Ϥ, possibly from Ⲉ, Ⲏ, Ⲡ, or Ⲥ; the second is probably from Ⲕ (shaped as in line 7 ⲔⲢⲒⲦⲎⲤ) or Ϩ; the third is probably from Ⲛ or Ⲡ; the fourth is probably from Ⲁ or Ⲕ. Ⲥ could also be Ⲉ̣.

3 ⲀⲤⲀⲢⲰⲐ ⲠⲚⲞϬ ⲈⲚⲬ[Ⲉ]ⲢⲞⲨⲂⲒⲚ: Compare Viktor Stegemann, *Die koptischen Zaubertexte*, 67 (no. 44:1–2); Angelicus M. Kropp, *Der Lobpreis des Erzengels Michael*, 35 (line 148 [= text 135 above]).

6 ⲚⲈⲦ: that is, Ⲛ̄Ⲧ, neg. I Present, requiring emendation of ⲂⲎⲖ ⲈⲂⲞⲖ to ⲂⲎⲖ ⲀⲚ ⲈⲂⲞⲖ.

7 ⲈⲘⲘⲎ[Ⲧ]: that is, Ⲙ̄ⲘⲈ, but possibly restore ⲈⲘⲘⲎ[ⲚⲈ].

9 ⲠⳊⲰⲘ[Ⲁ] ϪⲆ: Compare line 14.

11 ⲘⲈⲦ: that is, Ⲙ̄Ⲛ̄Ⲧ.

11–12 ⲉⲣⲙⲟⲉⲧ: that is, ⲡⲙⲟⲛⲧ, hence perhaps to be emended to ⲉⲣⲙⲟⲛⲉⲧ (ⲟ at the end of line 11 is deformed, but no attempt was made to write ⲟ̄ for ⲟⲛ).

12 For the restoration, compare line 19 (ⲧⲉⲙⲟⲛⲓⲁⲕⲟⲥ).

13 ϣⲃⲉ ⲉⲛⲅⲓ ⲉⲛϣⲱⲛⲉ: that is, ϣϥⲉ ⲛ̄ⲅⲓⲛϣⲱⲛⲉ. ⲉⲩⲉⲓ ⲉⲛⲕⲉⲛⲧⲟⲩ: that is, ⲉⲩⲉⲉⲓ ⲛ̄ⲧⲛ̄ⲧⲟⲩ.

14 ⲉϫⲉⲛⲡ[ⲥⲱ]ⲙⲁ ⲁⲁ: The traces are very ambiguous, but compare lines 8–9.

15 ϫⲉⲛⲉ: that is, ϫⲉⲛ̄ⲛⲉ.

18 ⲉⲧⲉⲙⲁ: that is, ⲁⲓⲧⲏⲙⲁ.

19 Of the undeciphered traces, the first and second are probably to be read ⲭⲓ or ⲭⲏ (ⲭ could also be ϫ), but possibly ϩⲉ etc.; the third and fourth traces are very ambiguous.

5. P.CtYBR inv. 2124

Paper, 10.9 x 8.4 cm; donated by Hans P. Kraus, December 1966. The text is written in Bohairic. The back is blank.

A translation appears as text 58 above.

TEXT

    ⲧⲱⲃϩ ⲉ́ϫⲉⲛⲛⲉⲛ
2 ⲓⲱϯ ⲛⲉⲙⲛⲉⲛⲥ̀ⲛ
    ⲛⲟⲩ ⲉⲧⲁⲩϣ̈ⲱⲓⲛⲓ
4 ⲃⲉⲛⲡ̈ϣⲱⲛⲓ ⲛⲓ
    ⲃⲉⲛ ϩⲓⲧⲉ ⲃⲉⲛⲡⲓ
6 ⲑⲱⲡⲟⲥ ϩⲓⲧⲁ ⲃⲉⲛ
    ⲡⲓ ⲛⲓⲃⲉⲛ ⲛⲉⲛⲧⲉ
8 ⲡ̄ⲭ̄ⲥ ⲡⲉⲛⲛⲟⲩ
    ϯ ⲁ́ⲣⲓϩ̣ⲙⲟⲧ ⲛⲱ
10 ⲛⲉⲙⲟⲩⲱϫⲁⲓ ⲛⲉ
    ⲙ̇ⲡⲁⲧⲉⲗϣ̈ⲱⲓ
12 ⲧⲏⲣⲟⲩ ⲛ̇ⲧⲉϥ
    ⲭⲉⲛⲉⲛⲛⲟⲩⲃⲓ
14 ⲛⲉⲛ ⲃⲟϫ

NOTES

3 ⲏ added in the margin at the beginning of the line. ϣ̇ⲱⲓⲛⲓ: that is, ϣⲱⲛⲓ.

4 ⲡ̇ϣ̅ⲱⲛⲓ: that is, ϣⲱⲛⲓ.

6 ⲑⲱⲡⲟⲥ: that is, ⲧⲟⲡⲟⲥ.

7 ⲡⲓ: probably an error for ⲏⲓ. ⲛⲉⲛⲧⲉ: that is, ⲛ̇ⲧⲉ.

9 ⲛⲱ: that is, ⲛⲱⲟⲩ.

10–11 ⲛⲉⲙ̇: that is, ⲛⲉⲙ.

11 ⲡ is a correction over ⲙ. ⲉⲗ̅ϣⲱⲓ: that is, ⲉⲣ̅ϣⲱⲛⲓ.

14 ⲃⲟⲗ: that is, ⲉⲃⲟⲗ.

TEXTUAL NOTES

1. A woman's complaint *(Old Coptic Schmidt Papyrus)*

9   "*<before> him*": that is, before you, the god.

10   "*Hor . . .* ": possibly "Hor . . . my Tirter" or "Hor . . . he of (that is, son of) Tirter."

17   "*of . . .* ": possibly "of the [gods] . . . " or "of our [Ti]rter" followed by "my Mouhrker" or "they of (that is, children of) Mouhrker." Line 18 opens with Coptic letters that may possibly be translated "they of (that is, children of) Horus. . . ."

2. Invocation of Egyptian and Jewish deities *(Great Magical Papyrus of Paris, 1–25)*

12   "*who give answer*": Coptic ⲉⲧⲁⲓⲟⲩⲱ (not ⲉⲧⲁⲓⲟⲩⲱ, as printed in Karl Preisendanz, *Papyri Graecae Magicae*, 1.66).

13   "*the noubs tree*": or, "the shade of the noubs tree."

25   "*The usual*": The manuscript has ⲟ over ⲕ, probably for κοινόν (or κοινῶς? καλῶς?). Terrence DuQuesne, *A Coptic Initiatory Invocation*, 15, translates the final clause as follows: "about which I enquire of them clearly." Here Marvin Meyer's interpretation is that the abbreviation provides the user the opportunity to suggest a personal request.

3. Isis love spell *(Great Magical Papyrus of Paris, 94–153)*

99   "*He is not with me*": or, "It is not of my doing."

108   "*those who trample (?)*": Coptic ⲛϩⲑⲟⲙ (compare ϩⲱⲙ, "trample"; Walter E. Crum, *A Coptic Dictionary*, 674b–675a).

110   "*forge*": Read ⲙⲟⲩⲧ (rather than ⲙⲟⲩⲧ, as mistakenly printed in Karl Preisendanz, *Papyri Graecae Magicae*, 1.72), for ⲙⲟⲩⲛⲕ, "make, form" (Crum, 174b–175a).

114   "*this flame . . .* ": The Coptic not translated here is ⲉⲧⲉⲙⲉⲥⲕⲁⲧⲉ, which F. Ll. Griffith, "The Old Coptic Magical Texts of Paris," 90, translates "which is mysterious."

124   "*arouse god (after) N.*": or, "arouse every god (after N.)."

152   "*what is in her heart*": Read ⲉⲡⲉⲧⲉⲙⲡⲉⲥϩⲧ (rather than ⲉⲙⲉⲧⲉⲙⲡⲉⲥϩⲧ, as mistakenly printed in Preisendanz, 1.76).

4. Spells and healing legends *(Oxyrhynchus 1384)*

12   "*silphium (?)*": Greek φοίλλου (for φύλλου), "leaf"; in medical texts the word often refers to silphium, that is, laserwort.

26 *"The son of the lord"*: Greek ὁ κ⟨υρίο⟩υ; possibly read ὁ κ⟨ύριο⟩ς, "The lord" (so Bernard P. Grenfell and Arthur S. Hunt, *The Oxyrhynchus Papyri*, 11.240).

30 *"difficulty in urination"*: or, strangury, Greek στραγγουριτία (for στραγγουρητία, compare στραγγουρία).

6. Healing ostracon *(Paris, ostracon from the Egger collection)*

1 *"Soloam"*: Read "Siloam."
2 *"Bedsaida"*: Read "Bethsaida."

8. Amulet for help *(Berlin 11858)*

1 *"[When a strong . . . came up]"*: restored before the existing line 1.
30 *"bless"*: or, "you bless."

10. Spell invoking Christ *(Cairo, Egyptian Museum 10263)*

1 *"the fullness of the aeon"*: Greek τὸ πλήρωμα τοῦ αἰῶνο[ς].
17 *"the figure"*: Greek τῆς εἰκόνος, "the image."

12. Amulet to heal and protect Megas *(Amsterdam 173)*

2 *"heal"*: or, "is healed."

20. Amulet to protect against evil spirits *(Vienna G 337, Rainer 1)*

14 *"it"*: that is, the evil spirit or demon.
27 *"beams"*: Greek δοκούς, "beams" of houses or "bars" of doors.

21. Protective spell *(Ianda 14)*

18 *"<our> debtors"*: after "debtors," Greek ὀφιλέταις, the scribe neglected to add an additional line: ἡμῶν, καὶ μὴ ἄγε ἡμᾶς εἰς πειρασμόν, ἀλλὰ ῥῦσαι ἡμᾶς ἀπὸ τοῦ πον-, "our (debtors). And do not lead us into temptation, but deliver us from the e-" (for "evil one," compare line 3).

22. Spell for protection against evil spirits *(Cairo, Egyptian Museum 67188)*

2 *"[. . .]"*: Greek [. . .]ϲτεφανη; compare (with Karl Preisendanz, *Papyri Graecae Magicae*, 2.222) PGM IV.2271–72, χρυσοστεφή, "crowned with gold."

25. Amulet to protect the entrance to a house *(Oxyrhynchus 1060)*

5 *"arte<m>isian"*: Greek ἀρτερήσιε; read ἀρτε<μί>σιε (compare Oslo 1.5, 3 [text 26]).

26. Amulet to protect a house and its occupants *(Oslo 1.5)*

2 *"Salaman:"* "Solomon"?
7 *"Naias"*: Naiad, "river nymph"?
"Meli": Greek μέλι, "honey"?
8 *"KORE"*: Greek κόρη, "girl"? In Greek mythology the daughter of Demeter, sometimes named Persephone, was called Κόρη, "girl" or "daughter."

37. Biblical names of power *(Heidelberg G 1359)*

2 *"of god"*: Greek θεοῦ; perhaps read θεός, "(is) god," with Karl Preisendanz, *Papyri Graecae Magicae*, 2.223.
4 *" . . . "*: According to Adolf Deissmann, *Light from the Ancient East*, 405, a word has been crossed out.
10 *"Judah"*: Greek Ἰούδα; Deissmann, 406, suggests Ἰουδα[ς], "Judas."

16 *"[Es]aiou"*: Greek transcription [Ησ]αιου (so Deissmann, 406).

18 *"Jachaz"*: "Joachaz"?

19 *"[J]akin"*: "Joakin"? (for Joakim).

26 *". . . . el"*: Deissmann, 406, suggests the Greek transcription Ηλ[ι], "my god."

39. Spell for ascending through the heavens *(Second Book of Jeu, chapter 52)*

passim The text gives the numbers both in numerals and in words.

40. The Gospel of the Egyptians *(Nag Hammadi Codex III)*

66,8 *"IE"*: probably an abbreviation for ΙΕCCЄΟC or similar; Codex IV spells it out.

66,22 *"EIOEI EIOSEI"*: The editors suggest that the letters are a variation of Exodus 3:14 in the Greek Septuagint, ἐγώ εἰμι ὁ ὤν "I am the one who exists"; however, long supralinear strokes divide these vowels into the two words indicated here.

67,14 *"IES"*: The editors see ΙЄC and ΙC as the standard abbreviations for Jesus.

41. The First Stele of Seth *(Nag Hammadi Codex VII)*

119,16 *"self-produced one"*: While page 118, line 28, uses Coptic ϪΠΟ for "produced," here the text uses αὐτογενής.

42. Prayers, hymns, and invocations *(Zostrianos, Nag Hammadi Codex VIII)*

4,25 *"[I] was rescued"*: restoring Ϫ[ЄΙ], "I," not Ϫ[Ν], "we," as in the critical edition.

4,28 *"[by] their angelhood"*: restoring [ϨΝ], "by," not [ΜΝ], "and," as in the critical edition.

51,24ff. *"You are one . . . "*: This seems similar to a hymn in the Gospel of the Egyptians, NHC IV 59, 19ff.

43. Book of ritual spells *(Michigan 136)*

1 *"a little"*: Coptic ΚΟΥΪ; William H. Worrell, "Coptic Magical and Medical Texts," 17, suggests the reading ΚΟΥΪ ΚΟΥΪ "little by little."

5-6 *" . . . petala Kenon"*: Worrell, 17, suggests πέταλον καινόν, "new metal leaf."

17ff. Compare *PGM* VII. 490–504; Jacques van der Vliet, "Varia Magica Coptica," 228–31.

29 *"the (condition) from god*: Coptic ΤΟ ΚΑΤΑϤϮ; Worrell, 29, offers the translation "the natural position" and also cites (18) a suggestion of Campbell Bonner, ΚΑΤΑϤΡ, κατάφορον (?), "downward position" (?).

33 *"under it"*: that is, under the womb or vagina.

44 *" . . . . "*: Here the Coptic reads ΚΤΡΙΤЄ, the meaning of which is unknown; Worrell, 19, 29, speculates that it could be Κ̄ τρίτη, "twenty-third."

64-66 The Coptic text in these lines seems to be defective.

75-76 *"(for) four days of how many . . . "*: The translation is tentative.

79 Something seems to be missing at the end of page 5.

80 *"her spine"*: Coptic ΠϪЄΒЄΝ ΝΤЄCϪΙСЄ, perhaps "the cord of her back"; the translation is tentative.

95-97 *"with their garments torn . . . "*: The text and translation of these lines remain uncertain; note the emendations of Elizabeth Stefanski in Worrell, 22.

97   " . . . ": Coptic ⲗⲁϩⲙⲉϥ, meaning unknown (compare Walter E. Crum, *A Coptic Dictionary*, 150a).

102   *"7 great cows"*: Coptic ⲍ̄ ⲛϩⲉⲱ̄; Crum (in Worrell, 22) suggests ⲍ̄ ⲉϩⲉ ⲱ. It is also possible to derive ϩⲉⲱ̄ from a form of ⲉⲓⲱ (Crum, *A Coptic Dictionary*, 75b) and translate the phrase "7 asses."

133   *"the malignant disease"*: Coptic ⲡϣⲱⲛⲟⲩⲙ̄ⲏ; Crum (in Worrell, 23) suggests ⲡ̄ϣⲛⲟⲩⲁⲙⲟⲙⲉ "the disease of cancer / gangrene" (compare Greek καρκίνος, "eating sore, ulcer, cancer").

135   *"measures of Ebriaam"*: Coptic ϣⲓ ⲛ̄ⲉⲃⲣⲓⲁⲁⲙ; compare ϣⲉ ⲛ̄ⲁⲃⲣⲁϩⲁⲙ, "wood of Abraham," in other Coptic texts of ritual power.

145   *"in the . . . "*: Coptic ϩⲛ̄ ⲧⲕⲉⲗⲓⲥⲧⲣⲁ; Worrell, 34, proposes that ⲕⲉⲗⲓⲥⲧⲣⲁ may be from the Greek κλεῖστρον/κλεῖθρον, "bar, bolt," and that the word may communicate the sense of "room."

147–48   *"stretch them out . . . "*: Coptic ⲛ̄ϭⲉⲡⲁϩⲟⲩ ⲉϫ̄ⲛ ⲡⲉⲕⲣⲁⲧϥ̄. The translation is uncertain. Worrell, 24, wonders whether ⲡⲉⲕⲣⲁⲧϥ̄ could possibly be translated "your bed" (from ⲣⲱⲧⲉⲃ, "lie down"). In that case the clause could be translated "stretch them out on your bed." Compare also ⲣⲁⲧ- as "bottom, part that is down."

195   *"neck"*: or, "shoulders."

206–7   *"calf <marrow>"*: Here the Coptic text reads ⲁⲛⲑⲁ̄ⲙ̄ ⲙ̄ⲙⲁⲥⲉ, "calf skull" (compare line 209). The textual emendation to <ⲁⲧⲕⲁⲥ> (again compare line 209) is suggested by Worrell, 27.

214–15   *"pint"*: Coptic ϫⲉⲥⲧⲏⲥ; the Greek ξέστης is from the Latin *sextarius*, a Roman measure of about a pint.

219   *"is mixed in"*: Coptic ⲉⲓ ⲉϩⲟⲩⲛ, literally "goes in."

224   *"vegetable oil"*: Coptic ⲛⲉϩ ⲛ̄ⲥⲓⲙ, perhaps "radish oil."

44.   Spells for medical problems *(Vienna K 8303)*

Recto

7   *"bone (?)"*: Coptic ⲕⲁⲥ; ⲧⲕⲁⲥ, "pain," is a problematic emendation since "it" in the same line is feminine in gender and ⲧⲕⲁⲥ is masculine.

Verso

9   *". . ."*: perhaps "on a bone" or even "prayers" (Coptic ⲉⲩⲭⲁⲥ—so Walter Till); otherwise, "it will stop" (Coptic ⲉϥⲛⲁϩⲟ—so Viktor Stegemann).

10   *"Alaoth"*: Compare "aloes," from Greek ἀλόη? See Friedrich Bilabel and Adolf Grohmann, *Griechische, koptische und arabische Texte*, 402, regarding ⲁⲗⲟⲩⲑ in a similar context in Heidelberg Kopt. 681 (text 105). In this and other instances Bilabel translates ⲁⲗⲟⲩⲑ as "aloes."

47.   Spell to bring sleep *(Berlin 5565)*

1–2   *"you will go . . . you will stay"*: perhaps "will you go . . . will you stay . . . ?" *"stay"*: Coptic ⲙ̄ⲙⲟⲥ, perhaps for ϩⲙⲟⲟⲥ.

8   *"to confine them (?)"*: Coptic ⲉϫⲁⲗⲁⲩ (ϫⲁⲗⲁ′, from ϫⲱ(ⲱ)ⲗⲉ, ϭⲱⲗ?). On the question of the placement and meaning of this word see Angelicus M. Kropp, *Ausgewählte koptische Zaubertexte*, 2.14; Walter E. Crum, *A Coptic Dictionary*, 769a (referring to 561a).

48.   Another spell to bring sleep *(Schmidt 1)*

14–15   *"Even <if> [you] . . . "*: The restoration follows Angelicus M. Kropp, *Ausgewählte koptische Zaubertexte*, 2.5, and parallel Berlin 8313, verso, 3 (text 49).

49. Spells for pain of childbirth and stomach pain *(Berlin 8313)*

1,5–6   *"found a doe . . . in pain [. . .] in labor pains"*: The Coptic is difficult. Angelicus M. Kropp suggests "giving birth in a cave of stone."

13   *"[wand]"*: Kropp restores [ⲡⲁϥⲁⲟⲥ], "wand," but Walter Beltz leaves this blank.

14   *"[it]"*: "It" is masculine, thus "upon the offering" (not upon the doe, who is feminine).

15   *"whatever is crooked, let it be straight"*: Compare Isaiah 40:4 and Luke 3:4; here the imagery of the biblical words is applied to the birth passage.

2,1   *"Jesus! Horus"*: or, "Jesus Horus." In this connection it may be noted that in the Coptic Museum in Old Cairo there is a wooden crucifix with the crucified figure of Jesus together with a falcon (Horus).

2   *"[Bank bird]"*: Jacques van der Vliet notes that if the Bank bird is understood to be a phoenix, then Horus may be described as getting a stomachache from committing the sacrilege of eating three sacred birds.

7   *"to him"*: The manuscript has ⲉⲡⲟⲓ, "to me."

15   *"to him"*: The manuscript (line 14) has ϣⲁⲣⲟⲓ, "to me."

19   *"crown"*: Coptic ⲕⲉⲫⲁⲗⲏ (κεφαλή), perhaps "head" or "helmet."

23   *"Bank bird"*: See note to 2,2.

50. Amulet to heal and protect a woman *(Vienna K 7093)*

6   *"Kiraheu"*: or, "lady Heu."

9   *"THIO"*: The reading is uncertain; perhaps read ⲑϥ, = ϥⲑ (the Coptic designation for the number 99) = "Amen" (a common convention in Coptic texts of ritual power)? Compare Moen 3, end (text 117), and Michigan 593, page 12, line 6 (text 133).

51. Amulet to heal and protect Poulpehepus *(Oxyrhynchus 39 5B.125/A)*

5   *"take away"*: Anthony Alcock, "A Coptic Magical Text," 98, erroneously reads ⲱⲧⲛ̄ⲣⲱ (from line 4—compare ⲱⲧⲏⲣⲱ); from the plate on page 103 it seems likely that the manuscript here reads ϥⲓ ⲉϥⲱⲗ (for ϥⲓ ⲉⲃⲟⲗ) or something similar (compare below, lines 22, 39–40, 49).

12–13   *"tertian fever"*: so Walter E. Crum, according to Alcock, 101; Coptic ϣⲟⲩⲙⲉⲧϣⲱⲙⲉⲧ, literally "three three."

18   *"driven into (?)"*: Coptic ⲧⲱϫⲟⲩ, perhaps from ⲧⲱⲕⲥ (so Alcock, 101).

32   *" . . . "*: Alcock, 100, offers the translation "old," which presupposes the Coptic ⲡⲗⲗ rather than the ⲅⲗⲗ that he mistakenly includes in his transcription (99; compare the photographic reproduction on 103, which almost certainly should be read with a ⲡ rather than a ⲅ).

52–53   *"tertian fever"*: Coptic ϣⲟⲩⲙⲉⲧⲧ̄ (see above, note to lines 12–13).

52. Amulet to heal and protect Phoibammon *(amulet from the Moen collection)*

8   *"Phoibammon, the son"*: Possibly read "Phoibammon son <of Maria>" (compare lines 24–25).

53. Another amulet against fever *(Heidelberg Kopt. 564)*

1   *"[As]arias"*: or, "[Az]arias."

3   *"B[. . .]"*: Perhaps restore to read "B[oulal]" (but Hans Quecke suggests that there was a ⲕ in the restored position).

8 "*malady*": Coptic ⲁⲥⲓⲕ, a periodic malady or fever (so Walter E. Crum, *A Coptic Dictionary*, 18a).

54. Amulet to heal Ahmed *(Heidelberg Kopt. 544)*

12–13 "*slight chill*"; Coptic ⲡⲓⲕⲁ ⲛⲥⲁϩⲧⲉ (on ⲡⲓⲕⲁ compare ⲡⲁⲕⲉ in Walter E. Crum, *A Coptic Dictionary*, 261a).

19 "*you*": that is, the powers that are invoked and worn on the amulet.

58. A monk's prayer for good health *(Yale 2124)*

12 "*him*": that is, Christ.

59. Invocation of the sun for protection *(Cologne 20826)*

21 "*as*": Read ⲛⲑⲏ ⲛ- rather than ⲕⲑⲏⲛ (the latter is read by Cornelia Römer and Heinz J. Thissen, "Eine magische Anrufung in koptischer Sprache," 176); see Tafel VIIIa.

60. Invocation of god for protection *(Freer collection, fragment 10)*

1,1 "*lord*": Coptic ⲡⲟⲥ (compare ⲡ̄ⲟ̄ⲥ̄); William H. Worrell, *The Coptic Manuscripts in the Freer Collection*, 323, suggests in a note that the scribe may have meant to write ⲡⲑ̄ⲥ̄, "god."

2–3 "*above*": Coptic ⲥⲁϩ[ⲣ]ⲁⲓ; Worrell, 381, translates the Coptic as "beneath."

3 "*[the] soul*": Coptic [ⲧ]ⲯ̄ⲏ̄ⲭ̄ⲓ; plural? (compare 2,11).

5 "*by fate*": Coptic ϩⲉⲛ ⲟⲩⲁⲛⲁⲛⲕⲏ (Greek ἀνάγκη); or, "with distress."

15 "*supply [the] restraints*": Coptic ⲥⲉϩⲛⲓ ⲛⲛⲓⲙⲉⲁ[ⲓ] (Fayumic for ⲙⲏⲣⲉ); Worrell, 382, translates this "dispensest the floods."

17 "*overturn them . . .*": Coptic ⲡⲟⲛⲉ ⲙⲙⲁⲟⲩ ⲉⲧⲁⲗⲉⲩ ⲉⲛⲓϭⲁⲙ; Worrell, 382, suggests the translation "poureth (from ⲡⲱⲛ, see Walter E. Crum, *A Coptic Dictionary*, 263ab) them out." Also possible is the translation "overturn those who are lifted over the powers" (compare Angelicus M. Kropp, *Ausgewählte koptische Zaubertexte*, 2.118).

2,1 "*ages*": or, "aeons."

5 "*laid low*": Coptic ⲕⲁⲏⲥⲟⲑⲉ, perhaps from κλίνω (so Carl Schmidt in Kropp, 2.119); Worrell, 325, proposes that the word may derive from ἐγκλείω/ἐγκλεῖσθαι, "shut in."

10 "*asks*": Coptic ⲁⲓⲧⲉ ⲙⲟ followed by ⲛⲧⲁⲕ (see Worrell, 325, with reference to αἰτέω followed by ⲙⲙⲁⲕ, "you"). Kropp, 2.119, wishes to see a form of δαίμων, "demon," in the Coptic.

61. Spell for protection against illness *(Vienna K 8302)*

16–17 "*the city {the city}*": "the city of cities"? Also possibly "the city, the city of Edessa (?)," but "Edessa" remains a very difficult reading.

21 " . . . ": Coptic ⲛⲩⲟⲩ (compare ⲛ̄ⲩ̄ⲟⲧ, "difficult"?).

26 "*It*": or, "He"(?).

" . . . ": Coptic ⲉⲧⲉⲕⲧⲛⲁϥ; Viktor Stegemann, *Die koptischen Zaubertexten*, 73, tentatively suggests that these letters may derive from ⲕⲱⲧⲉ and that the expression may be translated "the one who seeks." Walter Till, "Zu den Wiener koptischen Zaubertexten," 217, provides a different reading for the whole line and suggests that it refers to Abdemelek (compare Jeremiah 38:7ff.).

27 "*It bore him*": or, "He bore it"(?).

29 "*by myself*": Stegemann reads "by her alone."

43 "*MOUNTHARAHA*": or, "NOUNTHARAHA."

62. Amulet to protect Philoxenos *(amulet from the collection of M. Robert Nahman)*

1 *"Aio Sabaoth"*: compare Iao (= Yao) Sabaoth. Taken by itself ⲁⲓⲟ, "Aio," may be translated "yea." Compare text 127, line 45.

63. Ritual spell to heal and protect *(Berlin 11347)*

Recto

5 *"you (?)"*: Coptic [. . .] ⲧⲱⲧⲛ; Angelicus M. Kropp, *Ausgewählte koptische Zaubertexte*, 2.113, apparently assumes the transcription and reconstruction [ⲁⲛⲁ]ⲧⲟⲗⲏ (or [ⲁⲛⲁ]ⲧⲱⲗⲏ), "east."

31 *"etc."*: Coptic ⲛ̄ⲧ̄ (here and elsewhere in the text). This abbreviation means to indicate the trinitarian formula.

Verso

4 *"who have walked"*: or, "who walk."

10 *"sides"*: or, "directions."

64. Exorcistic spell *(London Oriental Manuscript 5525)*

22 *"devil"*: The Coptic ⲉⲛⲉⲏⲣ is translated "devil" to differentiate it from the Greek δαιμόνιον, which is translated "demon" at line 46.

32 *"Aberselia"*: On Aberselia or Berzelia as the child-killing demoness against whom St. Sisinnios fought, see Jacques van der Vliet, "Varia Magica Coptica," 232–33.

"Sura daughter of Pelca": This is a later addition that does not fit syntactically and is written with a different pen. It is, however, written by the same hand that wrote the spell.

34 *" . . . "*: Coptic ⲧⲟⲩⲧⲟⲩ; this may be a word but its meaning is uncertain. Kropp puts ellipsis points.

38–40 *"Miksanther"*: Kropp analyzes as Greek μίγνυμι plus Coptic ⲁⲛⲉⲏⲣ, "mixed-up demons."

50–51 *"Sara= Mar= Bi= Sara= Mar= Thar= Thathrar="*: The hatchmarks following these names indicate that they are abbreviations: For example, Sara= (Coptic ⲥⲁⲣⲁʼ) may be for Sorochata.

53ff. *"DD"*: The Deltas are probably just decorative triangles.

56 *"Christ . . . †"*: The monogram combines the standard abbreviations for "Christ" and "cross."

75ff. The parchment is very dark. See the parallel at lines 24–27 for a possible restoration.

94–108 These lines are written to the right and left of the "wing formations."

95 *"by your . . . "*: Coptic ⲙ̄ⲧⲁⲟⲩ; the reading is uncertain, as are the following two lines.

107 *"The sun"*: Greek Ἥλιος, name of the sun god.

111 *"Escho Sabao"*: Kropp suggests ἰσχυρός σαβαώθ, "mighty hosts," a name that echoes Septuagint titles of the lord.

112 *"Sariel"*: a name that appears in several angel lists in the Old Testament Pseudepigrapha.

119 *"Saraphuel, the . . . "*: Coptic ϩⲏⲥⲉ; meaning unknown.

129–130 *"Susunkus . . . Barpharankus"*: a variation of another common name in Greek and Coptic texts of ritual power, Sesengen Barpharanges.

130 *"Marioth"*: with -ⲱⲉ squeezed in under the line, which cramps the end of line 131, ⲡⲉⲣⲁⲛⲉⲩ . . . (perhaps -ⲱⲉ).

66. Spell for protection during childbirth *(Michigan 1190)*

5 *"the other"*: grammatically feminine, that is, the female client.

12–13 *"attain <her> right side"*: The intransitive ⲡⲱϩ + locative ⲛ̄-, "reach, attain," is only attested in Bohairic in Walter E. Crum, *A Coptic Dictionary*, 281a–282a. To see such usage here moves the text from the realm of miraculous caesarean section (so Worrell) to that of the stereotypical assembly of protective angels on each side of a client in distress. Worrell opts for the attested, transitive meaning of ⲡⲱϩ, "split," with the direct object indicated by the ⲛ̄-. Thus he translates, "A pregnant woman, mayest thou split her right side and bring forth her child" ("Coptic Magical and Medical Texts," 11).

Recto, column 2

24 *"Amin"*: or, "Pamin."

Verso

19 *"(ring signs and letters)"*: Worrell, 10, notes, "Below the text and at right angles to it: ⲱⲱⲱⲱⲭ seven times in one column, five times in another. Below this: ⲕ̄ with a small circle on the right lower extremity. Horizontal line. Below this: 'ring signs,' ⲡ (?) three times, ⲃ in horizontal position three times, ⲃ in normal position three times, more 'ring signs,' ⲕⲟ̄." One may note the similarity of ⲱⲱⲱⲱⲭ to the controlled breathing punctuated by pushing that characterizes some modern techniques of childbirth.

67. Spell for the well-being of a child *(Vienna K 70)*

2 *"Prescribe"*: or, perhaps, "with" (linked to the previous clause).

14 *"flatulence"*: Coptic ⲛⲉϥⲓ, literally "breath, wind, vapor." Perhaps compare, above, the introduction to text 46.

15–16 *" . . . "*: Coptic ⲛⲟⲩϩⲏϣⲧⲉⲓ, meaning unknown; possibly from ⲛⲁϣⲧⲉ, "strength, protection" (Walter E. Crum, *A Coptic Dictionary*, 238a). Walter Till, "Zu den Wiener koptischen Zaubertexten," 214–15, suggests that rather than translating these lines "Provide . . . ," we translate as follows (continuing from the previous sentence): "whether it is an Eshi . . . " (a disease? Compare text 128, note to line 24).

69. Spell for protection against violent attack *(London Oriental Manuscript 4721 [5])*

5–7 The restorations of lacunae are based on lines 10–11.

20 *"bloodshed"*: Coptic ⲕⲱⲁ ⲛⲥⲛⲟⲩϥ; the translation follows Walter E. Crum's suggestion, but the meaning of ⲕⲱⲁ is "uncertain" according to his *Coptic Dictionary*, 102a.

70. Spell to protect from filthy demons *(London Oriental Manuscript 5987)*

1 *"Baktiotha"*: This appears to be a name of Christ; Angelicus M. Kropp suggests that it is based on the Hebrew בכירותא, "firstborn." See also line 94.

3–9 The appropriation of such credal fragments by these texts generally results in pronominal slips between the second and third persons, as here.

16,97,125 *"distributors"*: Coptic ⲣⲙ̄ⲉⲡⲱϣ; compare (First) Apocalypse of James (Nag Hammadi Codex V) 26,21, "these are they who were distributed (ⲡⲱϣ)," referring to the distribution of the powers of the seventy-two heavens by the twelve archons.

20 *"There is"*: The text has simply ⲛ-; Walter E. Crum suggests ⲟⲩⲛ-.

21 *"Lake Acherousia"*: This term appears in Apocalypse of Peter 14, Apocalypse of Paul 22, and Sibylline Oracles II, as a lake in the Elysian Fields by the city of Christ. Also related are apocalyptic descriptions of the throne of god. The actual River Acheron in northwest Greece and a lake on the Acherusian plain were thought to be the entrance to Hades in ancient times.

24 *"faith"*: or, perhaps personified "Pistis."

25–26 The translation is uncertain; perhaps compare, with Kropp, Luke 11:21.

26 *"Kabaoth"*: Kropp suggests that the word is derived from Kyrios Sabaoth, "lord of hosts."

32 *"within <him>"*: The text reads "within them," Coptic Ⲛ̅Ⲅ̅ⲎⲦⲞⲨ.

33 Most of this line is missing, and the reading of line 34 is uncertain.

39ff. In this list of names are included a few of the twenty-four elders, Charuel, Yoel, and Thiel.

61 *"your"*: feminine singular; the antecedent is probably "Mary" at line 10. Does this indicate that the spell is to be cast by a woman?

81–87 This parallels lines 4–9, but note the variant credal formula.

88 *"and divided the day"*: as god divided the day from the night in Genesis 1:4.

97,115 *"Spell"*: The text has ⲔⲞⲬ, which may mean "spell" (like ἀπολογία); compare also Bainchooch, etc. (ⲔⲁⲔⲉ is Coptic for "darkness"). See below, note to text 113, line 6.

98 *"two arms (?) of Seth"*: Coptic Ⲅ.ⲂⲈ ⳝ̅ⲚⲦⲈ ϪⲎⲦ. Crum suggests ⲄⲃⲞⳝ, "arm," but Kropp rejects this and puts ellipsis points. ϪⲎⲦ is not the normal spelling of Seth, either.

102 *"<You>"*: Coptic ⲀⲚⲞⲔ; Crum and Kropp are both uncertain about this word; Kropp suggests ⲚⲦⲞⲔ, "you."

111 *" . . . "*: "Adonai" probably goes in the ellipsis; compare line 46.

134–144 These lines are in a different hand. Crum says that these lines, which provide "the directions for application, are particularly illegible."

71. Rossi's "Gnostic" tractate *(from the Biblioteca Nazionale, Turin)*

1,12 *"(of) the names"*: Coptic ⲚⲒⲣⲀ; probably read (Ⲛ̅)ⲚⲒⲣⲀⲚ.

2,13 *"bowls"*: Coptic ⲔⲣⲎⲔⲦⲎⲣⳝⲞⲚ; probably read ⲔⲣⲀⲦⲎⲣⳝⲞⲚ/ ⲔⲣⲎⲦⲎⲣⳝⲞⲚ.

2,19 *"the . . . "*: Coptic ⲚⲈⲀⲎ...ⲚⲎ.. ; perhaps restore ⲚⲈⲀⲎ[ⲔⲀ]ⲚⲎ.., "the vessels . . . ." Angelicus M. Kropp, *Ausgewählte koptische Zaubertexte*, 2.194, tentatively suggests ⲚⲈⲀⲎ[ⲔⲀ]ⲚⲎ [Ⲛ̅ⲀⲀ], "the vessels [of hailstones]" (compare the meteorological references in 2,16–3,3).

4,21 *"An . . . baom"*: Kropp, 1.66, reads ⲀⲚ . . . ‾ⲂⲀⲰⲘ but transliterates the name An . . . raom (2.178); Francesco Rossi, "Di alcuni manoscritti copti," 129, reads . . . ‾ⲣⲀⲰⲘ.

7,12 *"the holy one(s?)"*: Coptic ⲠⲈⲦⲞⲨⲀⲀϤ (sg.); also possible is the translation "the only one(s?)."

8,2 *"appear"*: or, "reveal."

12,21 *"its [. . .]"*: Perhaps restore Ⲛ̅ⲈϤⲦ[ⲣⲞⲬⲞⲤ], "its [wheels]" (compare Kropp, 2.197). On this description of the throne of god, with wheels, compare Jewish (and Christian) portrayals of the divine throne-chariot.

13,22 *"[of (your) holy] . . . "*: Coptic/Greek [ⲦⲎⲤ ⲢⲀⳝⳝ]ⲀⲤ ⲈⲨⲦⲀ . . . ; instead of ⲈⲨⲦⲀ. . . . We expect ⲀⲞϪⲎⲤ ⲤⲞⲨ, "your . . . glory" (compare 3,20–21).

15,4 *"through which"*: or "through whom."

17,6 *"Babam"*: Kropp, 1.75, reads $\overline{\text{Ⲃⲁⲃⲁⲙ}}$ but transliterates the name as Balam (2.188); Rossi, 139, also reads $\overline{\text{Ⲃⲁⲃⲁⲙ}}$.

17,9 *"Pantocrator"*: or, "almighty."

19,1–2 *". . . . ma Chamariel"*: Probably restore to read "[Agra]ma Chamariel" (but compare Chamariel as an independent name at 21,10).

73. Erotic spell of Cyprian of Antioch *(Heidelberg Kopt. 684)*

54 *"snorted"*: evidently a reference to something like the bellowing, hissing, or other sound effects attested elsewhere in ancient descriptions of acts of ritual power.

65 *"AMOU AMOU"*: perhaps Coptic for "come, come."

65–66 *"the spirit you have deposited"*: Justina's spirit, deposited in a body.

74–75 *"that fire which is your divinity"*: Compare Exodus 24:17; Deuteronomy 4:24; 9:3; Psalm 50:3; Isaiah 29:6; 30:27, 30; 33:14.

78–79 *"the river of fire "*: Compare Daniel 7:10.

83 *"He "*: that is, Gabriel. It later becomes more apparent that Gabriel is the angel to arouse love in Justina because of his role in the annuciation to Mary (compare Luke 1:26–38).

115–16 *"a . . . upon her . . . "*: Both are unknown animals.

125 *"for the burning summer heat"*: So ablaze with love is she. Stephen Emmel offers the following variant translation for lines 120–25: "desperate for the desire and love of N. son of N. as for a drop of water that one sees dangling from the lip of a jar while fasting in the burning heat of summer" (see above, pages 352–53, note on lines 15–17).

141–42 *"without any land, empty-handed"*: It remains unclear to what this refers. The Coptic translated "without any land" can also mean "without any earth" or even "off the ground," but these alternative possibilities do not help matters much.

174–75 *"you tore the veil of the temple"*: Compare Matthew 27:51; Mark 15:38; Luke 23:45.

182–83 *"the holy"*: or, "the pure."

184–86 *"the judgment . . . in the valley of Josaphat"*: Compare Joel 4:2.

190–91 *"your sign of the zodiac . . . "*: The reference is obscure. Perhaps this means to refer to the sign of Virgo, standing for the virgin Justina: Cyprian is trying to enflame both of them with desire.

233 *"together with every day and every night"*: The meaning is unclear. Friedrich Bilabel suggests the reference may be either to the day on which she sees her servitude to Cyprian or to the day on which she bears a child. It may simply be a matter of the great effort that she will expend on beautifying herself.

250 *"and you must not . . . "*: Lacunae in the manuscript set in at this point.

74. Erotic spell to attract a woman *(Yale 1791 [second text])*

1 *"charm"*: The translation is entirely conjectural; literally the word probably means "tyrant."

2 *"wild herb"*: possibly rather "asphalt" (that is, bitumen, mineral pitch).

4 *"it"*: that is, the offering.

"(signs and letters)": The signs to be written (see line 2) occur on the papyrus between lines 4 and 5, where the following strings of letters occur together with various signs and figures: "RIBIETIODTHFPHORARSTHELOAPOAE FAIKON AAAAAAA EEEEEEE EEEEEEE IIIIIII OOOOOOO UUUUUUU OOOOOOO AEEIOUOTAEN."

11 *"Bersebour"*: that is, the devil (Beelzebul).

12 " . . . ": The beginning of this line is badly damaged.

14 "a [black (?)] dog": Compare Berlin 8314 (text 75), lines 8-10.

15-17 "and, as for a drop of water . . . , desperate [for the] soul of N. son of N.": This commonplace image of longing is most fully expressed in Heidelberg Kopt. 684 (text 73), lines 120-25 (see note on line 125).

17-18 " . . . ": The last clause of the text is damaged and incomprehensible.

75. Another erotic spell *(Berlin 8314)*

6 "*portion*": Coptic ⲟⲓⲡⲉ, "ephah," a unit for measuring grain and other items.

6-8 " . . . ": The meanings of these three words (ⲁⲉⲡⲁⲓⲡ / ⲥⲁⲉⲡⲁⲓⲡ, ⲟⲩⲱⲥ, ⲁ̣ⲅⲁⲁⲧ) are not known. They may refer to parts of animals (so Walter E. Crum, *A Coptic Dictionary*, 331b, 492a); they may also indicate emotive powers of animals (ⲁⲉⲡⲁⲓⲡ may be a form of ⲅⲁⲟⲡⲁ(ⲉ)ⲡ, "distress"; could ⲟⲩⲱⲥ = ⲟⲩⲱⲩ, "desire"?).

12 "*flesh*": Coptic ⲥⲁⲣⲉⲝ, possibly an earthy expression for the female sexual organs.

18 "*You are a god also*": In a similar text, Berlin 8320 (not translated in this volume), a woman's heart and flesh are to be bound to a man after she eats and drinks of certain items. In this text the devil Satan is said to beat the earth with his staff against "the living god" and say, "I am a god also" (compare Isaiah 14:13-14; Ezekiel 28:2).

76. Another erotic spell (Berlin 8325)

4-5 "*[pieces of fruit (?)]*": Coptic ⲅⲟⲩⲡ[...]ⲁ̣ⲓ; perhaps read ⲅⲟⲩⲡ[ⲱⲣ]ⲁ̣ⲓ, from the Greek ὀπῶραι (compare Walter Beltz, "Die koptischen Zauberpapyri," 75; Angelicus M. Kropp, *Ausgewählte koptische Zaubertexte*, 2.25).

77. Another erotic spell *(Heidelberg Kopt. 518)*

20 " . . . . ": Coptic ⲉⲧⲁⲣⲣⲁⲕ, perhaps "on a (piece of) paper," from Arabic *arraq* (compare Friedrich Bilabel in *Griechische, koptische und arabische Texte*, 380).

26 "*Thymas*": perhaps read ⲑⲩ ⲙⲁⲥ, "Off(ering): mas(tic)" or "Off(er) mas(tic)."

78. Another erotic spell *(London Hay 10376)*

15 "*Mastema*": On Prince Mastema as a diabolical power compare Jubilees 49:2.

16-17 "*the source of the four rivers*": The source of the four rivers is Eden. According to Questions of Bartholomew 59, Satan washed himself in "the spring of water from which the four rivers flow," and when Eve drank from the spring "desire came upon her. For if she had not drunk of that water, [Satan] should not have been able to deceive her."

17 "*He [washed (?)] in it*": Coptic ⲁϥⲝⲟⲟⲕⲁⲕⲓ ⲉⲃⲟⲗ ⲛ̄ϩⲏⲧⲥ. On the translation compare Questions of Bartholomew 59 and Walter E. Crum, *A Coptic Dictionary*, 763ab (ⲝⲱⲕⲙ, "wash").

79. Spells for sex and business *(London Hay 10414)*

Recto

1 " . . . ": Coptic ⲟⲛⲏ.

2 *"'suffers'"*: Coptic ϥⲓ ϩⲁ-; Walter E. Crum, "Magical Texts in Coptic—II," 196, translates this "beareth off (?)." See also Crum, *A Coptic Dictionary*, 621a. The translation given here assumes an ironic meaning.

"CHAHE": a word of ritual power?

3 *"their hymen(s)"*: Coptic ⲧⲟⲩⲙⲛⲧⲡⲁⲣⲑⲉⲛⲟⲥ.

5–6 *"KOK TPARKOKOK"*: a form of Bachuch? Also compare below, note to text 113, line 6.

18 *"tongs"*: Coptic ⳉⲁⲓⲕ (see Crum, *A Coptic Dictionary*, 558b): also possible is "bowls," from ⲗⲟⲕ / ⳉⲗⲟⲕ (see Crum, 138ab).

20 *"She will draw her robe to her neck"*: a gesture, known from passages in Herodotus and Diodorus Siculus, intended to display the genitals, apparently for purposes of fertility.

Verso

2, 19 *"spell-free"*: or "flower water"? See below, text 119, and James Drescher, "Two Coptic Magical Ingredients."

80. Spells for favor, honor, and passion (*London Hay 10434*)

Verso

7 *"Sebt-Hor"*: The angelic name seems to contain the name of the Egyptian god Horus. Robert K. Ritner suggests that it may be translated "one who equips Horus" (*Sbte-Hor*), otherwise unattested.

14 *"PHLEMNEKOK"*: Coptic Bachuch (with variations; note the preceding text)?

81. Spell for gathering, for menstrual flow (*London Hay 10122*)

Verso

bottom *"altar"*: Coptic ⳉⲟⲩⲣⲏ. Another possible translation: "censer."

82. Spell for mutual love (*Michigan 4932f*)

10–11 *"[like] a brother and sister, or a bear [who] wants to suckle her young"*: William H. Worrell (following an ingenious suggestion from Herbert C. Youtie) construes lines 10–11 thus: "[like] a brother and sister. {and a bear} [I] want to beget (?) her children." According to this understanding, the phrase "and a bear" is to be omitted as a translation of the Greek καὶ ἄρκτος, a garbled form of καὶ γὰρ οὕτως ("For thus"), which begins the next sentence. The reading followed in the present translation was proposed by Walter E. Crum, *A Coptic Dictionary*, 752a. This is a simpler reading that makes sense of the text as it stands. Unfortunately, it also vitiates Worrell's understanding of this text as a charm for "honest love and matrimony."

13–14 *"before whom is (what) is also under the Sheep (pl.) . . . "*: The text is somewhat unclear, although the basic intent of addressing the lord of the heavens is clear. The references are apparently astrological.

83. Spell to make a woman pregnant (*Pierpont Morgan Library M662B 22*)

5 *"At this time"*: Coptic ϩⲛⲡⲓⲟⲉⲓⳉ, here read as ϩⲛⲡⲓⲟⲩⲉⲓⳉ. Leslie S. B. MacCoull, "*P. Morgan Copt.*," 11, translates the phrase (as written) "(As a result of) your crying."

11 *" . . . "*: Coptic ϩⲁ.ⲁⲃ (or ϩⲁⲁⲃ); MacCoull, 11, translates the clause "so that it may be fulfilled (?) in N. daughter of N." Perhaps compare ϩⲁⲉ, "give," or ϩⲱⲃ, "send."

14 *"Elon"*: or, "Eloe."

"Sabaoth": clear in the photograph in Florence D. Friedman, *Beyond the Pharaohs*, 196; MacCoull, 11, supplies the erroneous transcription ⲭⲁⲃⲁⲱ̄ⲉ.

15 *"if (?)"*: Coptic ⲧⲁ̄ⲛ (for ⲕⲁⲓ ⲁ̄ⲛ?), here and in the following lines.

17 *". . ."*: Coptic ⲙⲟⲩⲧⲉ ("call"?); the chalice mentioned here refers to a potion that might be given to "bind" a person.

84. Spell for a man to obtain a male lover *(Ashmolean Museum 1981.940)*

14–15 *"his hand"*: David Frankfurter observes that "hand" is a common Hebrew euphemism for the penis, while Robert K. Ritner understands the clause ("his hand is full of all goodness") as a typical Egyptian description of generosity, in this case, of a man toward his lover.

85. Sexual curse *(Chicago Oriental Institute 13767)*

3 *"was . . . "*: Coptic ⲉⲛⲧⲁ̄ⲩⲣⲟⲡ; probably emend to read ⲉⲛⲧⲁ̄ⲩⲙⲟ̄ⲩⲣ, "was bound" (compare Heidelberg Kopt. 682, line 24 [text 86]).

4 *"Iliseus"*: Heidelberg Kopt. 682, line 29 reads Elias (that is, Elijah).

9 *"whether wild or domesticated"*: The Coptic ⲟⲩⲧⲉ ϩⲟⲟⲩⲧ ⲟⲩⲧⲉ ⲧⲉϥⲛⲏ could also be translated "or man or (domestic) animal" (translation preferred by Robert K. Ritner).

86. Another sexual curse *(Heidelberg Kopt. 682)*

12 *"Aios Baiot Atonas"*: or, "Aio Sbaiot Atonas," probably from Yao Sabaoth Adonai.

35ff. *"He . . . he . . . he . . . he . . . he"*: perhaps "It . . . it . . . it . . . it . . . it" (that is, the penis).

38–39 *"it must stay"*: probably the semen.

45 *"wild"*: Coptic ⲛϩⲟⲟⲧ, literally "male."

87. Another sexual curse *(Strasbourg Coptic Manuscript 135)*

3 *"chariot (?)"*: Walter E. Crum, "La magie copte," 541–42, reads ϩⲁⲣⲓⲁ, "holy one"(?), but also suggests the reading adopted here, ϩⲁⲣⲙⲁ, "chariot." On the devil being cast into outer darkness, see Jacques van der Vliet, "Satan's Fall in Coptic Magic." Robert K. Ritner has proposed another possible translation: "the one who has found his state of blessedness untimely (from ἄωρος)," that is, one who has died an untimely death, for example, a martyr.

88. Curse against Victor Hatre, David, and Papnoute *(London Oriental Manuscript 5986)*

1ff. *"in <it>"*: literally, "in me."

5ff. *"My father Michael"*: The opening of London Oriental Manuscript 6794 (text 129) also may address the angel Michael as "father."

"Papnoute": as the name of one of the enemies, with Walter E. Crum, but Angelicus M. Kropp simply translates this as "Gott."

10ff. *"those who . . . "*: The verb is missing.

15ff. *"my [prayer]"*: Kropp's suggested restoration.

20ff. *"spirit of the world"*: probably Satan (so Kropp).

25ff. *"<his> brother"*: The manuscript reads "her brother."

89. A widow's curse *(Munich Coptic Papyrus 5)*

2 *"a burned . . . "*: Coptic ⲦⲂⲦ . . . ⲦⲘϦ**ꞯ**Ⲏ**ꞯ**, possibly "a grilled fish" (reading <ⲈⲦ>ⲦⲘϦ**ꞯ**Ⲏ**ꞯ**).

"nine . . .": Coptic ⲠϬ**ꞯ**Ϭ ⲚⲤⲘ̄ . . ., possibly "nine [appeals] . . . " (reading ⲤⲘ̄ⲘⲈ as in line 3).

5 *"[care upon me]"*: reading with Angelicus M. Kropp, *Ausgewählte koptische Zaubertexte*, 2.229.

13 *" . . . "*: W. Hengstenberg, "Koptische Papyri," 13*, suggests that the sense of this reference may be that Lot was saved on account of his sinlessness (ⲘⲚ̄ⲦⲀⲦⲚⲞⲂⲈ).

18 *"you"*: or, "it" (that is, the chariot).

20 *"[. . .]"*: The lacuna must allude to the four creatures around god's throne (compare Ezekiel 1).

21 *"their face . . . [their feet]"*: literally, "his face . . . [his feet]."

23 *"[. . .]"*: Hengstenberg, 10*, tentatively suggests [Ⲡ Ⲍ̄ Ⲥ ⲤⲀⲂⲀⲰⲐ], "[the lord Sabaoth]."

33–34 *"The mummy . . . "*: The restorations depend upon Kropp, 2.230.

90. Curse against several violent people *(Papyrus Lichačev)*

3 *"you"*: or, "it" (that is, the chariot).

11–12 *"Prestasia and Tnounte and Eboneh"*: Oscar von Lemm, "Koptische Miscellen," 1086, understands these words not to be names but rather characteristics of a person: "the appearance and the root of his life."

92. Curse against perjurers *(Berlin 10587)*

Column 1

4 *" . . . punishments"*: The uncertain word before "punishments" (in the English translation) appears to be ⲚⲘⲀⲦ**ꞯ**ϛ; Angelicus M. Kropp translates "pitiless," and Walter Beltz "hard."

6 *"perjurers"*: Coptic ⲢⲈϤⲰⲢⲔ Ⲛ̄ⲚⲞⲨⲌ, literally, "false-swearers."

25 *"MMMMMMM"*: In Aeschylus's *Eumenides*, μυγμός, the repeated moaning of the letter Mu, is the sound made by the sleeping Furies as the ghost of Clytemnestra begins to evoke them.

Column 2

6–7 *"breaks . . . "*: The Coptic is difficult; perhaps something like "breaks in pieces and they tumble in a mess."

15 *"the twenty-one angels"*: Only twenty of the twenty-one are named.

18 *"who unjustly perjures the name of god"*: Here the perjury is "against the name of god," but in column 1, 20, it is "against my name."

22ff. This section is roughly the same as Zechariah 5:2–3a. In the Hebrew he sees a flying scroll, but the Septuagint reads, as here, "sickle."

31 The end is fragmentary, but the citation is helpful as well as appropriate; after "thieves," Zechariah continues "and everyone who swears falsely shall be cut off."

93. Curse of a mother *(London Oriental Manuscript 6172)*

4 *"strike"*: Coptic ⲢϬⲰⲦϦ ⲎⲦⲤ; the translation follows Walter E. Crum's suggestion.

5 *"[who will cast]"*: Crum's restoration.

9 "*cause . . . to err*": Coptic ⲀⲔⲀⲤⲣⲘⲣⲰⲤⲘ; the translation follows Crum's suggestion; Angelicus M. Kropp translates "lead her to destruction."

13f. The Deltas (DDD) may indicate a name or names to be inserted (N.).

94. Curse to make a man tongue-tied (*Cambridge University Library T. S. 12,207*)

11 " . . . ": Coptic ⲨⲐϨⲞⲨⲦ (meaning unknown).

22 "*I adjure the voice*": or, "I adjure (you) by the voice."

95. Abdullah's curses (*Berlin 8503*)

3 "*the one who has power*": that is, god.

9 "*SARTORIS . . .* ": probably meant to indicate a foreign language or words of power. Walter Beltz, "Die koptischen Zauberpergamente," 96, offers a partial translation: "Sartoris and the one who is with you, Kartoris" (with a different Coptic text in mind than the published text).

29–30 "*speechless (?)*": Coptic ⲔⲞⲨⲣⲈ, compare ⲔⲀⲣⲰⲒ (etc.), "speechlessness." Also possible is the translation "deaf" (Coptic ⲔⲞⲨⲣ).

35–36 "*this formula (?)*": Coptic ⲠⲣⲀⲚ ⲘⲘⲞⲤ ⲚⲀ; Angelicus M. Kropp, *Ausgewählte koptische Zaubertexte*, 2.245, suggests a Coptic form of the Greek word ὀνομασία.

40–42 According to Kropp, 2.247, after the phrase "The strong power of Ebbael" was written, the scribe subsequently added another curse against Mouflehalpahapani (41–51) and began by copying words into the available space on lines 39–40 before continuing on the next lines.

96. Lead curse (*lead tablet, Cologne T 10*)

3 "*Serbarbaraos*": perhaps meaning "they are foreign."

6 "*Cophibol*": perhaps meaning "outside instance, deed."

11 "*strong*": or, "destructive." The Coptic is ambiguous and may have been selected for its double meaning "power to scatter/destroy" or "strong power."

14 "*Penjeho*": a village probably in the vicinity of Ashmunein (Hermopolis).

29 "*until I*": Manfred Weber's Coptic transcription leaves out ⲨⲀⲚⲦⲒ, "until I," at the end of line 29.

31 "*hair . . . his personal effect*": the *ousia* or personal "relic" of the victim necessary for the transmission of the curse. Weber assumes that the hair is from the corpse.

97. Bone curse (*bone, Florence 5645*)

1 "*You shall say*": ⲈⲔ written for simple Ⲕ or second tense. Angelicus M. Kropp translates "While you say."

"*I invoke*": The text uses a form of ἐπιλαλέω, "charm," probably in error for the standard ἐπικαλέω, "invoke."

2 "*[which . . .]*": restoring Ⲉ[ⲦⲈ . . .]; Astorre Pellegrini and others read Ⲉ[ⲌⲰ . . .], "over."

4 "*praised one*": Coptic ϨⲤⲀⲒ for ϨⲀⲤⲒⲈ (compare Walter E. Crum, *A Coptic Dictionary*, 710a). Pellegrini and others consider this an error for ⲤϨⲀⲒ, "writing," which is spelled correctly in 1ine 8.

"*compel*": Coptic ϨⲰⲌ, "press."

"*[suffering]*": restoring Ⲛ[ϨⲒⲤ]Ⲉ; Kropp makes no restoration, but translates "[ein Leiden]."

6 "*May he tremble*": Coptic ⲘⲀⲣⲈϤⲤⲦⲞⲦⲞⲨ, from ⲤⲦⲰⲦ (Crum, *A Coptic Dictionary*, 366b).

98. Bone curse *(bones, Cairo A and B)*

Bone A

1 *"Chu"*: ⲭⲩ, perhaps only dittography for Kouchos, which begins the parallels. James Drescher translates the ⲭⲩ as "Christ (?)."

1–8 Among the names may be recognized: Luxury, Boasting (?) (from κόμπος ?), Sodomy, and War. The names are garbled in all three versions.

71 *"Depart"*: The verb of quick motion, ⲥⲱⲕ, has the basic nuance of "flow" or "glide" (used of water and air) and is thus appropriate for an incorporeal spirit.

Bone B, convex side

3 *"Aphonos"*: perhaps to be understood as "Voiceless," or in error for "Plentiful, Not Begrudged."

40 *"I call"*: The line begins with ⲧⲓⲱ, perhaps for "I call," or it is a defective first attempt to write the following "I adjure."

99. Spell for a bone and a corpse *(from the Liverpool Institute of Archaeology)*

4 *"child with flowing hair (?)"*: For ⲧⲉⲭⲛⲉ ⲡⲁⲣⲁⲭⲱⲙⲟⲥ, Angelicus M. Kropp translates "craft, earthen dike."

5 *"bone"*: Kropp conflates ⲕⲟⲥ, "bone," with ⲕⲱⲱⲥ, "corpse," in 1ine 7.

100. Mary's curse against Martha *(from Aberdeen)*

3 *"You"*: masculine singular, addressing the corpse on which the curse was placed.

3–4 *"bring her . . . "*: or, as Walter E. Crum and Roger Rémondon understand it, "bring her into the state of being ulcerous."

5–6 *"to put aside marriage"*: Coptic ⲁⲕⲁⲩⲁⲁⲧ ⲁⲭⲣⲏ, understood as ⲉⲕⲁ-ⲩⲉⲗⲉⲉⲧ ⲉⲉ̅ⲣⲁⲓ; misunderstood by Crum.

6 *"and send forth (?) punishment"*: Coptic ⲁⲩⲧⲟⲩⲅⲁⲗⲁⲧⲥⲉ, understood as ⲁⲩ(ⲱ) ⲧⲟⲩ (from ⲧⲉⲩⲟ, Crum, *A Coptic Dictionary*, 441b) ⲅⲁⲗⲁⲧⲥⲉ (from κολάζω); untranslated by Crum.

7 *"she"*: Coptic ⲩⲉ for ⲉⲥ? Otherwise, an instance of dittography from the preceding line; then translate as imperative, "Pour forth worms."

101. Jacob's curse *(from the Institut français d'archéologie orientale, Cairo)*

2–3 *"the sickle that comes forth from heaven"*: an image of divine vengeance (compare Zechariah 5:1–2; Joel 3:13; Revelation 14:14–20; Berlin 10587 [text 92]).

4 *"Hetiere (?)"*: perhaps a personal name (a form of ⲉ̅ⲁⲧⲣⲉ, "twin"?). *"who is in the father"*: that is, "deceased."

6–7 *"Mary, who bore Jesus, you"*: "you" is masculine singular, not in agreement with "Mary."

102. Victor's curse *(Würzburg 42)*

4 *"Phos"*: "Light."

5 *"Phipon"*: or "Phipop."

103. Invocation for blessing and cursing *(Cologne 10235)*

1–2 *"[. . . I pray . . .] of iron"*: restoration by Manfred Weber, "Ein koptischer Zaubertext aus der Kölner Papyrussammlung," 59, following the parallel in London Hay 10391, lines 12–13 (text 127).

8 *"face"*: Coptic ⲉ̅ⲟ, untranslated by Weber.

19 "*[your amulets of health]*": so restored by Weber.

21 "*burst*": reading ⲥⲟⲗⲡ; also possible is ϭⲟⲗⲡ, "uncover."
"*cloud*": Coptic ⲕⲗⲟⲟⲗⲉ; Weber understands "which you salve" (ⲗⲟⲟⲗⲉ), leaving no object for the verb ⲥⲟⲗⲡ/ϭⲟⲗⲡ.

35 "*[overthrowing]*": Coptic [ⲡⲱⲛⲉ] or [ⲡⲱⲱⲛⲉ], restored by Marvin Meyer on the basis of Coptic Museum 4960 (text 120).

104. Apa Victor's curse against Alo *(Michigan 3565)*

8 "*From afar (?)*": William H. Worrell suggests reading "Ye woes" instead of "From afar."

9 "*this one*": either Saot Sabaot or Ha[..]ouel.

17 "*Thib[am]on*": Worrell suggests that Thibamon should be corrected to read Phibamon. If this suggestion is followed, and if Victor's father is the same Phibamon who is cursed in line 12, then this text gives the reader a glimpse into a rather stormy family life. Unfortunately, the relation of Alo and Phibamon remains unknown.

105. Curse against a woman *(Heidelberg Kopt. 681)*

12 "*moustiaten*": Perhaps compare maschaton or muscatel (ⲙⲟⲩⲥⲭⲁⲧⲉⲛ) as ingredients in other recipes.

23-24 "*submission (?)*": Coptic ϩⲩⲡⲟⲥⲧⲓⲥⲙⲟⲥ, probably for ϩⲩⲡⲟⲑⲉⲥⲙⲟⲥ (ὑποθεσμός).

106. Curse to bring seventy diseases *(Yale 1800)*

1 " . . . *nas*": Probably the incantation began by naming one other divinity (or two?) before Psatael.

5 "*angel of the holy altar*": Traces of the Christian belief that angels are responsible for conveying to the heavenly altar the offerings presented during communion at altars in churches on earth can be found in liturgical texts both in Egypt and elsewhere; see Emmanuel Lanne, *Le grand euchologe*, 296–97 (Coptic p. 41:3–10); C. Detlef G. Müller, *Die Engellehre der koptischen Kirche*, 233; Oswald Hugh Ewart Burmester, *The Egyptian or Coptic Church*, 79, 341; Bernard Botte, "L'ange du sacrifice," esp. pp. 214–21; Erik Peterson, *The Angels and the Liturgy*, 33–34, with nn. 44–47 on pp. 65–66.

7 "*the true judge*": possibly rather "the judge daily."

8 "*until you have*": more literally, "since you have not."

9,14–17 "*it*": or, "him"; but if the Coptic masculine pronoun refers to the grammatically masculine noun "body," then it is not necessarily gender-specific and can refer to either a man or a woman.

15 "*sorcerer nor sorceress*": more literally, "male magician nor female magician," with "magician" expressed by two different words (ⲙⲁⲕⲟⲥ and ⲫⲁⲣⲙⲁⲅⲟⲥ), but neither of them gender-specific in and of itself.

18–19 "*Asmodeus the demon*": the evil demon, as in Tobit 3:8, 17.
" . . . *th*": Some magical name or word is to be restored (akin to Phelloth and Athes in line 20).

107. Possible curse through Shafriel *(Yale 882[A])*

2 Possibly the rest of the line after "angel" was meant to be deleted.

108. Curse against Joor and his wife (Michigan 1523)

2 "*injured party*": literally, "injured woman."

3 *"Joor"*: This name is attested with various spellings: ⲍⲟⲡ, ⲍⲟⲟⲡ, ⲍⲟ̄ⲡ̄, and ⲍⲱⲱⲡⲉ.

6 *"bring them to naught"*: Note the pun on the name ⲍⲟⲡ and the verb ⲍⲱⲡⲉ, "to bring to naught."

12 *"strong"*: Note the pun on the name ⲍⲟⲡ and the qualitative ⲍⲟⲟⲡ (from ⲍⲣⲟ, "strong"), which describes the instrument of his fate.

18 *"Koloje"*: perhaps the remnants of a personal name.

109. Curse to separate a man and a woman *(Louvre E.14.250)*

9 *"between . . . and . . . "*: Here and elsewhere in the text the Coptic employs the construction ⲛ̄- . . . ⲉ̄ⲟⲩⲛ ⲁ- (in line 43 the use of ⲉⲧⲙ[ⲏ]ⲧⲏ clarifies the sense of "between . . . and . . . "). Does this construction suggest that the man is to hate the woman (thus: ". . . hatred and separation in Sipa . . . toward Ouarteihla . . . ") or that the woman is to hate the man (thus: ". . . hatred and separation for Sipa . . . in Ouarteihla . . . "), or is a more general sense of mutual dislike intimated in the text?

13 *"[sheet]"*: Coptic [ⲕⲁⲣⲧⲁⲗⲟⲛ], from Greek χαρτάριον. Here and elsewhere Étienne Drioton, "Parchemin magique copte," 482ff., translates this word "grimoire." Conversely, Jacques van der Vliet, "Satan's Fall in Coptic Magic," suggests "with equal hesitation," the translation "strong one," and refers to Satan as the demonic power behind the spell. Then, as in other texts, Satan is the one to claim equality with god.

18–19 *"pass by . . . "*: The sense seems to be that ultimately Sipa is the one who is to pass by Ouarteihla and be rebuffed "for ever."

20 *"being [opened . . .]"*: Coptic ⲛⲛⲉⲩϣⲟ[ⲩⲱⲛ . . .] ⲉⲃⲟⲗ; the restoration is suggested by Drioton, 484. Drioton goes on to suggest, more tentatively, that the remaining portion of the lacuna may be restored to read [ⲉⲣϣⲁⲛⲧⲁ̄ϩⲙⲉ̄ϥ], "if one knocks."

29 *"Ei"*: The meaning of "Ei" in line 29 and again in line 31 is unclear.

31 *"Eloi Ei Elemas"*: probably the words of Jesus on the cross. On Elemas compare the figure of Elymas the practitioner of ritual power in Acts 13:8.

32 *"I myself am god"*: or, "I am god also" (compare text 75, line 18, and the note).

33 *"Apolle"*: or, "Apollo," as a demon.

"S[ipa]": Compare texts 96 and 98, in which the spell is placed under a corpse. Perhaps a different restoration would be preferable in the present text.

35 *"from [. . .] of Ouarteihla"*: Drioton, 487, suggests the restoration ⲉⲃⲟⲗ ϩⲓ̈ⲍ[ⲱϥ ⲉⲧⲡⲛ]ⲏ . . . , "from [him to the doorway] of Ouarteihla."

110. Curse to harm a person *(Heidelberg Kopt. 679)*

12–13 *"The people among all those [who] dwell in it"*: Hans J. Polotsky, "Zu einigen Heidelberger koptischen Zaubertexten," 424, prefers to read as follows: "People in whom is the breath of life."

30 The conclusion of the text may include the instructions "throw out" and "draw these things" and (in ring letters) the words of power "Bet Betha Be."

111. Curse to disable the body of an enemy *(Berlin 8321)*

1–2 *"I invoke you (sg.) today, Sourochchata. You (pl.) who are strong in your power"*: perhaps, "I invoke you (sg.) today. Sourochchata, you (pl.) who are strong in your power."

112. **Spell for the return of a stolen object** *(Vienna K 8304)*

4 *"until you return it"*: Coptic ϢⲀⲕⲧⲉⲕⲕⲧⲟϤ for ϢⲀⲚⲧⲉⲕⲕⲧⲟϤ (so Walter Till, "Zu den Wiener koptischen Zaubertexten," 219); Viktor Stegemann, *Die koptischen Zaubertexte*, 82, reads ϢⲀⲚⲧⲉϤⲕⲧⲟϤ, "until he returns it" or "until it returns."

7 *"to its place"*: Coptic ⲉⲡⲉϤⲙⲀ (so Till, 220); Stegemann, 82, reads ⲉⲡⲉⲓⲙⲀ, "to this place."

113. **Spell invoking Bathuriel** *(Cairo, Egyptian Museum 49547)*

5 *"Mizrael"*: Coptic ⲙⲓ̈ⲥⲧⲣⲀⲏⲀ.

6 *"Spell"*: Coptic ⲭⲱⲕ. *Chok* or *kok* may well be understood as "spell" (like ἀπολογία; see Angelicus M. Kropp, *Ausgewählte koptische Zaubertexte*, 3.138 [note 2]); or compare Bainchooch, etc. (ⲕⲀⲕⲉ is the Coptic word for "darkness").

7ff. *"the first seal . . . "*: The motif of seals upon Adam's body probably derives from the Jewish mystical tradition. The Coptic Book of Bartholomew describes—also in the context of a heavenly liturgy—a vision of the glorious body of Adam with esoteric signs and names written on it.

15 *"this vessel"*: either a cup (compare lines 33–34) or the body.

29,34 *"Spell"*: *Kok*; see the note to line 6.

35 *"the world"*: Coptic ⲧⲓ̈ⲕⲟⲩⲙⲉⲛⲉ (from Greek οἰκουμένη).

39–40 *"One holy father . . . "*: reconstructed by Louis Saint-Paul Girard, "Un fragment de liturgie magique copte sur ostracon," 66. As reconstructed, this acclamation (here and at line 27) is given in Greek.

115. **Spell of summons** *(Rylands 103)*

"vowels (?)": Walter E. Crum transcribes as ⲍ̅ . . . ⲏ̣; Angelicus M. Kropp suggests φωνή.

"I and my father . . . ": Compare John 10:30.

"Rabboni": Jesus is called "Rabboni" in Mark 10:51 and John 20:16.

"sealed": that is, made the sign of the cross over the cup.

116. **Spell for power to dominate adversaries** *(Berlin 8322)*

Recto

1 *" . . . "*: The Coptic reads, in part, ⲉⲧⲥⲱϣⲉ, "that/who creep"?

2 *"[I am (?)]"*: or, "[They are (?)]."

"indeed (?) weaker than the weak": perhaps, "weak with (ⲙⲉⲛ) the weak" (compare 1 Corinthians 9:22).

4 *"Louchme"*: "Elouchme"? Compare line 23.

12 *"[. . .]"*: The sense may be "If you do not restrain . . . ."

24 *"I shall do it"*: perhaps "We shall do it"?

Verso

1 *"his [body (?)]"*: Coptic ⲡⲉϤ..ⲙⲀ; probably restore to read ⲡⲉϤⲥⲱⲙⲀ.

117. **Spell invoking Michael and the heavenly powers** *(Moen 3)*

10 *"Spell"*: Coptic ⲕⲟⲭ (perhaps compare ⲀⲡⲟⲗⲟⲅⲓⲀ and the note to text 113, line 6, above).

50 *"Praiithel"*: or, "Praethel."

51 *"Paruthel"*: or, "Parithel."

74–75 *"of N., of N. child of N."*: Coptic ⲛⲓⲙ ⲆⲆ̅̅.

flesh side

19 *"Spell"*: See note 10.

23 *"bones"*: Coptic ⲚⲔⲀⲤ ⲂⲞⲚⲈ, perhaps "bones of a swallow (ⲂⲎⲚⲈ)" (compare line 24).

End

"*FTH*"; perhaps "99," = "Amen." Compare Vienna K 7093, line 9 (text 50), and Michigan 593, page 12, line 6 (text 133).

118. Spell invoking a thundering power *(from the H. O. Lange collection)*

11 *"Yea"*: Coptic ⲀⲒⲀ; H. O. Lange, "Ein faijumischer Beschwörungstext," 164–65, prefers to attach ⲀⲒⲀ to the previous sentence and translates the word "quickly."

16–17 *"Horasias Phankapres"*: This obscure phrase or name may possibly be translated "(in) appearance the head of a boar," Coptic ⲈⲰⲢⲀⲤⲒⲀⲤ (compare ὅρασις?) ⲪⲀ (compare ⲠⲢⲞ?) ⲚⲔⲀⲠⲢⲈⲤ (compare. κάπρος?). See Lange, 165.

20 *"feet"*: or, "foot."
    "toes": or, toe."

21 *"feet"*: or, foot."

35 *"Horasias Phankapres"*: see the note to lines 16–17.
    "Spell": Coptic ⲔⲞⲬ (perhaps compare ⲀⲠⲞⲖⲞⲦⲒⲀ and the note to text 113, line 6, above).

38 *"underworld"*: Coptic ⲀⲘⲦⲈ; read ⲀⲘ<Ⲛ>ⲦⲈ.

40 *"case (?)"*: The translation is based upon an uncertain reconstruction of the Coptic (ⲀⲠⲞⲔⲢ[ⲒⲤⲒⲤ]).

63 " . . . ": Coptic ⲦⲈⲔ[. . .]; Lange, 166, conjectures that the lacuna may possibly be reconstructed to read ⲦⲈⲔ[ⲈⲤ], "prod, drive" (compare Walter E. Crum, *A Coptic Dictionary*, 406b-407a).

64–65 " . . . ": These lines are fragmentary and cannot be reconstructed with confidence. The following is possible: "[of] the wheel, the wheel . . . ."

119. Spell invoking Aknator the Ethiopian *(Coptic Museum 4959)*

Fragment 1

"bowl": Greek φιάλε, a shallow libation bowl. In the first mention, the plural form must be a mistake. Setting the divination bowl upon a brick is a common instruction also in the Demotic texts of ritual power.

"bowl . . . of glass": The untranslated word is Coptic ⲚⲂⲎⳍⲈ.

"flower water:" or, "spell-free water." See above, text 79 verso, lines 2 and 19, and James Drescher, "Two Coptic Magical Ingredients."

"I have inquired": Coptic ⲀⲈⲒⳋⲒⲚⲈ; the verb is a technical term in texts of ritual power for "divination."

"those who are . . . ": The untranslated verb is Coptic ⲢⲦⲀⲢⲤ.

"hells": With this word the first scribe stops.

Between fragments 1 and 2 several lines are lost in lacunae and small fragments. The sequential relationship of fragments 1 and 2 is determined by the reverse (vertical fiber) side of the papyrus which has a drawing of a figure bearing a shield and several stafflike objects.

Between fragments 2 and 3 at least two lines are missing in lacunae. A parallel text (unedited), Coptic Museum 4956B, begins here, and many of the restorations have been enhanced by this other text.

The sequence of fragments 3 and 4 is determined by the parallel text 4956B. At least one line is missing in a lacuna.

120. Spell invoking the divine *(Coptic Museum 4960)*

1 *"Abrak..[ ]"*: perhaps "Abraksa[s]" or a similar name (the ink traces are ambiguous).

2 *"I adjure you . . . "*: Compare also London Hay 10391, lines 28–34 (text 127).

121. Spell for a good singing voice *(Berlin 8318)*

29 *" . . . in glory"*: Perhaps fill in the ellipsis with "may the sun before me bind me in glory," but this is uncertain.

42–43 *"23. Xanthios; 39. Sisinnios; 24. Priskos; 40. Aglaios"*: These four names are from a list of the forty martyrs of Sebastepolis. See the Coptic book of ritual power from Leiden (text 134).

122. Another spell for a good singing voice *(Yale 1791 [first text])*

6–9 *"calamus extract"*: or, "storax of calamus," "calamus storax."

"musk": or, "muscat wine," or "mastic."

13–17 To the right of these lines on the papyrus are the signs to be copied onto the chalice.

23–24 If this interpretation of the general import of these lines is correct, line 23 refers to the series of greetings with which the incantation begins, indicating either that it contains twenty-one greetings (of which only fifteen survive completely because of damage at the top of the manuscript), or that the entire series of however many greetings is to be recited twenty-one times. However, it is possible that these lines continue the list of ingredients, adding to the mixture in the chalice twenty-one measures each of two further items (neither of them identifiable).

27–28 The meaning of "kousht" is obscure, but the word occurs elsewhere in a magical ritual context, among items laid on an altar (Carl Schmidt and Violet MacDermot, *The Books of Jeu and the Untitled Text in the Bruce Codex*, 114:20 [see Walter E. Crum, *A Coptic Dictionary*, 113a]; perhaps also Angelicus M. Kropp, *Ausgewählte koptische Zaubertexte*, 1.59 [text M:59 = text 127] ⲕⲟϣⲧ; Kropp, *Der Lobpreis der Erzengels Michael*, 51–53 [= text 135, lines 256–57] ⲕⲟⲩϣ and white ⲕⲟⲩϣ). Probably here too the word specifies an offering.

29–31 An indeterminate number of lines might be lost between lines 28 and 29, and the beginnings of lines 29–31 are severely damaged.

40–41 *"the twelve powers that surround it"*: that is, the sun. Compare lines 62–63; the allusion is to the zodiac.

45–46 *"the heads . . . and it sends them after him"*: translation very uncertain.

48 *"pleasing like Philemon"*: The identity of this Philemon and the purport of the comparison are not clear.

52 *"like a . . . "*: A word here is too badly damaged to be read.

61 *"swear <by>"*: or, "adjure <you by>."

62 *"the seven stars"*: the seven planets of the solar system as known to the ancients? the Pleiades?

62–63 *"twelve stars"*: Compare lines 39–41.

123. Spell to silence a dog *(London Oriental Manuscript 1013A)*

26 *"the true . . . name"*: Coptic ⲡⲙⲏⲧ ⲛⲣⲁⲛ ⲙⲏⲧ; Adolf Erman, "Zauberspruch für einen Hund," 134, offers the translation "the ten (ⲙⲏⲧ) . . . true names."

124. Amulet with words and names of power *(Michigan 3023a)*

5–7 *"[AK]RAMMAJAMARI"*: The scribe apparently wrote ϫ instead of the usual χ.

8–10 *"AABLANAPHANALBAA"*: The scribe apparently wrote ⲫ instead of the usual ⲑ.

126. Collection of oracles *(Vatican Coptic Papyrus 1)*

207 *"He will delay . . . "*: possibly, "Its occurrence will be delayed."

210 *"live"*: or, "appear."

127. The London Hay "cookbook" *(London Hay 10391)*

12–13 *"O great <one>"*: Coptic ⲚⲚⲞϬ, "O great ones"; emend to read <ⲡ>ⲚⲞϬ.

14 *"You are the one who prepares your ears in . . . "*: The translation is tentative; the Coptic for "prepares" is ϩⲱⲕ, literally "girds." David Frankfurter suggests reading the concluding phrase ϩⲛ ⲛⲁⲭⲓⲁ as ϩⲛ ⲙⲁⲭⲓⲁ, "in battle," that is, in the struggle to triumph through the use of the spells.

18 *"before she is finished"*: or, "before she dies."

24 *"Miak"*: most likely the name of a power; less likely is the translation "Greetings to you" (compare Angelicus M. Kropp, *Ausgewählte koptische Zaubertexte*, 2.50; Walter E. Crum, *A Coptic Dictionary*, 158b–159a).

"[. . .]"; Coptic ⲁⲛⲉϥϫⲉⲛ[. . .]; perhaps another name?

26 *"[. . .] oil"*: Perhaps restore ⲛⲉϩ ⲛ̣[ⲥⲓⲙ], "[radish] oil" (compare line 37).

32 *"this Satan"*: Coptic ⲡⲁⲓⲍⲁⲇⲁⲛⲁⲥ.

34 *" . . . "*: Perhaps read ⲧⲁⲭⲏ, "at once."

35 *"male"*: or, "wild."

45 *"Aio Sabaoth"*: Compare Iao (= Yao) Sabaoth. Taken by itself ⲁⲓⲟ, "Aio," may be translated "yea." Compare text 62, line 1.

56 *"mas . . ."*: perhaps "mastic."

57 *"mela"*: "papyrus"(?).

"Choras": "places" (?).

"Chemera": "she-goat" or "Chimaera"(?).

65 *"For everything destructive"*: Coptic ⲉⲧⲃⲉ ⲫⲉⲛⲉⲙ. Less likely is the translation "For an enema," from the Greek ἔνεμα.

71 *"they heal every sickness"*: or, "every sickness is healed."

86 *"seize"*: or, "rob."

90 *"A . . . "*: Coptic ⲟⲩⲙⲉⲗⲱⲧ . . . , "A ceiling"(?).

96–97 *"love (?) . . . over her"*: The translation is tentative. Rather than ⲙⲛ ⲡⲱⲥ, "and hers," Kropp, 2.47, suggests μήπως, "lest"; but compare ⲙⲛⲡⲱⲥ in the transcription (1.61).

113 *"[. . .]"*: Coptic ⲛ[.]ⲁ̣(?); perhaps ⲛ[ⲇ]ⲇ(?), "[N.] child of N."

113–114 *"make his head go to the place of his foot"*: that is, overturn him.

119ff. The readings of many of the concluding names are tentative.

128. A "cookbook" from Cairo *(Cairo 45060)*

6–11 Some of the divisions among the powerful utterances have been made in order to identify known expressions.

21 *"Atamas"*: Probably read "Adamas."

24 "a sickness . . . ": Coptic ⲟⲩϣⲛⲓϣⲧ, that is, "a sickness ⲓϣⲧ," desig-nating some unknown disease (see Walter E. Crum, *A Coptic Dictionary*, 89a). Compare text 67, note to lines 15–16.

28 "with the finger of a mummy": If ⲧⲉⲃⲉ is not translated "finger" but rather "case" (compare Crum, 397a), then it is possible to read "on a mummy case."

29 "deception": or, "fraud," or perhaps a disease (?) (compare Crum, 649a).

30 " . . . ": Coptic ⲡⲟⲧⲏⲥⲟⲩ, from ποτήριον, "cup"? (compare Angelicus M. Kropp, *Ausgewählte koptische Zaubertexte*, 2.36).

31 "eye disease (?)": Coptic ⲥⲁⲕⲃⲁⲗ, for ⲕⲁⲕⲃⲁⲗ (?), "with bare eyes," that is, "without eyelashes" (compare Kropp, 2.36).

33 "let it go (?)": Coptic ⲛ̄ⲥ̄ⲃⲱⲃ, perhaps for ⲛ̄ⲥ̄ⲃⲱⲕ (compare Hans Dieter Betz, *The Greek Magical Papyri in Translation*, 94 [PGM IV.2943–44: "take the eyes of a bat and release it alive," . . . ζῶσαν αὐτὴν ἀπόλυσον]).

34 "strain": or, "torment"(?).

35 "coin": Coptic ⲥⲁⲧⲏⲣⲉ, compare Greek στατήρ, "stater."

37 "You must prepare it": Coptic ⲉⲕⲁⲧⲁⲁⲩ, probably for ⲉⲕⲁⲧⲁⲙⲓⲁⲩ (as elsewhere in the text).

"Make it full": most likely, fill or immerse the fly.

48 "wax figure": The nature of this wax object is unknown (compare Crum, 269ab).

52 "something of value": or, "treasure" (Coptic [and Greek] ⲭⲣⲏⲙⲁ).

56 "thorns (?)": Coptic ϣⲁⲡϣⲁⲡ; compare London Oriental Manuscript 6796, line 50 (text 132).

63 "Put a little in": Coptic ⲕⲟⲩ ⲟⲩⲕⲟⲩ ⲛ- (ⲕⲱ ⲟⲩⲕⲟⲩⲓ ⲛ-, "put a little in," or ⲕⲟⲩⲟⲩⲕⲟⲩ [from ⲕⲱⲕ] ⲛ-, "rub it off"; compare Kropp, 2.39). The first option suggests a curse upon the opponent; the second (less likely) op-tion suggests a means of purifying the hand of the person performing the spell.

69–73 These lines present a number of problems for translation. While the fol-lowing tentative suggestions (in Kropp, 2.39–40) remain quite speculative, they still may be noted: "present it before the sun ⲁⲥ̄ⲉⲡⲣⲓⲁⲓⲣ, that it come forth (?)" (from ⲡⲉⲓⲣⲉ/ⲡⲣ̄ⲣⲉ); "Take a ⲉⲙⲙⲉⲓⲏ, cat (?)" (from ⲉⲙⲟⲩ); "into netting" (or, "a thornbush," Coptic ϣⲛⲧⲉ); etc.

129. Spell to obtain a good singing voice (*London Oriental Manuscript 6794*)

2 "father": Angelicus M. Kropp suggests that "father" is addressed to Davithe, but see lines 25–27.

12 "Abael": The name is added above the line.

23–25 These threats echo Yahweh's words in Leviticus 26:19 and Deuteronomy 28:23.

35 "David": the psalmist; not spelled "Davithe" as elsewhere.

42 "A 7 (times), E 7 (times), E 7 (times), I 7 (times), O 7 (times), U 7 (times), O 7 (times)": Each of the seven Greek vowels is to be repeated seven times.

46 The names of these three decans are similar to those in London Hay 10391, line 21 (text 127).

51 These three names are written in large ring letters.

61 "Full up": Greek πλήρους, the absolute use of an adjective. Does it mean the cup, mentioned in line 16 and now assumed to be sitting in front of the prac-titioner, and which he is now supposed to drink (?), should be full to the top? Or, does it mean the spell is now complete?

130. Spell for good fishing *(London Oriental Manuscript 6795)*

33 *"Spell (?)"*: Coptic **o** (abbreviation for ὄνομα or ἀπολογία?)
35 *"Spell (?)"*: Coptic **ⲇ** (abbreviation for ἀπολογία?).

131. A prayer made by Mary *(London Oriental Manuscript 6796 [2], [3], [1])*

Recto

21 *"I am . . . "*: Beginning here, the text has many similarities with the one published in Walter E. Crum, "A Coptic Palimpsest I: Prayer of the Virgin in 'Bartos.'"

26 *"Let the [. . .]"*: Here Angelicus M. Kropp tentatively restores to read "Let the [honored helpers]." Marvin Meyer notes the translation, "let the powers of the light appear to me, let the angels and the archangels appear to me today," in a similar context in the unpublished manuscript Heidelberg Kopt. 685, page 3, lines 2–6 (on this manuscript see the introduction to chapter 13). In this manuscript reference is made, a few lines later (page 3, lines 9–10), to "my helper and my life."

37   Here the similarities to Crum's text end.

60 *"Spell (?)"*: Coptic **ⲇ** (abbreviation for ἀπολογία?).

61 *"Sanctus"*: given in Greek, then translated into Coptic. The translation "Sanctus" is used throughout the translations in this chapter when the Greek is followed by the Coptic for "holy."

69 *"<drew to themselves>"*: Kropp suggests restoring the omission based on line 78.

89–100 For a parallel to this, see London Oriental Manuscript 6796 (2), (3) verso, lines 43ff.

104 *"dew of heaven . . . fat of the land"*: Compare Genesis 27:28.

106 *"[is placed before me . . .]"*: The restoration of this lacuna is based on the phrase "descend upon this cup that is placed before me," which is contained in London Oriental Manuscript 6794, lines 16ff. (text 129) and London Hay 10391, lines 40ff. (text 127). Kropp, however, perceiving a eucharistic cup, suggests "this which [you gave to your holy apostles.]" His suggestion is not correct if this is a cup divination.

107 *"[. . . holy]."*: Kropp suggests restoring the lacuna "until [I complete my holy request]."

Verso

6 *"Eriel"*: or, Sriel."

9 *" . . . (today?)"*: The Coptic has ⲙ̄ⲙⲟⲕ (dittography?); possibly read ⲙ̄ⲡⲟⲟⲩ here or at the beginning of line 10.

13 *"drawn (?)"*: Coptic **ⲧⲟⲕϩ**, meaning unknown; perhaps read **ⲧⲟⲕⲙ̄** (from **ⲧⲱⲕⲙ̄**, "draw").

23 *"[that are established]"*: Compare line 66.

76 *"Leuei"*: Compare "Levi."

84 *"who is beside him?"*: or, "what is his name?"

92 *"Spell (?)"*: Coptic **ⲇ** (abbreviation for ἀπολογία?).

132. Spell to cast out every unclean spirit *(London Oriental Manuscript 6796 [4], 6796)*

3 *"Marmarimari"*: Angelicus M. Kropp's transcription is in error here.
21 *"Israel El"*: Coptic **ⲓ̄ⲏⲗ** **ⲏ̄ⲗ**.

133. The Coptic hoard of spells *(Michigan 593)*

2,15 *"our"*: the corporate first-person plural.

3,3–4 *"you whose names were first given to you"*: The meaning is obscure. The archangels may be the first of the angelic creations named by their creator, or the reference may be to the prayer itself in which the names of the seven archangels are the first of the secret Hebrew names spoken by the practitioner in the opening invocations.

3,6–7 *"Hebrew, the language of heaven"*: Hebrew as the holy language, the language of creation, is discussed in Jewish literature (compare Testament of Naphtali 8:3–6; Jubilees 12:25–27; Midrash Rabbah, Genesis 18.6; 31.8).

3,7–8 *"in order that they might hear the one who will activate this prayer"*: The assumption is that the twenty-one angelic powers understand the Hebrew language. Thus, the practitioner has access to and influence over the twenty-one powers because he can communicate with them in their primary language.

3,13 *"its"*: that is, the prayer's.

4,13 *"him"*: that is, the practitioner.

5,9 *"response"*: Coptic (from Greek) ⲘⲚ̄ⲦⲀⲠⲞⲔⲣⲓⲥⲓⲥ; the term suggests that the ritual is to be performed as a response to specific problems that might arise.

5,11–12 *"the anger of every married man"*: Note, here and elsewhere in the text, the general male orientation of the text.

6,13–14 *"oil of spanon"*: apparently a reference to "Spanish oil," an astringent oil known to medical authors and originally of Spanish origin but not necessarily produced there.

7,4–5 *"For one who does not usually sleep with (a) woman"*: for one whose perceived problem is either impotence, lack of interest, or homosexuality. The cure suggested is wine: Intoxication through an alcoholic aphrodisiac is thought to function as an effective cure. See also prescription 28 ("To cause someone to desire you").

12,6 *"FTHP"*: "FTH" (Coptic ϥⲑ or ⳓⲑ) is the alphabetic abbreviation for the number 99, representing the Greek "Amen." Compare Vienna K 7093, line 9 (text 50), and Moen 3, end (text 117).

13,8 *"this being of light"*: apparently the practitioner's endearing name for the client.

13,12 *"You"*: the great spirit whose virtues are praised seven times in this concluding aretalogical hymn.

14,3 *"the river of the ocean"*: or, "the river (which leads to) the ocean," possibly an allusion to traditional speculation on the source of the Nile River, which ultimately flows into the Mediterranean "Ocean."

14,3–5 *"shining until the end through the burning of the trees . . . "*: Morton Smith has suggested that the reference might be to "a setting star, like Sirius, signaling the beginning of summer, since its heat (mentioned here and in the next sentence) burns all of the trees."

134. The Coptic book of ritual power from Leiden *(Leiden, Anastasi No. 9)*

10 *"sorcery"*: Coptic ⲘⲚ̄Ⲧⲣⲉϥϩⲣ̄ⲓ̈ⲕⲛⲉ. This is one of the rare instances in these texts of the actual Coptic word for magic. It appears, moreover, as a force against which this text protects.

Page 1, recto

1 *"<of the living God>"*: Angelicus M. Kropp suggests that the scribe omitted this phrase.

7　*"morning star"*: Venus, associated with Christ in Revelation 22:16.

9　*"Adonai Eloei Elemas"*: These divine names, which also appear on page 2 verso, lines 5–6, are derived from the words of Jesus on the cross.

25–26　*"[You must give] salvation and [healing]"*: Kropp's restorations.

Page 2, recto

16　*"or in <trees with fruit>"*: The text is corrupt, but the following phrase suggests the restoration.

26　*" . . . "*: Kropp suggests the unreadable word . . . ⲦⲈ　be read as ϩ ⲞⲦⲈ, "is fearful."

27　*"trembling"*: reading ⲦⲰⲦ as ⳓ ⲦⲰⲦ.

Page 3, recto

1–5　*" . . . Chaldean . . . Hebrew . . . Egyptian . . . "*: These nationalities were all notorious for practicing magic. Kropp suggests that the implied writer must be Greek.

Page 3, verso

19　*"<them>"*: The text, ⲁ ⳓ Ⲧⲣⲉ ⳓ , "he made it," makes no sense.

27　*"The cause: I am Gregory . . . "*: or, "Yet again, I, Gregory, . . . invoke all you. . . ."

Page 4, verso

15–23　*"Michael . . . Gabriel . . . Raphael . . . Uriel . . . Sedekiel . . . Anael . . . Azael . . . "*: This list of the seven archangels and their attributes can be compared with London Oriental Manuscript 5525, lines 116–19 (text 64).

Page 5, recto

26–27　*"to the place where this prayer is deposited"*: This phrase also occurs on page 1, recto, lines 27–28.

Page 5, verso

20ff.　*"the word of the lord . . . "*: from Isaiah 9:1ff. (Septuagint).

23　*"< . . . >"*: As Kropp notices, something seems to be missing.

Page 6, recto

16–24　*"realizations . . . person"*: The Greek theological terms are ὑπόστασις and πρόσωπον.

Page 6, verso

1–11　This may be a standard list of sins, prototypical of the seven deadly sins. Such listings were popular beginning in the late fourth century, especially among Egyptian monastic writers.

26　*"seal"*: The "seal" was the amulet, in the sense that the sign of the cross was also a seal (Greek σφραγίς) that acted as protection (see page 3 recto, lines 10–15).

Page 8 (7), recto

14　*"creatures"*: The Coptic word Ⲥ Ⲱ ⲚⲦ probably equals the Greek ζῷον, a word used for theriomorphic astrological constellations.

Page 8, verso

16　*"the great star"*: Kropp suggests that the great star is Venus.

Page 9, recto

28　*"[S]edekiel"*: W. Pleyte and P. A. A. Boeser suggest reading [S]edekiel with page 9, verso, line 15.

Page 9, verso

14–16 *"Michael, Gabriel, Raphael, Uriel, Sedekiel, Anael, Setel, Azael"*: Eight rather than the usual seven archangels are named; Setel is the intruder.

19 *"heavens"*: Note the use of the plural "heavens." Up to this point in the text "heaven" (or simply "sky") has been used.

Page 10, recto and verso

28,1 *"Holy, holy, holy, lord of hosts . . ."* These rather elaborate quotations are probably derived from the liturgical chants of the eucharist rather than taken directly from the Bible.

Page 11, recto

3 *"wears"*: Greek φορέω; the amulet was probably meant to be rolled up and tied to the person.

6 *"Abgar"*: Here Abgar is spelled *Aukaros*.

Page 11, verso

3–16 *"The blind . . . after having been buried"*: This list is similar to the list in the letter quoted by Eusebius, which in turn may be based on the list of miracles in Matthew 11:5. Hardly any of the rest of the letter, except the request to come and cure his illness, is found in Eusebius.

Page 12, recto

8–10 *"come to us . . . our numerous illnesses"*: In the letter quoted by Eusebius, Abgar asks Jesus "to come to me and heal the suffering which I have," not the whole town.

Page 12, verso

1–6 *"What, however, is the people of Israel? . . . "*: Eusebius's letter simply says, "I heard that the Jews are treating you with contempt and want to mistreat you."

Pages 13, verso, 14, recto

27ff. *"Akrabi . . . Iel"*: Twenty-four names are invoked, but they are not the names of the twenty-four elders listed in other texts.

135. A Coptic book of ritual power from Heidelberg *(Heidelberg Kopt. 686)*

9 *"14"*: Coptic $\overline{3}$в, "twice 7."

33 *"Yea . . . "*: or, "I have come, I, Michael . . . and we offered adoration. . . ." Then the preceding clause "after he created Phausiel" may be taken to open the new paragraph.

35 *"Atoran"*: Probably emend to "Artoran" (compare line 76, and London Oriental Manuscript 5525, line 118 [text 64]).

37 *"Sanatael"*: Compare Satanael.

41 *"illness"*: Coptic ϢⲰⲚⲈ; Angelicus M. Kropp, *Der Lobpreis des Erzengels Michael*, 16, translates the Coptic word "deprivation," from ϢⲰⲰⲚⲈ (see Walter E. Crum, *A Coptic Dictionary*, 571ab).

44 *"month by month"*: Coptic ⲈⲒⲞⲢ ϢⲀⲢⲀ ⲈⲢ (for ⲈⲒⲞⲢ?); Kropp, 17, also suggests that ⲈⲢ may be read ⲈⲚⲢ, thus producing the phrase ϢⲀⲢⲀ ⲈⲚⲢ, "for ever."

70 *"amulets"*: Coptic ϥⲩ, for ϥⲩⲗⲀⲔⲦⲎⲢⲒⲞⲚ.

73 *"strength"*: Coptic ⲘⲞⲩⲦ, literally "sinew(s)."

77 *"it"*: that is, the church.

79 *"(adjure you)"*: Apparently these words were inadvertently omitted by the scribe.

82 *"there submit"*: Coptic ECⲰK, apparently corrupt.

88 *"the father"*: Coptic ⲠⲰT, probably emend to ⲠⲒⲰT; Kropp, 24–25, also suggests that ⲠⲰT may be read ⲠⲰTN, "what is yours."

92 *"the . . . support (?)"*: Coptic ⲠⲪⲈⲢⲘⲀ, perhaps from ⲈⲢⲘⲀ (ἕρμα), as is proposed by Kropp, 25–26.

93 *"beautiful (?)"*: Coptic ⲈT-ⲀⲈⲒ; Kropp, 27, suggests correcting ⲀⲈⲒ to CⲀⲈⲒ, "beautiful."

97 *"by the star(s)"*: Coptic ⲘⲠⲒⲞⲨ, from CⲒⲞⲨ (following Kropp, 27).
   "Thol": Kropp, 26, gives the spelling "Thoel" (compare line 94).

98 *"I adjure you . . . Stoel"*: Kropp, 26, omits this line from his German translation.

104 *"the (?) finger"*: The Coptic KNTHHⲂⲒ appears to be corrupt. In London Oriental Manuscript 6796, lines 41–42 (text 132) and elsewhere Orphamiel is described as "the great finger (ⲠNⲞ6 N̄THHⲂⲈ) of your right hand." Perhaps emend line 104 in the present manuscript to read similarly.

109–10 *"thirty"*: Coptic ⲘⲀⲀⲂ; taken together with the TⲀC in line 110, ⲘⲀⲀⲂ-TⲀC could be read as a form of "thirty-six" (see Crum, *A Coptic Dictionary*, 368b).

128 *"elders"*: Coptic ⲢⲈⳞ and ⲠⲢⲈⲂ.

133 *"fill them"*: Coptic ⲈⲂⲘⲀⳞⲞⲨ; Kropp, 32, prefers to read this as a passive, "that they may be filled."

149 *"forty-five thousand"*: thus Kropp; Coptic ⲘⲀⲞⲂ ⲘN ⲞⲨⲀ ⲞⲨⲄⲀC NTⲂ.

151 *"almighty"*: Coptic ⲠⲀNTⲰⲢ, for ⲠⲀNTⲞKⲢⲀTⲰⲢ.

157–58 *"May this be the way . . . Yeh, Hak, Hak"*: The translation is tentative and the Coptic text may well be corrupt. For the usual wording of these sorts of clauses see, for example, lines 70–74. The translation of line 157 assumes that the Coptic text be read as suggested by Kropp, 37: TⲈⳞⲒH ⲈTKⲀⲒ ⲘⲀⲒT.

163 *"Tirachael"*: or, "Tihrachael." Kropp, 36, transliterates this name as "Tiharachael."

168 *"If it is poured"*: Coptic ⲀⲨⲰⲰⲀNⲠⲀⳞⲂ; read ⲈⲨⲩⲀNⲠⲀⳞⲂ, with Kropp, 37 (in a note Kropp also emends the spelling of the verb and seems to prefer a plural pronominal suffix: ⲈⲨⲩⲀNⲠⲀⳞTⲞⲨ). As Kropp observes, ⲀⲨⲰ as "and" is not used in the manuscript.

174 *"You revealed"*: Kropp, 38, translates this "He revealed."

198 *"that were driven"*: Coptic NTⲀⲨTⲀⲂⲞⲨ; read NTⲀⲨTⲀⳤⲞⲨ with Kropp, 43 (compare Crum, *A Coptic Dictionary*, 406b–407a, under the word TⲰKC).

199–200 *"his . . . his . . . him"*: Perhaps read "your . . . your . . . you."

217 *"7"*: "6"?

222 *"glorify"*: Coptic ⲈKⲒ ⲈⲞⲞⲨ, read ⲈK† ⲈⲞⲞⲨ with Kropp, 45.

224 *"Anael . . . is hidden (?)"*: The translation of this line remains somewhat uncertain. ⲠNⲀ should probably be translated "the grace," but "spirit" is also possible. Kropp, 44–45, prefers to read the obscure ⲠⳞHⲠ ("hidden") as ⲈTⳞHⲠ, so that it may modify ⲠⲒⲰT ("father") in a construction like the one in line 242.

225 *"for"*: or, "and" (Coptic ⲘN); compare line 22, "dance to (Ⲉ-) the holy spirit."

230 *"withdraw"*: Coptic ⲀNⲀ⳦Ⲱ, read ⲀNⲀⲬⲰⲢⲈⲒ (or the like).

244 *"repentance"*: Coptic ⲘⲒTⲀNⲒ, identified by Kropp, 49, as derived from ⲘⲈTⲀNⲞⲒⲀ.

254 *"who ... "*: Coptic **ЄⲂⲰⲚⲔⲎⲚⲔⲂ**, the meaning of which is obscure. **ЄⲂ-** (= **ЄϤ-**) probably indicates the present circumstantial, and the other letters may designate a disease. Kropp, 51, also suggests that the letters could derive from **ⲂⲰⲀⲔ, ⲂⲰⲚⲔ**, "be angry," and that the clause could be translated, in part, "who is angry . . . ."

257 *"a chalice"*: that is, a drink or potion from a chalice.

259 *"on a mountain"*: perhaps to the wilderness, or to a monastery.

"At sunrise": literally, "At the first (light) of the sun."

"visit": Coptic **ⲔⲀⲀⲒ**; as noted by Kropp, 53, 80, **ⲔⲀⲀⲒ** could derive from either **ⲄⲞ(Є)ⲒⲀЄ**, "visit," or **ⲔⲀⲀЄⲒ** (καλέω), "call."

260 *"them"*: the signs of the figure?

"it": or, "him."

262 *"hastening toward"*: Coptic **ⲠⲎⲦ** Є-; Kropp, 54–55, 81, also suggests the translation "fleeing before."

"ruin": Coptic **(Ⲟ)ⲨⲘЄⲦⲀⲌЄⲨ**, compare **(Ⲟ)ⲨⲘⲚ̄ⲦⲀⲦϢⲀⲨ/ (Ⲟ)ⲨⲘЄⲦⲀⲦϢЄⲨ**, literally "worthlessness."

264 *"the power that is on the right side"*: an apparent reference to one of the drawings originally found at the end of the manuscript.

"No sorcery will deprive (you) of well-being (?)": The translation is tentative. Also possible is the translation "Surely (**ⲘⲀⲚ**) sorcery will be powerless (**ϢⲀⲚ**, from **ϢⲰⲚЄ**?). . . ." The Coptic translated "well-being" is **ⲞⲨⲌⲀⲨЄⲒ**; perhaps read **ⲞⲨⲌⲀⲒ**?

266 *"Take a broken basin"*: literally, "There is with you a broken basin."

268 *"is at odds with you"*: or, "is condemned to you," "is liable to you."

270 *"the power with the head of a bird"*: an apparent reference to one of the drawings originally found at the end of the manuscript.

"in it": that is, in the herd.

271 *"7 powers"*: Compare line 274?

272 *"For its release (?)"*: Coptic **ⲚⲀⲤⲂ**; Kropp, 59, suggests that **ⲀⲤ** may derive from **ⲞⲤЄ**, "damage, fine, ransom, price of release" (compare λύτρον).

"names": probably words of power.

273 *"barley (?)"*: Coptic ** Ï Ⲟ Ⲩ**; Kropp, 59, suggests that **Ï Ⲟ Ⲩ** may be read **ЄⲒⲰⲦ, ЄⲒⲞⲨⲦ**.

"Hidden water": perhaps water from underground, that is, from a well or cistern (compare Crum, *A Coptic Dictionary,* 696a).

"fasting": Coptic **ⲚЄϮⲀ**, from νηστεία.

GLoSSARY

Well-known biblical characters and those from Greek and Egyptian myths are not included in this glossary.

ABLANATHANALBA – A common word of power in Greek and Coptic texts. Correctly spelled it is a palindrome (reads both forward and backward). No satisfactory interpretation of the name has been proposed, though it may contain some Hebrew words (for example, "father, come to us"?)

ABRASAX, ABRASAXAX, ABRAXIEL, ETC. – A popular name of power among ritualists and Gnostics. Reading the letters as numbers (the mystical art of gematria), the name Abrasax totals 365. The name may derive from Hebrew, possibly Abra (for Arba?) Sabaoth, "Four (=YHWH, the tetragrammaton?) Sabaoth ("of hosts");" compare text 2.

ADONAI – Hebrew for "my lord." A name from the Hebrew Scriptures, linked to the ineffable name of god (YHWH, often vocalized as Yahweh).

AEEIOUO (AEĒIOUŌ) – The seven "holy vowels" of the Greek alphabet: Alpha, Epsilon, Eta, Iota, Omicron, Upsilon, and Omega. Frequently repeated, chanted, interpreted, etc.

AEON – The Greek word means "eternity," but in these texts aeons are personified heavenly beings.

AKRAMACHAMARI – A frequent word of power, with many variations in spelling. Gershom Scholem has proposed an Aramaic derivation, "uproot the magical spells."

ALPHA LEON PHONE ANER – The names of the four living creatures mentioned in Ezekiel, Revelation, etc.: bull (Hebrew *aleph*), lion (Greek *leon*), eagle (Greek *phone*, "voice"), and man (Greek *aner*).

AMULET – Usually translates the Greek *phylakterion:* something recited or worn for protection.

AO (AŌ) – Alpha Omega, the first and last letters of the Greek alphabet. In Christian lore, often related Christ as Alpha and Omega (compare Revelation 1:8 etc.; Isaiah 44:6).

ARCHANGELS – Seven in number, with Michael as their chief. Only Michael and Gabriel are mentioned in the Bible; the apocryphal book Tobit mentions Raphael. The remaining four names are taken from Jewish pseudepegripha, but there are many variations in the list: Suriel, Uriel, Raguel, Saraphuel, Sedekiel, Anael, etc.

ARCHON – Greek for "ruler." The archons are hostile powers in the heavens, especially in Gnostic texts.

BAINCHOOCH – A maleficent power whose name derives from the Egyptian phrase "spirit of darkness."

BATHURIEL, APABATHUEL – A power sometimes called "the great true name" or "the great power."

CHARACTER – The graphic symbol of a power, sometimes drawn in the bottom of a bowl or on a piece of papyrus as an inducement in invocations. Iamblichus says they could also be stood on.

CH M G – Chi Mu Gamma, an abbreviation or cryptogram used in Christian texts. Its interpretation is not clear, but the following suggestions have been made: "a writing of my hand" (Greek *cheiros mou graphe*); "Christ, Michael, Gabriel"; "one" (Greek CH M G visually resembles the Hebrew word for "one," *'ahad*); and "Mary gives birth to Christ" (Greek *Christon Maria genna*). Today most scholars seem to favor the last suggestion. It is also possible that the letters may have had a numerical meaning (for example, CH M G = 643, equivalent to the numerical value of an expression such as "god is the holy trinity" [Greek *he hagia trias th(eos)*]).

CHERUBIM – The living creatures who stand around god's throne (in Ezekiel, Revelation, etc.) and chant the heavenly liturgy.

CREED – A statement of faith recited as a part of Christian liturgies. Credal fragments are appropriated by texts of ritual power to address Christ and praise his virtues in the manner of ancient aretalogies.

DECAN – From the Greek word for "ten," a decan is a deity, originally prominent especially in Egyptian tradition, who governs ten degrees of the zodiac. There are thus thirty-six decans.

-EL – A Semitic word for god. Used as a suffix, it creates many Hebrew-sounding names of power, such as Abrasaxael, Yaoel, etc.

ELOI ELOI LAMA SABACHTHANI, with variations – The cry of Jesus from the cross, found in the Gospels of Matthew and Mark and based on the opening of Psalm 22. The cry may be understood in these texts as similar in power to the names of angels: Eloi Eloi Elemos Abaktane, Adonai Eloei Elemas Sabaoth, etc.

EVIL EYE – The ancient Mediterranean belief in the threatening power cast by an envious gaze. The evil eye thus required apotropaic precautions.

FIGURE – Greek *zodion*, a small drawn, painted, or carved depiction of a power to be invoked, along with the names.

FOUR LIGHTS – Beneficent powers derived from Sethian Gnosticism. Their names (with variations) are Davithe, Eleleth, Harmozel, and Oroiael.

FOUR LIVING CREATURES – These stand around and bear or draw the throne of god in Revelation, with the faces of a lion, an ox, a man, and an eagle. Sometimes they are named Paramara, Zorothion, Periton, and Akramata; sometimes they are called Alpha, Leon, Phone, and Aner.

HOLY HOLY HOLY – Called the trisagion or Sanctus, this is the chant of the cherubim in Isaiah 6:3 and Revelation 4:8. It became part of the Christian liturgy, from which it has been lifted into rituals of power.

INGREDIENTS – The recipes within the texts of ritual power include instructions for preparing offerings, incense, potions, oils, amulets, etc. The lists of ingredients enumerate a wide variety of animal and vegetable materials; even the types of water mentioned include honey water, laurel water, rose water, rainwater, salt water, spell-free (or flower?) water, Tobe water, bathwater, hidden water, and so on. Some of these ingredients are known and some are unknown, and of the former some are still in use as ingredients in Egyptian ritual power to the present day (see Gérard Viaud, *Magie et coutumes populaires chez les Coptes d'Égypte*). Among the more difficult items to identify: koush (various spellings), possibly the kostos root (see text 4); alouth (again, various spellings), perhaps aloes (so Friedrich Bilabel and Adolf Grohmann) or a kind of wood (of which several appear among the ingredients in recipes). Compare Angelicus M. Kropp, *Der Lobpreis des Erzengels Michael*, 85–86.

LAL MOULAL BOULAL – See SEDRAK.

LITURGY – The eucharistic service of the Christian church. Fragments of the liturgy are appropriated into texts of ritual power, such as the invocation over the cup, the Sanctus, the creed, etc.

MARMARIOTHA – A name derived from Syriac "lord of lords." There are several variations in spelling.

MITHRAS – Deity of a popular Greco-Roman mystery cult, he was originally a Persian solar god.

N. – Abbreviation for "Name." Here one is to insert the name of the user or the recipient of the spell.

ONNOPHRIS – An epithet of the Egyptian god Osiris, "beautiful one."

ORPHAMIEL – A power called "the great finger of the father," although text 123 calls Nathanael "the great finger."

PARAMARA ZOROTHION PERITON AKRAMATA – Names of the four living creatures.

RING SIGNS, RING LETTERS – Abstract or astrological diagrams or letters, with circles drawn at the ends of the lines.

SABAOTH – A title of god in the Hebrew Scriptures. Lord Sabaoth means "lord of hosts." The names Yao Sabaoth and lord almighty are all variations of the same title.

SAINTS – Many saints of the eastern Christian churches are invoked in ritual texts. Most of those named date from the fourth to the sixth centuries and are renowned for their miracles and healing powers. Cosmas and Damian, for example, were twin brothers born in Arabia and martyred in 303. Philoxenos was a famous Syrian bishop who died in 523. For individual entries see Aziz S. Atiya, ed., *The Coptic Encyclopedia*.

SATOR ARETO TENET OTERA ROTAS – Sometimes written as a word-square, this formula has been found throughout the ancient Christian world. Its interpretation is debated, and its origin is probably non-Christian. Some suggestions for interpretation: "The creator preserves his works" (from a Stoic-Pythagorean context); a *Pater Noster* ("Our Father") anagram (of Stoic origin?); and now (with Miroslav Marcovich, "SATOR AREPO"), "The sower Horus/Harpocrates checks (or, "binds") toils and tortures." See also Walter O. Moeller, *The Mithraic Origin and Meanings of the Rotas-Sator Square*.

SEDRAK MIZAK ABDENAKO, ANANIAS ASARIAS MIZAEL – With many spelling variations, these are the Babylonian and Hebrew names of the three friends of Daniel. God protected them in the fiery furnace, and they became names with which to conjure. Sometimes the names Lal Moulal Boulal are linked to these three youths; see Jacques van der Vliet, "Varia Magica Coptica," 236–39.

SEMESILAM, with variations – A name of power, probably derived from Semitic words for "eternal sun" or "sun of the world."

SENSENGENBARPHARANGES – A very common word in Greek and Coptic texts of ritual power, with many variations in spelling. Probably originally Aramaic (S. son of [bar-] P. ?); John G. Gager, *Curse Tablets and Binding Spells*, 269, suggests (with a reference to Josephus) a connection with a drug from a fig tree in "the Baaras ravine" (in Greek, *pharangos* [genitive]).

SERAPHIM – Winged angels who participate in the heavenly liturgy around the throne of god. They derive more from Jewish pseudepigrapha than the Bible.

SOLOMON – Early Jewish traditions, such as the Testament of Solomon, credited King Solomon with power to control the demons.

THREE HOLY ONES – See SEDRAK.

TOBE WATER – Several proposals have been made: "brick water," "rain-water of the month of Tobe" (January), "Epiphany water" (blessed during that feast in January), or perhaps even water from the Nile during Tobe. In these texts a connection with the feast of Epiphany is most probable. See James Drescher, "Two Coptic Magical Ingredients," 60–61; Oswald Hugh Ewart Burmester, *The Egyptian or Coptic Church*, 250–56.

TWENTY-FOUR ELDERS – Heavenly beings who surround the throne of god in Revelation; in ritual texts they are usually named in alphabetical order according to the twenty-four letters of the Greek alphabet: Achael, Banuel, etc.

WING FORMATION – The writing of a name of power in rows, dropping a letter at each row to form a triangular shaped "wing."

YAO, YAO SABAOTH – Yao or Iao is an attempt to write the ineffable name of the Hebrew god, YHWH, in Greek letters. Yahweh Sabaoth, "Lord of Hosts," is a frequently occurring name of god in the Hebrew Scriptures.

ZOE – In the Greek translation (Septuagint) of the Hebrew Scriptures, Zoe, "life," is the translation of Eve.

ZOROKOTHORA – Mentioned as the name of a demon in some brief texts from the Berlin collection; associated with Melchisedek in Gnostic texts; spelled Sorochata in text 131, SOROCHCHATTA in text 45.

ILLUSTRATION CREDITS

p. 64   Drawing of a seal, Second Book of Jeu. Adapted from Carl Schmidt and Violet MacDermot, *The Books of Jeu and the Untitled Text in the Bruce Codex*, 146.

p. 66   Drawing of a seal, Second Book of Jeu. Adapted from Carl Schmidt and Violet MacDermot, *The Books of Jeu and the Untitled Text in the Bruce Codex*, 152.

p. 67   Drawings of two seals, Second Book of Jeu. Adapted from Carl Schmidt and Violet MacDermot, *The Books of Jeu and the Untitled Text in the Bruce Codex*, 182.

p. 68   Drawing of a seal, Second Book of Jeu. Adapted from Carl Schmidt and Violet MacDermot, *The Books of Jeu and the Untitled Text in the Bruce Codex*, 184.

p. 121   Reconstructed drawing, London Oriental Manuscript 5525. Adapted from Angelicus M. Kropp, *Ausgewählte koptische Zaubertexte*, vol. 3, Tafel V, Abb. 9. Used with permission.

p. 133   Drawing of Davithe, London Oriental Manuscript 5987. Adapted from Angelicus M. Kropp, *Ausgewählte koptische Zaubertexte*, vol. 3, Tafel VII, Abb. 12. Used with permisson.

p. 146   Drawing of an angel, Rossi's "Gnostic" tractate. From Marvin Meyer, *Rossi's "Gnostic" Tractate*, 28. Used with the permission of the Institute for Antiquity and Christianity, Claremont Graduate School.

p. 158   Drawing of Gabriel, Heidelberg Kopt. 684. Adapted from Friedrich Bilabel and Adolf Grohmann, *Griechische, koptische und arabische Texte*, 314.

p. 168   Photograph of London Hay 10414 (lower part). Copyright British Museum. Used with permission.

p. 172   Photograph of London Hay 10122 (recto), upper part. Copyright British Museum. Used with permission.

p. 173   Photograph of London Hay 10122 (verso), upper part. Copyright British Museum. Used with permission.

p. 200   Photograph of Berlin 8503. Ägyptisches Museum und Papyrussammlung. Used with permission.

p. 214   Photograph of Heidelberg Kopt. 681. Photograph by Roland Zachmann, Institut für Papyrologie, Ruprecht-Karls-Universität, Heidelberg. Used with the permission of the Director of the Institut für Papyrologie.

p. 219   Photograph of Louvre E.14.250 (recto). Used with permission.

p. 220   Photograph of Louvre E.14.250 (verso). Used with permission.

p. 223   Drawing of a power, ring signs, and letters, Heidelberg Kopt. 679. Adapted from Friedrich Bilabel and Adolf Grohmann, *Griechische, koptische und arabische Texte*, 411–13.

p. 242   Photograph of Coptic Museum 4959, fragments 4–5 (rearranged). Used with the permission of the Coptic Museum.

p. 243   Photograph of Coptic Museum 4960 (text to the left). Used with the permission of the Coptic Museum.

p. 273   Drawings of roosters and ring signs, Cairo 45060. Adapted from Angelicus M. Kropp, *Ausgewählte koptische Zaubertexte*, 1.54. Used with permission.

p. 280   Drawing of David/Davithe the guitarist, London Oriental Manuscript 6794. Adapted from Angelicus M. Kropp, *Ausgewählte koptische Zaubertexte*, vol. 3, Tafel VIII, Abb. 15. Used with permission.

p. 282   Drawing of Jesus the fisherman, London Oriental Manuscript 6795. Adapted from Angelicus M. Kropp, *Ausgewählte koptische Zaubertexte*, vol. 3, Tafel II, Abb. 3. Used with permission.

p. 289   Drawing of Jesus, London Oriental Manuscript 6796 (3) verso. Adapted from Angelicus M. Kropp, *Ausgewählte koptische Zaubertexte*, vol. 3, Tafel VII, Abb. 14. Used with permission.

p. 292   Photograph of London Oriental Manuscript 6796 (lower part). Used by permission of the British Library.

BIBLIOGRAPHY

Alcock, Anthony. "A Coptic Magical Text." *Bulletin of the American Society of Papyrologists* 19 (1982): 97–103.

Amélineau, Émile. "Le christianisme chez les anciens coptes." *Revue d'histoire des religions* 14 (1886): 344–45.

———. *Le nouveau traité gnostique de Turin.* Paris: Chamuel, 1895.

———. "The Rôle of the Demon in the Ancient Coptic Religion." *The New World* 2 (1893): 518–35.

Atiya, Aziz S., ed. *The Coptic Encyclopedia.* 8 vols. New York: Macmillan Publishing Company, 1991.

Aubert, Jean-Jacques. "Threatened Words: Aspects of Ancient Uterine Magic." *Greek, Roman, and Byzantine Studies* 30 (1989): 421–49.

Aune, David E. "Magic in Early Christianity." In *Aufstieg und Niedergang der römischen Welt,* edited by Hildegard Temporini and Wolfgang Haase, II.23.2, 1507–57. Berlin and New York: Walter de Gruyter, 1980.

Barb, A. A. "St. Zacharias the Prophet and Martyr: A Study in Charms and Incantations." *Journal of the Warburg and Courtauld Institutes* 11 (1948): 35–67.

———. "The Survival of Magic Arts." In *The Conflict Between Paganism and Christianity in the Fourth Century,* edited by Arnaldo Momigliano, 100–125. Oxford: Clarendon Press, 1963.

Barry, L. "Une adjuration chrétienne." *Bulletin de l'Institut français d'archéologie orientale* 6 (1908): 61–63.

Baynes, Norman H. "St. Antony and the Demons." *Journal of Egyptian Archaeology* 40 (1954): 7–10.

Bell, Catherine. *Ritual Theory, Ritual Practice.* New York: Oxford University Press, 1992.

Beltz, Walter. "Katalog der koptischen Handschriften der Papyrus-Sammlung der Staatlichen Museen zu Berlin." *Archiv für Papyrusforschung und verwandte Gebiete* 26 (1978): 57–119; 27 (1980): 121–222.

———. "Die koptischen Zauberostraka der Papyrus-Sammlung der Staatlichen Museen zu Berlin." *Hallesche Beiträge zur Orientwissenschaft* 2 (1980): 59–75, 103–11.

———. "Die koptischen Zauberpapiere und Zauberostraka der Papyrus-Sammlung der Staatlichen Museen zu Berlin." *Archiv für Papyrusforschung und verwandte Gebiete* 31 (1985): 31–41.

———. "Die koptischen Zauberpapyri der Papyrus-Sammlung der Staatlichen Museen zu Berlin." *Archiv für Papyrusforschung und verwandte Gebiete* 29 (1983): 59–86.

——. "Die koptischen Zauberpergamente der Papyrus-Sammlung der Staatlichen Museen zu Berlin." *Archiv für Papyrusforschung und verwandte Gebiete* 30 (1984): 83–104.

——. "Die koptischen Zaubertexte der Papyrus-Sammlung der Staatlichen Museen zu Berlin: Register." *Archiv für Papyrusforschung und verwandte Gebiete* 32 (1986): 55–66.

——. "Noch zwei Berliner Sator-Amulette." *Archiv für Papyrusforschung und verwandte Gebiete* 24–25 (1976): 129–34.

Benko, Stephen. "Early Christian Magical Practices." In *Society of Biblical Literature 1982 Seminar Papers*, edited by Kent H. Richards, 9–14. Chico, CA: Scholars Press, 1982.

Betz, Hans Dieter, ed. *The Greek Magical Papyri in Translation, Including the Demotic Spells.* Chicago: University of Chicago Press, 1986. 2d ed., 1992.

Bilabel, Friedrich, and Adolf Grohmann. *Griechische, koptische und arabische Texte zur Religion und religiösen Literatur in Ägyptens Spätzeit.* 2 vols. Veröffentlichungen aus den badischen Papyrus-Sammlungen, vol. 5. Heidelberg: Verlag der Universitätsbibliothek, 1934.

Biondi, Alessandro. "Le citazioni bibliche nei papiri magici cristiani greci." *Studia Papyrologica* 20 (1981): 93–127.

Björck, Gudmund. *Der Fluch des Christen Sabinus: Papyrus Upsaliensis 8.* Arbeten utgivna med understöd av Vilhelm Ekmans universitetsfond, Uppsala, vol. 47. Uppsala: Almqvist & Wiksells, 1938.

Blackman, Winifred S. *The Fellahin of Upper Egypt: Their Religious, Social, and Industrial Life with Special Reference to Survivals from Ancient Times.* London: Frank Cass and Company Limited, 1968.

Böhlig, Alexander, and Frederik Wisse. *Nag Hammadi Codices III,2 and IV,2: The Gospel of the Egyptians.* Nag Hammadi Studies, vol. 4. Leiden: E. J. Brill, 1975.

Boeser, P. A. A. "Deux textes coptes du Musée d'antiquités des Pays-Bas à Leide." In *Recueil d'études égyptologiques dédiées à la mémoire de Jean-François Champollion à l'occasion du centenaire de la lettre à M. Dacier relative à l'alphabet des hiéroglyphes phonétiques lue à l'Académie des inscriptions et belles-lettres le 27 septembre 1822*, 529–35. Bibliothèque de l'École pratique des hautes études, IVᵉ section, sciences historiques et philologiques, vol. 234. Paris: Librairie ancienne Honoré Champion, Édouard Champion, 1922.

Bondi, J. H. "Koptische Fluchformeln aus jüdischer Quelle." *Zeitschrift für ägyptische Sprache und Altertumskunde* 35 (1897): 102–3.

Bonner, Campbell. "Amulets Chiefly in the British Museum." *Hesperia* 20 (1951): 301–45.

——. *Studies in Magical Amulets Chiefly Graeco-Egyptian.* University of Michigan Studies, Humanistic Series, vol. 49. Ann Arbor: University of Michigan Press, 1950.

Borghouts, J. F. *Ancient Egyptian Magical Texts.* Nisaba 9. Leiden: E. J. Brill, 1978.

——. *The Magical Texts of Papyrus Leiden I 348.* Oudheidkundige mededelingen, 51. Leiden: E. J. Brill, 1971.

Botte, Bernard. "L'ange du sacrifice." In *Cours et conférences des semaines liturgiques*, vol. 7 [Tournai, August 1928], 209–21. Louvain, 1929.

Bowman, A. K. *Egypt after the Pharaohs, 332 BC–AD 642: From Alexander to the Arab Conquest.* London: British Museum, 1986.

Brashear, William M. "The Coptic Three Wise Men." *Chronique d'Égypte* 58 (1983): 297–310.

——. "Die koptischen Heiligen Drei Könige." *Jahrbuch preußischer Kulturbesitz* 21 (1985): 131–41.

———. "Lesefrüchte." *Zeitschrift für Papyrologie und Epigraphik* 50 (1983): 97–107.

———. "Vier Berliner Zaubertexte." *Zeitschrift für Papyrologie und Epigraphik* 17 (1975): 25–33.

Brier, Bob. *Ancient Egyptian Magic.* New York: Morrow, 1980.

Brown, Peter. "Sorcery, Demons, and the Rise of Christianity from Late Antiquity into the Middle Ages." *Witchcraft Confessions and Accusations,* edited by Mary Douglas, 17–45. London and New York: Tavistock Publications, 1970.

———. *The World of Late Antiquity, A.D. 150–750.* New York: Harcourt Brace Jovanovich, 1971.

Brunsch, Wolfgang. "Ein koptischer Bindezauber." *Enchoria* 8 (1978): 151–57.

Budge, E. A. Wallis. *Amulets and Superstitions: The Original Texts with Translations and Descriptions of a Long Series of Egyptian, Sumerian, Assyrian, Hebrew, Christian, Gnostic, and Muslim Amulets.* London: Oxford University Press, 1930.

———. *Amulets and Talismans.* New Hyde Park, New York: University Books, 1961.

Burmester, Oswald Hugh Ewart. *The Egyptian or Coptic Church: A Detailed Description of Her Liturgical Services and the Rites and Ceremonies Observed in the Administration of Her Sacraments.* Publications de la Société d'archéologie copte: Textes et documents. Cairo: Printing Office of the French Institute of Oriental Archaeology, 1967.

Chadwick, Henry. *Origen: Contra Celsum.* Cambridge: Cambridge University Press, 1953.

Chassinat, Émile. *Le manuscrit magique copte n⁰ 42573 du musée égyptien du Caire.* Bibliothèque d'études coptes, vol. 4. Cairo: Imprimerie de l'Institut français d'archéologie orientale, 1955.

Clarysse, Willy. "A Coptic Invocation to the Angel Orphamiel." *Enchoria* 14 (1986): 155.

Crasta, Patrick. "Graeco-Christian Magical Papyri." *Studia Papyrologica* 18 (1979): 31–40.

Crum, Walter E. "A Bilingual Charm." *Proceedings of the Society of Biblical Archaeology* 24 (1902): 329–31.

———. "A Bilingual Charm." *Proceedings of the Society of Biblical Archaeology* 25 (1903): 89.

———. *Catalogue of the Coptic Manuscripts in the British Museum.* London: British Museum, 1905.

———. *Catalogue of the Coptic Manuscripts in the Collection of the John Rylands Library, Manchester.* Manchester and London: University Press, Bernard Quaritch, and Sherratt and Hughes, 1909.

———. *A Coptic Dictionary.* Oxford: Clarendon Press, 1939.

———. *Coptic Ostraca from the Collections of the Egypt Exploration Fund, the Cairo Museum and Others.* London: Egyptian Exploration Fund, 1902.

———. "A Coptic Palimpsest." *Proceedings of the Society of Biblical Archaeology* 19 (1897): 210–22.

———. "Magical Texts in Coptic—I." *Journal of Egyptian Archaeology* 20 (1934): 51–53.

———. "Magical Texts in Coptic—II." *Journal of Egyptian Archaeology* 20 (1934): 195–200.

———. "La magie copte: Nouveaux textes." In *Recueil d'études égyptologiques dédiées à la mémoire de Jean-François Champollion à l'occasion du centenaire de la lettre à M. Dacier relative à l'alphabet des hiéroglyphes phonétiques lue à l'Académie des inscriptions et belles-lettres le 27 septembre 1822,* 537–44. Bibliothèque de l'École pratique des hautes études, IVᵉ section, sciences historiques et philologiques, vol. 234. Paris: Librarie ancienne Honoré Champion, Édouard Champion, 1922.

———. *Short Texts from Coptic Ostraca and Papyri*. London: Oxford University Press, 1921.

———. "Eine Verfluchung." *Zeitschrift für ägyptische Sprache und Altertumskunde* 34 (1896): 85–89.

———, and H. I. Bell. "Medical, Magical." In *Wadi Sarga: Coptic and Greek Texts from the Excavations Undertaken by the Byzantine Research Account*, 50–53. Copenhagen: Gyldendalske Boghandel-Nordisk Forlag, 1922.

Daniel, Robert W., and Franco Maltomini, eds. *Supplementum Magicum*, 2 vols. Papyrologica Coloniensia, vol. 16. Abhandlungen der Rheinisch-Westfälischen Akademie der Wissenschaften. Opladen: Westdeutscher Verlag, 1990–92.

Deissmann, Adolf. *Light from the Ancient East: The New Testament Illustrated by Recently Discovered Texts of the Greco-Roman World*, translated by Lionel R. M. Strachan. Grand Rapids, MI: Baker Book House, 1978.

Delatte, Armand. *Herbarius: Recherches sur le cérémonial usité chez les anciens pour la cueillette des simples et des plantes magiques*, 3d ed. Académie Royale de Belgique, 54. Brussels: Palais des académies, 1961.

Devéria, Théodule. *Catalogue des manuscrits égyptiens écrits sur papyrus, toile, tablettes et ostraca en caractères hiéroglyphiques, hiératiques, démotiques, grecs, coptes, arabes et latins qui sont conservés au Musée égyptien du Louvre*. Paris: Charles de Mourgues Fréres, 1874.

Dodds, E. R. *The Greeks and the Irrational*. Berkeley: University of California Press, 1951.

Donadoni, Sergio. "Un incantesimo amatorio copto." *Atti della Reale Accademia delle Scienze di Torino*, scienze morali, storiche e filologiche, 100 (1965–66): 285–92.

Douglas, Mary. *Natural Symbols: Explorations in Cosmology*. New York: Pantheon Books, 1970.

———. *Purity and Danger: An Analysis of the Concepts of Pollution and Taboo*. New York: Praeger, 1966.

Drescher, James. "A Coptic Amulet." In *Coptic Studies in Honor of Walter Ewing Crum*, edited by Michel Malinine, 265–70. Bulletin of the Byzantine Institute of America, vol. 2. Boston: Byzantine Institute, 1950.

———. "A Coptic Malediction." *Annales du service des Antiquités de l'Égypte* 48 (1948): 267–76.

———. "Two Coptic Magical Ingredients." *Bulletin de la Société d'archéologie copte* 14 (1950–57): 59–61.

Drioton, Étienne. "Un apocryphe anti-arien: La version copte de la correspondance d'Abgar, roi d'Édesse, avec notre-seigneur." *Revue de l'Orient chrétien* 20, nos. 3 and 4 (1915–17): 306–26, 337–73.

———. "Parchemin magique copte provenant d'Edfou." *Muséon* 59 (1946): 479–89.

Du Bourguet, Pierre. "Diatribe de Chenouté contre le démon." *Bulletin de la Société d'archéologie copte* 16 (1961–62): 17–72.

Dunand, Françoise. *Religion populaire en Égypte romaine: Les terres cuites isiaques du musée du Caire*. Études préliminaires aux religions orientales dans l'Empire romain, vol. 70. Leiden: E. J. Brill, 1979.

DuQuesne, Terence. *A Coptic Initiatory Invocation (PGM IV 1–25)*. Oxfordshire Communications in Egyptology, 2. Thame Oxon: Darengo, 1991.

Durkheim, Émile. *The Elementary Forms of the Religious Life*. London: Allen and Unwin, 1915.

Edwards, I. E. S. *Hieratic Papyri in the British Museum*. 4th Series: *Oracular Amuletic Decrees of the Late New Kingdom*. London: British Museum, 1960.

Eitrem, Samson. "A New Christian Amulet." *Aegyptus* 3 (1922): 66–67.

———. *Papyri Osloenses*. Vol. 1: *Magical Papyri*. Oslo: Jacob Dybwad, 1925.

Erman, Adolf. "Die ägyptischen Beschwörungen des großen Pariser Zauberpapyrus." *Zeitschrift für ägyptische Sprache und Altertumskunde* 21 (1883): 89–109.

———. *Aegyptische Urkunden aus den Koeniglichen Museen zu Berlin: Koptische Urkunden*, vol. 1. Berlin: Weidmannsche Buchhandlung, 1895–1905.

———. "Drei Geister als Boten des Zauberers." *Mitteilungen der Vorderasiatischen Gesellschaft* 21 (1916): 301–4.

———. "Heidnisches bei den Kopten." *Zeitschrift für ägyptische Sprache und Altertumskunde* 33 (1895): 47–51.

———. "Ein koptischer Zauberer." *Zeitschrift für ägyptische Sprache und Altertumskunde* 33 (1895): 43–46.

———. "Zauberspruch für einen Hund." *Zeitschrift für ägyptische Sprache und Altertumskunde* 33 (1895): 132–35.

Ernštedt, Petr V. (= Jernstedt, P.). "Graeco-Coptica." *Zeitschrift für ägyptische Sprache und Altertumskunde* 64 (1929): 122–35.

———. *Koptskie teksty Gosudarstvennogo Èrmitaža* [Coptic Texts in the State Hermitage]. Moscow and Leningrad: Izdatel'stvo Akademii nauk SSSR, 1959.

———. *Koptskie teksty Gosudarstvennogo muzeja izobrazitel'nyx iskusstv imeni A. S. Puškina* [Coptic Texts in the A. S. Puškin State Museum of Fine Arts]. Moscow and Leningrad: Izdatel'stvo Akademii nauk SSSR, 1959.

Eusebius. *The Ecclesiastical History*, edited and translated by Kirsopp Lake. Loeb Classical Library. Cambridge: Harvard University Press, 1964–1965.

Faraone, Christopher A., and Dirk Obbink, eds. *Magika Hiera: Ancient Greek Magic and Religion*. New York and Oxford: Oxford University Press, 1991.

Fowden, Garth. *The Egyptian Hermes: A Historical Approach to the Late Pagan Mind*. Cambridge: Cambridge University Press, 1986.

Frankfurter, David. "Tabitha in the Apocalypse of Elijah." *Journal of Theological Studies* 41 (1990): 13–25.

Frazer, James George. *The Golden Bough: A Study in Magic and Religion*, 3rd ed. London: Macmillan, 1900.

Freire-Marreco, Barbara. "Charms and Amulets (Introductory and Primitive)." In *Encyclopedia of Religion and Ethics*, 3:392–98. New York: Scribner's, 1911.

Freud, Sigmund. *Totem and Taboo*. Harmondsworth: Penguin, 1913.

Friedman, Florence D., et al. *Beyond the Pharaohs: Egypt and the Copts in the Second to Seventh Centuries A.D.* Providence: Rhode Island School of Design, 1989.

Gager, John G., ed. *Curse Tablets and Binding Spells from the Ancient World*. New York and Oxford: Oxford University Press, 1992.

Girard, Louis Saint-Paul. "Un fragment de liturgie magique copte sur ostrakon." *Annales du service des Antiquités de l'Égypte* 27 (1927): 62–68.

Godbey, Allen H. "Incense and Poison Ordeals in the Ancient Orient." *The American Journal of Semitic Languages and Literatures* 46 (1930): 217–38.

Goedicke, Hans. "Was Magic Used in the Harim Conspiracy against Ramesses III?" *Journal of Egyptian Archaeology* 49 (1963): 71–92.

Grenfell, Bernard P., and Arthur S. Hunt, ed. *The Oxyrhynchus Papyri*. London: Egypt Exploration Fund, 1898–.

Griffith, F. Ll. "The Date of the Old Coptic Texts and Their Relation to Christian Coptic." *Zeitschrift für ägyptische Sprache und Altertumskunde* 39 (1901): 78–82.

———. "The Old Coptic Magical Texts of Paris." *Zeitschrift für ägyptische Sprache und Altertumskunde* 38 (1900): 85–93.

———, and Herbert Thompson, eds. *The Leyden Papyrus: An Egyptian Magical Book.* New York: Dover, 1974. Reprint of *The Demotic Magical Papyrus of London and Leiden.* London: H. Grevel, 1904.

Grumach, Irene. "On the History of a Coptic Figura Magica." *Proceedings of the Twelfth International Congress of Papyrology,* edited by Deborah H. Samuel, 169–81. American Studies in Papyrology, vol. 7. Toronto: Hakkert, 1970.

Hall, H. R. *Coptic and Greek Texts of the Christian Period from Ostraka, Stelae, etc. in the British Museum.* London: British Museum, 1905.

Hengstenberg, W. "Koptische Papyri." In *Beiträge zur Forschung: Studien und Mitteilungen aus dem Antiquariat Jacques Rosenthal, München,* vol. 1 (= "erste Folge"), edited by Jacques Rosenthal, 92–100, 1*–22*. Munich: Verlag von Jacques Rosenthal, 1915.

Horsley, G. H. R. *New Documents Illustrating Early Christianity: A Review of Greek Inscriptions and Papyri Published in 1976.* North Ryde, N.S.W., Australia: Ancient History Documentary Research Center, Macquarie University, 1981.

———. *New Documents Illustrating Early Christianity: A Review of Greek Inscriptions and Papyri Published in 1977.* North Ryde, N.S.W., Australia: Ancient History Documentary Research Center, Macquarie University, 1982.

———. *New Documents Illustrating Early Christianity: A Review of Greek Inscriptions and Papyri Published in 1978.* North Ryde, N.S.W., Australia: Ancient History Documentary Research Center, Macquarie University, 1983.

———. *New Documents Illustrating Early Christianity: A Review of Greek Inscriptions and Papyri Published in 1979.* North Ryde, N.S.W., Australia: Ancient History Documentary Research Center, Macquarie University, 1987.

Hull, John M. *Hellenistic Magic and the Synoptic Tradition.* Studies in Biblical Theology, 2d ed., ser. 28. Naperville, IL: A. R. Allenson, 1974.

Jackson, Howard M. "A Contribution toward an Edition of the *Confession* of Cyprian of Antioch: The *Secreta Cypriani*." *Muséon* 101 (1988): 33–41.

Jacoby, Adolph. "Zu pap. Graec. mag. III 479ff." *Archiv für Religionswissenschaft* 29 (1931): 204–5.

Judge, Edwin A. "The Magical Use of Scripture in the Papyri." In *Perspectives on Language and Text,* edited by Edgar W. Conrad and Edward G. Newing, 339–49. Winona Lake, IN: Eisenbrauns, 1987.

Kahle, Paul E. *Bala'izah: Coptic Texts from Deir el-Bala'izah in Upper Egypt.* 2 vols. Oxford and London: Oxford University Press, 1954.

Kákosy, L. "Remarks on the Interpretation of a Coptic Magical Text." *Acta Orientalia* (Budapest) 13 (1961): 325–28.

Khater, Antoine. "L'emploi des psaumes en thérapie avec formules en caractères cryptographiques." *Bulletin de la Société d'archéologie copte* 19 (1967–68): 123–76.

Kolenkow, Anitra Bingham. "A Problem of Power: How Miracle-Doers Counter Charges of Magic in the Hellenistic World." In *Society of Biblical Literature 1976 Seminar Papers,* edited by George MacRae, 105–10. Missoula, MT: Scholars Press, 1976.

Kosack, Wolfgang. *Lehrbuch des Koptischen.* Graz, Austria: Akademische Druck- u. Verlagsanstalt, 1974.

Kotansky, Roy. "Incantations and Prayers for Salvation on Inscribed Greek Amulets." In *Magika Hiera: Ancient Greek Magic and Religion,* edited by Christopher A. Faraone and Dirk Obbink, 107–37. New York and Oxford: Oxford University Press, 1991.

Krall, Jacob. "Koptische Amulete." In *Mittheilungen aus der Sammlung Papyrus Erzherzog Rainer*, edited by J. Karabacek, 115–22. Mittheilungen aus der Sammlung der Papyrus Erzherzog Rainer, vol. 5. Vienna: Verlag der K. K. Hof- und Staatsdruckerei, 1892.

Kropp, Angelicus M. *Ausgewählte koptische Zaubertexte*. 3 vols. Brussels: Fondation égyptologique reine Élisabeth, 1930–31.

———. *Der Lobpreis des Erzengels Michael (vormals P. Heidelberg Inv. Nr. 1686)*. Brussels: Fondation égyptologique reine Élisabeth, 1966.

———. *Oratio Mariae ad Bartos: Ein koptischer Gebetstext aus den Giessener Papyrus-Sammlungen*. Berichte und Arbeiten aus der Universitätsbibliothek Giessen, vol. 7. Giessen: Universitätsbibliothek, 1965.

———. "Oratio Mariae ad Bartos: Ein koptischer Gebetstext aus den Giessener Papyrus-Sammlungen (P. Jand. Inv. Nr. 9 A. B.)." *Nachrichten der Giessener Hochschulgesellschaft* 34 (1965): 145–80.

Kühner, Ruth. "Gnostische Aspekte in den koptischen Zaubertexten." *Bulletin de la Société d'égyptologie de Genève* 4 (1980): 61–64.

Lacau, P. "Les statues 'guérisseuses' dans l'ancienne Égypte." In *Académie des inscriptions et belles-lettres, histoire, prix, et fondations, publications (Commission de la fondation Piot, Monuments et mémoires)* 25 (1921–22): 189–209.

Lange, H. O. "Ein faijumischer Beschwörungstext." In *Studies Presented to F. Ll. Griffith*, edited by S. R. K. Glanville, 161–66. London: Egyptian Exploration Society, 1925.

Lanne, Emmanuel. *Le grand euchologe du monastère blanc*. Patrologia Orientalis, vol. 28, fasc. 2, 267–407. Paris: Firmin-Didot, 1958.

Lantschoot, A. van. "Une collection sahidique de sortes sanctorum (Payprus Vatican Copte 1)." *Muséon* 69 (1956): 35–52.

Leclercq, H. "Amulettes." In *Dictionaire d'archéologie chrétienne et de liturgie*, 1:1784–860. Paris: Librairie Letouzey et Ané, 1931–53.

———. "Magie." In *Dictionnaire d'archéologie chrétienne et de liturgie*, 10:1067–1114. Paris: Librarie Letouzey et Ané, 1931–53.

Lee, G. M. "Demotica et Coptica." *Aegyptus* 48 (1968): 139–40.

Legge, F. "A Coptic Spell of the Second Century." *Proceedings of the Society of Biblical Archaeology* 29 (1897): 183–87.

Lemm, Oscar von. "Kleine koptische Studien LIV: Ein koptischer Zauberspruch." *Mémoires de l'Académie impériale des sciences de Saint-Pétersbourg*, classe des sciences historico-philologiques, 8th ser., 8.12 (1907): 50–57.

———. "Koptische Miscellen L: Zu einigen von Turajev edierten Texten 2–5." *Bulletin de l'Académie impériale des sciences de Saint-Pétersbourg*, classe des sciences sociales, 6th ser., 2 (1908): 1076–89.

Lévi-Strauss, Claude. "The Effectiveness of Symbols." In *Structural Anthropology*, translated by Claire Jacobson and Brooke Grundfest Schoepf, 186–205. New York: Basic Books, 1963.

———. "The Sorcerer and His Magic." In *Structural Anthropology*, translated by Claire Jacobson and Brooke Grundfast Schoepf, 167–85. New York: Basic Books, 1963.

Lexa, François (or Frantisek). *La magie dans l'Égypte antique de l'ancien empire jusqu'a l'époque copte*. 3 vols. in 2 books. Paris: Librairie Orientaliste Paul Geuthner, 1925.

Maas, Max. "Ein koptisch-christlicher Fluchpapyrus." *Theologische Literaturzeitung* 39 (1914): 446.

MacCoull, Leslie S. B. "*P. Morgan Copt.*: Documentary Texts from the Pierpont Morgan Library." *Bulletin de la Société d'archéologie copte* 24 (1979–82): 1–19.

——. "Three Coptic Papyri in the Duke University Collection." *Bulletin of the American Society of Papyrologists* 20 (1983): 137–41.

MacMullen, Ramsay. "Magicians." In *Enemies of the Roman Order: Treason, Unrest and Alienation in the Empire,* 95–127. Cambridge, MA: Harvard University Press, 1966.

Malinowski, Bronislaw. *Coral Gardens and Their Magic.* 2 vols. Indiana University Studies in the History and Theory of Linguistics. Bloomington, IN: Indiana University Press, 1965.

——. *Magic, Science and Religion.* Garden City, NY: Doubleday, 1954.

Marcovich, Miroslav. "SATOR AREPO." *Zeitschrift für Papyrologie und Epigraphik* 50 (1983): 155–71.

Mauss, Marcel. *A General Theory of Magic.* NY: W. W. Norton, 1975.

Meyer, Marvin. "The Love Spell of *PGM* IV. 94–153: Introduction and Structure." In *Acts of the Second International Congress of Coptic Studies,* edited by Tito Orlandi and Frederik Wisse, 193–201. Rome: C. I. M., 1985.

——. "O. Moen 34: A Second Look." *Bulletin de la Société d'archéologie copte* 27 (1985): 71–72.

——. *Rossi's 'Gnostic' Tractate.* Occasional Paper 13. Claremont, CA: Institute for Antiquity and Christianity, 1988.

——. "A Sixth-Century Christian Amulet." *Bulletin of the Institute for Antiquity and Christianity* 8 (1981): 9.

——. *Who Do People Say I Am? The Interpretation of Jesus in the New Testament Gospels.* Grand Rapids, MI: William B. Eerdmans, 1983.

——, and Paul Allan Mirecki, eds. *Magic in the Ancient World.* In preparation.

——, and Richard Smith. "Invoking Aknator the Ethiopian." *Bulletin of the Institute for Antiquity and Christianity* 18 (1991): 10–12.

Mirecki, Paul Allan. "The Figure of Seth in a Coptic Magical Text." In *Acts of the Fifth International Congress of Coptic Studies, Washington, 12–15 August 1992. Vol. 2: Papers from the Sections,* edited by David W. Johnson. Rome: C.I.M., 1993.

Moeller, Walter O. *The Mithraic Origin and Meanings of the Rotas-Sator Square.* Études préliminaries aux religions orientales dans l'Empire Romain, vol. 38. Leiden: E. J. Brill, 1973.

Moritz, B. "A Bilingual Charm." *Proceedings of the Society of Biblical Archaeology* 25 (1903): 89.

Müller, C. Detlef G. *Die Engellehre der koptischen Kirche: Untersuchungen zur Geschichte der christlichen Frömmigkeit in Ägypten.* Wiesbaden: Otto Harrassowitz, 1959.

Müller, Wolfgang. "Die koptischen Handschriften der Berliner Papyrussammlung." In *Koptologische Studien in der DDR: Zusammengestellt und herausgegeben vom Institut für Byzantinistik der Martin-Luther-Universität Halle-Wittenberg,* 65–84. Halle and Wittenberg: Wissenschaftliche Zeitschrift der Martin-Luther-Universität, 1965.

Murray, Gilbert. *Five Stages of Greek Religion.* New York: Columbia University Press, 1925.

Parássoglou, George M. "Artificial Scripts and Magical Papyri." *Studia Papyrologica* 13 (1974): 57–60.

——. "A Christian Amulet against Snakebite." *Studia Papyrologica* 13 (1974): 107–10.

Pearson, Birger A. *Nag Hammadi Codex VII.* Nag Hammadi Studies. Leiden: E. J. Brill, in preparation.

Pellegrini, Astorre. "Piccoli testi copto-sa'îdici del Museo Archeologico di Firenze. *Sphinx* 10 (1906): 141–59.

Pernigotti, Sergio. "Il codice copto." In "Nuovi papiri magici in copto, greco e aramaico," by Edda Bresciani et al., 19–53. *Studi classici e orientali* 29 (1979): 15–130.

——. "Una tavoletta lignea con un testo magico in copto." *Eggitto e Vicino Oriente* 6 (1983): 75–92.

Petersen, Theodore C. *A Collection of Papyri: Egyptian, Greek, Coptic, Arabic.* Kraus Catalogue, no. 105. New York: H. P. Kraus, [1964].

Peterson, Erik. *The Angels and the Liturgy: The Status and Significance of the Holy Angels in Worship,* translated by Ronald Walls. London: Darton, Longman and Todd, 1964.

Petropoulos, J. C. B. "The Erotic Magical Papyri." In *Proceedings of the XVIII International Congress of Papyrology,* 2:215–22. Athens, 1988.

Pezin, Michel. "Les manuscrits coptes inédits du Collège de France." In *Écritures et traditions dans la littérature copte,* edited by Jacques É. Ménard et al., 23–27. Cahiers de la bibliothèque copte, vol. 1. Louvain: Éditions Peeters, 1983.

Pleyte, W., and P. A. A. Boeser. *Manuscrits coptes du musée d'antiquités des Pays-Bas à Leide.* Leiden: E. J. Brill, 1897.

Polotsky, Hans J. Review of Stegemann, *Die koptischen Zaubertexte der Sammlung Papyrus Erzherzog Rainer in Wien. Orientalistische Literaturzeitung* 38 (1935): 88–91.

——. "Suriel der Trompeter." *Muséon* 49 (1936): 231–43.

——. "Zu einigen Heidelberger koptischen Zaubertexten." *Orientalia* 4 (1935): 416–25.

——. "Zwei koptische Liebeszauber." *Orientalia* 6 (1937): 119–31.

Preisendanz, Karl. "Deux papyrus magiques de la collection de la Fondation égyptologique (P. Bruxelles inv. E 6390 et 6391)." *Chronique d'Égypte* 6 (1931): 137–40.

——, ed. *Papyri Graecae Magicae: Die griechischen Zauberpapyri.* 2 vols., 2d ed., edited by Albert Henrichs. Stuttgart: B. G. Teubner, 1973.

Quecke, Hans. "Ein Fragment eines koptischen Zaubertextes (PPalau Rib. Inv. 137)." *Studia Papyrologica* 8 (1969): 97–100.

——. "Palimpsestfragmente eines koptischen Lektionars (P. Heid. Kopt. Nr. 685)." *Muséon* 85 (1972) 5–24.

——. "Zwei koptische Amulette der Papyrussammlung der Universität Heidelberg (Inv. Nr. 544b und 564a)." *Muséon* 76 (1963): 247–65.

Ray, John. "Ancient Egypt." In *Divination and Oracles,* edited by Michael Loewe and Carmen Blacker, 174–90. London and Boston: Allen and Unwin, 1981.

Rémondon, Roger. "Un papyrus magique copte." *Bulletin de l'Institut français d'archéologie orientale* 52 (1953): 157–61.

Remus, Harold. "Does Terminology Distinguish Early Christian from Pagan Miracles?" *Journal of Biblical Literature* 101 (1982): 531–51.

——. "'Magic or Miracle'? Some Second-Century Instances." *The Second Century* 2 (1982): 127–56.

Ritner, Robert K. *The Mechanics of Ancient Egyptian Magical Practice.* Studies in Ancient Oriental Civilization, no. 54, edited by Thomas A. Holland. Chicago: Oriental Institute of the University of Chicago, 1993.

Römer, Cornelia, and Heinz J. Thissen. "Eine magische Anrufung in koptischer Sprache." *Zeitschrift für Papyrologie und Epigraphik* 84 (1990): 175–81.

Rossi, Francesco. "Di alcuni manoscritti copti che si conservano nella Biblioteca Nazionale di Torino." *Memorie della Reale Accademia delle Scienze di Torino, scienze morali, storiche e filologiche,* 2d ser., 43 (1893): 223–340; 44 (1894): 21–70.

Rudolph, Kurt. *Gnosis: The Nature and History of Gnosticism.* Translated by R. McL. Wilson, P. W. Coxon, and K. H. Kuhn. San Francisco: Harper and Row, 1983.

Satzinger, Helmut. "Magische Texte." *Ägyptische Urkunden aus den Staatlichen Museen Berlin: Koptische Urkunden,* 3:113–26. Berlin: B. Hessling, 1968.

——. "The Old Coptic Schmidt Papyrus." *Journal of the American Research Center in Egypt* 12 (1975): 37–51.

——, and Pieter J. Sijpesteijn. "Koptisches Zauberpergament Moen III." *Muséon* 101 (1988): 51–63.

Sauneron, Serge. "Aspects et sort d'un thème magique égyptien: Les menaces incluant les dieux." *Bulletin de la Société française d'égyptologie* 8 (1951): 11–21.

——. "Le monde du magicien égyptien." In *Le monde du sorcier,* 27–65. Sources orientales, vol. 7. Paris: Editions du Seuil, 1966.

Schiffman, Lawrence H., and Michael D. Swartz. *Hebrew and Aramaic Incantation Texts from the Cairo Genizeh: Selected Texts from Taylor-Schechter Box K1.* Semitic Texts and Studies, vol. 1. Sheffield: JSOT, 1992.

Schiller, A. Arthur. "A Coptic Charm. Columbia Coptic Parchment, Numbers 1 and 2." *Journal of the Society of Oriental Research* 12 (1928): 25–34.

Schmidt, Carl. *Gnostische Schriften in koptischer Sprache aus dem Codex Brucianus.* Texte und Untersuchungen zur Geschichte der altchristlichen Literatur, vol. 8, nos. 1–2. Leipzig: J. C. Hinrichs, 1892.

——, and Violet MacDermot. *The Books of Jeu and the Untitled Text in the Bruce Codex.* Nag Hammadi Studies, vol. 13. Leiden: E. J. Brill, 1978.

Sieber, John H. *Nag Hammadi Codex VIII.* Nag Hammadi Studies, vol. 31. Leiden: E. J. Brill, 1991.

Sijpesteijn, Pieter J. "Amulet against Fever." *Chronique d'Égypte* 57 (1982): 377–81.

——. "Ein christliches Amulett aus der Amsterdamer Papyrussammlung." *Zeitschrift für Papyrologie und Epigraphik* 5 (1970): 57–59.

——. "A Coptic Magical Amulet." *Chronique d'Égypte* 57 (1982): 183–84.

——. "Two Coptic Ostraca from the Moen Collection." *Bulletin de la Société d'archéologie copte* 26 (1984): 95–97.

Smith, Jonathan Z. "Good News Is No News: Aretalogy and Gospel." In *Christianity, Judaism, and Other Greco-Roman Cults: Studies for Morton Smith at Sixty,* part 1, *New Testament,* edited by Jacob Neusner, 21–38. Studies in Judaism in Late Antiquity, vol. 12. Leiden: E.J. Brill, 1975.

——. "The Bare Facts of Ritual." In *Imaging Religion: From Babylon to Jamestown,* 53–65. Chicago: University of Chicago Press, 1982.

——. "The Temple and the Magician." In *Map Is Not Territory: Studies in the History of Religions,* 172–189. Leiden: E. J. Brill, 1978.

——. *To Take Place: Toward Theory in Ritual.* Chicago: University of Chicago Press, 1987.

——. "Towards Interpreting Demonic Powers in Hellenistic and Roman Antiquity." In *Aufstieg und Niedergang der römischen Welt,* edited by Hildegard Temporini and Wolfgang Haase, II.16.1, 425–39. Berlin and New York: Walter de Gruyter, 1978.

Smith, Morton. *Jesus the Magician.* New York: Harper and Row, 1978.

——. "The Jewish Elements in the Magical Papyri." In *Society of Biblical Literature 1986 Seminar Papers,* edited by Kent H. Richards, 455–62. Atlanta, GA: Scholars Press, 1986.

Smither, Paul C. "A Coptic Love-Charm." *Journal of Egyptian Archaeology* 25 (1939): 173–74.

Sobhy, Geo. P. G. "The Persistence of Ancient Coptic Methods of Medical Treatment in Present-Day Egypt." In *Coptic Studies in Honor of Walter Ewing Crum,* edited by Michel Malinine, 185–88. Bulletin of the Byzantine Institute of America, vol. 2. Boston: Byzantine Institute, 1950.

Sørensen, Jørgen Podemann. "The Argument in Ancient Egyptian Magical Formulae." *Acta Orientalia* (Copenhagen) 45 (1984): 5–19.

Staal, Frits. "The Meaninglessness of Ritual." *Numen* 26 (1980): 2–22.

——. *Rules without Meaning: Ritual, Mantras, and the Human Sciences.* New York: Peter Lang, 1989.

Stefanski, Elizabeth. "A Coptic Magical Text." *American Journal of Semitic Languages and Literatures* 56 (1939): 305–7.

Stegemann, Viktor. *Die Gestalt Christi in den koptischen Zaubertexten.* Heidelberg: Bilabel, 1934.

——. *Die koptischen Zaubertexte der Sammlung Papyrus Erzherzog Rainer in Wien.* Sitzungsberichte der Heidelberger Akademie der Wissenschaften, philosophisch-historische Klasse, 1933–34, no. 1. Heidelberg: Carl Winters Universitätsbuchhandlung, 1934.

——. "Neue Zauber- und Gebetstexte aus koptischer Zeit in Heidelberg und Wien." *Muséon* 51 (1938): 73–87.

——. Review of Kropp, *Ausgewählte koptische Zaubertexte. Orientalistische Literaturzeitung* 37 (1934): 16–21.

——. "Zur Textgestaltung und zum Textverständnis koptischer Zaubertexte." *Zeitschrift für ägyptische Sprache und Altertumskunde* 70 (1934): 125–31.

——. "Über Astronimisches in den koptischen Zaubertexten." *Orientalia* 4 (1935): 391–410.

Stern, Ludwig. "Faijumische Papyri im Ägyptischen Museum zu Berlin." *Zeitschrift für ägyptische Sprache und Altertumskunde* 23 (1885): 23–44.

——. "Fragment eines koptischen Tractates über Alchimie." *Zeitschrift für ägyptische Sprache und Altertumskunde* 23 (1885): 102–19.

Tambiah, Stanley J. "Form and Meaning of Magical Acts: A Point of View." In *Modes of Thought: Essays on Thinking in Western and Non-Western Societies,* edited by Robin Horton and Ruth Finnegan, 199–229. London: Faber, 1973.

——. *Magic, Science, Religion, and the Scope of Rationality.* Cambridge: Cambridge University Press, 1990.

Te Velde, Herman. "Funerary Mythology." In *Mummies and Magic: The Funerary Arts of Ancient Egypt,* organized by Sue D'Auria et al. Boston: Museum of Fine Arts, 1988.

——. "The God Heka in Egyptian Theology." *Jaarbericht van het Vooraziatisch-Egyptisch Genootschap "Ex oriente Lux"* 21 (1969–70): 71–92.

Till, Walter. "Eine koptische Alimentenforderung." *Bulletin de la Société d'archéologie copte* 4 (1938): 71–78.

——. "Koptische Kleinliteratur 1–4." *Zeitschrift für ägyptische Sprache und Altertumskunde* 77 (1942): 101–11.

——, ed. *Die koptischen Ostraka der Papyrussammlung der Österreichischen Nationalbibliothek.* Denkschriften (Österreichische Akademie der Wissenschaften, philosophisch-historische Klasse), vol. 78, 1. Vienna: Hermann Böhlaus Nachf, 1960.

——. "Koptische Rezepte." *Bulletin de la Société d'archéologie copte* 12 (1946–47): 43–55.

——. "Zu den Wiener koptischen Zaubertexten." *Orientalia* 4 (1935): 195–221.

Trachtenberg, Joshua. *Jewish Magic and Superstition: A Study in Folk Religion.* New York: Atheneum, 1975.

Treu, Kurt. "Varia Christiana I." *Archiv für Papyrusforschung und verwandte Gebiete* 24–25 (1976): 120.

———. "Varia Christiana II." *Archiv für Papyrusforschung und verwandte Gebiete* 32 (1986): 29–30.

Turaev, B. A. "Axmimskij papirus iz kollekščin N. P. Lixačev" [An Akhmimic Papyrus in the Collection of N. P. Lixačev]. *Zapiski Vostočnogo otdelenija Imperatorskogo Russkogo Arxeologičeskogo obščestva* 18.1 (1907–8): 028–030.

Turner, Eric G. *Greek Papyri: An Introduction.* Oxford: Clarendon, 1968.

Tylor, Edward Burnett. *Primitive Culture.* London: J. Murray, 1871.

Valentasis, Richard. "Daemons and the Perfecting of the Monk's Body: Monastic Anthropology, Daemonology, and Asceticism." *Semeia* 58 (1992): 47–79.

Vasconcellos-Abreu, G. de. "La symbolique des nombres dans les recettes magique des traditions et des usages populaire en Europe." In *Mélanges Charles de Harlez: Recueil de travaux d'érudition offert à Charles de Harlez à l'occasion du vingt-cinquième anniversaire de son professorat à l'Université de Louvain 1871–1896,* 330–35. Leiden: E. J. Brill, 1896.

Viaud, Gérard. *Magie et coutumes populaires chez les coptes d'Égypte.* Saint-Vincent-sur-Jabron: Editions Présence, 1978.

Vikan, Gary. *Byzantine Pilgrimage Art.* Washington, D.C.: Dumbarton Oaks Center for Byzantine Studies, 1982.

Vliet, Jacques van der. "Demons in Early Coptic Monasticism: Image and Reality." In *Coptic Art and Culture,* edited by H. Hondelink, 135–56. Cairo: Shouhdy Publishing House, 1990.

———. "Satan's Fall in Coptic Magic." In *Magic in the Ancient World,* edited by Marvin Meyer and Paul Allan Mirecki. In preparation.

———. "Varia Magica Coptica." *Aegyptus* 71 (1991): 217–42.

Vycichl, Werner. "Die Aleph-Beth Regel im Demotischen und Koptischen: Eine Untersuchung an ägyptischen und koptischen Zauberspruchen." *Archiv für ägyptische Archäologie* 1 (1938): 224–26.

———. "Magic." In *The Coptic Encyclopedia,* edited by Aziz S. Atiya, 1499–1509. New York: Macmillan Publishing Company, 1991.

Wassef, Cérès Wissa. *Pratiques rituelles et alimentaires des coptes.* Bibliothèque d'études coptes, vol. 9. Cairo: Publications de l'Institut français d'archéologie orientale du Caire, 1971.

Weber, Manfred. "Ein koptischer Liebeszauber." *Enchoria* 5 (1975): 115–18.

———. "Ein koptischer Zaubertext aus der Kölner Papyrussammlung." *Enchoria* 2 (1972): 55–63.

———. "11. Schadenzauber." In *Kölner ägyptische Papyri (P. Köln ägypt.).* Papyrologica Coloniensia 9, vol. 1, edited by Dieter Kurth et al., 109–12. Opladen: Westdeutscher Verlag, 1980.

Wessely, Carl. *Les plus anciens monuments du christianisme écrits sur papyrus.* Patrologia Orientalis, vol. 18. Paris: Firmin-Didot, 1924; reprinted, Turnhout, Belgium: Brepols, 1974.

Wessetzky, Wilhelm. "Die Wirkung des Altägyptischen in einem koptischen Zauberspruch." *Acta Orientalia* 1 (1950): 26–30.

Wilsdorf, Helmut. "Die koptischen Zaubertexte in der Bearbeitung von Pater Angelicus Kropp." In *Griechen und Kopten im Byzantinischen Ägypten,* 85–101. Graeco-Coptica. Halle-Wittenberg: Martin Luther Universität, 1984.

———. "Bemerkungen zu den mineralogischen Pharmazeutika der Kopten." *Berliner Byzantinistische Arbeiten* 45 (1974): 77–100.

Winkler, John J. "The Constraints of Eros." In *Magika Hiera: Ancient Greek Magic and Religion,* edited by Christopher A. Faraone and Dirk Obbink, 214–43. New York and Oxford: Oxford University Press, 1991.

Wisse, Frederik. "Language Mysticism in the Nag Hammadi Texts and in Early Coptic Monasticism I: Cryptography." *Enchoria* 9 (1979): 101–20.

Wolinski, Arelene. "Egyptian Masks: The Priest and His Role." *Archaeology* 40 (1987):22–29.

Worrell, William H. "Coptic Magical and Medical Texts." *Orientalia* 4 (1935): 1–37; 184–94.

——. *The Coptic Manuscripts in the Freer Collection.* University of Michigan Studies, Humanistic Series, vol. 10. New York and London: Macmillan, 1923.

——. "A Coptic Wizard's Hoard." *American Journal of Semitic Languages and Literatures* 46 (1929–30): 239–62.

Wortmann, Dierk. "Der weisse Wolf." *Philologus* 107 (1963): 157–61.

Youtie, Herbert C. "Questions to a Christian Oracle." *Zeitschrift für Papyrologie und Epigraphik* 18 (1975): 253–57.